World-Regional Social Policy and Global Governance

This volume explores the case and the prospects for the development of world-regional social policies as integral elements of a pluralistic, equitable and effective system of global governance.

Focusing on transnational regionalism, this book examines the trajectory and crossing over of the three strands of scholarly analysis within the past decade which have given rise to this volume: the perceived negative impact of neo-liberal globalization upon national social policy; the need for but the difficulty of securing reforms in the institutions of global social governance; and the increasing salience of the world-regional level of governance in handling cross-border issues.

The authors develop an intellectual and research agenda that will also inform the political development of an international programme concerned with the social policy dimensions of regional governance. Combining the perspectives and collective expertise of a team of international scholars and activists, the book features:

- theoretical and policy cases for a focus on regionalism and social policy;
- a mapping and analysis of social policy dimensions of regional integration processes and formations in four continents;
- an assessment of the regional dimensions of global agencies, in particular of the UN (ILO, WHO, UNESCO, UNDP) including the approach to regional social policy of the UN Regional Economic Commissions and Development Banks;
- an articulation of a multi-level conceptualization of global social governance within which regional associations of countries play a significant part.

The book will be of interest to students and scholars of social policy, development studies, international relations and political science, especially those focused on the public policy dimensions of globalization, regionalization and international development.

Bob Deacon is Director of the Globalism and Social Policy Programme, Professor of International Social Policy at the University of Sheffield, UK and Senior Visiting Fellow attached to the Programme for Comparative Regional Integration Studies of the United Nations University (UNU-CRIS) in Bruges. **Luk Van Langenhove** is Director of the Programme for Comparative Regional Integration Studies of the United Nations University and Vice-President of the International Social Science Council. **Maria Cristina Macovei** is research officer of the UNU-CRIS programme. **Nicola Yeates** is Senior Lecturer in Social Policy at the Open University in the UK. She is author and editor of key texts on Global Social Policy including in 2008 *Understanding Global Social Policy* (Policy Press), and co-editor of *Global Social Policy* (Sage).

Routledge advances in international relations and global politics

1 **Foreign Policy and Discourse Analysis**
France, Britain and Europe
Henrik Larsen

2 **Agency, Structure and International Politics**
From ontology to empirical enquiry
Gil Friedman and Harvey Starr

3 **The Political Economy of Regional Co-operation in the Middle East**
Ali Carkoglu, Mine Eder and Kemal Kirisci

4 **Peace Maintenance**
The evolution of international political authority
Jarat Chopra

5 **International Relations and Historical Sociology**
Breaking down boundaries
Stephen Hobden

6 **Equivalence in Comparative Politics**
Edited by Jan W. van Deth

7 **The Politics of Central Banks**
Robert Elgie and Helen Thompson

8 **Politics and Globalisation**
Knowledge, ethics and agency
Martin Shaw

9 **History and International Relations**
Thomas W. Smith

10 **Idealism and Realism in International Relations**
Robert M. A. Crawford

11 **National and International Conflicts, 1945–1995**
New empirical and theoretical approaches
Frank Pfetsch and Christoph Rohloff

12 **Party Systems and Voter Alignments Revisited**
Edited by Lauri Karvonen and Stein Kuhnle

13 **Ethics, Justice & International Relations**
Constructing an international community
Peter Sutch

14 **Capturing Globalization**
Edited by James H. Mittelman and Norani Othman

15 **Uncertain Europe**
Building a new European security order?
Edited by Martin A. Smith and Graham Timmins

16 **Power, Postcolonialism and International Relations**
Reading race, gender and class
Edited by Geeta Chowdhry and Sheila Nair

17 **Constituting Human Rights**
Global civil society and the society of democratic states
Mervyn Frost

18 **US Economic Statecraft for Survival 1933–1991**
Of sanctions, embargoes and economic warfare
Alan P. Dobson

19 **The EU and NATO Enlargement**
Richard McAllister and Roland Dannreuther

20 **Spatializing International Politics**
Analysing activism on the internet
Jayne Rodgers

21 **Ethnonationalism in the Contemporary World**
Walker Connor and the study of nationalism
Edited by Daniele Conversi

22 **Meaning and International Relations**
Edited by Peter Mandaville and Andrew Williams

23 **Political Loyalty and the Nation-State**
Edited by Michael Waller and Andrew Linklater

24 **Russian Foreign Policy and the CIS**
Theories, debates and actions
Nicole J. Jackson

25 **Asia and Europe**
Development and different dimensions of ASEM
Yeo Lay Hwee

26 **Global Instability and Strategic Crisis**
Neville Brown

27 **Africa in International Politics**
External involvement on the continent
Edited by Ian Taylor and Paul Williams

28 **Global Governmentality**
Governing international spaces
Edited by Wendy Larner and William Walters

29 **Political Learning and Citizenship Education Under Conflict**
The political socialization of Israeli and Palestinian youngsters
Orit Ichilov

30 **Gender and Civil Society**
Transcending boundaries
Edited by Jude Howell and Diane Mulligan

31 **State Crises, Globalisation and National Movements in North-East Africa**
The Horn's dilemma
Edited by Asafa Jalata

32 **Diplomacy and Developing Nations**
Post-Cold War foreign policy-making structures and processes
Edited by Justin Robertson and Maurice A. East

33 **Autonomy, Self-governance and Conflict Resolution**
Innovative approaches to institutional design in divided societies
Edited by Marc Weller and Stefan Wolff

34 **Mediating International Crises**
Jonathan Wilkenfeld, Kathleen J. Young, David M. Quinn and Victor Asal

35 **Postcolonial Politics, the Internet and Everyday Life**
Pacific traversals online
M. I. Franklin

36 **Reconstituting the Global Liberal Order**
Legitimacy and regulation
Kanishka Jayasuriya

37 **International Relations, Security and Jeremy Bentham**
Gunhild Hoogensen

38 **Interregionalism and International Relations**
Edited by Heiner Hänggi, Ralf Roloff and Jürgen Rüland

39 **The International Criminal Court**
A global civil society achievement
Marlies Glasius

40 **A Human Security Doctrine for Europe**
Project, principles, practicalities
Edited by Marlies Glasius and Mary Kaldor

41 **The History and Politics of UN Security Council Reform**
Dimitris Bourantonis

42 **Russia and NATO Since 1991**
From Cold War through cold peace to partnership?
Martin A. Smith

43 **The Politics of Protection**
Sites of insecurity and political agency
Edited by Jef Huysmans, Andrew Dobson and Raia Prokhovnik

44 **International Relations in Europe**
Traditions, perspectives and destinations
Edited by Knud Erik Jørgensen and Tonny Brems Knudsen

45 **The Empire of Security and the Safety of the People**
Edited by William Bain

46 **Globalization and Religious Nationalism in India**
The search for ontological security
Catrina Kinnvall

47 Culture and International Relations
Narratives, natives and tourists
Julie Reeves

48 Global Civil Society
Contested futures
Edited by Gideon Baker and David Chandler

49 Rethinking Ethical Foreign Policy
Pitfalls, possibilities and paradoxes
Edited by David Chandler and Volker Heins

50 International Cooperation and Arctic Governance
Regime effectiveness and northern region building
Edited by Olav Schram Stokke and Geir Hønneland

51 Human Security
Concepts and implications
Shahrbanou Tadjbakhsh and Anuradha Chenoy

52 International Relations and Security in the Digital Age
Edited by Johan Eriksson and Giampiero Giacomello

53 State-Building
Theory and practice
Edited by Aidan Hehir and Neil Robinson

54 Violence and Non-Violence in Africa
Edited by Pal Ahluwalia, Louise Bethlehem and Ruth Ginio

55 Developing Countries and Global Trade Negotiations
Edited by Larry Crump and S. Javed Maswood

56 Civil Society, Religion and Global Governance
Paradigms of power and persuasion
Edited by Helen James

57 War, Peace and Hegemony in a Globalized World
The changing balance of power in the 21st century
Edited by Chandra Chari

58 Economic Globalisation as Religious War
Tragic convergence
Michael McKinley

59 Globalization, Prostitution and Sex-trafficking
Corporeal politics
Elina Penttinen

60 Peacebuilding
Women in international perspective
Elisabeth Porter

61 Ethics, Liberalism and Realism in International Relations
Mark D. Gismondi

62 Law and Legalization in Transnational Relations
Edited by Christian Brütsch and Dirk Lehmkuhl

63 Fighting Terrorism and Drugs
Europe and international police cooperation
Jörg Friedrichs

64 **Identity Politics in the Age of Genocide**
The holocaust and historical representation
David B. MacDonald

65 **Globalisation, Public Opinion and the State**
Western Europe and East and Southeast Asia
Edited by Takashi Inoguchi and Ian Marsh

66 **Urbicide**
The politics of urban destruction
Martin Coward

67 **Transnational Activism in the UN and the EU**
A comparative study
Jutta Joachim and Birgit Locher

68 **Gender Inclusive**
Essays on violence, men and feminist international relations
Adam Jones

69 **Capitalism, Democracy and the Prevention of War and Poverty**
Edited by Peter Graeff and Guido Mehlkop

70 **Environmental Change and Foreign Policy**
Theory and practice
Edited by Paul G. Harris

71 **Climate Change and Foreign Policy**
Case studies from East to West
Edited by Paul G. Harris

72 **Securitizations of Citizenship**
Edited by Peter Nyers

73 **The Power of Ideology**
From the Roman Empire to Al-Qaeda
Alex Roberto Hybel

74 **The Securitization of Humanitarian Migration**
Digging moats and sinking boats
Scott D. Watson

75 **Mediation in the Asia-Pacific Region**
Transforming conflicts and building peace
Edited by Dale Bagshaw and Elisabeth Porter

76 **United Nations Reform**
Heading North or South?
Spencer Zifcak

77 **New Norms and Knowledge in World Politics**
Protecting people, intellectual property and the environment
Preslava Stoeva

78 **Power, Resistance and Conflict in the Contemporary World**
Social movements, networks and hierarchies
Athina Karatzogianni and Andrew Robinson

79 **World-Regional Social Policy and Global Governance**
New research and policy agendas in Africa, Asia, Europe and Latin America
Edited by Bob Deacon, Maria Cristina Macovei, Luk Van Langenhove and Nicola Yeates

World-Regional Social Policy and Global Governance

New research and policy agendas in Africa, Asia, Europe and Latin America

Edited by Bob Deacon, Maria Cristina Macovei, Luk Van Langenhove and Nicola Yeates

Routledge
Taylor & Francis Group
LONDON AND NEW YORK

First published 2010
by Routledge
2 Park Square, Milton Park, Abingdon, Oxon OX14 4RN

Simultaneously published in the USA and Canada
by Routledge
270 Madison Ave, New York, NY 10016

Routledge is an imprint of the Taylor & Francis Group, an informa business

Typeset in Times by Wearset Ltd, Boldon, Tyne and Wear

British Library Cataloguing in Publication Data
A catalogue record for this book is available from the British Library

Library of Congress Cataloging in Publication Data
World-regional social policy and global governance: new research and policy agendas in Africa, Asia, Europe, and Latin America/edited by Bob Deacon ... [et al.].
p. cm. – (Routledge advances in international relations and global politics ; 79)
1. Social policy. 2. Regionalism (International organization) 3. International agencies. 4. Globalization–Social aspects. I. Deacon, Bob.
HN18.3.W665 2009
320.6–dc22 2009018168

ISBN10: 0-415-45659-2 (hbk)
ISBN10: 0-203-86650-9 (ebk)

ISBN13: 978-0-415-45659-3 (hbk)
ISBN13: 978-0-203-86650-4 (ebk)

Contents

Illustrations

Figure

Tables

Contributors

Brid Brennan is a fellow of the Transnational Institute based in the Netherlands and coordinates its Alternative Regionalisms Programme.

Jenina Joy Chavez is Senior Associate of the Focus on the Global South and heads its Philippines Programme.

Bob Deacon is Director of the Globalism and Social Policy Programme, Professor of International Social Policy at the University of Sheffield, UK, and Senior Visiting Fellow attached to the Programme for Comparative Regional Integration Studies of the United Nations University (UNU-CRIS).

Maria Cristina Macovei is Researcher, United Nations University–Comparative Regional Integration Studies (UNU-CRIS), Bruges, Belgium.

Cecilia Olivet is a Research Associate with the Alternative Regionalisms Programme of the Transnational Institute, where she participates in coordinating the initiative People's Agenda for Alternative Regionalisms (PAAR) and the work around the European's Union's trade relations with the South. She is involved in the work of networks such as Our World Is Not for Sale, Seattle to Brussels, Europe–Latin America and the Caribbean bi-regional network Enlazando Alternativas.

Manuel Riesco is Vice-President of the Centre for National Studies of Alternative Development (CENDA), Chile. He is editor of *Latin America: A New Developmental Welfare State Modem in the Making.*

Monica Threlfall is Reader in European Politics at the Institute for the Study of European Transformations (INSET), London Metropolitan University. She is editor of the *International Journal of Iberian Studies*.

Luk Van Langenhove is Director, United Nations University–Comparative Regional Integration Studies (UNU-CRIS), Bruges, Belgium, Vice-President of the International Social Science Council and author of several books on comparative regionalism.

Nicola Yeates is Senior Lecturer in Social Policy at the Open University in the United Kingdom and author/editor of several volumes on aspects of globalization and social policy. She is joint editor of the *Global Social Policy* journal.

Foreword

This timely and remarkable book provides an excellent example of how social scientists and policy-makers can collaborate to push back the frontiers of knowledge and set new policy agendas. As such, it is a perfect illustration of what UNESCO aims to achieve through its programme Management of Social Transformations (MOST), and I am glad to say that MOST played a significant role in making this book possible.

In February 2006 UNESCO organized the Buenos Aires International Forum on the Social Science – Policy Nexus (IFSP) in Argentina and Uruguay, with the explicit purpose of creating an innovative space for dialogue between social scientists and actors from the worlds of both policy-making and civil society. The IFSP was attended by some 2,000 participants from eighty countries, including thirteen social development and education ministers and six secretaries general from regional organizations. Among the key issues discussed were both social policies and regional integration.

The United Nations University, through its programme on Comparative Regional Integration Studies (UNU-CRIS), took the initiative to organize at the IFSP in Montevideo a high-level symposium on the Social Dimensions of Regional Integration, in collaboration with UNESCO, MERCOSUR, GASPP and the Open University Centre for Citizenship, Identities and Governance. It was on that occasion that some of the contributors to this book had their first scientific discussions and the idea of a volume on regional integration and social policy emerged.

The IFSP also adopted the Buenos Aires Declaration, calling for a concerted, enduring attempt to improve linkages between policy-makers and social scientists. Part of this declaration focused upon the social dimensions of regional integration and called upon regional organizations, in association with social scientists and civil society, to extend research in this area. The UN was also called upon to facilitate inter-regional dialogue on regional social policies.

The United Nations University took this call seriously and, in partnership with policy scholars from all over the world, UNU-CRIS further developed its research and training activities on the social dimensions of regional integration.

In March 2007 UNU-CRIS, together with the Open University's CCIG and GASPP, organized a two-day workshop in Bruges that further developed the research and debates of the Montevideo meetings. The result is the present book, which investigates the prospects for the development of world-regional social policies as integral elements of an effective system of global governance.

Meanwhile, MOST's regional fora of ministers in charge of social development have been further developed by UNESCO. Fourteen such fora have been organized in Latin America, South Asia and the Arab states, and in the context of African regional integration organizations such as ECOWAS, the SADC and the EAC. I am convinced that the present book will prove to be a valuable input to the next fora of ministers and will help to shape debates on diverse topics such as the importance of solidarity in achieving social development, the need for corporate social responsibility for social development and effective regional migration policies.

But the research–policy linkage is a two-way process. Therefore I also hope that the fora outcomes will fit into research programming so that the social dimensions of regional integration as a field of intellectual and policy study can be further developed.

Pierre Sané
Assistant Director-General for Social and Human Sciences
UNESCO

Acknowledgements

This volume was conceived after we had been invited by Pierre Sané of UNESCO to organize in February 2004 a High-Level Symposium on the Social Dimension of Regionalism in Uruguay within the context of its International Social Sciences – Policy Nexus taking place in Buenos Aires. Most of the authors of these chapters were involved in that Symposium. Subsequently the United Nations University programme for Comparative Regional Integration Studies (UNU-CRIS) agreed to host a workshop in Bruges on 23–25 May 2007 on this theme. This was jointly organized by UNU-CRIS, the UK Open University and the Globalism and Social Policy Programme (GASPP). We are grateful to the UK British Academy for funding this conference. At that workshop first drafts of the chapters of this volume were tabled. We are grateful for the constructive comments provided at that event by Denys Correll (ICSW), Isabel Ortiz (UNDESA), Eric Maertens (ILO), Timo Voipio (Finnish government), Rudi DelaRue (European Commission) and others. Subsequently UNU-CRIS worked with the ILO International Training Centre on a project to strengthen the social dimension of the SADC and ECOWAS. This experience informed Chapter 8 of this volume. We therefore acknowledge the valuable contributions of the spokespersons of many organizations within the SADC and ECOWAS regions. The authors of the other regional chapters owe a debt of gratitude to their numerous informants too.

While each of the editors wishes to thank his/her own institution for providing some resources and time to work on this volume, our main debt of gratitude must be to the staff of UNU-CRIS who hosted editorial meetings and, more importantly, provided technical assistance in the later stages of the production process. We owe a special thank you to Liesbeth Martens for formatting all the chapters and preparing the merged bibliography. Thanks also to the support and patience of our publishers.

Permission to reproduce Tables 6.2–6.6, originally published in Manuel Riesco, *Latin America, a New Developmental Welfare State Model in the Making*, 2007, Palgrave Macmillan/UNRISD, has been granted by Palgrave Macmillan.

Abbreviations

ABAC	ASEAN Business Advisory Council
ACP	Africa, Caribbean and Pacific countries
ACSC	ASEAN Civil Society Conference
ADB	Asian Development Bank
ADF	ASEAN Development Fund
AEC	ASEAN Economic Community
AEPF	Asia Europe People's Forum
AfDB	African Development Bank
AFP	Administradoras de Fondos de Pensiones
AFSR	ASEAN's Food Security Reserve
AFTA	ASEAN Free Trade Area
AGE	European Older People's Platform
AIDS	acquired immune deficiency syndrome
AIPO	ASEAN Inter-Parliamentary Organization
ALAC	Andean Labour Advisory Council
ALADI	Asociación Latinoamericana de Integración (Latin American Integration Association)
ALALC	Asociación Latinoamericana de Libre Comercio (Latin American Free Trade Association)
ALBA	Alianza Bolivariana para los Pueblos de Nuestra América (Bolivarian Alternatives for the Americas)
ALIDES	Alianza para el Desarrollo Ostensible de Centroamérica (Alliance for the Sustainable Development of Central America)
AMU	Arab Maghreb Union
ANSA	Alternatives to Neo-Liberalism in Southern Africa
APA	ASEAN People's Assembly
APEC	Asia Pacific Economic Cooperation
ARIA	Assessing Regional Integration in Africa
ASC	ASEAN Security Community
ASCC	ASEAN Socio-Cultural Community
ASEAN	Association of South East Asian Nations
ASEAN-ISIS	ASEAN Institutes of Strategic and International Studies
ASEAN5	Indonesia, Malaysia, Philippines, Singapore and Thailand

ASEAN+3	ASEAN + China, Japan and South Korea
ASEM	Asia–Europe Meeting
ATN	Africa Trade Network
AU	African Union
AUPF	ASEAN–UNDP Partnership Facility
BBVA	Banco Bilbao Vizcaya Argentaria
BCLMV	Brunei Darussalam, Cambodia, Lao PDR, Myanmar and Vietnam
BID	Banco Interamericano de Desarrollo (Inter-American Development Bank)
BIT	bilateral investment treaties
BLA	bilateral labour agreement
BUSA	Business Unity of South Africa
BWI	Bretton Woods institutions
CACM	Central American Common Market
CAN	Comunidad Andina de Naciones (Andean Community)
CANTA	Caribbean Association of National Training Agencies
CAREC	Central Asia Regional Economic Cooperation
CARICOM	Caribbean Community
CARIFORUM	Caribbean Forum of African, Caribbean and Pacific States
CCEA	Conseyo Consultivo Empresarial Andino (Andean Business Advisory Council)
CCIG	Centre for Citizenship, Identities and Governance
CCSCS	Coordination of Trade Unions of the Southern Cone
CECODHAS	Comité Européen de Coordination de l'Habitat Social (European Liaison Committee for Social Housing)
CECOP	European Confederation of Workers Cooperatives, Social Cooperatives and Participative Enterprises
CEEAC	Communauté Economique des Etats de l'Afrique Centrale (Economic Community of Central Africa States)
CELADE	Centro Latinoamericano de Demografía (Latin American Demographic Center)
CEMAC	Communauté Economique et Monétaire de l'Afrique Centrale (Economic and Monetary Community of Central Africa)
CENSAD	Community of Sahel–-Saharan States
CET	Common External Tariff
CIAPPEP	Curso Intensivo de Evaluación Económica de Proyectos Públicos (Intensive Course for Economic Evaluation of Public Projects)
CLAC	Cumbre de Latinoamerica y el Caribe
CLMV	Cambodia, Laos, Myanmar and Vietnam
CLS	core labour standards
CMC	Council of the Common Market
COHSOD	Council for Human and Social Development
COMESA	Common Market for Eastern and Southern Africa

CSME	Caribbean Community Single Market and Economy
CSO	civil society organization
DfID	Department for International Development (UK)
DPA	Development Partnership Agreement
EAC	East African Community
EAERR	East Asian Emergency Rice Reserve
EAP	economically active population
ECA	Economic Commission for Africa (United Nations)
ECCAS	Economic Community of Central African States
ECDPM	European Centre for Development Policy Management
ECE	Economic Commission for Europe (United Nations)
ECJ	European Court of Justice
ECLAC	Economic Commission for Latin America and the Caribbean (United Nations)
ECOSOC	Economic and Social Council (United Nations)
ECOSOCC	Economic, Social and Cultural Council
ECOTECH	economic and technical cooperation
ECOWAS	Economic Community of West African States
EDF	European Disability Forum
EEC	European Economic Community
EECCA	Countries of Eastern Europe, the Caucasus and Central Asia
EERC	Economic Education and Research Consortium
EES	European Employment Strategy
EESC	European Economic and Social Committee
EID	emerging infectious diseases
EJN	Economic Justice Network
EMRO	Eastern Mediterranean Region
ENAR	European Network Against Racism
ENQA	European Association for Quality Assurance in Higher Education
EP	European Parliament
EPA	Economic Partnership Agreement
EPG	Eminent Persons Group
ERIO	European Roma Information Office
ESCAP	Economic and Social Commission for Asia and the Pacific (United Nations)
ESCWA	Economic and Social Commission for Western Asia (United Nations)
ESF	European Social Fund
ETUC	European Trade Union Confederation
EU	European Union
EU–LAC	European Union and the Latin America and the Caribbean countries
EWL	European Women's Lobby
FARE	Forum for Associations Recognized by ECOWAS

FCES	Foro Consultivo Económico y Social del Mercosur (Economic and Social Consultation Forum)
FDI	foreign direct investment
FEALAC	Forum for East Asia Latin America Cooperation
FEFAF	European Federation of Unpaid Parents and Carers at Home
FLS	frontline states
FOCEM	Fund for Structural Convergence of MERCOSUR
FTA	free trade agreement
FTAA	Free Trade Area of the Americas
GAFTA	Greater Arab Free Trade Area
GASPP	Globalism and Social Policy Programme
GATS	General Agreement on Trade in Services
GDP	gross domestic product
GENTA	Gender and Trade Network
GISM	Grupo para la Creación del Instituto Social
GMS	Greater Mekong Sub-region
GNP	gross national product
GRULAC	Group of Latin America and Caribbean Countries
GSP	Generalized System of Preferences
GTZ	Deutsche Gesellschaft für Technische Zusammenarbeit
GURN	Global Union Research Network
HDI	human development index
HIV/AIDS	human immunodeficiency virus/acquired immune deficiency syndrome
HLP	High-Level Panel
HLTF	High-Level Task Force
HRD	Human Resources Development
HRDWG	Human Resources Development Working Group
HSA	Hemispheric Social Alliance
IADB	Inter-American Development Bank
IAI	Initiative for ASEAN Integration
ICFTU	International Confederation of Free Trade Unions
ICRY	Ibero-American Convention on the Rights of Youth
ICSW	International Council on Social Welfare
IDB	Inter-American Development Bank
IGAD	Inter-Governmental Authority for Development
IILS	International Institute of Labour Studies
ILGA-Europe	European Region of the International Lesbian and Gay Association
ILO	International Labour Organization
IMF	International Monetary Fund
INDES	Inter-American Institute for Social Development
IOC	Indian Ocean Commission
IPA	Integrated Programme of Action
IsDB	Islamic Development Bank

ISFD	Islamic Solidarity Fund for Development
ISI	import-substitution industrialization
ITC	International Training Centre of the ILO
LA	Latin America
LAC	Latin America and the Caribbean
LAS	League of Arab States
LDCs	least developed countries
LSPN	Labour and Social Protection Network
MDGs	Millennium Development Goals
MERCOSUR	Common Market of the South
MEXA	Movimiento Estudiantil Xicano de Aztlan
MFN	Most Favoured Nation
MOST	Management of Social Transformations (UNESCO)
MRA	Mutual Recognition Arrangement
NAFTA	North American Free Trade Agreement
NAM	Non-Aligned Movement
NAWO	National Alliance of Women's Organizations
NEPAD	New Partnership for Africa's Development
NGO	non-governmental organization
OAU	Organization of African Unity
ODA	overseas development assistance
ODI	Overseas Development Institute
OECS	Organization of Eastern Caribbean States
OIC	Organization of the Islamic Conference
OMC	Open Method of Coordination
PAHO	Pan American Health Organization
PIFS	Pacific Islands Forum Secretariat
PPP	purchasing power parity
PRODIAF	Promotion of Social Dialogue in Francophone Africa
PRSPs	Poverty Reduction Strategy Papers
PT	Partido dos Trabalhadores (Workers' Party)
PTA	Preferential Trade Agreement
PUC	Pontificia Universidad Católica (Catholic University of Chile)
PYME	pequeña y mediana empresas (small and medium enterprises)
RCI	regional cooperation and integration
RECs	Regional Economic Communities
RI	regional integration
RIACES	Red Iberoamericana para la Acreditación de la Calidad de la Educación Superior
RISDP	Regional Indicative Strategic Development Plan
ROSA	Regional Office for South Asia (UNICEF)
RPGs	regional public goods
RTA	Regional Trade Agreement
SAARC	South Asian Association for Regional Cooperation
SACN	South American Community of Nations

SACU	Southern African Customs Union
SADC	Southern African Development Community
SADCC	Southern African Development Coordination Conference
SAFA	South Asian Federation of Accountants
SAFTA	South Asian Free Trade Area
SAPA	Solidarity for Asian Peoples' Advocacy
SAPSN	Southern African Peoples' Solidarity Network
SARS	Severe Acute Respiratory Syndrome
SASEC	South Asia Subregional Economic Cooperation
SATUCC	Southern Africa Trade Union Coordination Council
SC	Security Council (United Nations)
SCCI	SAARC Chamber of Commerce and Industry
SCE	Steering Committee on Economical and Technical Cooperation
SDF	SAARC Development Fund
SDGs	SAARC Development Goals
SEATO	Southeast Asia Treaty Organization
SEG	Southern African Employers Group
SELA	Sistema Económico Latinoamericano y del Caribe (Latin American Economic System)
SFSR	SAARC's Food Security Reserve
SHSS	Social and Human Sciences Sector
SIDA	Swedish International Development Cooperation Agency
SIPO	Strategic Indicative Plan for the Organ
SPA	SADC Programme of Action
SPARC	Support to Poverty Assessment and Reduction in the Caribbean
SPC	Secretariat of the Pacific Community
SPF	Social Policy Framework for Africa
SRO	Sub-regional Programme Office
SSD	Social Development Division
TB	tuberculosis
TCP	Tratado Comercio de los Pueblos (Trade Treaty of the People)
TLS	Trade Liberalization Scheme
TNC	trans-national corporation
TNI	Transnational Institute
UDEAC	Union Douanière et Economique de l'Afrique Centrale (Customs and Economic Union of Central Africa)
UEMOA	Union Economique et Monétaire Ouest Africaine (West African Economic and Monetary Union)
UN	United Nations
UNASUR	Union of South American Nations
UNCTAD	United Nations Conference on Trade and Development
UNDESA	United Nations Department of Economic and Social Affairs
UNDP	United Nations Development Programme
UNESCO	United Nations Educational, Scientific and Cultural Organization

UNFPA	United Nations Population Fund
UNICE	Union of Industrial and Employers' Confederations of Europe
UNICEF	United Nations Children's Fund
UNILA	Universidade Federal da Integração Latino-Americana (Federal University of Latin-American Integration)
UNRISD	United Nations Research Institute for Social Development
UNU-CRIS	United Nations University – Comparative Regional Integration Studies
US	United States
VAP	Vientiane Action Programme
WB	World Bank
WCSDG	World Commission on the Social Dimension of Globalization
WG-ASEAN	Working Group on ASEAN
WHO	World Health Organization
WTO	World Trade Organization

Introduction

Nicola Yeates, Bob Deacon, Luk Van Langenhove and Maria Cristina Macovei

Aims and purposes of the volume

This volume explores the case and the prospects for the development of world-regional social policies as integral elements of a pluralistic, equitable and effective system of global governance. Combining the perspectives and collective expertise of a team of international scholars and activists, we bring together in one place for the first time: (i) the theoretical and policy cases for a focus on regionalism and social policy; (ii) a mapping and analysis of social policy dimensions of regional integration processes and formations in four continents; (iii) an assessment of the regional dimensions of global agencies, in particular of the United Nations (UN) system, including the approach to regional social policy of the UN regional economic commissions and development banks; and (iv) an articulation of a multi-levelled conceptualization of global social governance within which regional associations of countries play a significant part.

For the purpose of clarity, it is worth specifying at this early stage what we mean by the terms region, regionalism and regionalization. This volume is very specifically concerned with trans-national or cross-border regional formations. Our use of the term world-regionalism, as in the title of the book and elsewhere, is consciously used to clearly distinguish our approach from sub-national regionalisms (as in cities, municipalities, provinces, etc.), which our book neither addresses nor is concerned with. In regional integration studies, a 'region' can be defined as any geographical area that is not a state but in which there are extant statehood properties. So regions are not states, but they look to some extent 'as if' they were. Regions can be found at all territorial levels. There are regions within countries, so-called sub-national regions. There are cross-border regions that stretch over different countries, and there are regions that are made up of different countries, namely supra-national regions. Regionalism is a 'state-led or states-led project designed to reorganize a particular regional space along defined economic and political lines' (Gamble and Payne 1996: 2). Regionalism is thus often associated with state strategies but it may also encompass non-state actors acting on a regional scale to the extent that they formulate clear organizational structures. Regionalization, on the other hand, is defined as the *outcome* of state and non-state strategies to lock in regional divisions of labour, trade and production (Hout 1996).

Contexts

Three strands of scholarly study and political development within the past decade gave rise to the work that forms the basis of this volume. One is the perceived negative impact of neo-liberal globalization upon national social policy. Neo-liberal globalization has generated a vigorous debate amongst scholars, policy-makers and activists about how to preserve existing, and develop new, social policies to provide for the social needs of populations. Much of this debate focused on identifying appropriate national-level social policy responses and strategies in the context of increasing the international mobility of people, finance and ideas and increasing global production and delivery of goods and services. A major concern is the negative consequences of 'free trade' and international competition on the funding and provision of public social provision as well as on access to public services by citizens and residents. Increasingly, attention is turning to address the kinds of policies necessary to achieve socially equitable development under contemporary conditions of globalization – a socially just globalization (Yeates 2001). One response to the perceived threat to public social provision at the national level has been to argue for more coherent cooperation and coordination at the world-regional level.

A second response concerns the need for – but the difficulty of – securing reforms to the institutions of global social governance. Formidable obstacles to enhanced *global* redistribution, regulation and social rights through a strengthened UN-based global social governance system are involved. Many governments and non-governmental bodies in the Global North and Global South alike are unsure about the appropriateness of a Northern-driven reformed globalization imposing 'inappropriate' global social and labour standards, while many actors in the South are reluctant to buy into even the more progressive forms of conditionality. This is where the construction and strengthening of regional organizations of countries enter the picture. Rather than seeking to develop a case for a global social policy of redistribution, regulation and rights that would also imply a strengthening of Northern-based institutions, it is now being argued that the focus should perhaps be on building several *regional social policies* of redistribution, regulation and rights. Equally, rather than seek to win the World Bank (WB) over to a European perspective on social policy, the point should be to forge a policy space where Southern governments and civil society can construct their own policy choices. Reforming global social governance should perhaps imply building a pluralistic federation of world regions each with competence in its own location.

The third strand is the increasing salience of the supra-national regional level of governance in handling cross-border issues. Regionalism can prove to be an important tool in managing globalization in the interests of social protection and, thus, an important level of governance that complements states and international organizations. Regionalism facilitates the reaching of inter-state agreements as it entails more proximity, both geographically and culturally. Regional identity can play a major role in fostering good cooperation among states, even though sometimes regionalization processes themselves help forge a common identity.

Beyond trade integration, regional integration initiatives have the potential to fulfil other important functions, including the creation of an appropriate enabling environment for economic and social development; the development of infrastructure programmes in support of economic growth and regional integration; the development of strong public sector institutions and good governance; and the reduction of social exclusion and the development of inclusive civil society.

The social policy dimensions of regional integration: research and policy agendas

By the opening years of the twenty-first century, a number of specific initiatives were taking place, testifying to the increased salience of these perspectives and policy issues in the agendas of international research and governmental organizations. One was the interest shown by United Nations Research Institute for Social Development (UNRISD) in the world-regional dimensions of social policy in its Social Policy in a Development Context research programme (Yeates 2005). A second was the interest of United Nations Educational, Scientific and Cultural Organization (UNESCO) in these issues, facilitating the High-Level Symposium on the Social Dimension of Regional Integration co-organized by UNU-CRIS, the Open University CCIG and the Globalism and Social Policy Programme (GASPP). The invitation to Symposium participants expressed the logic in the following terms:

> At this point, the processes of regional integration are mainly analyzed in terms of economic and trade issues. Therefore most initial forms of regional integration see them as free trade areas or customs unions. This development has experienced a recent acceleration in all regions of the world, partially in response to globalization. The aim of this Symposium will be to analyze the social dimensions and consequences of integration mechanisms. In this context, the regional level is an appropriate frame for scientific analysis of social policies. Increasingly, regions should be considered as an emerging space for the formulation and implementation of social policies. Although social welfare has been largely addressed at the global level and has even been codified into clear development goals by the global community (e.g. the MDGs), the main level of implementation for these goals remains the nation state. Since the social dimensions of regional integration are more than just the circumstantial consequences of economic integration, this should be an occasion to address the topic of the social impact of regional processes. Indeed, recent examples of free trade areas such as NAFTA have directly impacted on the social livelihood of populations by creating new forms of migration and disparities of labour protection. These consequences are not adequately addressed by the international agreements that often lack the necessary social clause. Just as economic integration necessitates a number of consequent policy changes at the national level, the social dimension of integration also calls for adequate social policies.
>
> (Sané 2004)

Steps in this direction had been undertaken by both the research communities and the regional integration bodies through a diverse set of initiatives like a Draft Social Charter for ASEAN, the European Union Social Agenda, the Economic and Social Consultative Forum of MERCOSUR, the Social and Economic Council in the case of ECOWAS or the social aspects in the Pacific Plan drafted by the Forum of Pacific States. The purpose of the High-Level Symposium was to identify policy gaps regarding the social dimension and consequences of regional integration projects and to articulate research and policy agendas following their detailed analysis of current situations. One outcome of the Symposium was the inclusion of a recommendation in the Buenos Aires Declaration Calling for a New Approach to the Social Sciences – Policy Nexus that research and policy organizations focus their efforts on the regional dimensions of social policy:

> Article 6: We call upon the regional organizations such as MERCOSUR and the African Union, in association with social scientists and civil society, to further develop the social dimensions of regional integration, and call upon the United Nations to facilitate inter-regional dialogues on regional social policies.
>
> Article 7: We call upon existing funding programmes, in particular donor agencies and multilateral and regional development banks, to participate in these new spaces of dialogue.
>
> (UNESCO 2006)

Policy-orientated research and scholarly work that flowed from the Symposium included a special issue of *Global Social Policy* (2007, 7(3)) on the social policy dimensions of world-regional dimensions, edited by Nicola Yeates. UNU-CRIS was subsequently commissioned by the International Labour Organization (ILO) to contribute an assessment of the extent to which a social dimension was being realized in regional contexts. The paper *Deepening the Social Dimensions of Regional Integration: An Overview of Recent Trends and Future Challenges in Light of the Recommendations of the Report of the World Commission on the Social Dimension of Globalization* (UNU-CRIS 2008) was the outcome of this work. This was followed by collaboration between UNU-CRIS and the International Training Centre (ITC) of the ILO on a scoping project designed to assess the need in two African sub-regions (ECOWAS and the SADC) for capacity building and training in order to enable them to better address the social consequences of trade deals and European Partnership Agreements (EPAs) in those regions. The 2008 report *Regional Integration, Decent Work, and Labour and Social Policies in West and Southern Africa* (Deacon *et al.* 2008) is the first outcome. Training is now taking place in ECOWAS.

UNU-CRIS was also invited to contribute its views on the regional dimension of social policy at an expert meeting preceding the meeting of the AU Ministers of Development who agreed in November 2008 *A New Social Policy Framework for Africa* (AU 2008b). At the same time UNESCO, under the auspices of its

Management of Social Transformations programme (MOST), had continued its promotion of the case for regional social integration by convening meetings of Ministers of Social Development in Latin America, Asia and all sub-regions of Africa. The United Nations Department of Economic and Social Affairs (UNDESA) became alerted to the significance of these developments and published its own *Regional Social Policy* working paper in 2007 (UNDESA 2007).

The immediate precursor to this volume was a seminar on the Social Dimension of Regional Integration, convened at UNU-CRIS in 2007, which brought together all the authors of this volume, together with different experts from the European Union (EU), UNDESA, the ILO, ICSW and other institutions.

Organization of the volume

The volume is organized into three main parts. Part I essentially sets out the context of and the case for regionalism with a social dimension. Chapter 1, by Luk van Langenhove and Maria Cristina Macovei, reviews the literature and recent developments in regional integration and governance, drawing attention to the missing social and policy dimensions of regional integration to date. Chapter 2, by Nicola Yeates and Bob Deacon, establishes the political and intellectual case for a focus on regional social policy within the context of the globalization, global social governance and social policy debates. Chapter 3, by Bob Deacon and Maria Cristina Macovei, examines what role the UN regional economic and social commissions, the UN social agencies and the regional development banks play in fostering the social dimension of regional integration. Chapter 4, by Cecilia Olivet and Brid Brennan, focuses on regionalism 'from below': they develop existing analyses of social movements and civil society organizations' engagement with trans-national governmental formations by focusing on civil society organizations at world-regional level. This chapter reviews and discusses the development of regional civil society associations, the extent to and ways in which they organize regionally, engage with regional formations and the institutional and policy reforms they are advocating in the field of regional social policy.

In Part II the book proceeds to consider case studies of the social policy dimensions of regional integration and governance through a focus on four continents. Thus, Chapter 5 by Monica Threlfall focuses on Europe, in particular the European Union and the Council of Europe. Chapter 6 by Manuel Riesco focuses on Central and Latin America. Chapter 7 by Jenina Joy Chavez focuses on Asia, in particular ASEAN and SAARC. Chapter 8 by Bob Deacon focuses on African regionalisms and their relationship to continent-wide social governance arrangements. Across these four extended chapters, the authors survey and discuss the substance of the social policy dimensions of regional formations, evaluate the extent to which they have developed regional mechanisms of redistribution, regulation and rights, and developed cross-border mechanisms for collaboration in health, education and social protection.

Part III comprises discussion of additional sets of issues and considerations not discussed earlier in the book. Chapter 9, by Nicola Yeates, Maria Cristina

Macovei and Luk Van Langenhove, addresses a number of issues that have a bearing upon the prospects for the development of regions with a strong social agenda and effective social policies which were not the focus of attention in the earlier chapters. These include inter-regional open trading formations and bilateral trading arrangements and the impact of these cross-cutting developments upon regional social policies, together with the inter-regional dialogues and support processes taking place on a North–South basis. Chapter 10, by the editors, reviews the evidence for the emergence of regional social policies on four continents, suggesting the conditions best suited to their development and the factors which militate against their development. It reviews the shortcomings of the emerging system of global social governance, develops the case for a reformed system of international social governance based upon mutual cooperation between regional formations, and indicates the steps that need to be taken to advance this agenda. It ends with a call for further policy-related research on this topic.

Part I

The case for regionalism with a strong social dimension

In some – still limited – cases economic regionalization has been broadened towards other areas of society because it is believed that true economic integration cannot be achieved if trade and the economy are isolated from the rest of society. If, for instance, one wants to create a competitive economic union, this implies achieving a good innovation system, which in turn is linked to research and development. So one might consider a move away from national socio-economic policy research and towards a regional research area. Consequently, as research is linked to the higher education system, so again there can be a tendency towards unifying the educational system, without having a centralized educational body. Some scholars have called this 'new regionalism': a form of supranational regional integration that involves deep economic integration as well as integration in many other domains.

Once again, the European Union is the first and most developed example of such integration that is not only multi-dimensional but also based upon building a strong institutional and legal framework. It is a political model that challenges conventional assumptions about governance all over the world and is related to a transformation of the nation state and 'the dispersion of authoritative decision-making across multiple territorial levels' (Hooghe and Marks 2001: xi).

Regional integration by building a geopolitical identity and actorness

The two ways of achieving integration described above both focus upon internal procedures. Nevertheless, a trans-national region can also act in the international arena in a more or less unified way. This implies working towards a recognized regional identity at the geopolitical level as well as achieving regional coherence in how to address global issues. Such a form of regional integration is difficult to achieve as it goes against one of the main pillars of state sovereignty, its foreign policy.

However, regional integration that could have at least three main characteristics, which would distinguish it from the previous manifestation. First, the institutional environment for dealing with 'out of area' consequences of regional policies would become fully consolidated, by for instance organizing a regional 'diplomatic force'. Second, regions would become more proactive, engaging in inter-regional arrangements and agreements with a multidimensional character, going beyond purely trade issues and having the potential to affect a range of relations at the global level. Finally, regions would become more actively engaged as a single entity at the UN and in other world bodies.

In other words, while the first generation of regional integration was of an 'introverted' and protectionist nature, exclusively focusing on the creation of economic benefits for its members, the second generation brought in a more extroverted form of regionalism, extending integration to new domains although still mainly focusing on the consolidation of internal political integration. Finally, the third generation would introduce an extroverted level of regionalism, with a clear focus on the external projection of the region and inter-regionalism. Even though second-generation integration is still a limited phenomenon, the EU

1 Regional formations and global governance

Luk Van Langenhove and Maria Cristina Macovei

This chapter aims to provide a framework for understanding the growth and changing character of regional governance. This lays the basis for considering in Chapter 2 how social policy might be affected by the world-wide rise of regional governance. The first section explores how governance has evolved from an essentially state-led preoccupation into a complex phenomenon that involves many other actors and that is characterized by interlinkages between different (geographical) levels of policy-making. It will be argued that we are witnessing the transition from a single world of states towards a multiple world of states and regions. Important actors in this new world order are the world regional organizations and regional arrangements between states that have resulted from regional integration processes. The second section discusses three main varieties of regional integration that currently exist. First, there is regional integration by removing economic obstacles, a process that has resulted in a multitude of regional trade arrangements all over the world. Second, there is regional integration by building institutions and regulations that often go beyond economic and trade policies and that can be described as a 'pooling' of sovereignty at a transnational level. Third, there is regional integration by building a geopolitical identity and actorness. Here the 'world region'[1] behaves as an actor on the global scene, both through its own 'foreign' policy and through its presence in global institutions. The third and final section will then begin the exploration of the consequences of these varieties of regionalism for social policy. It will be argued that regionalism aimed only at creating free trade areas can put severe pressures on the existing national social policies of the countries involved. On the other hand, the development of a broader and deeper form of regionalism (often referred to as 'new regionalism') can act as a driver towards regional social policies. Moreover, in those – rare – cases where regionalism involves global actorness the regional external policy can contribute to the development of global social policies as well. By way of conclusion, it will be argued that in theory regional integration can act both as a building block and as a stumbling block on the way towards a global social policy that makes globalization 'fairer'.

The changing face of governance

In our globalized world, societies are affected more and more extensively and deeply by events in other societies. Debates on globalization raise questions regarding the appropriate political response to deal with both its negative and its positive effects. One of the fundamental questions is at what level action should be situated. Action can be taken by national and local authorities but it is often the case that these authorities are limited in their ability to tackle global and thus trans-national problems. On the other hand, there are the global world-wide institutions such as the UN and the Bretton Woods institutions. And in between these levels are the regional institutions (such as the EU, MERCOSUR, the Association of South East Asian Nations (ASEAN), Asia Pacific Economic Cooperation (APEC), the Southern African Development Community (SADC), the African Union (AU), the North American Free Trade Agreement (NAFTA), etc.), and perhaps at precisely that level there is increasing interest in and focus on dealing with the effects of globalization.

This may seem surprising as at first sight it could only be the UN which as a global institution offers a political answer to globalization. After all, the UN was founded in 1945 in an attempt to create a multilateral world forum where sovereign states could resolve differing opinions and where common actions about peace and development can be stimulated. Today, however, the world is dramatically different from that of the post-Second World War period in which the UN was founded. First of all, the geopolitical stability of that system disappeared with the end of the Cold War. Second, a lot more countries are now members of the UN than used to be the case (from the original fifty-one, the number has now risen to 192 member states), which means that the functioning of the General Assembly is not getting easier. Third, states now have to share their hegemony and their capacity to regulate economic transformation more and more with local governments, supra-national groupings and non-governmental actors.

One can observe that nowadays there are emerging problems that are beyond national or regional borders. Therefore, the problématique is how to deal with the rapid emergence of collective problems with cross-border dimensions, in particular those that are global in scope or potentially so. Global governance can be an answer to this problématique, as it refers to 'cooperative problem solving arrangements on a global plane' (Thakur and Van Langenhove 2006: 233). Global governance is characterized by a complex matrix of institutions, both formal and informal, of mechanisms, of processes between and among states, markets and citizens, and of organizations, both intergovernmental and non-governmental. In the global governance system collective interests are wrought, rights and obligations are set up, and differences are mediated (Thakur and Van Langenhove 2006). The need for global governance is very present in today's world; however, the idea of a centralized world government is not embraced by many people. In this respect, as underlined by Thakur and Van Langenhove (2008: 22), the goal of global governance 'is not the creation of world government, but an additional layer of consultation and decision-making' in governments and intergovernmental organizations. The organizing principle of global governance is multilateralism, and the UN represents the hub of the multilateral system of global governance. The world needs global governance in order to deal with non-passport issues, like human rights, chronic poverty, migration and other social problems. Global governance can be seen as a 'chameleon-like' concept that can be adapted to different meanings. The goals of global economic governance, for instance, are to manage the economic activity of the world without undermining state sovereignty, to preserve international financial stability, and to promote cooperative solutions to global problems, among others. Global security governance aims to minimize conflicts and violence across the planet, again respecting the sovereignty of the nation state (Thakur and Van Langenhove 2006). By the same token, global social governance, without harming the sovereignty of nations, seeks to protect the well-being of all people, including issues like social protection, education and health, and to try to solve the inequality and poverty dilemmas via intergovernmental modalities. Indeed, the world is 'stumbling towards the articulation of global social policy of global redistribution, global social regulation, and global social rights' (Deacon 2007). Global redistribution can be achieved via tax and income transfers, regional funds and overseas development assistance (ODA). Global social regulation is encompassing the core labour standards advanced by the ILO in 1998 and by UN Conventions. Global social rights are about citizenship empowerment, which refers to UN Conventions on the Rights of the Child and the UN International Covenant on Economic, Social and Cultural Rights (Deacon 2007, 2008).

The current debate (WCSDG 2004, Farrell *et al.* 2005, Thakur and Van Langenhove 2006, 2008, UNU-CRIS 2008) is advocating a global governance built on regional integration. This approach is of particular interest for the debate on advancing (regional) social policy (Deacon 2007, Yeates 2005, 2008, Yeates and Deacon 2006, Deacon *et al.* 2007). The regional level is becoming a level of governance actively involved in policy implementation and elaboration. Multi-level governance or 'the dispersion of authoritative decision-making across multiple territorial levels' (Hooghe and Marks 2001: xi) is the new paradigm to explain this phenomenon. From this perspective, European integration, for example, is a 'polity-creating process in which authority and policy-making influence are shared across multiple levels of government – sub-national, national, and supranational' (Hooghe and Marks 2001: 2). The weakening of the state and the shift of competences to the new sub-national and supra-national levels of government result from a dual process:

> European integration has shifted authority in several key areas of policy-making from national states up to European-level institutions. Regionalization in several countries, including the most populous ones, has shifted political authority from the national level down to the sub-national level of government.
>
> (Hooghe and Marks 2001: xi)

One of the main characteristics of the sovereign state is that it has long had a quasi-monopoly on the provision of public goods within its territory. The beneficiaries of public goods are not limited to a single consumer or a specific group or consumers; they are available to all. The benefits of different public goods, like legal systems and institutions, defence systems and nationwide highways, extend to the entire population of a specific state (Musgrave and Musgrave 2003: xi). Some of these public goods also deal with social policy. National poverty eradication programmes, national education programmes, national social security systems, etc. are examples in this sense.

A main debate has always been on how far a state should go in developing instruments of social policy. The two extreme positions in that debate have been: (i) states need to be strong to tame the negative consequences of market forces; and (ii) states need to refrain from interfering where markets can do a better job. States versus markets has been a dominating political theme and has long been the main point of difference between left and right. But recently, two major (interrelated) events have shaken that old paradigm of state/market balance. On the one hand, markets have increasingly become globalized. As a result, many aspects of industrial production and of trade have escaped the control of national states. On the other hand, states have increasingly become stripped of some of their powers and competences as a result of a double movement. In many cases, there has been devolution of power from the (central) state level to federalized entities. In a country such as Belgium, the majority of governmental policy domains are now situated at the level of regions. Next to that, there have been strong tendencies to somehow 'pool' sovereignty across states into larger regional entities. The EU is the most developed example of this trend, though other examples of how this pooling/cooperation is taking place across world-regions are provided in each of the chapters in Part II of this book. As a result, a complex web of interrelated levels and spheres of governance with many actors has emerged. For a person living in Belgium, for example, this means that policies are situated at the local level of the commune, the level of the provinces, the regional level, the level of the language community, the national (federal) level, the level of the Benelux group of countries, the European level and the global level.[2]

Notwithstanding the above, in the foreseeable future states will remain important centres of governance. Nevertheless, in an attempt to face the challenges of globalization, states can turn to sub-national and world regions to complement and even strengthen their power. The world of states would thus gradually become a world of states and regions. A world of states and regions could be an innovative approach that holds the promise of a renewed and better system of global and local governance. Within this development, regional integration has taken an important place since the mid-1980s. There has been not only a proliferation of various forms of regional integration processes on a global scale but also an unprecedented deepening of the process of European integration. The EU is the world's most advanced form of supranational regionalism. It has managed to develop a model that incorporates political elements in a system of deep economic integration, and as such challenges existing assumptions about governance.

This has important consequences for social policy. On the one hand, there is the issue of migration of some elements of social policy from the state level to either the supranational or the sub-national level. On the other hand, there is the problématique of the interaction between these different governance levels. Progressively, the idea that the EU should strengthen its competences in the social area over the national member states has indeed gained ground. In this sense, the first steps made have been the introduction of the legally enforceable 'acquis communautaire', the softer 'acquis' and the Open Method of Coordination (OMC)[3] (see also Chapter 5) to promote coordinated social policy-making. But all in all, the European integration process is not as advanced in social policy as in other policy domains.

Although not the model for the rest of the world, the EU can be seen as an example of regional integration with cooperation spanning culture, politics, security, economics, social policies and diplomacy. It is often taken as a model for political and economic efforts in other regions to achieve stability and prosperity. Not surprisingly then, those interested in the social dimension of regional integration turn to the EU to see how social policy has been handled in the European integration process (see Chapter 5).

But regional integration is a world-wide phenomenon, and the regions should not be seen just as formal institutions but rather as (re)constructed organizations in the process of global transformation. The regions, therefore, should be seen as 'dynamic in their development and open to change and adaptation' (Farrell 2005: 8).

In Latin America, for instance, the idea of Latin American unity achieved by regional economic integration has been on the agenda since the end of the Second World War. Prominent organizations in the region are MERCOSUR and the Andean Community, next to other forms of regional integration. MERCOSUR can be considered as a 'network regionalization' scheme, where regional identity is a response to globalization, and relies primarily on non-institutionalized or intergovernmental working methods (Warleigh-Lack 2008). The Asunción Treaty establishing MERCOSUR in 1991 does not provide for a special cluster of integration-related social issues. In 2004, however, the issue of the institutionalization of the social dimension began to form part of the agenda, with proposals and actions in this connection. This resulted in the creation in 2000 of the Social MERCOSUR, which consists of ministers and authorities in charge of the social development of MERCOSUR. The social dimension of MERCOSUR underlines the importance of an integration process that has real implications for human and social development (SELA 2008). In contrast with MERCOSUR, the social dimension of integration was part of the Andean Community (CAN) from its conception in 1969. The whole Andean integration process involved social and labour issues, followed by health-related ones. CAN has also started to deal with border problems and education-related issues, and in 2003 and 2004 the Andean Community approved its first decisions regarding its social development plan (SELA 2008) (see Chapter 6).

In Asia and the Pacific, the most notable examples of regional integration are ASEAN and APEC. According to Warleigh-Lack (2008), ASEAN, like MERCOSUR, is a network regionalization process. With its *ASEAN Vision 2020* (ASEAN Leaders 1997), ASEAN leaders vowed to establish a community of caring societies with a common regional identity. In October 2003, they returned to Bali to update the original Bali Concord that laid the foundation for their cooperation. The declaration ASEAN Concord II (Bali Concord II) provided for the establishment of an ASEAN community with three pillars, the ASEAN Security Community (ASC), the ASEAN Economic Community (AEC) and the ASEAN Socio-Cultural Community (ASCC). APEC is basically a forum to facilitate trade and investment. Labour issues in APEC have been mostly limited to human resources, productivity, worker training and education issues. A Human Resources Development Working Group (HRDWG), established in 1990, aims at facilitating recognition of qualifications between the participating members. It also fosters links and strengthens collaborative initiatives between the members by organizing regular meetings of education ministers. One major outcome in the field of professional recognition so far has been the APEC Engineers Register (see Chapters 7 and 9).

In the African continent regional integration schemes are taking place at both continental and sub-continental levels. The main drivers of continental integration are the UN Economic Commission for Africa (ECA) and the Organization of African Unity (OAU), now known as the African Union (AU). The second wave of African regionalization started in the 1980s and led to the creation of a patchwork of overlapping sub-continental organizations, such as the Southern African Development Community (SADC) and the Economic Community of West African States (ECOWAS). The ECOWAS Treaty provided for a Social and Cultural Affairs Commission designed to 'provide a forum for consultation generally on social and cultural matters affecting the member states' (Art. 49). The AU is the umbrella organization for all African regional arrangements.[5] It was designed as an intergovernmental organization and was established in 2002 to promote the unity and solidarity of African states, to spur economic development, and to promote international cooperation (see Chapter 8).

On a world scale the picture of regionalization is thus complex. There exist many regional organizations, and quite a lot of them overlap with other regional integration schemes (i.e. the overlapping membership in the case of Regional Economic Communities (RECs) in Africa). Most of the existing schemes, however, are little more than 'paper tigers': they have weak structures and powers, and all too often there is a gap between the integration discourses and the actual practices. Nevertheless, it is possible to identify differences in the nature of the ongoing integration processes.

Varieties of regional integration

Regional integration is a complex process of interactions between a group of (mostly) neighbouring countries that can be driven by state interventions or by interactions between citizens. As a merely European endeavour after the Second World War, regional integration has its origins in a political preoccupation to bring peace and security to Europe, based upon a common economic policy. Since then the idea has not only spread around the globe but it has also developed instruments of economic cooperation. As a result, regional integration schemes come in many different forms. Based upon the three generations of regional integration identified by Van Langenhove and Costea (2007), one can classify the many varieties of regionalism into three broad categories: (i) regional integration by removing economic obstacles; (ii) regional integration by building institutions and regulations; and finally (iii) regional integration by building a geopolitical identity and actorness.

Regional integration by removing economic obstacles

The building of a supranational region faces several obstacles, perhaps the most important being the concept of sovereignty as it limits – *de jure* – the possibility of 'interference' in the internal affairs of each of the member states. Identity can also be a major obstacle, as it – *de facto* –limits the urge towards integration. And then there are borders: fixed boundaries that limit the jurisdiction of each state and that can be used to control and limit the flow of goods, people and money across them.

One of the main drivers towards regional integration has always been trade. This is for obvious reasons: if one has goods to sell, why limit oneself to a market that coincides with a certain national territory? In principle, market expansion does not want to be limited by borders. States have long had a general tendency to limit free trade across borders, partly out of protectionism (limiting the inflow of goods should increase internal sales) and partly because trade across borders can generate income for the state through tariffs and custom duties. However, during the 1980s and 1990s most policy-makers agreed that allowing a maximum of free trade across borders would generate more benefits for all parties involved. More recently, this approach has come to be questioned and some now put forward a case for a degree of regional protectionism for the purposes of social development.

Not surprisingly, then, an important manifestation of regional integration has been and still is the economic integration of neighbouring states which involves the incremental lowering of all internal boundaries for trade and the establishment of common external boundaries. Such a form of regional integration is based upon the idea of a linear process of economic integration by which separate (national) economies are merged into larger world economic regions. This process begins with a Free Trade Area in which states agree to remove all custom duties and quotas on trade passing between them, keeping, however, the right to determine unilaterally the level of custom duties on imports coming from outside the region. The next stage is the Customs Union where a common level of duty on external trade arrangements is applied. The following stage is the Common Market where the free movement of goods and factors of production are added to the agreement on free trade. And finally there is the Economic Union: a common market is installed, including complete unification of monetary and fiscal policy. Mattli (1999: 41) has defined such economic regional integration as 'the voluntary linking in the economic domain of two or more formerly independent states to the extent that authority over key areas of domestic regulation and policy is shifted to the supranational level'.

The classic example of this linear evolution to economic integration is offered by Western Europe after the Second World War: the creation of the European Economic Community (EEC) under the Treaty of Rome in 1957 which removed the tariffs and quotas on intra-EEC trade; the achievement of a Customs Union in 1968 with the establishment of a Common External Tariff (CET; the creation of a Single European Market in the mid-1980s, eliminating the barriers still existing to trade and establishing the 'four freedoms' of circulation (persons, goods, services and capital). The economic union is in the process of being completed following the creation of a single currency, although, even in the EU, unification is still needed in important fields such as fiscal policy.

There are nevertheless numerous other examples world-wide of agreements at different levels of the above-mentioned spectrum of economic integration. European market integration became a trigger for the creation of similar common markets and free trade areas in the Middle East, Africa, the Pacific and the Americas during the 1960s and early 1970s. The surge in these agreements has continued since the early 1990s. With the current suspension of the Doha global trade negotiations in 2008, the road towards more economic regionalism lies open as it seems that such regionalism is a 'natural response to the diversity in the world of economy' (Ahearne *et al.* 2006).

Regional integration by building institutions and regulations

Economic integration as described above is not the only possible driver for building a world region. There are also domains in which states can cooperate in order to facilitate their approach to common problems or in order to create win-win situations. In addition, feelings of belonging to joint cultural or language groups can foster regional integration. In principle, there is not a single aspect of the social realm that cannot be the subject of integration processes. This implies not only state-driven integration but also integration from below, when the initiative comes from citizens. Of course, much citizen-driven integration can only occur to the extent that states allow it (see other chapters in this book, especially Chapter 4).

While economic integration in the strict sense is mostly a process of removing obstacles, non-economic integration more readily involves specific institution-building or regulations that promote or facilitate integration in fields such as justice, security, culture, education, social protection, etc. For instance, if two or more countries want to build a common security policy, this need not necessarily involve merging their separate armies but it will necessitate building a common security infrastructure such as a centralized command.

shows that the contours of a third generation of regionalism are becoming apparent. It recognizes that economic and internal political integration may be followed by integration in external policy with the ambition to participate in global institutions as a single entity with a single voice and to promote inter-regionalism.

While first-generation regional integration was generally a top-down process led by national governments and economic élites, with a strong emphasis on the process of government, the 'new regionalism' is characterized by the multiplication of actors involved in regional integration building, including national and regional civil society actors in a bottom-up process focusing on regional governance. Third-generation regional integration would go further in this respect, adding as a new category the trans-national actors involved in the processes of inter-regional cooperation. The emphasis is rather on the promotion of the region's identity in global governance and in countries and geographical regions outside its own continent.

Is the EU moving towards third-generation regionalism?

Despite the difficulties in ratifying the Lisbon Treaty, the EU is consolidating its position as the most advanced integration scheme in the world and is moving further towards third-generation regionalism. This is visible in the two domains discussed below, as well in the EU's growing role in inter-regional relations (see Chapter 9).

The development of an adequate foreign policy institutional design

In 'third-generation' regionalism the institutional environment for dealing with 'out of area' consequences of regional policies would become fully consolidated. Despite the problems of ratification, the European Constitutional Treaty, signed in Rome on 29 October 2004, was the first step towards bringing the EU closer than ever to unifying its foreign policy representation through the intermediary of several institutional innovations. The proposed Treaty of Lisbon to replace the Constitutional Treaty would represent a further major step in developing a unified foreign policy.

The Treaty creates a new High Representative for the Union in Foreign Affairs and Security Policy, who will conduct the Union's common foreign and security policy, presiding over the Foreign Affairs Council while also acting as a full member and Vice-President of the European Commission. This should ensure better coordination between the Council's foreign policy and security competences, ruled at present by a purely intergovernmental method, and the Commission's work in external relations, development and foreign trade, already dominated by the supranational method. In fulfilling this mandate, the High Representative shall be assisted by a European External Action Service, made up of officials from relevant departments of the General Secretariat of the Council and of the Commission, as well as staff seconded from the national diplomatic services of the member states. Furthermore, the European Council will become a fully fledged institution with a President appointed for two and a half years. The possibility of more closely structured cooperation in the field of defence policy is a new feature. At the same time, the Treaty of Lisbon, if ratified, will offer the EU a legal personality and therefore create the first ever regional organization that has the jurisdiction to act as a supranational organization within the framework of the UN.

If ratified and implemented by all member states, these institutional innovations have the potential to unify the European foreign policies which are currently fragmented between the Council, the Presidency and the Commission. This could also help to address the current 'frustrating ambiguity' (Telò 2005) about the EU's foreign policy identity between 'civilian power' and military power. By achieving a complete 'package of capabilities',[6] combining both 'soft power' and 'hard power' elements, the EU could promote a unique vision of international affairs in which multilateralism would prevail over unilateralism, and a specific strategy of conflict prevention combining civilian and military aspects.

The role of regions as actors within global institutions such as the UN

Finally, in third-generation form, regions would become more actively engaged at the UN. The European Union's commitment to multilateralism has gradually been consolidated as a defining principle of its foreign policy identity. The European Commission Communication of 9 September 2003, *The European Union and the United Nations: The Choice of multilateralism*, underlines Europe's attachment to multilateralism – and to the United Nations as the pivot of the multilateral system. This communication also highlighted two aspects in particular of the EU's contribution to the effectiveness of multilateral legal instruments and commitments established under UN auspices that could be further developed. The first is 'the EU's ability to act as a "front-runner" in developing and implementing multilateral instruments and commitments. And the second is support, where necessary, for the capacity of other countries to implement their multilateral commitments effectively' (European Commission 2003: 5). The communication also stated the need to lay the foundations for a wider EU–UN partnership going beyond development, and to build cooperation in security, conflict prevention, crisis management, peacekeeping and peace building. However, the presence of the EU in the UN will always be limited to the extent that the UN is an organization that brings together states and the EU is not a state.

Nevertheless, in the context of debates on UN reform, a number of developments are in progress that could pave the way for this aspect of third-generation regionalism (Thakur and Van Langenhove 2006: 233–40). The High-Level Panel on Threats, Challenges and Change (UN 2004) recognized that regional organizations can be a vital part of the multilateral system and this was confirmed by the former UN Secretary General Kofi Annan, in his 2005 report *In Larger*

Freedom. Towards Security, Development and Human Rights for All (UNSG 2005). In addition, the UN member states have called for a stronger relationship between the UN and regional organizations at the Millennium Review Summit in 2005. It was even suggested that regional organizations should be involved in the proceedings of the Security Council. Meanwhile, the existing high-level meetings between the UN and regional organizations have become annual since 2006 and coordinated with meetings of the Security Council (SC). This decision was taken in October 2005, when the Council adopted resolution 1631, in which it expressed its intention to have regular meetings with regional and sub-regional organizations. This is the first resolution on the UN and regional organizations.[7] The main areas for discussion specified in the resolution are standby arrangements, rapid deployment, small arms and light weapons, counter-terrorism and capacity-building assistance. Though 'some action has been taken and a number of countries have committed funds to African organizations, in particular ECOWAS, progress at the general level is minimal' (Thakur and Van Langenhove 2006: 233–40). Moreover, the Secretary General asked to submit a report on the issue to the Security Council. As a result, in July 2006 the report *A Regional–Global Security Partnership: Challenges and Opportunities* was issued (UN 2006a).

All these recent developments go back to the UN Charter, Chapter VIII of which predicted a specific role for regional organizations. Scholars such as Graham and Felício (2006) and Tavares (2006) have argued that the time is ripe to take Chapter VIII as the basis of a new global-regional security system. Of course, this cannot be seen independently of the hot issue of the reform of the SC. A regional framework for SC membership could facilitate UN–regional organization cooperation and allow regional actors such as the EU to play a greater role in international politics.

In other words, a number of developments within the UN are gradually allowing regional organizations to act much like international actors, just as states do.[8] One would expect the EU, currently the most advanced second-generation entity in the world to take full advantage of this and support UN reform processes designed to create a space where it will be able to manifest itself as a third-generation integration scheme. This seems, however, not to be the case, mainly because the EU does not apparently want to be identified as a Chapter VIII agency. Given its current special status within the UN, accepting Chapter VIII status would somehow be perceived as a demotion putting the EU on the same level as, say, the African Union or the League of Arab States (Graham and Felício 2006).

Regional social policies

Regional integration thus comes in many varieties. On the one hand, there are the pure Regional Trade Agreements (RTAs). More than 400 RTAs are currently notified to the WTO. On the other hand, there are supranational regional arrangements that go beyond pure economic integration. Such integration schemes exist and the EU is currently the most developed example. And finally a kind of regionalism seems to be emerging and taking its place as an actor in the multilateral system, next to nation states; again, the EU is in the forefront of this process, its objection to Chapter VIII[9] status and its failure to ratify the Lisbon Treaty notwithstanding.

All of these developments present challenges to social policies: first, the impact of the proliferation of first-generation integration schemes on national social policies; second, the development of regional social policies in the framework of second-generation integration schemes; and third, the emergence of regional integration as a catalyst for global social policies.

Regional integration as a factor affecting national social policies

Whether regional integration has positive or negative impacts upon national social policy is a question much contested with claims and counterclaims. Some draw attention to the downward pressure on social and labour standards resulting from economic competition. Others draw attention to the levelling up of national policies through legally binding regional directives.

Downward pressures

Regional trade agreements have brought with them increasing openness to global competition. It has been argued that this has imposed costs on unskilled labour in industrial countries through downward pressure on wages, erosion of social security systems, and weakening of trade unions and labour standards. The creation of 'internal' regional markets has given birth to a fundamental economic dilemma:

- It is in the interest of companies to move business from high-wage to low-wage countries.
- It is in the interest of workers to move from low-wage to high-wage countries.

Furthermore, companies move from countries with high labour standards to countries with low labour standards. In developing countries, this increased openness has exacerbated the prevalence child labour and other violations of core labour standards as established by the ILO (Granger and Siroën 2006).

Incorporating labour rights provisions into regional trade agreements

Attempts by the ILO to establish at a global scale legally binding regimes of social standards have not hitherto been successful. Opposition to a multilateral regime for social standards has come from developing countries which feared that it would undermine their comparative advantages in low-wage, labour-intensive industries (Dasgupta 2000). The possibility of such standards being developed at a regional level has opened up.

At the regional level, however, even in the EU, the most advanced example of regional integration with a social dimension, member states still have maintained a large degree of sovereignty over labour legislation. Nevertheless, the EU has developed a series of directives governing social issues that deal with free movement of labour, social security, equal treatment of men and women, protection of safety and health at the workplace and the introduction of a 'social dialogue' between industrial management and labour representatives at the European level. The European Charter of Fundamental Social Rights, incorporated into the 1993 Maastricht Treaty, has given enlarged competence to the EU to legislate in a number of areas.

Regional integration as a driver towards regional social policies

The main characteristic of 'second-generation' regionalism or 'new regionalism' is the development of the political dimension. The political dimension has to be understood according to Hettne's (1999) definition of 'new regionalism':

> [a] multidimensional form of integration which includes economic, political, social, and cultural aspects and thus goes far beyond the goal of creating region-based free trade regimes or security alliances. Rather, the political ambition of establishing regional coherence and identity seems to be of primary importance.

As underlined by Van Langenhove and Costea (2007), the ideas behind 'new regionalism' rely on the fact that trade and the economy cannot be isolated from the rest of the society. Integration is also about non-economic matters, like social, cultural and environmental issues. The more the economies become integrated the more common policies in the social field will be needed.

Regional integration through institution building has been most prominent in Europe. Nevertheless, the EU institutions have played a relatively minor role in social policy when compared to their powers in purely economic matters such as trade, competition and monetary policy. Since the 1980s, under pressure from social groups, EU social policy has been gradually developed. However, the key moment for developing a coherent set of regional social policies was the Lisbon Summit in 2000. The heads of the member states adopted the Lisbon Strategy, aiming to turn the EU into 'the most competitive and knowledge based economy in the world capable of sustainable economic growth with more and better jobs and greater social cohesion' (Zeitlin *et al.* 2005). Therefore, the EU model has been redefined to include high economic growth and a high level of social and economic cohesion. This is Europe's response to globalization, designed to make its business and labour more competitive and better able to take advantage of the opportunities created in a globalized world.

The Lisbon Strategy, however, represents the materialization of progressive EU initiatives regarding labour and employment issues. The 1992 Maastricht Treaty was the moment when it was decided to form the Monetary Union. Moreover, a multilateral surveillance procedure was introduced for aligning national decisions. Based on the new provisions of the Amsterdam Treaty in 1997, which included for the first time a chapter on employment policy, the Luxembourg European Council in 1997 paved the way for the European Employment Strategy (EES). The EES is designed to function as the main tool to give direction to and ensure coordination of the employment policy priorities to which member states should subscribe at EU level.

The EES represents the foundation of a new soft working method at EU level – the Open Method of Coordination (OMC), launched at the Lisbon Summit in 2000. The OMC is a new and broadly applicable instrument of EU governance that addresses common European concerns while taking into consideration national diversity. Moreover, it is a tool that translates the European guidelines into national and regional policies. The main areas covered are employment, social inclusion, pensions, health, research and innovation, and education and training (see also Chapter 5 below).

Regional integration as catalyst of global social policies

The EU is our most developed example of a region as an actor seeking to influence global policy. Since the beginning of the millennium the EU 'has indeed taken a more systematic and assertive approach to advancing the social dimension of globalization' (Orbie and Tortell 2008: 21). Together with the ILO, the EU as a global player has been instrumental in injecting decent work (including social protection) into the Millennium Development Goals (MDGs), and, since 2005, has included social cohesion in its external development assistance (Delarue 2006). Moreover, the EU plays an important role in promoting social clauses throughout its trade and development policies. A significant objective of the EU's global social agenda is deepening its cooperation with the ILO. Thus the EU as a global actor is promoting the effective application of core labour standards at global level. Moreover, its strategy aims at helping developing countries to apply core labour standards for achieving social development (European Commission 2001). An example of this is the Cotonou Agreement, signed in 2000 with the ACP countries, which makes specific reference to the ILO core labour standards (CLS).

The EU's international position on health, gender, children's rights and corporate social responsibility has many progressive features. The European Commission is cited as an important example to follow in the World Commission on the Social Dimension of Globalization (WCSDG), which issued the report, *A Fair Globalization. Creating Opportunities for all* (2004). The 'European social model', the Lisbon Strategy and the Open Method of Coordination are given as models for international social governance.

In the field of development, the EU supports the UN sustainable development policies and is committed to achieving the UN MDGs. By adopting *The European Community's Development Policy*, the European Commission (2000) strengthened the role of the EU in promoting regional integration, alongside five other activities. In this respect, 'the EU has clearly acknowledged [the] link between regional integration and development in its policies towards African countries [...] by including regional integration among the focal priorities for poverty reduction mentioned in the Cotonou Agreement' (Van Langenhove and Costea 2007: 71).

However, Orbie and Tortell (2008: 21) note that:

> in relation to initiatives such as the inclusion of labour standards in bilateral agreements, the social dimension of the Union's enlargement and neighbourhood policies, the implementation of gender mainstreaming in development aid and the achievements of the MDG, the EU's actions are still at a preliminary stage.

Moreover, it has been argued that the EU is an *obstacle* to fair globalization in its trade policies even as it argues for fairer globalization. Thus, it has been claimed that the EU's attempts at creating Economic Priority Areas between itself and former ACP states is not conducive to enabling African and other poorer countries to develop the social and labour dimensions of their own regional integration (Keet 2007a). This aspect of the EU's inter-regional strategy will be examined further in Chapter 9 below.

A third position argues that the EU as a global social policy player is neither an effective actor for progressive global social policies based upon the EU model nor an obstacle because of its trade policies, but is indeed irrelevant because European social welfare ideas and ideals are not transferable to other world regions. Thus

> In the light of the peculiar religious-historical roots of social policy in the West, we must reassess the transferability of Western institutions to countries with a different cultural foundation as well as standards of measurement of progress in the development of a welfare state.
>
> (Rieger and Leibfried 2003: 326)

In fairness, the EU insists it does not seek to export its own social model or to promote harmonization with its own social standards. In addition, together with the World Commission on the Social Dimension of Globalization, it strictly refuses any sanctions-based approach to labour standards in international trade agreements (European Commission 2004c).

The question of whether the EU is an agent for progressive change in social policy in other world regions will be returned to in Chapter 9 below.

Conclusions

Regional integration can act both as a building block and as a stumbling block on the way to a global social policy that makes globalization more 'fair'. The report of the WCSDG, *A Fair Globalization. Creating Opportunities for All*

(2004), strengthens the idea that regional integration can contribute to a more equitable pattern of globalization, but only if regional integration has a strong social dimension. The WCSDG referred quite extensively to the need to strengthen regional governance, based on principles of participation and democratic accountability:

> Representative bodies, such as regional parliaments, have an important role to play. We believe that regional integration should be advanced through social dialogue between representative organizations of workers and employers, and wider dialogue with other important social actors, on the basis of strong institutions for democratic and judicial accountability. The creation of tripartite or wider councils and forums at the regional level ... provides an important institutional framework for such dialogue.
>
> (WCSDG 2004: 73)

At least in theory, regional integration offers a number of possibilities for the development of

> regional social, *regulation, rights and redistribution schemes* (Yeates and Deacon 2006) in the form of regional *social, health and labour regulations*, regional mechanisms that give citizens a voice to challenge their governments in terms of *social rights*; regional intergovernmental forms of *co-operation in social policy*; regional cross-border *investments* in the area of social policy; regional *coordination of economic and developmental policies*; regional initiatives in *capacity building and innovation* to strengthen the capabilities of people; or *inter-regional* agreements and arrangements related to social issues.
>
> (UNU-CRIS 2008: 1)

These issues are explored in Chapter 2 below.

A general tendency that can be observed is the need for more initiatives in the area of social policy at the regional level. Shallower forms of regional integration and inter-regional relations introduce social issues as part of the broader attempts to manage and regulate intra- or inter-regional flows of goods and services (trade), capital (investment) and people (migration). In deeper, broader and more institutionalized forms of regionalism, more or less embryonic forms of what could be called regional social policies can and do emerge, through policy approximation, coordination and/or convergence. However, policy spill-over mechanisms and policy sequencing within regional integration processes are still not very well understood, mainly because they remain under-studied – even if some new trends in regionalism studies are emerging to address these important questions.

Notes

1 In the text 'world region' refers to supranational entities.

2 While this concept of levels captures an element of the emerging process of multi-levelled governance it is also important to recognize that higher-level actors can and do take part in lower-level decisions and vice versa. Some kinds of actors are more likely to jump scale, such as representatives of global financial institutions or policy consultants.

3 See also Deacon (2007: 165).

4 See APEC website: www.apec.org.

5 Eight RECs are accredited to the AU: ECOWAS, COMESA, ECCAS, SADC, AMU, IGAD, CEN-SAD, EAC (First Conference of African Ministers of Economic Integration in March 2006, Ouagadougou, Burkina Faso, CAMEI/Consol. Report (I)).

6 In 2002, Javier Solana, the EU High Representative for Common Foreign Security Policy, stated in the Spanish journal *Politica Exterior*:

> The best way to confront many of the challenges that have appeared in the twenty-first century regarding security will be by the coordinated and coherent application of a 'package of capacities' that includes economic, diplomatic, civilian and military resources. The EU is gradually putting such a package together.
>
> (Javier Solana, *Politica Exterior*, Marzo/Abril 2002, XVI (86): 10)

7 See www.securitycouncilreport.org/site/c.glKWLeMTIsG/b.2616247/k.893B/Update_Report_No_3BR_The_UN_and_Regional_OrganisationsBR_23_March_2007.htm.

8 See also Van Langenhove (2003: 1–4).

9 The Charter of the UN refers to regional arrangements in its Chapter VIII. Article 52.1 of Chapter VIII states that:

> Nothing in the present Charter precludes the existence of regional arrangements or agencies for dealing with such matters relating to the maintenance of international peace and security as are appropriate for regional action, provided that such arrangements or agencies and their activities are consistent with the Purposes and Principles of the United Nations.

For more information see www.unhchr.ch/html/menu3/b/ch-chp8.htm.

2 Globalization, regional integration and social policy

Nicola Yeates and Bob Deacon

This chapter establishes the case for strengthened regional social policy as a necessary element of effective global social governance. The discussion is organized around four main sections. First, we set out the context of a research and policy focus on regional social policy, rehearsing arguments about the possible impacts of existing forms of globalization upon *national* social policy on the one hand and the difficulties of securing a *global* social contract with effective global social policies on the other. We then proceed to set out the case in principle for a *regional* social policy and several advantages of regional social policy and regional social integration are identified. The next section proposes possible social policy mechanisms along the axes of regional social redistribution, regional social regulation and regional social rights, and elaborates idealized examples of regional standard-setting, regional policy coordination and regional identity mobilization. Finally, the chapter considers some of the challenges and issues for advocates of regional social policy.

The limits of global social policy

The global system that has emerged in the opening years of the twenty-first century has generated a vigorous debate amongst scholars, policy-makers and activists about how to preserve existing, and develop new, policies that adequately provide for the social needs of populations. Much of the context and impetus for this debate stems from the Northern-driven neo-liberal social experiments of the 1980s and 1990s that supported increased global production, global trade and the global delivery of a wide range of goods and services to respond to the preferences and demands of an expanding global consumer market. This strategy encouraged increased commercialization, informalization and privatization of welfare services to meet unmet social needs more cost-effectively, and involved lighter- touch social regulation conducive to a more flexible economic environment. The dynamics unleashed by these policies are manifesting themselves in the welfare arena: national social contracts are being undermined as welfare states are set in competition with one another and as global health and welfare markets are created. Extant systems of public service provision are less able to respond to social needs, and the idea of comprehensive public services is under threat. Overall, it has been clear that the supposed opportunities that such experiments were designed to create have been unevenly distributed; furthermore, they have created new and widespread social risks for populations as a whole, increasing the incidence of poverty and exacerbating social inequality, polarization and conflict.

Growing concerns with the negative and widespread social consequences of neo-liberal 'free' trade-driven globalization are feeding alternative global social policy imaginaries. Increasingly, attention is turning to address the kinds of systems and policies necessary for a socially just globalization, one that maximizes the satisfaction of the human needs and rights of everyone, irrespective of their country of origin or residence, or their social background and position. One response to a perceived threat to public social provision at the national level has been to argue for more coherent trans-national policy cooperation and coordination. One expression of trans-national social policy involves *global* redistribution, regulation and social rights, involving reformed global institutions with 'teeth' and capable of tackling global social problems. One version of this global social reform agenda involves strengthened UN-based global social governance, giving more powers to the Economic and Social Council (ECOSOC), as a means of curtailing the global influence of the World Bank. Another version involves more extended inter-organizational cooperation and policy dialogue between the Bank and the UN agencies, as advocated by the ILO-sponsored World Commission on the Social Dimension of Globalization which reported in 2004 (Deacon 2007). Yet another version would build upon the G20 as a more representative gathering of countries and strengthen it with a permanent secretariat (ODI 2009).

However, formidable obstacles are involved. Many governments and non-governmental bodies in the Global North and Global South alike are unsure about the appropriateness of a Northern-driven reformed globalization strategy imposing 'inappropriate' global social and labour standards, while many actors in the South are reluctant to buy into even the more progressive forms of conditionality. For some in the Global South (Keet and Bello 2004, Bello 2004), the point is not so much to reform and strengthen extant 'global' institutions that are controlled by and operate in the interests of the North, but to undermine and outflank them by creating new countervailing and pluralistic sources of power properly serving the interests of the Global South:

> [W]hat developing countries and international civil society should aim at is not to reform the TNC-driven WTO and Bretton Woods institutions, but ... [a strategy that] would include strengthening diverse actors and institutions such as UNCTAD, multilateral environmental agreements, the International Labour Organization and regional economic blocs.
>
> (Bello 2004: 116–17)

As this quote suggests, it is here that the construction and strengthening of regional organizations of countries enter the picture. Rather than seeking to develop a case for a *global social policy of redistribution, regulation and rights* that would also imply a strengthening of Northern-based and Northern-controlled institutions, or seeking to win the Bretton Woods institutions over to a European progressive perspective on social policy so that the World Bank and the UN concur on the advice to give national governments about the best social policies, the point should be to liberate a policy space where Southern governments and civil society can make their own policy choices. Thus, the focus should perhaps be on building several *regionally based social policies of redistribution, regulation and rights* as part of a more general strategy of global economic governance based on economic devolution (Bello 2004: 117). Thus, reforming global social governance should perhaps imply building a world federation of regions, in which the role of international organizations is 'to express and protect local and national cultures by embodying and sheltering their distinctive practices' (John Gray, cited in Bello 2004: 118).

International civil society and several emerging trading blocs and other regional associations in the South are showing signs of concretely engaging with this regionalist global governance reform agenda. They are confronting key policy questions such as: (i) how to forge an appropriately balanced relationship between trade and social (labour, welfare, health) standards?; (ii) how to maintain levels of taxation and progressive tax structures in the face of international competition to attract and maintain inward capital investment?; and (iii) how to balance national risk- and resource-pooling systems and mechanisms with regional ones? In the next part of this chapter we turn our attention to the principles of and arguments in favour of forging a social policy dimension of regional integration.

The advantages of regional cooperation and social policy[1]

Countries may find several potential advantages in building a social policy dimension to regional groupings of nations. In this section we first set out these advantages in principle and relate them to current examples. These include: (i) creating a stronger voice in international negotiations and agreements; (ii) stronger protection from global market forces; and (iii) international economies of scale and risk pooling. We then proceed to discuss some of the ways in which the case for strengthened regional social policy is being taken up by global commissions and agencies.

In terms of *a stronger voice in international negotiations*, since regional formations often entail groups of countries with similar (or at least less diverse) cultural, legal and political characteristics and legacies, agreement on the scope and nature of collaboration may be more feasible and progress can potentially be made more quickly than in global multilateral negotiations involving a wide diversity of countries. Because of this greater similarity, regional formations can offer countries access to a broader menu of policy alternatives (Yeates 2005). For smaller and developing countries in particular, regional formations offer enhanced access to and influence over policy developments (Yeates 2005). In the EU, for example, small countries can have a strong blocking effect on the development of social policy. These national influences on regional formations are not necessarily negative: more socially developed countries can force social standards upwards in the poorer members of the formation. Regional formations offer further advantages to countries within global multilateral negotiations and fora: by having earlier consultations and building common positions, regional formations offer significant advantages to countries within global multilateral negotiations and fora, namely avoiding rushed decisions and amplifying their expression of regional circumstances and positions. Finally, given the aforementioned difficulties involved in the forging of global multilateral standards, regional formations might give countries, especially those in the South, a stronger voice to advance their own social standards and at a faster rate than would be possible in global fora (Yeates 2005).

In terms of *protection from global market forces*, in addition to grouped countries having a louder voice in the global discourse on economic and social policy in the UN and other fora, such an approach affords protection from global market forces that might erode national social entitlements. Regional formations also offer a means of 'locking in' internationalizing flows of finance, production and labour on a regional basis. Regionalist trading strategies are an effective means of protecting, promoting and reshaping a regional division of labour, trade and production. Nurturing and protecting internationalizing trade flows enable fiscal resources to be generated for national and regional social policy purposes. Too often global trade comes with tax exemptions for local and global companies that erode such fiscal resources. At the same time Southern regional formations can become a 'transmission belt' that receives increased overseas development assistance (ODA) or revenue from projected global taxes. In this way the social policy conditions placed upon countries in receipt of such global funds can be managed and determined through peer review mechanisms of countries within the same region. The offer by the African Union to manage the increased flows of ODA to Africa is one such example. Such strengthened regional formations can also provide a career move for Southern civil servants who might otherwise be lost to the World Bank or other Northern agencies.

A third main set of advantages to countries of a regionalist social policy strategy relates to *economies of scale and risk pooling*. On the first of these, in a context of pressing social needs and limited resources, there are benefits from developing economies of scale whenever possible. For instance, where not all countries can develop expensive high-quality universities and research centres, there is a major argument for uniting forces across neighbouring countries and agreeing to create regional educational training/research centres. Cross-border agreements on education and the mobility of educators, scholars and students can also foster regional identity.

Regional integration can also redress some of the limitations of national social policies and schemes. One of the reasons why agricultural insurance experiments have failed across the world is because of their small size, meaning they collapse when a major catastrophe occurs (e.g. drought, plant pest or cattle disease affecting a whole country); in these situations, insurance funds have been unable to cover all losses. However, by pooling risks internationally, and by adequate reinsurance, schemes can work. During disasters of widespread proportion when a nation's finances are at a low ebb, other countries can share the burden (Ortiz 2001). Apart from agricultural insurance, there is the more basic question of natural disasters. The precarious conditions under which poor populations live generate catastrophic human and economic losses when natural disasters occur (e.g. earthquakes, typhoons, floods, volcanic eruptions). Regional social policies offer the possibility of increased rapid response for disaster mitigation, management and preparedness (Deacon *et al.* 2007).

Many of these arguments have found expression in ongoing debates at the level of global commissions. The report of the World Commission on the Social Dimension of Globalization (WCSDG 2004) claimed that regional integration can contribute to a more equitable pattern of globalization, but only if regional integration has a strong social dimension. According to the Commission, regional arrangements can achieve this by empowering people and countries to better manage global economic forces, by helping to build the capabilities needed to take advantage of global opportunities, and by improving the conditions under which people connect to the global economy (WCSDG 2004: 71). The WCSDG refers to *the regional governance level* with respect to: (i) the need to build representative regional institutions and organize regional social dialogues; (ii) the importance of linking trade liberalization (at the global and regional levels) to respect for labour rights; (iii) the need to make investment rules more development-friendly; and (iv) the urgency of providing a more appropriate regulatory framework for migration.

In terms of *regional social dialogues* it argues that

> Representative bodies, such as regional parliaments, have an important role to play. We believe that regional integration should be advanced through social dialogue between representative organisations of workers and employers, and wider dialogue with other important social actors, on the basis of strong institutions for democratic and judicial accountability. The creation of tripartite or wider councils and forums at the regional level ... provides an important institutional framework for such dialogue.
>
> (WCSDG 2004: 73)

In terms of *labour standards*, as we noted earlier, increasing openness to global competition has imposed costs on labour in industrial countries through downward pressure on wages, the erosion of social security systems, and the weakening of trade unions and labour standards. While the trade–labour linkage has been side-stepped at the multilateral level, labour standards are now increasingly incorporated into RTAs and bilateral FTAs, led by the United States and the EU (see Chapter 9 in this volume).

In terms of *investment rules*, regional collective action and rule-making, as suggested by the Commission, could indeed reproduce a number of the potential benefits of a multilateral investment regime (greater transparency and fewer incompatibilities, leading to lower transaction costs and fewer rules on competition among capital-importing countries), while at the same time making progress on, for example, finding a new balance between domestic policy objectives and investment provisions and reaching more transparency and balance in dispute settlement. Collective renegotiation of bilateral investment treaties at the regional level might be an interesting option, although the economic and political 'optimal size' of the regions remains to be established, as well as the legal bases for such collective action.

In terms of *cross-border migration* patterns, problems (forced migration, remittances, etc.) may differ between regions. Regional specificities exist, related to the nature of migration in the different regions, for example regards integration or return policies or, more generally, immigration or emigration policies. Nonetheless, much more emphasis is now put, at this regional level, on the positive effects of cross-border movements of people, for example on migration as compensating for the demographic deficit of ageing populations in industrialized countries. The current debate focuses on the means of reaping these benefits by managing migration in an orderly and efficient way. In its final report, acknowledging these changes in migration patterns and policies, the WCSDG (2004) recommends the development of a multilateral framework for 'orderly and managed' cross-border movements of people, a framework that could help to 'enhance global productivity' and 'eliminate exploitative practices' by 'complementing measures to achieve a more balanced strategy for global growth and full employment'. According to the World Commission, given a global framework based on more democratic rules and respect for the human rights of migrants, the countries of origin and destination, as well as the migrants themselves, could maximize the benefits of migration and minimize the negative sides: this framework could 'provide uniform and transparent rules for cross-border movements of people' and 'balance the interests of both migrants themselves and of countries of origin and destination'. The WCSDG insisted further on the fact that 'the issues and problems associated with the movement of people across national borders cannot be addressed by single countries acting in isolation or on a unilateral basis'. Thus, this implies the development of effective cooperation arenas at the regional level (WCSDG 2004: 94, 96–9).

Within the UN system too, such ideas about reinforcing the regional level in order to 'tame' globalization are increasingly popular. In the July 2006 session of ECOSOC the UN Secretary General declared that multi-stakeholder policy dialogues at the national and regional levels have to be developed 'with the objective of building national and regional capacity to develop a multi-disciplinary approach to economic and social issues' (UNSG 2006). This came on the back of ongoing initiatives within other parts of the UN. In 2005, UNESCO organized a High-Level Symposium on the Social Policy Dimension of Regionalism in Montevideo in the context of the UNESCO International Social Sciences Policy Nexus Forum (Deacon *et al.* 2006). The resulting *Buenos Aires Declaration* called upon 'the regional organisations such as MERCOSUR and the African Union, in association with social scientists and civil society, to further develop the social dimension of regional integration and [called] upon the UN to facilitate inter-regional dialogues' (UNESCO 2006). Since then, arguments for strengthening the regional dimensions of their social policies have continued to gather pace. The UNDESA commissioned a working paper arguing the case for regional social policies as a contribution to poverty alleviation (Deacon *et al.* 2007), while the proposals of the High-Level Panel on UN Reform calling for 'One UN' at national level also call for the regional UN economic commissions and the UN social agencies to rationalize their regional structures and better target their efforts on actually existing regional associations of countries (UN 2006). There is some evidence that donors are taking up these ideas too. The new consensus on comprehensive social policies for development (Wiman *et al.* 2007) arising out of a meeting of donors paid significant attention to the case for regional as well as national and global social policies.

The content and mechanisms of regional social policy

In principle, therefore, through intergovernmental agreements, regionalism would make possible the development of regional social policy mechanisms of cross-border redistribution, regulation and rights, as well as facilitating a number of other cross-border cooperation mechanisms. In this section we outline the form that such mechanisms could take. This discussion refers both to idealized forms and actually existing ones.

- Regional social *redistribution* mechanisms. Regionally financed funds can take several forms, ranging from targeting particularly depressed localities, to tackling particularly significant health or food shortage issues or stimulating cross-border cooperation. Capacity-building of weaker governments by stronger ones is another approach. If such mechanisms are in place, then North–South transfers funded either by ODA or by global taxes could be transmitted to specific localities via the regional structure.
- Regional social, health and labour *regulations.* These can include standardized regulations to combat an intra-regional 'race to the bottom'. Such regulations are commonly thought of as relating to health and safety, labour and social protection, and agreements on the equal treatment of men and women, and majority and minority (including indigenous) groups, but they could also extend to a range of other areas including food production and handling standards and utilities. Regional formations may also in principle be in a stronger position in relation to private suppliers to set, monitor and enforce cross-border rules regarding, for example, access rights to commercial services.
- Regional mechanisms that give citizens a voice to challenge their governments in terms of social *rights.* Principles of social policy and levels of social provision could be articulated and used as benchmarks for countries to aspire to. In the long term the EU's European Court of Justice or the Council of Europe's Court of Human Rights could serve as useful models of mechanisms by which citizens can be empowered to challenge the perceived failures to fulfil such rights.

- Regional *intergovernmental cooperation.* Governments within a region could cooperate in social policy in terms of regional health specialization, regional education cooperation, regional food and livelihood cooperation and regional recognition of social security entitlements.

  The possibilities for the sharing of specialist health services are numerous. Cross-border agreements on education mobility can foster regional identity. Cross-border labour mobility issues can be managed more effectively and with greater justice if there are social protection-related mobility rights. Regional cooperation can also create an opportunity to learn from good practices that have worked at national level through intergovernmental policy dialogue.

There are a range of different mechanisms and methods of regional social policy to bring about redistribution, regulation and rights and cross-border cooperation and sharing, including standard-setting, policy coordination, legislation and regional identity mobilization. The UNDESA working paper, 'Regional Social Policy' (Deacon *et al.* 2007), focused primarily on developing countries and lists some possible policies in different social sectors. The following is based upon part of the recommendations of that working paper.

Employment and decent work

Creating decent employment is a result of employment-sensitive economic policies, combined with adequate labour market interventions at the national level. However, this can be fast-tracked with regional support. The EU offers a good example of how harmonization of labour regulations under the EU *acquis communautaire* and EU regional funds can promote employment and decent work at the local level. For developing countries, the two critical priorities are to ensure, first, that policy-makers understand the links between economic and social policies, and, second, that regional funds are created to promote employment in poorer areas that otherwise could not be supported by national administrations. Among specific policies in this domain are: enhanced inter-ministerial cooperation (economic and social sectors) to ensure that economic policies are employment generating; sharing of experiences and best practice in the areas of employment, sustainable livelihoods and labour standards; establishing regional funds for programmes for employment generation and for promoting formalization of informal work (promoting small and medium enterprises, cooperatives, wage subsidies, public works, guaranteed job schemes, and special employment programmes for women, youth and persons with disabilities); and skills development programmes (training and retraining of labour to enhance employability and productivity).

Health

The cross-border spread of diseases (e.g. HIV/AIDS, SARS, tuberculosis, malaria, avian flu, etc.) must be prevented and collaborative efforts between governments strengthened. Extending coverage of health is a priority in most countries and international cooperation on the development of accessible and affordable quality health care can effectively support national health systems. Additionally, there are benefits from economies of scale in the regional production of cheaper generic drugs. A good example can be found in South America's MERCOSUR harmonization of pharmaceutical legislation and regulations to facilitate economies of scale among Argentina, Brazil, Paraguay, Uruguay and Venezuela. Regional policies could include regional early warning systems of epidemics, coupled to the regional coordination of specialists for rapid deployment to affected areas; bolstering of the ability of border controls to monitor the movement of persons from and into affected areas; establishing effective procedures for disinfecting people, livestock and vehicles; facilitating regional access of citizens to specialized health care facilities through partnerships; coordination of regional procurement and production of pharmaceuticals and benefits from economies of scale; investigating the viability of mobile medical and health care units to ensure that remote rural communities have access to diagnosis and treatment; and coordinating approaches to global health funds.

Social protection

Social protection instruments, particularly social security systems, social pensions and social assistance, are priority instruments to expedite poverty reduction. If well designed, social protection instruments are highly redistributive and important for raising incomes and initiating a positive spiral of aggregate demand in domestic markets. Like employment, social protection is mostly a national issue; however, there are benefits from regional cooperation. An example can be found in the decision by the Andean Community (Bolivia, Colombia, Ecuador and Peru) to strengthen and harmonize members' social security systems and create an Andean Social Humanitarian Fund and an Integral Plan for Social Development, to unite efforts to fight poverty, exclusion and inequality. Potential regional programmes include (i) cross-border social protection programmes to address remote communities' development needs (e.g. distant areas near borders, ethnic minorities, etc.); (ii) regional funds to ensure social transfers to vulnerable populations like children (child benefits), elderly and disabled persons and rural areas (social pensions); and (iii) development of cross-border cooperation in social security and social protection policies that include provision for low-skilled and casual economic migrants, as well as the highly skilled mobile labourers, including portability of benefits.

Higher education and research

The erosion of public expenditures on higher education in many developing countries due to structural adjustment, combined with the brain drain of the few highly trained experts into the aid industry, has led to the reduction of research capacity in the field of social policy. Addressing lack of funding is an urgent priority. Given resource limitations, there are major advantages from a regional division of labour in research and education; not all countries need to develop expensive high-quality research – advantages are to be found in regional cooperation, creating regional centres with higher-quality research addressing local topics. Potential regional programmes include: funds for regional academic fellowships to build research capacity in national and regional institutions; support for regional tertiary education; and academic networks.

Regional social policy: challenges and issues

The opportunities for, and practice of, developing a regional social policy are not without their difficulties and challenges. These are discussed under four headings: elite origins and orientations of regional formations; competition from trans-continental open and bilateral trading arrangements; financing; and long-term policy-making.

Elite origins and orientations of regional formations

There has been little popular demand for regionalist projects,[2] and such formations have tended to originate in discussions and negotiations within restricted policy-making circles involving trade and finance ministers and economists. This problem of extant regional formations originating as regional elite projects does not deny or curtail the possibilities for subsequent involvement by labour organizations, development agencies and wider civil society actors in regionalist political processes, or the fact that such organizations and agencies can use these processes to demand a stronger social dimension to national and regional policies. However, it has meant that these formations mostly exist primarily as trade (or political) agreements of various kinds; their purpose is not primarily a social developmental one, nor are they conceived of as being a social union (Yeates 2005). Even in the EU, which has by world standards an advanced regional social policy and relatively extensive involvement by non-state actors in policy-making, the difficulties of forging a comprehensive regional social policy have been significant. Here, the absence of a vision for a regional social union in the founding articles and treaties has been apparent in the inhibited development of social integration processes (Threlfall 2003). The conception of regional integration as an elite project means, moreover, that most regional formations exist purely as intergovernmental trade agreements or semi-institutionalized regional fora and consequently have limited or no supranational-level political authority or set of institutions which, many argue, is necessary for a coherent, binding and effective regional social policy (Yeates 2005).

Competition from trans-continental open and bilateral trading arrangements

The rise of free trade agendas within US-led mega-regional formations, such as the attempted Free Trade Area of the Americas (FTAA) and the Asia Pacific

Economic Cooperation (APEC), is also a concern for those in favour of regional social policies. To what extent are relatively 'closed' regions that currently have, or might develop, a social dimension cut across by relatively 'open' regions that exist essentially as global trading blocs which downplay these social equity and social policy dimensions? MERCOSUR provides one illustration of this issue. The question is whether its social dimension could have survived the creation of the mega-regionalist free trade project of the FTAA. While both MERCOSUR and the FTAA aimed to promote international trade, the model of economic integration underpinning these formations was quite different (Yeates 2005). Thus, whereas MERCOSUR aims at the free movement of production factors, the FTAA was concerned with market access (goods, services and investment) and sought to internationalize the North American Free Trade Agreement (NAFTA) model across the Americas (Vaz, cited in Yeates 2005, and Chapter 6 of this volume). The FTAA's lack of a social agenda did not go unchallenged. Indeed, the FTAA generated the mobilization of social forces nationally and transnationally to oppose the FTAA (Chapter 4 of this volume). The derailment of the FTAA in favour of a Latin America-only trading bloc hinged on the ability of these forces to forge 'multilateralism from below'. Recent developments within Latin America (see Chapter 6) indicate the increased awareness of the limitations of pursuing free trade policies through such mega-regionalist mechanisms. Indeed, there has been a strategic resurgence of affiliation with existing regional groupings (MERCOSUR combining with the Andean Community) as a means through which to pursue regionalist internationalization (including social policy) strategies.

Bilateral trade agreements generate similar pressures on regional policies. For example, there is a concern that the separate trade deal between South Africa and the EU might undermine regional solidarity within the SADC. The US's Africa Opportunity Act encouraging bilateral deals between African countries and the US may have such an effect too. Additionally, bilateral trade agreements benefit wealthy countries more than developing countries (UNDESA 2005). The use of bilateral trade agreements to undermine regional agreements, and attempts to insert free trade clauses into them, also cuts across and potentially undermines attempts to develop social policy on a regional basis. These issues are discussed in greater depth in Chapter 9 of this volume.

Overall, the multiplicity of bilateral trade agreements and trans-national open trading agreements cuts in a bewildering way across systematic attempts to develop a strong social dimension to regional formations – and can potentially undermine achievements made at regional level. In a major review of Southern regionalism, Page (2000: 290) concluded that: 'So far … regions have moved more in the direction of extending their liberalization to the rest of the world than finding ways of discriminating more tightly'. At issue here is the overall coherence of the multi-level strategies that governments pursue, and the possible tensions arising from this multiplicity.

Financing

Financing is a major challenge to regional social policies. Developing countries are starved of capital, so regional policies should not displace necessary expenditures for national social development. Developing regional policies and programmes require funding. Funding may originate at the regional level, if some countries in the region are prepared to cover the costs of regional integration. This has been the case for Germany and other wealthier northern European countries, which accepted the role of supporting the less developed countries of the EU periphery in view of the common public interest. This is also the case for oil-rich Venezuela, supporting the development of less prosperous ALBA countries, and the Gulf States and their neighbouring Arab countries. However, other regional groupings do not have the benefit of including one or more wealthy financier partners (Deacon *et al.* 2007).

The paper commissioned by UNDESA (2008) outlines two main financing sources for regional social policies: international funds and intra-regional transfers. In what follows we highlight key points of that discussion. In terms of international funds, the official channel for international redistribution is ODA. Given the limited scale of ODA, aid has focused on national interventions, and regional policies have not been a priority. Generally, bilateral donors have been reluctant to finance multi-country programmes given the lack of a single interlocutor that can be held accountable. This could be overcome by forming accountable implementing institutions, such as were created in post-war Europe (to disburse Marshall Aid) and in Africa (the New Partnership for Africa's Development (NEPAD)).

Since the mid-1990s more innovative international financing mechanisms have emerged, mostly a variety of public–private partnerships in the area of health. Examples are the Global Health Program of the Gates Foundation (started 1994), the Global TB Vaccine Foundation (1997) and the Drugs for Neglected Diseases Initiative (2003). These institutions are a potential source of funds for selected cross-border social policies in specific areas. New international sources of development finance have been proposed (Atkinson 2005), mainly taxing luxury activities or activities with negative social/environmental externalities. If operative, these could become sources of funding for global and regional social policies.

Intra-regional transfers are another source of finance for regional social policies. These require, of course, participation by at least one higher-income country in the regional association, as well as willingness to pay for regional solidarity. Such is the case of the EU, ALBA and the League of Arab States (LAS). In Europe, intra-regional redistribution has emerged from a policy to develop the EU internal market. The EU set a range of policy instruments, known collectively as Structural Funds, to direct transfers from wealthy to poor regions, and thus assist lagging areas to build infrastructure, human capital and jobs. Thus intra-European redistribution is a central element of the EU's policies. Regional solidarity appears also to be a component in Chavez's vision for

Latin America's ALBA. Although ALBA as yet lacks any accountable democratic regional institutions, oil-rich Venezuela has been funding a number of social policies among ALBA member countries (literacy and health programmes, emergency relief). Gulf states have also redistributed wealth among members of the LAS, funding mosques and educational services. The main issue for ALBA and LAS is sustainability: their redistributive policies depend on the price of oil. Diversification of regional contributions and less dependency on a single resource are advised to ensure sustainability. Financing regional social policies will require adequate institutional arrangements and good governance to attract either international or intra-regional funding. The degree of institutional complexity will change from case to case; however, what is essential is that sound management practices and controls are put in place to ensure prudent and efficient use of resources.

Long-term policy-making

Regional policies are based on the political will of governments to jointly commit to a common interest. Interstate cooperation in social policy is a voluntary accession to policies and codes that does not challenge the principle of sovereignty in a fundamental sense. Nevertheless, styles of leadership, entrepreneurial cultures, stereotypes, rivalries and mistrust may hinder negotiations.

A great obstacle to regional social policies comes in the short-term goals of policy-makers. Democratic systems have many benefits, but one of the pitfalls is that administrations focus on short-term policies, that is, policies that provide results within the four or five years of their mandate. Regional social policies require a long-term vision to which not all administrations may be prepared to adhere. Leadership for longer-term issues is not common. Anti-imperialism and 'affirmative regionalism' can play an important role, as in the case of the Venezuela-led ALBA or, in a rather more muted style, of the EU. Ideologies such as pan-Arabism or pan-Africanism could consolidate regional social policies in these parts of the world (Deacon *et al.* 2007).

The subsequent chapters of this volume explore the extent to which regional social policies are being developed despite the obstacles created by the elite origins of the regions, competition from more open inter-regional trading blocs, lack of financing and the downplaying of long-term regional policy making.

Notes

1 This section borrows heavily from two UNU-CRIS Working Papers on the social dimension of regional integration: Yeates and Deacon (2006) prepared for the UNESCO High-Level Symposium, and UNU-CRIS (2008).

2 See Chapter 4 below for the role of social movements, especially in Latin America, in pressing for regionalism with a social dimension.

3 Regional social policy from above

International organizations and regional social policy

Bob Deacon and Maria Cristina Macovei

Regional associations of governments are the key actors determining the extent to which their regional formations include a social dimension in their regional integration strategy. Their policy decisions are influenced by a number of regional factors and economic and social forces, as well as the extent to which member governments are willing to cede sovereignty in this policy domain. However, of some importance in influencing policy will be the role played by a number of international organizations. Among these are three sets of international organizations: the regional economic commissions of the UN, the regional development banks, and the regional offices of the UN social agencies, primarily the United Nations Development Programme (UNDP), UNESCO, the ILO, the World Health Organization (WHO) and the United Nations Children's Fund (UNICEF). This chapter examines the extent to which each of these sets of actors includes a focus on the social policy dimension of regional association and integration among its policy advisory armoury and among its budget line activities. Existing analysis suggests we will find quite a low commitment to these cross-border social issues. When analysing the percentage of overseas development assistance (ODA) supporting regional policies, Birdsall (2006) reports that, surprisingly, the regional development banks – the African, Asian, European and Inter-American Development Banks – have invested less than UN agencies. Regional development banks have concentrated their portfolios on country loans, despite their original regional mission.

Some regional programmes have been supported (e.g. the Mekong Initiative by the ADB or Controlling Transmittable Diseases in Latin America by the IDB) but they did not account for more than 1.2 per cent of the banks' portfolio in the early 2000s. If we add UN agencies such as the WHO or UNDP, regional interventions as a percentage of the total portfolio increase to 2.3 per cent, still a low figure (Birdsall 2006, Deacon *et al.* 2007). This chapter proceeds to consider each set of actors in turn in more detail.

Regional development banks

Asian Development Bank

The ADB has recently increased the resources it commits to the process of regional integration. In particular, a Technical Assistance Programme for 2007–2010 was agreed between the ADB and Association of South East Asian Nations (ASEAN) to strengthen the capacity of the ASEAN Secretariat. Some $720,000 have been allocated to this work which is focused only on pillars two and three of ASEAN, those dealing with trade and investment, and with monetary cooperation (ADB 2007a). The ADB has also addressed sub-regional cooperation below the level of ASEAN but again not with a particular focus on social protection. For the ADB, such sub-regional cooperation addresses the needs of countries that could gain substantially by facilitating movement across international boundaries. These initiatives included the Greater Mekong Sub-region (GMS) Economic Cooperation Program, the Central Asia Regional Economic Cooperation (CAREC), the South Asia Sub-regional Economic Cooperation and the Pacific sub-region.

In terms of social protection, on the other hand, the ADB produced excellent work culminating in the report *Social Protection in Asia and the Pacific* (Ortiz 2001) presented to and endorsed by the Asia-Pacific Forum on Poverty in Manila in 2001. However, the report focused on country-level policy and did not address in any detail cross-border issues at the level of ASEAN.

A review of projects funded in 2004–7 in the health, nutrition, population and social protection sector of the ADB reveals a number of regional projects in the fields of avian flu, communicable diseases and HIV/AIDS, and on civil society participation, and on combating the trafficking of women and children. These cross-border projects are not necessarily associated with policies addressed to the supranational level but may simply involve recommendations for bilateral sharing and cooperation.

In July 2006, the ADB adopted a strategy to guide its work on regional cooperation and integration (RCI). It is designed on four pillars, the fourth of which is enhancing regional public goods such as the prevention of communicable diseases and environmental degradation. Issues such as trade, investment, finance, transport, health, communications and environment transcend borders and must be handled on a regional basis to bring the greatest benefit to the most people. By taking joint action on shared concerns, countries improve economic prospects and better address complex goals such as reducing poverty and promoting trade (ADB 2006a).

However an examination of the *Regional Co-operation Strategy for South Asia 2006–2008* (ADB 2006b), which is focused both on the South Asian Association for Regional Cooperation (SAARC) and on its sub-region, South Asia Subregional Economic Cooperation (SASEC), reveals a programme of work involving five activities designed to increase connectivity, trade and investment, regional tourism, private sector cooperation and energy cooperation. The social dimension of regional integration is noteworthy by its absence, as is any talk of regional public goods.

One cross-border issue recently addressed by the ADB is that of migration in terms of the use to which remittances might be put. The report (ADB 2007b) notes that migrant remittances represent the most direct, immediate and far-reaching benefit to migrants, their families and their countries of origin. They are a constant source of income to developing countries including the Philippines. This study takes the perspective of remittances as a critical source of capital and resources that have impacted, and will probably continue to impact, on the development of millions of households in the Philippines. The two main areas of this study include a review of the flows of remittances by overseas Filipino workers from two representative source countries (Singapore and the United States) and the identification of the constraints in the policy, regulatory and institutional framework that influence or impact on these flows. The principal objective was to develop proposals that address the problems and constraints with a view to increasing remittance volumes, facilitating the shift from informal to formal channels, and leveraging the use of remittances for sustainable poverty reduction.

Inter-American Development Bank

The IDB has a long tradition of advancing regional programmes in Latin America and the Caribbean. The IDB supports regional initiatives by offering the 'know-how' support for policy discussions and funding technical cooperation to strengthen regional integration. In its institutional strategy the IDB places regional integration as one of the four priority areas. Two initiatives call attention to the importance of regional integration on the IDB agenda, namely the Regional Policy Dialogue and the Initiative for the Promotion of Regional Public Goods.

In 1999, the Bank created the Regional Policy Dialogue, aiming at fostering a forum for dialogue between the borrowing countries. Through the eight different networks that were created, including the networks on Poverty Reduction and Social Protection and on Trade and Integration, the IDB members have the opportunity to share experiences and to explore new modalities of regional cooperation in areas that are of most interest. The IDB Regional Technical Cooperation Division coordinates the Regional Policy Dialogue Networks.

The Poverty and Inequality Unit of the IDB is responsible for the technical coordination of the Poverty Reduction and Social Protection Network. Between 2000 and 2007, the Network organized five sub-regional and nine hemispheric meetings, where the permanent secretariats or the vice-ministers responsible for social policy and poverty reduction strategies in Latin America and the Caribbean discussed the policy challenges they are facing. During the Ninth Hemispheric Meeting – Employment and Labour Insertion Policies to Overcome Poverty – held in Washington DC in September 2007, the main topics on the agenda were: (i) social protection and income generation; (ii) quality of employment and informality; and (iii) experiences and lessons learned to improve the performance of labour markets. Here it was argued that 'social policy ... might be creating inappropriate incentives towards informality and the creation of low productivity jobs, and might be limiting aggregate growth' (IDB 2007). Social policy should count on complementary interventions favouring labour insertion and increased social protection levels. The meeting acknowledged the importance of appropriate complementary policies aiming at the 'ensuring more integral transition strategies to allow a greater amount of the beneficiaries' families to overcome poverty' (IDB 2007).

In 2006, two sub-regional meetings of the Poverty and Social Protection Network took place. The topic of the Andean sub-regional meeting was Poverty and Social Protection, focusing on identifying areas of horizontal cooperation among the countries of the region, sharing best practices in the implementation of effective social protection policies, and studying how the IDB can enhance its support to diminish poverty and promote equality in the region. The Caribbean meeting fostered a discussion on Effective Policies to Meet the MDGs (Millennium Development Goals) Agenda in the Caribbean. The meeting had three themes: (i) how to adapt the MDGs' agenda to the Caribbean context; (ii) lessons learned from the Caribbean programmes to reach the MDGs; and (iii) expanding the availability and use of micro data to monitor the MDGs (IDB 2006).

The Initiative for the Promotion of Regional Public Goods (RPGs) was established by the IDB in 2004, in response to the increased demand for regional public goods created by policy reforms oriented to open internal markets and to encourage competitiveness in a global economy. Moreover, this initiative of the IDB to promote RPGs aimed to contribute to the worldwide debate on public goods which envisaged the regional dimension as one of its key elements. As a general rule, when applying for different proposals under the Programme, the 'regional' criteria stipulate a minimum of three countries to constitute a subregion, these countries producing the RPGs collectively. However, in 2004 under the social development cluster, the IDB granted the Single-based Social Security for MERCOSUR project, aiming at better integration of the social security systems of the MERCOSUR countries. It was proposed that this would be achieved 'developing and implementing a Regional Public Good consisting of a system to transfer and validate the data needed to process benefits granted under the MERCOSUR Multilateral Social Security Agreement' (IDB 2004a), namely the Single Social Security Database. Another project financed by the IDB is the Common Population Census in CARICOM. The public good envisaged consists of 'the establishment of technical standards, methodologies and a common framework survey for conducting population censuses in the 15 member countries of the Caribbean Community and Common Market in the census year (2010)' (IDB 2004b).

Additionally, as part of the contribution to the regional public goods debate, the IDB in collaboration with the Asian Development Bank published in 2004 the book *Regional Public Goods. From Theory to Practice* (Estevadeordal *et al.* 2004). The publication 'is intended to broaden the discussion on strategic and operational issues related to the provision of regional public goods, and in doing so support efforts to improve regional development assistance' (Estevadeordal *et al.* 2004: vi).

Furthermore, the IDB created the Inter-American Institute for Social Development (INDES), a training institute seeking to strengthen the capacities of social managers in Latin America and the Caribbean. By means of social management training, INDES promotes social policies committed to the reduction of poverty and inequality in Latin America and the Caribbean.

African Development Bank

The AfDB is a multilateral development finance institution seeking to contribute to the economic and social development of its regional member states. In 2007, the AfDB approved several projects supporting economic cooperation and regional integration in Africa. Approvals by the Bank for the social sector represented 2.6 per cent of the total loans and grants (AfDB 2008). The Policy on Poverty Reduction division is designed 'to articulate the poverty reduction potential, including contributions to the achievements of the MDGs, of Bank-financed lending and non-lending operations to maximize improvements in the welfare of the poor' (AfDB 2008: 23).

However, most of the projects running under the Social Development, Gender and Inclusion Division of the AfDB focus on the national level. Nevertheless, the Gender Plan of Action for 2004–2007 underlines the role of The New Partnership for Africa's Development (NEPAD) and the AfDB in promoting gender and female empowerment issues. NEPAD's strategy focuses on promoting the role of women in all activities, while gender issues are explicitly included in the Bank's Strategic Plan.

In 2006, the AfDB approved the SADC Support to Communicable Diseases Project, aiming to build the capacities of the SADC Secretariat to harmonize efforts at regional communicable disease control. The SADC and the AfDB signed on 19 June 2006 an agreement for US$29.42 million, in support of intervention against major communicable diseases such as HIV/AIDS, TB and malaria, as outlined in the Regional Indicative Strategic Development Plan's (RISDP) health-related priorities. Moreover, this project aims to establish an effective regional system for the surveillance of communicable diseases (SADC 2006).

The AfDB has a strategic plan to support statistical development in Africa, and aims to establish a statistical network in the sub-region concerning COMESA, ECOWAS and the SADC.

Islamic Development Bank

The IsDB is a multilateral development bank set up to foster the economic development and social progress of its member countries. The fight against poverty represents the dominant objective of the IsDB group. In 2006, in line with the

MDGs agenda, the IsDB launched the report *A Vision for Human Dignity* (IsDB 2006). Its thirty-third Annual Report (*1428H*) underlines that with the launch of the report *A Vision for Human Dignity* the IsDB takes a leading role in fostering socio-economic development, alleviating poverty and promoting human development in the region (IsDB 2008).

Furthermore, aware of the need for accelerating progress towards the accomplishment of the MDGs, the IsDB launched in 2007 the poverty reduction fund officially known as the Islamic Solidarity Fund for Development (ISFD). The Fund also represents an aspect of the Organization of the Islamic Conference (OIC) New Vision, adopted in 2005. The main purpose of the Fund, with a targeted capital of $10 billion, is to contribute to poverty alleviation, by reducing unemployment, fighting disease and epidemics, eliminating illiteracy and building capacities in member countries (Cisse 2008). The IsDB will provide support via the ISFD in areas like education, health, agriculture, sanitation and institutional capacity building. The Fund's aim is 'achieving social justice by targeting individuals and groups that are socially excluded, marginalized, vulnerable, and disadvantaged' (Cisse 2008).

During 2001–7, the IsDB supported the work of the OIC in Sierra Leone. It initiated various socio-economic projects, including the construction and reconstruction of primary schools ($4.617 million) and a social action support project ($9.580 million).

The focus of the IsDB's work appears to be on African countries rather than on the continent's sub-regional groupings.

Summary of regional development banks

With the possible exception of the Islamic Development Bank, each of the regional banks surveyed includes a focus upon regional and sub-regional social policy issues within their work and lending programmes. The bulk of the work of these banks does, however, continue to focus upon countries *within* geographically defined regions rather than on the regional associations of governments themselves. Where there is a focus on cross-border, supranational regional and sub-regional social policy issues, these tend to be in the policy fields of:

1 labour migration management;
2 monitoring of communicable diseases;
3 prevention of the trafficking of women and children;
4 social protection and social security transferability;
5 capacity building of the secretariats of regional and sub-regional associations of governments (particularly ASEAN, SAARC, MERCOSUR, CARICOM and the SADC).

At the interface of interventions and advice to countries and interventions and advice to regions is the common thread in the work of the banks: encouraging the sharing of best practice across borders in sub-regions.

UN regional economic commissions

ESCAP

The United Nations Economic and Social Commission for Asia and the Pacific (ESCAP) is the regional development constituent of the United Nations for the Asia-Pacific region. The envisaged role of ESCAP is to meet some of the region's greatest challenges and it focuses on issues that are most effectively addressed through regional cooperation. ESCAP's area of work is threefold: poverty reduction, managing globalization, and tackling emerging social issues. An important role in promoting regional support is undertaken by the ESCAP Technical Cooperation Activities, which also includes Regional Advisory Services, a body that offers support for social development and planning policy to governments of the ESCAP regional member states. Regarding the first area, ESCAP provides advisory services on how to address the emerging social issues and strengthen regional coordination in the social sector. The development policy unit provides support for integrating the MDGs into national development policies and reviews poverty reduction programmes in partnership with civil society. One ESCAP-led project in 2006–7 extended to all other UN regional economic commissions.[1] The project, Interregional Cooperation to Strengthen Social Inclusion, Gender Equality and Health Promotion in the Millennium Development, which involves all five regional commissions, aimed to enhance the capacity of member states in all five regions to design and implement development policies and programmes in a manner that substantially contributes to social inclusion, achievement of gender equality and health promotion. Once again, the focus of activities is primarily on individual countries.

The role of the Emerging Social Issues Division is to boost the capacity of ESCAP member countries to develop and implement policies and programmes addressing emerging social issues, especially those directly affecting the poor and other disadvantaged people in the region. The Population and Social Integration section has a special focus on social policy. The social policy programme promotes the implementation of the Copenhagen Declaration and Programme of Action of the World Summit for Social Development. Moreover, the programme 'strives to develop national capacity in planning, monitoring and evaluating programmes for sustainable social development, emphasizing social integration, social protection, efficient delivery of social services and the empowerment of disadvantaged groups'.[2] Social development and social integration are key priorities on the ESCAP agenda, 'as poverty and social inequalities … continue to affect far too many people in the region' (ESCAP 2007a). In 2001, the Social Policy and Integration of Disadvantaged Groups Section issued a Social Policy Paper, *Working Towards Social Integration in the ESCAP Region*. Social integration is defined as 'a goal and a process which aims at a society for all, promoting social inclusion based on human rights and countering the social exclusion of individuals or groups by reasons of age, sex, lifestyle, belief system, physical characteristics and diseases' (ESCAP 2001: 5). However, the social dimension of regional integration is not specifically tackled in this paper. In the section 'Regional support' the main ESCAP initiatives to advance international cooperation for social development in the Asian and Pacific region are highlighted.

ESCAP is engaged in several activities in the ASEAN countries. In 2007 the project Enhancing Capacity toward Regional Cooperation on International Migration in East and South East Asia was designed to develop a more effective and constructive dialogue on regional cooperation on international migration in the region. The expected outcome was to implement the key policy recommendations for national and regional frameworks to manage international migration. During 2007–8, two projects called attention to access to basic health care: Promoting Sustainable Strategies to Develop and Improve Universal Access to Basic Health Care in the Asian and Pacific Region, and Promoting Sustainable Social Protection Strategies to Improve Access to Health Care in the Greater Mekong Sub-region (GMS). Both the projects focus on the promotion of basic health care services to vulnerable groups, including women, through improved dialogue and cooperation.

At the end of 2007, ESCAP released the study *Ten as One: Challenges and Opportunities for ASEAN Integration* (ESCAP 2007b), which coincided with the ASEAN Summit. The study is the first of a new ESCAP series on inclusive and sustainable development that seeks to contribute to regional and sub-regional policy dialogue and solutions. Even though the study reaffirms that ASEAN represents a successful example of regional organization, it also stresses 'the need for ASEAN to narrow the development gaps among its members, through mutual assistance and cooperation, for the benefit of the citizens of all 10 countries' (ESCAP 2007b: 5). The report calls on ASEAN to advance a regional strategy for managing the migration phenomenon in a coordinated and integrated manner. Furthermore, it states that 'inadequate social protection systems and standards will make it difficult for poorer countries to cope with the effects of investment integration and to achieve their potential in attracting investment' (ESCAP 2007b: 32). According to ESCAP's recommendations, ASEAN should formulate a coherent policy on the freedom of movement of people. This will only be sustainable if supported by a coherent policy aimed at 'narrowing the gaps between winners and losers of the integration process. The policy requires financial transfers for social, economic, and environmental development and strengthening social safety nets'.

ECLAC

The United Nations Economic Commission for Latin America and the Caribbean (ECLAC) has a deserved reputation among the regional economic commissions for excellent policy analysis and policy advocacy, including work in the fields of social policy and social protection. *Globalization and Development: A Latin American and Caribbean Perspective* (Ocampo and Martin 2003: xv) argued for an agenda for the global era 'to achieve three foremost objectives of a new international order: a supply of global public goods, the gradual correction of international asymmetries, and the progressive construction of a rights-based international social agenda'. Ocampo went on to become Under Secretary General for Economic and Social Affairs under Kofi Annan but he retained links with ECLAC, for which he compiled *Regional Financial Co-operation* (Ocampo 2006). This text noted that the Monterrey Consensus, adopted by the 2002 International Conference on Financing for Development, highlighted in its paragraph 45 'the vital role that multilateral and regional development banks continue to play in serving the development needs of developing countries and countries with economies in transition'. It went on to note:

> They should contribute to providing an adequate supply of finance to countries that are challenged by poverty, follow sound economic policies and may lack adequate access to capital markets. They should also mitigate the impact of excessive volatility of financial markets. Strengthened regional development banks and sub-regional financial institutions add flexible financial support to national and regional development efforts, enhancing ownership and overall efficiency. They also serve as a vital source of knowledge and expertise on economic growth and development for their developing member countries.
>
> (UNDESA 2003)

The experiences reviewed in the book indicate that regional cooperation can be a very effective means of surmounting the difficulties posed by the shortfall in the financial services provided by the current international financial architecture.

The social dimension is not directly addressed in this book but it is the main theme in the recent ECLAC (2006a) volume, *Shaping the Future of Social Protection: Access, Finance, and Solidarity*. The foreword to the volume by Jose Luis Macinea, Executive Secretary of ECLAC, notes:

> From a social perspective, ECLAC has placed special emphasis on promoting greater equality of opportunities through education and the benefits it brings to poor families, addressing and reversing the exclusionary dynamics of structurally heterogeneous labour markets, redistributing assets through social spending and promoting the full exercise of citizenship ... the ultimate aim being to strengthen democracy while laying the political foundations for the consolidation of more inclusive societies. ECLAC now proposes to take this line of thought a step further by focusing on social protection.... The main reason why solidarity based social protection mechanisms need to be rethought is that the labour market has not demonstrated a capacity for greater inclusiveness either through the creation of decent job opportunities or in terms of the level of social protection contributions.... The structural changes reflected in the current situation call for a fresh

> approach to social protection within a framework of integral solidarity that combines contributory and non-contributory mechanisms. A new social covenant must therefore be formed in which social rights are seen as the normative horizon.
>
> (ECLAC 2006a: 11)

All that said, the ECLAC texts referred to say little on supranational regional social policies such as MERCOSUR's cross-border agreements on social security or the Andean Community's cross-border social funds, let alone Venezuela's new cross-border largess funding anti-poverty programmes in its neighbouring country. This is surprising, given that regional integration in Latin America has its origins in the developmental theory that ECLAC promulgated in the 1950s. In this theoretical framework, regional integration would serve as a strategy to increase intra-regional trade, decrease economic and political dependence on the main superpowers, and achieve development. The strategy proposed for this was the broadening of national markets into regional ones. It sought to protect these markets from global trade via import-substitution industrialization (ISI) and aimed to achieve industrialization (Iglesias 2000).

However, a number of recent examples showed that ECLAC is seeking to reinject a concern with the social dimension of regional economic integration into the agenda. In June 2006, the ECLAC sub-office in the Caribbean convened a High-Level Ministerial Dialogue on Social Security and Sustainable Social Development, item seven on the agenda of which was the Social Dimension of Regional Integration in CARICOM. The discussion dealt with cross-border social security agreements, harmonization of industrial relations, etc. (ECLAC 2006b).

The leadership role in promoting the social dimension of regional integration in Latin America seems to have been taken on by the Latin American and Caribbean Economic System (Sistema Económico Latinoamericano y del Caribe) (SELA), a regional intergovernmental body established in 1975. In July 2008 it convened in Caracas, Venezuela, a Regional Seminar for Consultation on the Social Dimension of Integration in Latin America and the Caribbean. The seminar was attended by representatives of MERCOSUR, the Andean Community, CARICOM, ALBA, the WHO, the ILO, UNESCO, UNDESA and a number of regional think tanks and civil society organizations. It received a report from the Permanent Secretariat of SELA, entitled *The Social Dimension of Integration: Guidelines for an Action Plan in the Areas of Health, Education, Housing and Employment* (SELA 2008). The seminar concluded that:

> Little progress has been made as regards the social component of Latin American and Caribbean integration; nevertheless, changes have occurred recently on the regional political scene, but the commitments and declarations adopted in relation to the social dimension of development and integration do not always lead to concrete action.
>
> (SELA 2008: 2)

Therefore, it continued:

> SELA must become the forum for debates and regional rapprochement aimed at coordinating and exchanging ideas concerning the achievements and lessons learned about social development and [the] social dimension of integration in LAC, and specific tasks to be undertaken in order to achieve the aforementioned goal include: (a) to promote, in SELA, the exchange of experiences, particularly best practices, at the sub-regional level, so as to analyze the feasibility of expanding them to a regional level; (b) to support training activities for public- and private-sector actors, so as to allow for facing the challenges posed by poverty and social exclusion; (c) to foster the creation of new funds for social projects with a regional scope; and (d) to identify national … networks in the region, which could be grouped together into a network with a Latin American and Caribbean scope.
>
> (SELA 2008: 2)

ECA

Regional integration represents an important topic on the United Nations Economic Commission for Africa (ECA) agenda. The 2006 African Union Summit reaffirmed the role of the ECA as a 'key African institution to assist and facilitate the work of the African Union and the Regional Economic Communities (RECs) in advancing the development agenda of the continent' (ECA 2007: 1). In its structural design, the five sub-regional offices of ECA play an important role in implementing regional integration programmes.

In 2004, the ECA delivered one of a series of policy research reports, *Assessing Regional Integration in Africa* (*ARIA*). However, even though the report is considered to be 'a tool for monitoring and tracking progress in achieving integration in key sectors at the sub-regional and regional levels' (ECA 2007: 5), the social dimension of regional integration is not addressed in a separate chapter. The chapter 'Human Resources and Labour Mobility' emphasizes the progress achieved in labour mobility within the RECs. Subsequent editions of *ARIA* have looked at the crucial issue of rationalization of the RECs (2005) and macroeconomic policy convergence (2008).

ESCWA

Since 2002, the United Nations Economic and Social Commission for Western Asia (ESCWA) 'has focused on the issue of integrated social policies with a view to promoting a coordinated and effective social vision that encompasses both the social and the economic priorities of countries in the region' (ESCWA 2005).

The Social Development Division (SDD) is responsible for promoting an integrated and viable social policy, policy formulation mechanisms and implementation and monitoring tools. Furthermore, it seeks to advise ESCWA member countries on how to achieve a higher level of social equity and well-being for the people in the region. SDD has four main programmes: Social Policy Framework and Instruments, Social Policy and Participatory Development, Population and Social Policy, and Social Policy in the City. These programmes are designed to cover critical complementary dimensions of the integrated social policy approach.

In 2005, ESCWA issued a report entitled *Towards Integrated Social Policies in Arab Countries: Framework and Comparative Analysis*, which underlines advantage and disadvantage affecting the formulation and implementation of social policies in developing countries. One of the recommendations of the report is 'to initiate "regional social reports" based on regional surveys conducted by ESCWA in cooperation with member countries' (ESCWA 2005: 94). It is argued that ESCWA 'should be responsible for planning, data collection and analysis and that the reports would provide a valuable barometer for development in the region' (ESCWA 2005: 94).

In January 2008, the Policy Frameworks and Instruments team of the Social Development Division convened an Expert Group Meeting in Amman. The meeting was attended by regional and international experts in the area of social policy. A new ESCWA report 'Integrated Social Policy Report II: From Concept to Practice', was produced as an aide-mémoire for the meeting. It was designed to serve as 'an advocacy tool providing practical direction for social policy makers and practitioners in the region' (ESCWA 2008a: 1). Notably, this report was envisaged as the basis of a subsequent 'regional social policy forum' (ESCWA 2008b: 4). However, no concrete details are provided. It is important to note that the report tackles the issue of financing social policy in the ESCWA region, which 'remains a challenge for the … countries in the region' (ESCWA 2008b: 39). Furthermore, the report claims that 'each country needs to examine or re-examine its entire budget process – from revenue collection, to allocations, to outcomes – in prioritizing social policy' (ESCWA 2008b: 39). Nevertheless, the social dimension of regional integration is not directly addressed in the report; one of the recommendations is to strengthen regional dialogue on integrated social policies. Prior to this meeting, in 2007 ESCWA organized a peer-review meeting under the auspices of the SDD, as a preliminary step to preparing the Social Policy Report No. 2, *Operationalizing Social Policy in the ESCWA Region*. It is stated that:

> ESCWA should build on its role and mandate as a regional organization by tackling the regional dimension of social policy. The Report could address such regional thematic issues as the status of refugees, the status of migrant workers in the Arab countries, and social policies for an integrated market.
>
> (ESCWA 2007: 5)

ECE

The major aim of the United Nations Economic Commission for Europe (ECE) is to promote 'pan-European economic integration'.[3] The Commission's experts provide technical assistance to the countries of Eastern Europe, the Caucasus and

Central Asia (EECCA) and south-east Europe. The sectors covered by the ECE's work include economic cooperation and integration, energy, environment, housing and land management, population, statistics, timber, trade and transport. It is important to underline that housing policies are seen as relevant for 'safeguarding social cohesion in the UNECE countries'.[4] The Committee on Housing and Land Management also focuses on the basic mechanisms for social housing development. In this context, the ECE produced its report *Guidelines on Social Housing. Principles and Examples* (2006), work on which started in 2003 at the ECE Workshop on Social Housing in Prague, in cooperation with the Comité Européen de Coordination de l'Habitat Social (CECODHAS), and concluded at the ECE Symposium on Social Housing in Vienna in 2004.

This report represents the initiative of the countries in the region to share experience on social housing polices and practices. Due to

> the increasing challenges faced by the socially vulnerable in the housing sector and the importance of affordable housing for socially cohesive societies, countries of the UNECE region are beginning to realize the need for a renewed and stronger role of the state in the provision of social housing.
>
> (ECE 2006: v)

The *Guidelines* deal with the institutional, legal and economic outlines for social housing policy design. The four major areas of the guidelines are: (i) the role and evolution of social housing in society; (ii) the institutional and legal framework; (iii) the macro-economic framework and social housing finance; and (iv) social cohesion and social housing design.

The relationship between social cohesion and social housing is highlighted in a separate chapter of the Guidelines, 'The Role of Social Housing in Social Cohesion'. It is stated that the ECE Committee on Human Settlements and the European Commission have acknowledged 'the need for governments to compensate for the deficiencies of the unregulated housing market to combat exclusion' (ECE 2006: 75). This idea is supported, for example, by the *ECE Strategy for a Sustainable Quality of Life in Human Settlements in the 21st Century* (ECE 2001), and the *European Commission's Joint Report on Social Inclusion* (2004). It is generally agreed that specific groups of the population, i.e. the unemployed, refugees, ethnic minorities, etc., are 'particularly vulnerable to social exclusion and in some countries live almost in slum settlements' (ECE 2001: 12) and that

> All Member States, because of the deficiencies in their housing markets, need to intervene in order to combat the exclusion of persons or families affected by social problems or living in certain geographical areas. Such state aid, although not allocated on a non-discriminatory basis, is a legitimate element of public policy.
>
> (ECE 2004: 6)

The ECE also plays an important role in advancing sustainable development through education. In 2003, the ECE Environment Ministers adopted a Statement on Education for Sustainable Development, which calls on countries to integrate sustainable development in all levels of their education systems, education being a 'key agent for change'. Moreover, the ministers invited the ECE, in collaboration with UNESCO, the Council of Europe and other relevant actors, to develop a strategy for education for sustainable development. In 2005, at the High-Level Meeting of Education and Environment Ministries in Vilnius the *UNECE Strategy for Education for Sustainable Development* (ECE 2005) was endorsed. The objective of the Strategy is to incorporate key elements of sustainable development in all education systems, i.e. poverty alleviation, security, peace, human rights, health, social equity, cultural diversity, economy, environmental protection, etc. (ECE 2005).

Once again, however, the focus of the work of the ECE is on countries in the region rather than the regional groupings of countries.

Summary of UN regional economic commissions

There is remarkably little focus within the work of the UN regional economic commissions on cross-border, supranational regional and sub-regional social policies. Despite being constituted as an arm of the UN with a regional focus, the work of UN regional economic commissions remains concentrated on countries and, within that country-focused work, social policy issues do not receive enough emphasis. The understanding of regions within the thinking of these commissions is as geographical space, not as existing regional associations of countries.

Among the exceptions are the focus of ESCAP on ASEAN capacity-building in the field of migration management, ECA's work in terms of the importance it attributes to the sub-regional communities, and the work of ECLAC on cross-border social security issues in the Caribbean. ESCWA's very important work on social policy in the countries of the Arab region only extends to the truly regional level when it focuses on lesson learning and policy dialogue across borders.

It was noted that the surprising underdevelopment of the work of ECLAC in recent years on the supranational level of sub-regional governance was due to the replacement of its earlier regional development strategy with an open and neo-liberal-driven regionalism. This explanation probably applies to the other UN economic commissions as well.

UN social agencies

ILO

The issue of regional social integration has received increasing attention in the ILO particularly since the report of the World Commission on the Social Dimension of Globalization (WCSDG 2004) which it sponsored. This report referred to the regional governance level in relation to (i) the need to build representative institutions and organize regional social dialogues; (ii) the need to link trade liberalization and the regional level to labour standards; and (iii) the need to provide a regulatory framework for migration. It argued that regional integration might be a stepping stone to fair globalization so long as it embodied a social dimension. Indeed as a follow-up to this, UNU-CRIS (United Nations University – programme for Comparative Regional Integration Studies) was commissioned by the ILO to report on progress on the social dimension of regional integration (UNU-CRIS 2008). The proposition that regional integration might be a stepping stone to fair globalization has informed much of the ILO's work on the topic although no unit has specific responsibility for regional integration, nor has a systematic approach or policy been developed on the issue. The ILO has, however, signed agreements with fourteen different regional communities over the years on the sharing of information and cooperation on matters of shared concern. In practice, the day-to-day interaction between the ILO and the RECs varies dramatically from one region to the next. The social dimension of regional integration (RI) is largely dealt with on an ad hoc basis (through a mixture of projects and research) whenever sub-regional developments correspond to ILO policy priorities (e.g. regional labour migration protocols, the Economic Partnership Agreements (EPAs) process, regional Poverty Reduction Strategy Papers (PRSPs) or related development plans, skills and social security portability, regional labour law harmonization or regional social dialogue). Because of the scattered nature of this work, a survey was initiated in early 2007 to find out what was being done both at the field level and in Geneva on regional integration over the past few years (mainly 2006–7). This revealed that despite the lack of coordination, there is in fact a great deal being done. Among the projects were: (i) the labour law harmonization project in CARICOM; (ii) Promotion of Social Dialogue in Francophone Africa (PRODIAF); (iii) ILO–ASEAN Occupational Health and Safety Network; (iv) Joint ILO–ASEAN Study on the impact on labour of the ASEAN Free Trade Agreement; (v) labour migration for integration and development in the Euromed context and West and East Africa; (vi) strengthening the capacity of the SADC to promote social dialogue and corporate social responsibility; (vii) Ouagadougou Summit of the African Union on employment and poverty alleviation; (viii) ILO–ASEAN study on HIV/AIDS in the world of work, and (ix) comparative analysis of child labour legislation in MERCOSUR.

To take one region as an example, we focus here on Africa. In Africa, the ILO regional office is conveniently located in Addis Ababa, which is home to both the African Union (AU) and to ECA. This enabled close cooperation between the ILO and African governments at the Summit of Heads of State and Governments in Ouagadougou in 2004 on Poverty Alleviation and Employment. Subsequently, the AU organized a series of five sub-regional meetings in 2006 aimed at supporting capacity-building in the regional economic communities. Regional frameworks for integrated employment strategies were agreed at each of these. The ILO signed memoranda of understanding with ECOWAS in 2005 and with the Communauté Economique des Etats de l'Afrique Centrale (CEEAC) in 2006. In 2007 the ILO International Training Centre secured funds from the French and Flemish governments to provide, in association with UNU-CRIS, capacity-building activities for the regional employment and social protection policies of ECOWAS and the SADC (Deacon *et al.* 2008). While the ILO regional office in Addis Ababa appears therefore to be driving an agenda directed at the regional economic communities in the African sub-regions, the sub-regional ILO offices in Abidjan, Harare, Cairo, Dakar, etc., which are not co-terminous with existing sub-regional associations, are finding it harder to pursue this agenda and ensure it is followed up in each sub-region.

In the case of SADC, this geographic problem was overcome when a Senior Programme Manager (Employment, Productivity, Labour, and Social Security) was seconded to Gaborone in 2008 to coordinate labour and employment programmes within the SADC Secretariat. Among the areas in which assistance is being provided to the SADC are: (i) the development of monitoring and evaluation mechanisms/instruments for the SADC standards on employment and labour, and popularization of the provision of the newly adopted Code on Social Security in the SADC; and (ii) the promotion of compliance with the provisions of Social Security Convention 102 in the sub-region.

In the case of ECOWAS, the geographic problem persists in that the ILO office in Dakar (Senegal) is responsible for ECOWAS, rather than the ILO office based in Abuja (Nigeria) where ECOWAS has its headquarters. However, the projected work programme of the Humanitarian and Social Affairs Department of ECOWAS includes a plan to establish an ECOWAS Social Dialogue Forum in 2009. This initiative derives from a joint ILO–ECOWAS meeting in December 2007, organized within the framework of the ILO–ECOWAS Memorandum of Understanding signed in 2005. ECOWAS is encouraging the harmonization of labour laws and social security legislation. It commissioned a study on issues involved in the formulation of a labour policy for the ECOWAS region. The report comprises an exhaustive and comprehensive set of recommendations for an ECOWAS labour policy in line with ILO policy and based on consultations with ILO colleagues in Geneva. It also calls for a regional social fund.

UNESCO

UNESCO has been surprisingly active in the field of regional social policy and development through the agency of its Social and Human Sciences Sector (SHSS). This sector of UNESCO convened in February 2004 in Uruguay a High-Level Symposium on the Social Dimension of Regionalism within the context of its International Social Sciences – Policy Nexus event. At this symposium, some regional secretariats engaged with scholars from the Transnational Institute (TNI) programme, UNU-CRIS and Globalism and Social Policy Programme (GASPP) on the topic of regional social policy. The Buenos Aires Declaration resulting from the Policy Nexus

> call[ed] upon the regional organizations such as MERCOSUR and the African Union, in association with social scientists and civil society, to

> further develop the social dimension of regional integration, and call[ed] upon the United Nations to facilitate inter-regional dialogues on regional social policies.
>
> (UNESCO 2006)

UNESCO itself through its MOST (Management of Social Transformations) programme has subsequently organized regional meetings of Ministers of Social Development in three continents. Zola S. Skweyiya, Minister for Social Development in South Africa and chair of MOST, has ensured that the focus of such meetings in Africa has been on regional integration. The MOST programme's initiative emphasizes some very important aspects of this new dynamic in Africa's regional integration processes, notably: promoting awareness of the added value that social sciences can bring to the process of regional integration, and fostering dialogue between decision makers and social scientists. It is within this perspective that MOST organized a series of seminars on regional integration policies in the ECOWAS region, called 'Nation-States and the Challenges of Regional Integration in West Africa', which ended with a call to establish a regional integration studies centre in Cape Verde (Barry 2008). The first Forum of Ministers of Social Development of the East African Community (EAC) took place in Kigali, Rwanda, in September 2008 with the objective of sharing experiences and harmonizing policies.

The second meeting of the Ministers of Social Development from the Arab Region also took place in 2008 under MOST auspices and focused on fostering regional corporate social responsibility. This followed a first meeting in 2007 at which the Marrakesh declaration[5] was agreed.

Beside these projects, UNESCO is collaborating with regional organizations, in the fields of education and social and human development. In 1980, UNESCO signed an agreement with CARICOM, which envisaged cooperation in the spheres of education, science and culture. This agreement was renewed in 2003 with a new Memorandum of Understanding. This agreement places a new emphasis on increased participation by young people in policy-making and the implementation of projects 'as a key expected outcome of planed activities in the area of social and human sciences'.[6] In 2007, UNESCO launched a new capacity-building project dealing with educational statistics for the English-speaking countries of the Caribbean. In collaboration with UNESCO, the South Asia Foundation organized the conference Youth in Contemporary Information Society – Needs, Role and Policies, in New Delhi, attended by representatives of youth NGOs and youth policy-makers from SAARC. The meeting was designed to assess the conditions affecting the development of the information society in the region, and to develop an information network and partnership among youth movements in order to share experience and update national youth policies in the region.

UNDP

The United Nations Development Programme is the UN's global development network. One of the focal points of the UNDP's work is the Poverty Reduction Unit, which focuses on strategies and policies for poverty reduction, inclusive globalization, MDGs support,[7] and gender inequality and poverty reduction. At the regional level, the UNDP is involved in different projects that are linked with regional social policies. For instance, the UNDP Regional Centres in Bangkok and Colombo (Asia and the Pacific region) are involved in several projects that are worth mentioning. The *2007 Work Plan* (UNDP 2007) refers to capacity development programmes directly linked to poverty reduction and achieving the MDGs, and to HIV/AIDS. These programmes include Support for SAARC: Prepared Regional Poverty Profile; Data Bank for Best Practices and Technical Support, Capacity Support Provided to ASEAN, SAARC, Secretariat of the Pacific Community (SPC) and Pacific Islands Forum Secretariat (PIFS) for Regional and Inter-Country Collaboration on HIV, Implementation of ASEAN Work Programme III; SAARC HIV Strategy and SPC and PIFS ADIS Strategy, Assessment of the Legal Situation in Relation to Trafficking, Sex Work and HIV Conducted in SAARC Countries and Regional Consultation Organized on Enabling Ethical and Legal Environment in ASEAN and SAARC (UNDP 2007).

The ASEAN–UNDP sub-regional programme represents the base for the dialogue between the two institutions. In 2003, it started a three-year ASEAN–UNDP Partnership Facility (AUPF) project aiming to offer 'analytical and advisory support services to ASEAN for deepening and broadening regional economic integration in a way that leads to reduction in poverty and socio-economic disparities, and to narrowing of the development gap within and across ASEAN member countries'. One of the sub-projects in the pipeline is an 'analysis of labour and employment impact of economic integration'.[8]

In Latin America and the Caribbean region, the UNDP Barbados unit has a special programme entitled *Support to Poverty Assessment and Reduction in the Caribbean* (SPARC). The programme is designed to deliver capacity-building inputs to support poverty and MDGs monitoring and social policy development systems in the Caribbean region. SPARC has five distinctive areas, one being regional coordination and the development of a legislative framework for policy development. It operates via a Regional Programme, managed by UNDP/SRO (Sub-regional Programme Office) Barbados and the Organization of Eastern Caribbean States (OECS) and implemented by CARICOM, UNDP, the UN system, and other donors.

Other UN agencies and initiatives

UNDESA

The UN Department of Economic and Social Affairs (UNDESA) based in New York 'promotes and supports international cooperation to achieve development for all, and assists governments in agenda-setting and decision-making on development issues at the global level'.[9] UNDESA builds international and national consensus and commitments to a specific course of action, through UN summits, conferences and meetings. UNDESA's Division for Social Policy and Development aims at strengthening international cooperation for social development focusing on poverty eradication, employment generation and social integration, family, youth, persons in situations of conflict, and indigenous peoples. UNDESA's Division of Social Policy and Development has been supporting the Ibero-American Convention on the Rights of Youth (ICRY) that entered into force on 1 March 2008. This 'is so far the only international treaty in the world that specifically recognizes the rights of young people' (UNDESA 2008: 1). The Convention includes forty-four articles which convey a set of civil, political, economical, social and cultural rights. The righs of young people to education, employment, shelter, culture and art are explicitly underlined. The Convention was developed and promoted by the Ibero-American Youth Organization with the support of UNDESA and the United Nations Population Fund (UNFPA).

In its work to advance regional social policies, UNDESA issued in 2007 a Working Paper titled *Regional Social Policy* (Deacon *et al.* 2007), which explains why countries should prioritize the development of cross-border regional social policies. Furthermore, the authors provide an overview of the concepts and dimensions of regional social policies, highlighting how the social dimension of regionalism can provide an alternative to neo-liberal globalization.

In its work with regional organizations, UNDESA offered support for an equitable and socially inclusive Bank of the South in 2007 and for the SADC Regional Social Policy Meeting in Johannesburg, held in 2006. The Bank of the South is a result of a collective agreement of several Latin American countries, and it was discussed in 2007 during a technical meeting of MERCOSUR and UNASUR.

In 2006, the UNDESA Division for Social Policy and Development issued a pioneering draft document on regional social policy in Africa, which was finalized at a Ministerial Meeting of the SADC, organized by UNDESA and the government of South Africa. The Ministerial Meeting stressed the need 'to strengthen the African Union, NEPAD and SADC institutions dealing with social policy' (UNDESA 2007). The document 'Towards an African Regional Social Policy' was endorsed during the meeting and represents important progress towards framing SADC sub-regional social policy. UNDESA officials[10] involved in organizing the ministerial meeting stress that the 'rationale for a sub-regional social policy is precisely the inability of most countries to put these measures in place on their own due to limited capacity'. Furthermore, they stress that 'a regional social policy does not deny the concept of national sovereignty' and that the two layers of social policy – national and regional – 'do not compete with each other'. The financing of the plan of action to implement the new goals would in principle be undertaken by the New Partnership for Africa's Development, the socio-economic programme of the African Union (UNDESA 2007). Subsequently, in October 2008, at the first AU meeting of Ministers Responsible for Social Development a Social Policy Framework for Africa was agreed which endorsed the significance of regional and sub-regional social policies.

UNDESA is also involved in providing advisory services, and formulating and executing multidisciplinary programmes and action plans for the advancement of the economic, social and environmental agendas. For instance, in July 2008, the Permanent Secretariat of SELA organized a regional seminar for consultation on the social dimension of integration in Latin America and the Caribbean, to which UNDESA was invited. UNDESA and its Division for Social Policy and Development is 'working to develop cross-sectoral approaches that link development activities in a holistic manner, and works in close cooperation with United Nations regional commissions, funds, programmes and specialized agencies'.[11]

UNICEF

The United Nations Children's Fund issued in 2006 the report *State of the SAARC Child* (UNICEF ROSA 2006). This report is a result of collaboration between SAARC and UNICEF, which started in 1993 with a Memorandum of Understanding. The report focuses on the rate of progress of girls' education in SAARC. In 2006, UNICEF and the United Nations Research Institute for Social Development (UNRISD) delivered a report called *Social Policy in South Asia* (Köhler and Keane 2006).

In April 2008, the UNICEF Regional Office for South Asia (ROSA) hosted a meeting which resulted in the report 'Regional Policy Makers' Symposium on Social Protection in South Asia' (UNICEF 2008). 'The symposium focused on how expanded social protection could serve as a strategy to transform social policy and reduce economic and social vulnerability, especially for children'. The Regional Adviser on Social Policy, Gabriele Köhler, underlined that SAARC could play an essential role in line with its Social Charter. As a follow-up to the symposium, the participants urged the establishment of a 'South Asian social protection network for knowledge sharing. The network would be composed of governments, academics and others, with a research hub to continue analysis of child-sensitive social protection strategies'. In July 2008 it produced the first draft of a Synthesis Report of the Symposium, highlighting: (i) the opportunities for introducing and expanding the space for social protection; (ii) the challenges to social protection systems; and (iii) the emerging policy ideas and progress towards transformative child-sensitive social protection systems (UNICEF 2008).

In April 2008 the UNICEF Regional Office for Latin America and the Caribbean organized a visiting delegation of children from Guyana, Trinidad and Tobago, and Suriname to attend the Second Special Session on Children of the CARICOM Council of Human and Social Development (COHSOD). The child delegates presented a common statement calling on all CARICOM countries to make the necessary transformations to support the rights of children in the region.

WHO

In 2005, World Health Organization launched the Commission on Social Determinants of Health. One of the aims of the Commission is 'to help build up a sustainable global movement for action on health equity and social determinants, linking governments, international organizations, research institutes, civil society and communities'.[125] In close cooperation with WHO, ASEAN implemented the ASEAN Plus Three Emerging Infectious Diseases Programme. The Ouagadougou Declaration on Primary Health Care and Health Systems in Africa in April 2008 called on WHO in consultation with the member states and other UN agencies to establish a regional health observatory.

The office for the Eastern Mediterranean Region (EMRO) of WHO is also very active. In 2003, the Regional Committee for the Eastern Mediterranean approved the regional strategy paper *Investing in Health of the Poor: Regional Strategy for Sustainable Health Development and Poverty Reduction* (WHO 2003). In Latin America, WHO, in partnership with the Pan American Health Organization (PAHO), supported the First Summit of CARICOM Heads of Governments on Chronic, Non-communicable Diseases that took place in September 2007. This was the first time that the heads of government collectively committed 'to stem the tide of chronic diseases in their countries, as these diseases seriously undermine economic growth and well-being across society, and perpetuate chronic poverty at household level'. However, the collaboration between WHO/PAHO and CARICOM is not new, as in 1999 the two institutions in partnership with the UNDP delivered a complex policy document 'Managing and Financing Health to Reduce the Impact of Poverty in the Caribbean. Implementing Decentralization and Financing Strategies while Protecting the Poor'.[13] In 2006, CARICOM in partnership with WHO/PAHO issued a new Report of the Caribbean Commission on Health and Development.[14] The report seeks to analyse different dimensions of the health situation in the Caribbean, to present the nature of the problems faced by the region, and to offer possible solutions for consideration. Moreover, the report synthesizes the material contained in the Working Papers prepared specifically for the Commission and presents some of the arguments for 'propelling health to the centre of development' (PAHO/WHO and CARICOM 2006).

Summary of UN social agencies

The extent to which the social agencies of the UN are focused on the work of actually existing regional associations of governments as distinct from merely working within a geographical region with national governments appears to vary considerably. Even in the case of the ILO, which after all argued for the importance of working at the regional level in its World Report on the Social Dimension of Globalization (WCSDG 2004), what important work there is of this kind is uncoordinated and does not appear to flow from a central policy drive. The initiatives of individuals in UNICEF, UNESCO, the ILO or the UNDP appear to be a key factor in determining whether work of this kind takes place.

Where UN social agencies work with regional associations of countries the following policy fields and processes appear to be given most attention:

1 migration of labour
2 social security collaboration
3 communicable diseases
4 child labour and social protection
5 social dialogue mechanisms at sub-region institutional level
6 policy dialogue and best practice learning
7 regional social integration
8 capacity building (e.g. of ASEAN, SADC, ECOWAS, SAARC, CARICOM).

Conclusions

We have shown that all of the three categories of organizations surveyed – regional development banks, regional economic commissions and regional branches of the UN social agencies – address aspects of regional social policies and regional social integration. However, much of this analytical work and policy prescriptive work is focused on the region defined merely as a collection of individual countries that happen to occupy a particular regional territory. In other words, what is observed is:

- First, the continued focus of the agencies is *on advice to countries within regions rather then advice to regional associations of countries.*
- Second, where there is advice to regional associations, *the advice often neglects the social policy dimension of regional social integrations.*
- Third, where the genuinely regional dimension comes in it is in the useful form of *lesson learning across borders* from countries within the regions.
- It is the exceptional intervention which is designed to contribute to *the building of the capacities of the regional associations of countries* in the field of social policy.

Where there is a focus on cross-border, supranational regional and sub-regional social policy issues by the agencies surveyed, these tend to be in the policy fields of:

- economic and labour migration management;
- communicable diseases monitoring;
- regulation of the trafficking of women and children;
- social protection and social security transferability and commonality;
- capacity-building of the secretariats of regional and sub-regional associations of governments; and
- social dialogue mechanisms at the sub-regional institutional level.

Explanations for this limited focus on regional social policy on the part of these agencies can probably be found in a combination of (i) the constitutionally driven focus of the UN system on individual countries; (ii) the general ideological drift towards global free trade in the later part of the twentieth century which eschewed any kind of regional protectionism; and (iii) the absence of calls from regional associations of countries for such a focus. Where more effort towards the fostering of regional social policies was evident it could be attributed to the purchase within some parts of, and among certain individuals in, the ILO, UNESCO, UNICEF and UNDESA of the 'idea' of regional social policy as an alternative to neo-liberal globalization. The drive to foster regional social policy in these organizations was an ideological one motivated by a desire to attend to the negative social consequences of globalization.

In terms of the few actual initiatives that were being fostered, these were in general driven by a politics of *reaction* to the emerging cross-border employment and health problems consequent on unplanned economic migration and, in the case of the focus on trafficking and on social dialogue, by the concerns of cross-border social movements active especially in parts of Asia and Latin America.

The findings and conclusions of this chapter have implications for UN reform to ensure that the work of UN social agencies and of the UN economic commissions is better focused on the institutions of regional associations of governments rather than merely on countries within geographical regions. These are addressed in Chapter 10.

Notes

1 The five UN regional economic commissions are: ESCAP, ECLAC, ECA, ESCWA and ECE.
2 See ESCAP website: http://www.unescap.org/esid/psis/social/index.asp (accessed May 2008).
3 See ECE website: http://www.unece.org/.
4 See ECE website: http://www.unece.org/.
5 Subsequent activities in the Maghreb region can be found at: http://www.mostmaghreb.org.tn.
6 See CARICOM website: http://www.caricom.org/jsp/secretariat/legal_instruments/mou_caricom_unesco_03.jsp?menu=secretariat.
7 A more elaborated work on the UNDP's role in advancing MDGs can be found in Deacon (2007).
8 See ASEAN website: http://www.aseansec.org/14842.htm.
9 See UNDESA website: http://www.un.org/esa/about_esa.html.
10 UNDESA officials were Sergei Zelenev and Isabel Ortiz.
11 See UNDESA website: http://www.un.org/esa/socdev/.
12 See WHO website: http://www.who.int/social_determinants/en/.
13 The document can be consulted at: http://www.paho.org/English/HDP/HDD/policy-greeneonline.pdf.
14 The Caribbean Health and Development Commission was launched in 2003 by the PAHO/WHO and CARICOM.

4 Regional social policy from below

Reclaiming regional integration: social movements and civil society organizations as key protagonists

Cecilia Olivet and Brid Brennan

Introduction

The current conjuncture of intense crisis in neo-liberal economic globalization – in the fields of finance, food, energy and the environment – is fuelling what some commentators call the phenomenon of 'Globalization in Retreat' (Bello 2007). The key institutions at the epicentre of neo-liberal economic globalization, the International Monetary Fund (IMF), World Bank (WB) and World Trade Organization (WTO), are likewise experiencing an ever deepening crisis of legitimacy. While the credibility of the WB and IMF continues to unravel, the WTO has been held in stalemate by broad resistance from many governments of the South as well as the 'alterglobalization' movement. The new generation of 'bilateral' free trade agreements, proposed by both the US and the EU, and being pursued at the national and regional level, are also confronting strong resistance. From Mar del Plata, to Costa Rica, to Senegal, Nigeria and South Africa and from Chiang Mai to Seoul, national and region-wide mobilizations protest and reject the aggressive neo-liberal trade and investment agenda being imposed on the South.

In this chapter we focus on the regional social movements which have emerged in the context of confronting the global neo-liberal agenda as it is being pursued in the South in the guise of 'new regionalism'. These movements are imagining and reclaiming a different people-centred regional integration. In particular, we analyse the regional coalitions of social movements and civil society organizations (CSOs) which have emerged in three regions of the South: the Hemispheric Social Alliance (HSA) in Latin America; the Southern African Peoples' Solidarity Network (SAPSN) in Southern Africa; and the ASEAN Civil Society Conference (ACSC) and Solidarity for Asian Peoples' Advocacy (SAPA) in the South East Asian region.

As noted by Hettne (2006: 141), 'Civil Societies are still generally neglected in the description and explanation of new regionalism'. This view is shared by the few scholars who have made attempts to address this gap (Grugel 2006, Söderbaum 2007). This chapter, therefore, seeks to further contribute to the debate on the role of civil society at the regional level. It will argue that social movements have been able to establish their role as a counter-hegemonic force and as key protagonists in challenging the dominant paradigm.

In the second section of this chapter the trajectory and current development of neo-liberal regionalisms in the Latin American, Southern African and South East Asian regions are analysed. The third section deals with the conjunctures and struggles against neo-liberal regionalisms in which a new generation of regional social movements have emerged. In the fourth section, the role of regional alliances and coalitions in advancing proposals for alternatives to the dominant neo-liberal paradigm will be discussed. Finally, the concluding section draws some overall conclusions and perspectives on the challenges and opportunities that are currently available to social movements and CSOs in terms of articulating an alternative vision of regional integration and of promoting the concretization of projects that place the social dimension and the interest of people at its centre.

This chapter argues that regional integration as originally conceived in the 1950s and 1960s was premised on a more encompassing vision and intended to pursue political and security as well as development objectives. It was during the 1990s that the earlier processes got hijacked by neo-liberalism and the goals of regional formations became very narrowly defined in economic terms and centred on markets under the free trade and investment paradigm. The new generation of social movements and CSOs in Latin America, Southern Africa and South East Asia, shaped particularly over the past ten years by their strong resistance to trade liberalization and privatization and by the development of alternatives from below, are positioning themselves as key agents and players in regional integration processes. They have asserted the need to reclaim regional integration from the forces of neo-liberalism and to shape future regional integration processes that are responsive to the interests of the people.

Developmental regionalism derailed

Regional integration is not new in Asia, Africa or Latin America. Already in the 1950s and 1960s, African as well as Latin American and Asian countries started to develop proposals for regional integration. These proposals were built on a sub-regional basis, and were developed mainly as projects that pursued different political, developmental and security aims. As Mansfield and Milner (1999: 600) have signalled, 'These arrangements were initiated against the backdrop of the Cold War, the rash of decolonization following World War II, and a multilateral commercial framework'. This wave of regional processes has been labelled 'old regionalism' in contrast to the wave of the 1980s and 1990s, driven by neo-liberal economic globalization, which was characterized as 'new regionalism'.[1]

In Latin America, regional integration has its origins in the developmental theory that the United Nations Economic Commission for Latin America and the Caribbean (ECLAC), and particularly Raúl Prebisch, proposed in the 1950s. In this theoretical framework, regional integration was intended to serve as a strategy to increase intra-regional trade, decrease economic and political dependence on the main superpowers and achieve development. The strategy proposed for this was the expansion of markets from the national to the regional scale. The strategy sought to protect these markets from global trade via import-substitution industrialization (ISI) and aimed to achieve industrialization. It became quite influential and as a result several regional projects were created, such as: the Andean Pact in 1969, later changed into the Andean Community of Nations, the Central American Common Market (CACM) and the Caribbean Free Trade Association, which developed into the Caribbean Community (CARICOM) in 1973 (Iglesias 2000).

In the case of South East Asia, ASEAN was formed in 1967, at the period when the South East Asia Treaty Organization (SEATO) – which had been developed as an anti-communist military alliance – was in decline. The ASEAN Declaration of 1967, while identifying its main goals as economic, political and social cooperation, also carried an implicit objective 'to ensure the survival of regimes which had by then retreated significantly from their postcolonial experiments of liberal democracy' (Acharya 2003: 375).

Examples can also be found in Africa, where the origins of the Southern African Development Community (SADC) can be traced back to the 1970s with the formation of the Frontline States (FLS), which in 1980 set in motion the creation of the Southern African Development Coordination Conference (SADCC). This was converted into the Southern African Development Community (SADC) in 1992. As Schoeman (2002: 2) noted, 'to treat SADCC purely as an attempt at economic regionalism or development coordination and cooperation would be to miss much about the original driving forces behind the establishment of the organisation'. The SADCC's geo-strategic objective was to gain economic independence from and to isolate apartheid South Africa (Gibb 2007).

During the mid-1980s and the 1990s, a new wave of regional integration processes emerged. This new trend can be seen either as a response to or as a result of neo-liberal globalization and, as Breslin and Higgot (2003: 170) noted, 'Globalisation, moreover, was thought to be a spur to regional cooperation to the extent that participants in regional schemes thought it might make them more globally competitive'. The strategy at the core of these initiatives aimed to open and liberalize markets and convert the countries' economics to being export-led and investment-driven. The ultimate goal was the competitive insertion of the developing countries into the world economy. Enrique Iglesias (2000: 2–4), President of the Inter-American Development Bank, stated clearly: 'New Regionalism of today is an integral part of the structural reform process which is designed to make our economies more open, more market-based, more sociably equitable and democratic and more internationally competitive in a globalizing world economy'. Furthermore, Mansfield and Milner (1999: 606) have pointed out: 'Using PTA (Preferential Trade Agreements) membership to stimulate liberal economic and political reforms is a distinctive feature of the latest wave of regionalism'.

Ironically, it was ECLAC (which had advocated a developmental approach to regional integration) that launched in the 1990s the 'open regionalism theory'.[2] This was the theory driving regional processes in the 1990s which promoted market-led, export-driven regional integration. As Bergsten (1997: 545) put it: 'the concept seeks to assure that regional agreements will in practice be building blocks for further global liberalisation rather than stumbling blocks that deter such progress'. Open regionalism was widely adopted in the 1990s as the theoretical framework that led governments, not only in Latin America but in all the regions being discussed, to introduce vigorous market deregulation, a widespread privatization drive, and a frantic search to attract foreign direct investments (FDI). As a consequence of this neo-liberal trend, the regional processes that were created in the 1950s and 1960s were restructured to accommodate the demands being made by neo-liberal globalization. Consequently, the new regional integration processes of the 1990s emerged with the main purpose of facilitating the integration of the member countries into world markets and the global economy. Africa, Asia and Latin America were all caught up in this trend. In Latin America, a clear example was the launching in 1991 of the Common Market of the South (MERCOSUR) in South America, which was conceived, in the words of Richards (1997: 133), to 'serve[s] the function of more thoroughly incorporating them [its members] within the world capitalist system while preserving their subordinate status in that system'. The earlier regional projects such as Andean Pact and the CACM were also transformed to 'meet the new challenges'. In Asia, ASEAN experienced a change in direction, when the member countries decided in 1993 to launch an ASEAN Free Trade Area (AFTA). As argued by Nesadurai (2003: 235), 'AFTA has conventionally been explained as a project of open regionalism, adopted by the ASEAN member governments as an instrument to attract foreign direct investment'. This shift in policy marked the moment when ASEAN became part of the 'new wave' of regionalisms (Bowles 1997: 225).

A similar story can be found in Southern Africa, where three of the most important regional formations – the Southern African Customs Union (SACU), the SADC and the Common Market for Eastern and Southern Africa (COMESA) – have undergone structural changes (Gibb 2007) which can be explained by the comment:

> the great majority of present-day regionalist schemes in Africa are founded on the notion that the regional economic integration project should be market driven and outward looking and should remove obstacles to the free movement of goods, services, capital, and investment within the regions as well as to the rest of the world. The overall intention is to ensure a closer integration into the world economy.
>
> (Söderbaum 2004: 423)

These shifts in the policy and structures of regional blocs in Asia, Africa and Latin America show how neo-liberal economic globalization and the forces behind it (mainly transnational corporations, local elites and governments) have hijacked the processes of regional integration to serve their interests. So to treat regional integration as an economic and technical issue only would be to fall into the neo-liberal trap and should therefore be avoided (Gibb 2007).

Two decades of privatization, liberalization and deregulation in Asia, Africa and Latin America have left a trail of social and environmental destruction. As noted by Scholte (2005), neo-liberal globalization has not helped to end poverty – on the contrary, the gaps between rich and poor have widened; it has failed to resolve the unemployment question and has brought a deterioration of working conditions; it has contributed to the destruction of the global environment; and it can be linked to persistent or increased insecurity. By the end of the 1990s, the severe effects of neo-liberal globalization and the widespread resistance and rejection shown (at national and global levels) by social movements and CSOs gave urgency to the need to develop economic and social alternatives. In responding to this challenge to address the failure of neo-liberal globalization, social movements and CSOs, as well as some governments, were impelled to *reclaim regional integration* from the neo-liberal trend, and to recreate or create regional integration processes based on different principles and policies.

In this context, a new kind of regional integration, referred to as alternative regionalism, is being conceptualized and concrete alternative regional proposals are being developed, although at different intensities and levels, by social movements and CSOs in Africa, Asia and Latin America. The possibility of developing regional alternatives to the neo-liberal paradigm has gained strength, especially in the past few years, to the extent that Latin America, a continent deeply penetrated by neo-liberal globalization for two decades and very hard hit by its effects, is today the context where not only social movements and civil society, but also some governments, are starting to experiment with new forms of regional integration. A key feature of these processes in Latin America is new initiatives aimed at regaining sovereignty – mainly in terms of economy, politics and natural resources.

While the wave of regional processes of the 1950s and 1960s was originally aimed at reducing North–South dependence, the wave of regionalism that emerged in the 1990s was, on the contrary, preoccupied with serving as a mechanism for countries to integrate into world markets. However, a common characteristic of both the 'old' and the 'new' wave of regional processes is that civil society is kept largely at the margins of the regional agendas. The only exception to this was the effort to create consultative mechanisms which involved mainly trade unions. Conversely, the 'alternative regional integration' processes which are now being conceptualized (and in some cases, in Latin America for example, concretized) create more space for social movement and CSO engagement.

Over the last ten years, social movements and CSOs have been centrally involved in processes of change and have positioned themselves more strategically in the relations of power that could eventually lead to a transformation of the regional integration model and spur what could be called a third wave of regional processes.

Reclaiming regional development and integration: the role of regional civil society

A new body of research is growing rapidly around the issue of global civil society and transnational activist coalitions (Keck and Sikkink 1999, Tarrow 2001, Evans 2005, Serbin 2004). There is a general consensus that the emergence and strengthening of civil society and social movements should be seen as a political response to the social and economic grievances created by neo-liberal globalization (Veltmeyer 2004). However, most of these researchers have focused on the global level, and how 'global civil society' engages with global governance institutions (i.e. World Trade Organization) or creates specific sectoral issue coalitions (e.g. women's movements). Very little research has been dedicated to the role of civil society in the process of regionalization and even less attention has been given to the emergence of networks operating at a regional level and engaging with the question of regional integration processes.[3]

It is only recently that some scholars have begun to recognize that 'States are not the only regionalising actors' (Söderbaum 2007: 324). One reason for the research gap is indeed the lack of possible case studies. Until recently, social movements and civil society have been largely excluded from regional processes. A democratic deficit has been a common feature of regionalism. Even in bodies such as MERCOSUR, ASEAN and the SADC, regarded as 'developmental regionalism' (Hettne 2006: 138), civil society engagement has met with institutional barriers and it has been limited to participation by trade unions in some consultative mechanisms, where the agendas for discussion have already been set by governments.

This situation started changing at the end of the 1990s. The emergence of regional civil society alliances can be attributed to the combination of two crucial factors: on the one hand, the neo-liberalization of regional processes and, on the other, the strengthening and emergence of social movements and CSOs which saw the regional arena as a space where it was needed to (i) resist the hegemonic neo-liberal agenda, and (ii) engage in reclaiming the regional space with the objective of developing alternatives.

Over the past two decades, as the neo-liberal processes deepened, social movements and CSOs underwent major transformations in two important respects. On the one hand, new social movements emerged in both rural and urban contexts comprising, for example, the landless, farmers and, in Latin America, indigenous communities, as well as the unemployed and the urban poor. These movements were born primarily as a consequence of the privatization of public services, the extraction of natural resources and delocalization, and they took the lead in resistance to the dominant neo-liberal policies (Seoane *et al.* 2005). On the other hand, these new popular movements also pursued a strategy of transnational multi-sectoral alliances.

All across the global South, the 1990s witnessed the emergence of alliances that brought together social movements – such as the indigenous, the landless, the farmers, women, fisherfolk, migrants, youth and environmentalists – with other fractions of the civil society spectrum such as non-governmental organizations (NGOs) but also the more established trade unions and political parties (Seoane *et al.* 2005, Veltmeyer 2004, Söderbaum 2007, Keet 2007b).

The participation of trade unions in these alliances is of particular importance. In the face of diminished power in the 1990s, the labour movement found a new source of mobilization and strength through the strategy of making alliances with social movements and NGOs around issues of common concern, such as free trade and economic governance (Anner and Evans 2004, Spooner 2004, Saguier 2007).

This convergence of sectoral and multi-sectoral alliances laid the basis for social movements to become key actors in the social and political conjuncture at local and global levels. At the same time, the regional arena was increasingly seen by social movements and CSOs as a very strategic space to demand a break with the neo-liberal paradigm and put forward people-centred regional alternatives.

The focus on regional arenas and regional alternatives is directly linked with and at the same time embedded in the struggles of resistance and search for alternatives at the global level. Even when neo-liberalism has had similar impacts in all three regions, there are different regional realities, which demand particular regional responses. Furthermore, regional social alliances have identified very specific reasons why they need to centre their attention at the regional level. First of all, sovereignty and independence are at the core of the alternative regional integration proposals. These proposals are designed to strengthen the nation states and to build capacity to act with autonomy when facing pressures from neo-liberal forces (either TNCs, global capital or the main powers such as the US and EU).

However, no country alone, no matter how strong and autonomous, will be able to challenge current global corporate power and neo-liberal forces. Only a united front of many countries studying together with the same political will could resist the pressures from the global free trade institutions and the big powers whose business interests will be strongly impacted by these alternative proposals.

Furthermore, social movements and civil society organizations have realized that, beyond the heterogeneity among the countries in each region, there is great potential for coordination, cooperation and indeed complementarity – both at the governmental and the people's level. Alternative regional integration proposals therefore point to the prospects of a redefinition of the production, infrastructure, communication and energy (among others) structures, in order to develop each region into a unit oriented to the real needs of its people. Latin America, Asia and Africa have enormous natural and human resources (such as raw materials, energy, water, minerals, and oil/gas) which, if better coordinated, could be used for the development of the region.

These factors have led to the emergence and configuration of regional civil society in Africa, Asia and Latin America, the key actors of which are positioning themselves in the debate on and definition of an alternative regional integration, which also demands a new configuration and commitment from political forces, particularly governments, to implement actual alternatives.

People-centred regionalism: regional alliances and alternatives proposed in Africa, Asia and Latin America

The most significant regional civil society networks addressing regional integration which have developed in recent years are: the Hemispheric Social Alliance (HSA) in Latin America, the Southern African Peoples' Solidarity Network (SAPSN) in Southern Africa, and Solidarity for Asian Peoples' Advocacy (SAPA) and the ASEAN Civil Society Conference (ACSC) in South East Asia. In assessing their role and significance, it is crucial first to analyse the contexts in which they have emerged, their strategies of action, their processes of engagement and their articulation of institutional and policy alternatives in the specific regions where they are based.

Context of emergence of regional networks

Hemispheric Social Alliance

The HSA, a networks umbrella organization, articulates social movements (of peasants, indigenous peoples, environmentalists, women and students), NGOs and trade unions across the whole of the Americas, from Canada to Argentina. It was created in 1997, with the purpose of resisting the negotiations towards a Free Trade Area of the Americas (FTAA) promoted by the US. In parallel to the process of resistance to the FTAA, the HSA started the construction of alternatives to that project in particular and to neo-liberal globalization in general. As Saguier (2007: 257) notes in his in-depth analysis of the formation of the HSA, the building of a common agenda of political alternatives was a more complex process than that of coordinating a common front of resistance. However, 'efforts to reconcile some of these differences in a continental vision of development resulted in the first version of the HSA policy document *Alternative for the Americas*', launched in 1998.

In 2005, during the Mar del Plata Summit of the Americas in Argentina, the first major success after eight years of campaigning materialized when the FTAA project was defeated by the MERCOSUR countries' (Brazil, Argentina, Uruguay and Paraguay) and Venezuela's refusal to sign the agreement, supported by the mass mobilization organized by the HSA during the event. This moment marked the first signs of a breakdown in the hemispheric governmental consensus of adhesion to the neo-liberal model. Furthermore, the HSA served as a catalyst for mounting social protests. It has been recognized that in the years immediately before and since the defeat of the FTAA project in 2005, popular uprisings have 'in some cases … entailed the toppling of governments, the creation of deep political crisis, or the failure of undertakings of neoliberal character' (Seoane *et al.* 2005). This scenario of change was consolidated with the coming to power of newly elected 'progressive' governments in Venezuela, Brazil, Argentina, Uruguay, Ecuador and Bolivia. With these changes, civil society and social movements in Latin America began to encounter 'interlocutors that will propose dialogues and alliances in the construction of an autonomous vision of the continent and the countries' (Berrón 2007: 14).

The political context that Latin America has experienced since 2005 is key to understanding the shifts that the HSA has undergone. As Grugel (2006: 221) observed, 'once resources had been deployed and concentrated at hemispheric level – where so much appears to be at stake – there was less energy and less interest left over for sub-regionalism'. But this immediately changed after the FTAA was defeated and with the emergence of new 'friendly' governments. With the FTAA out of the way, the HSA embarked on a new stage. It was confronted with the challenge, particularly from the new governments, to start engaging directly with the new regional initiatives such as the Bolivarian Alternatives for the Americas (ALBA), the Trade Treaty of the People (TCP), and the South American Community of Nations (later named UNASUR – Union of South American Nations), as well as with the more established organizations such as MERCOSUR. Even more important, this included the challenge to concretize proposals in the policy terrain (Berrón 2007).

With the opening of this new political scenario where governments started to put regional integration high on the agenda, social movements and CSOs in Latin America also saw the new proposals for regional integration as an opportunity to rethink their models of development and the possibility of active participation and engagement in its construction. Therefore, they embarked on a continuous process of debate on the type of regional integration they desired (Mello 2006). These broad debates served to generate a significant number of concrete initiatives in the different areas under discussion (energy, trade, militarization, migration, environment, financing, corporations and water among others). As Berrón (2007: 3) remarked: 'the launching of the South American Community of Nations (renamed UNASUR), and in particular the Summit in Cochabamba,[4] offered the ideal scenario for social movements to discuss integration in a more systematic fashion'. This does not mean that social movements in Latin America have reached a consensual vision on the kind of regional integration they want, but they have certainly moved the debate forward.

The Southern African Peoples' Solidarity Network

The SAPSN was formed in 1999 to challenge the interlinked issues of debt, structural adjustment and globalization. The SAPSN developed into a network drawing together a broad range of organizations and movements (from trade unions to faith-based organizations) from the Southern African region. Three major African networks are part of SAPSN: the Africa Trade Network (ATN), the Gender and Trade Network (GENTA) and Jubilee South (which campaigns for debt cancellation and development).

At the heart of the SAPSN lies a 'history of colonisation and mutual support in our struggles for national liberation, as well as our shared experience of the depredations of apartheid' (SAPSN, 2000). The main reasons motivated certain regional groups which were working on debt, trade, structural adjustment and globalization to propose the creation of the SAPSN were: (i) the realization that civil society did not have any real space for engagement with the SADC's processes and structures, in spite of its many declarations on the need to engage civil society; (ii) the increasingly neo-liberal character of the SADC, which meant that its policies were not helping to address the needs of poor and marginalized communities. Thus, the SAPSN is unequivocally critical of the current corporate-driven regionalism within the SADC. As Söderbaum (2007: 332) observed, 'the ... SAPSN has rapidly become one of the key nodes in Southern Africa of the so-called "anti-globalisation movement".'

What draws SAPSN members together is their commitment to regional solidarity, to the building of people-based regional cooperation and integration, to a genuinely united and developmental Southern African community of states (SAPSN 2000) and to the urgent need to reclaim the SADC from its current neo-liberal path (SAPSN 2006, 2007). The SAPSN also identified the free trade agenda embedded in the Economic Partnership Agreements (EPAs) as a direct threat to the SADC's regional integrity. Furthermore, it was envisaged that taking the resistance to the regional level could significantly strengthen the search for a more just Southern Africa.

In order to fulfil these purposes, the SAPSN has concentrated on the promotion of sharing experiences, developing capacity, exchanging information, increasing awareness and consciousness on its focus issues, and contributing to the mobilization and building of mass movements. At the core of these strategies lies the organization of a series of SADC People's Summits in parallel with the Inter-governmental and Heads of State SADC Summit. These are core moments when the networks converge and open up key spaces to let the voices and proposals of SAPSN member organizations and networks be heard by the governments. The first SADC People's Summit was organized in August 2000 in parallel with the SADC Heads of State Summit in Windhoek, Namibia. This was followed by the People's Summit held under the theme Reclaiming SADC for People's Development: Assessing the Impact of Neoliberal Policies on the People's Livelihoods in Maseru in 2006, and in 2007 by the Lusaka People's Summit held under the banner 'Reclaiming SADC for People's Development and Solidarity: Let the People Speak'. The most recent SADC People's Summit was held in Johannesburg, South Africa, in August 2008. At the end of each of these Summits strong declarations were released containing the key demands and proposals put forward by SAPSN members and later submitted to the SADC Heads of State.

ASEAN Civil Society Conference /Solidarity for Asian Peoples' Advocacy

Close-knit dynamic networks of social movements and CSOs developed in South East Asia in the context of the anti-dictatorship struggles which dominated ASEAN countries during the 1970s and 1980s, the time when the so-called 'Asian Tiger economies' were established. Strong sectoral and thematic movements developed in the midst of human rights and labour rights struggles, as well as campaigns on freedom from debt and military bases. It was in 1989 that social movements and networks initiated a People's Plan for the 21st Century (PP21) to build a 'People's Alliance ... exercising transborder participatory democracy' to address more comprehensively the prevailing economic and political system which later became widely known as the 'neo-liberal globalisation regime' (Ichiyo 2002). The PP21 initiative had a strong Asia-wide character and in some ways anticipated the agendas of the alterglobalization movement which converged in Seattle (Feffer 2007).

However, despite these region-wide initiatives, social movements and CSOs have until recently remained quite resistant to engaging with ASEAN, although business (ASEAN Business Chamber–ASEAN Chamber of Commerce and Industry) and academic (ASEAN-ISIS) networks began to address ASEAN in the 1970s and 1980s. ASEAN was seen by civil society in South East Asia as 'a "club of elites", disconnected from the people in the region' (Caballero-Anthony 2004: 577). As observed by Chandra (2006: 72), 'It was only after the financial crisis in 1997 that the involvement of a wider range of non-state actors in the association intensified, partly due to the process of democratization in the region'.

The first initiative that resulted in wider civil society mobilization in ASEAN came with the launching of the ASEAN People's Assembly (APA) in 2000 in Batam, Indonesia,[5] under the initiative of the ASEAN-ISIS academic network, which subsequently organized five APAs. Even when the first APA conference was described as a 'historic event in building an ASEAN society' (APA 2001: 12), civil society organizations felt that APA had not achieved real engagement with the ASEAN agendas, and that a more inclusive and socially rooted civil society network was needed.

Therefore on the eve of the eleventh official ASEAN Summit the first ASEAN Civil Society Conference (ACSC) was organized in Kuala Lumpur in December 2005. Under the theme Building a Common Future Together, the first ACSC called for the transformation of ASEAN from a purely intergovernmental association into a genuine people-centred community of nations and peoples (ACSC 2007a: 5). During this Summit, for the first time in the thirty-eight year life of ASEAN, 'a civil society representative read a statement prepared and approved in a wider civil society conference held several days earlier' (Chavez 2005). Even though the ACSC was meant to be a one-off event and, unlike APA, was not recognized officially by ASEAN, the importance of maintaining this open civil society forum was acknowledged, and the decision was taken to hold a conference every year in parallel with the official ASEAN Summits.

In this way, 'civil society not only claimed the ACSC; it enhanced the ACSC process as well' (ACSC 2007a: 5). ACSC conferences were organized independently by civil society in Cebu, Philippines (December 2006), and in Singapore (November 2007). Each of these conferences mobilized a broad range of civil society organizations, trade unions and social movements and gave impetus to building consensus on a vision of ASEAN that would serve the interests of the people and lead to the creation of a people-centred and people-driven ASEAN.

Overall, the ACSC started the process of demythologizing ASEAN and underlining the importance of regional spaces for advancing struggles and alternatives. Nonetheless, it was clear that the ACSC also had its limitations. Since it was conceived as an open forum rather than a network, the need was identified to create a more permanent 'open platform for consultation, cooperation, and coordination between Asian social movements and CSOs that are engaged in action, advocacy, and lobbying at the level of intergovernmental processes and organizations' (Rillorta 2007: 15). This is what defines the platform Solidarity for Asean Peoples' Advocacy (SAPA), which was launched in February 2006 and rapidly expanded to include more than 100 organizations (SAPA 2008).

The creation of SAPA and the Working Group on ASEAN (WG-ASEAN)[6] took place in the context of responding to the official process of drafting an ASEAN Charter by 2007. The SAPA working group on ASEAN, in conjunction with the ACSC, undertook a series of regional consultations aimed at producing a concrete set of proposals on the three pillars identified by ASEAN as central to the Charter: the security pillar, the economic pillar and the socio-cultural pillar. While their submissions were initially well received by the Eminent Persons Group (EPG) in charge of making recommendations on the ASEAN Charter, they did not get beyond the High-Level Task Force (HLTF) which was finally responsible for the actual drafting (Nuera 2007: 6). As Chavez (2007a) noted: 'the initial expectation and hope, however, soon turned into concern when it became apparent that the ASEAN charter was not to be the subject of wide-ranging discussions, and that it was not to be made public until after it is signed by ASEAN leaders'.

Finally the ASEAN governments failed to give due acknowledgement to the civil society engagement with the Charter process. In fact, ASEAN did not make public the draft of the ASEAN Charter prior to its signing. Then, when the Draft Charter was leaked to the media[7] it became clear that civil society inputs had been largely ignored (SAPA 2007).

Despite this negative experience, SAPA member organizations recognized the positive outcomes of the process of engaging with ASEAN and acknowledged that this provided the opportunity to 'look into regional governance', to address the 'need to develop some notion of regionalism', and to advance the much needed 'consensus building at regional level'. It was also emphasized that 'engagement doesn't mean supporting' (ACSC 2007a: 24). In fact it means the opposite, confronting ASEAN when the policies adopted are felt not to be conducive to the welfare of the people in the region.

The importance of sustaining engagement with ASEAN was reiterated during the ACSC III with the decision to 'launch a process of drafting an ASEAN

People's Charter' to be prepared for the ACSC IV which was held in Thailand in February 2009 (ACSC 2007).

HSA, SAPSN and ACSC/SAPA: parallels and divergences

When comparing SAPSN, ACSC/SAPA and HSA, several common characteristics may be observed. They are all built as multi-sectoral alliances aimed at resisting corporate-driven neo-liberal globalization. Likewise, all have identified the regional arena as key to pursuing the people's struggles and to mobilizing their organizations to embark together on a process of developing regional alternatives. The three networks share a general critique of the economic market-driven approach to regional integration processes; they all criticize the trend to liberalization, privatization and deregulation and continue to monitor and warn of the impacts of these on people and the environment. They share the view that is imperative for the improvement of people's lives to reclaim regional integration and push for 'alternative regionalisms' that go beyond pure economic and trade agendas and instead comprehensively serve the interests of the people. The regional arena is perceived by all three networks as a key space in which to push for and influence social transformation and changes in national government policies. Additionally, all three networks combine a political strategy of resistance and mobilization for social change together with the articulation of regional development alternatives.

Furthermore, the three alliances have engaged with governments, though in different ways and at different levels. Given the recent configuration of political forces and progressive governments in Latin America, social movements and CSOs within the HSA have had the possibility of constructing dialogues with governments and therefore have achieved a higher level of policy space to put forward their alternative proposals. The ACSC/SAPA has also had the possibility of submitting proposals on the three pillars of the ASEAN Charter and has been able to access a very short direct dialogue with ASEAN government officials. On the other hand, the SAPSN has not encountered the same level of openness from SADC governments, and in some instances has experienced hostility. For instance, the participants at the SADC People's Summit in Lusaka were denied space to express their views and were prevented from holding a peaceful march to deliver their resolutions.

In terms of the articulation of regional alternative proposals, social movements and civil society in the three regions have developed more or less detailed policy proposals. This can partly be explained by whether or not they were confronted by new regional developments and direct challenges that demanded immediate concrete responses. In the case of the HSA, the opening of space to influence the building and shaping of UNASUR triggered movements and civil society to embrace a process of in-depth discussion on the substantive content of its advocacy on the 'integration of the people'. Likewise, the ACSC/SAPA seized its opportunity when ASEAN declared its intention to introduce a Charter.

Another common feature of the HSA and the ACSC/SAPA is that both are developing alternatives that go beyond their engagement with governments. The HSA, for instance, is not only thinking in terms of what UNASUR or ALBA should look like, but is continuously giving content to its own ideal 'integration of the people' initiative. The ASCS/SAPA, even though it started the development of alternatives concentrating on the submission of proposals to the ASEAN Charter process, has now, after its initial negative experience, embarked on the formulation of an ASEAN People's Charter.

Alternative policy proposals

The range of statements, declarations, reports and official submissions produced over the last years by the HSA, SAPSN and ASC/SAPA form an impressive corpus of documents from which it is possible to extract the key regional proposals which are being advocated by each. These documents reflect advances in the elaboration and concretization of key proposals for a different development model as well as identifying the specific policy challenges that social movements and civil society face in each region.

Principles of alternative regionalism

Even when the concrete initiatives being proposed by these networks vary according to the political realities of each region, we can see commonalities among the three networks in the way they articulate the overall principles of 'alternative regional integration'. First of all, they strongly affirm that alternative forms of regional integration need to be based on a different model of development that must move away from the economic neo-liberal globalization architecture (mainly driven by the WTO, WB and IMF) and must break with the current trade and investment paradigm. In particular, they advocate the rejection of the free trade model pursued by the US and EU as a first step towards gaining national/regional policy space (ACSC 2006, HSA 2006, 2006i, SAPSN 2000, 2006, 2007). Furthermore, the rejection of economic neo-liberal policies is also reflected in the rejection of privatization of essential public services (such as access to water, housing, health care, education, etc.) and advocacy of public policies that address basic public needs (HSA 2007a, SAPSN 2006, ACSC 2006, SAPA 2006b). The repossession of natural resources is also a common shared concern and goal, which in Latin America is being articulated as direct advocacy for nationalization (ACSC 2006, HSA 2006d).

In addition, alternative regionalism is being advocated not only in relation to economic policy but as a multi-dimensional process, in which the social, environmental, cultural and political dimensions are not subordinated to the interests of trade and finance and their main beneficiaries, the local and transnational elites (SAPSN 2000, ACSC 2006, SAPA 2006b, HSA 2006j). Therefore, the advocacy for regional development rejects the current export-led model of exploitation of primary resources and instead proposes a development strategy at the service of the people. A new development model embedded in the concept of social justice and based on principles of cooperation and solidarity instead of competition is promoted. This sustainable and equitable model of development, placing poverty reduction and the protection of the environment at its core, takes precedence over models based on competition and the accumulation of wealth by transnational corporations (HSA 2006j, 2008, SAPA 2006a).

The regional integration advocated by the social movements and civil society networks in each region coincide in their demand for a 'people-centred regionalism' (as it is described in Asia) or 'integration of the peoples' (as it is called in Latin America) or a 'people-based regional development' (as it is referred to in Africa). All in all, the regionalism that is envisaged would place social movements and civil society at its centre and would promote the interests of the people rather than corporations (HSA 2007, SAPSN 2000, ACSC 2005). All the networks have stated in one way or another their conviction that 'alternative regional integration' should be based on the recognition and celebration of cultural diversity as well as the people's unity based on solidarity (HSA 2007a, SAPSN 2000, ACSC 2006).

Equally important are those key principles which are given particular emphasis (identified as unique) in each specific region. In the case of South East Asia where human rights violations are a main concern in all countries, the ACSC/SAPA indicate that the 'protection of human rights and dignity should be the primary goal of all efforts for regional integration and cooperation' (SAPA 2006b). They also call for integration that redefines democracy in the sense of 'extending citizenship' to serve as a guardian for 'free and honest elections, participatory governance, basic liberties and a free and plural media'. They also aim for regional integration that reinterprets the principle of non-intervention, on the understanding that the application of this principle within ASEAN has blocked the possibility of solving regional and national conflicts (ACSC 2006).

Similarly, in Latin America, the current realities have also led the social movements and civil societies to articulate principles for the 'integration of the peoples' that are unique to the region. Above all, they see in alternative regional integration a strategy that will allow the Latin American countries to regain sovereignty (i.e. over their natural resources, financial and energy independence, and the right to regulate markets in the interest of balanced social and economic development) and from this basis, engage in reconstructing a multi-polar global space.

Regional socio-economic policies

A further analysis of the documents of these regional networks also reveals specific regional socio-economic policy proposals concretizing the principles and vision of an alternative regional integration. In many instances these call for the setting up of regional mechanisms for the coordination and implementation of policy priorities.

In terms of human, economic, social, and cultural rights, SAPA (2006b) has proposed an ASEAN Regional Human Rights Body responsible for: 'monitoring and reporting human rights conditions within the region; investigating human rights violations; developing awareness on human rights among people in the region; and, providing effective compliance and redress mechanisms'. The HSA (2006c) has proposed a South American Social Charter which guarantees the human, social, cultural and environmental rights of the people. This would be based on the already proposed Social Charter for the Americas and it would reaffirm the rights to: a decent life, food sovereignty, universal health care, education, employment, land ownership and family agriculture, and universal access to water, social protection and housing. It would also include environmental rights, indigenous people's rights, and rights to cultural and sexual diversity, gender equality, social inclusion and the right to migrate and not to migrate. For Southern Africa, the SAPSN (2007) is promoting an 'SADC protocol on human rights and gender'.

Specific proposals have also been put forward to defend workers' rights and decent work. In ASEAN, SAPA (2006a) has proposed the need for a regional mechanism to ensure standards and certifications recognizing workers' rights – formal and informal –and protection of the labour movement. In Latin America, the proposal has been advanced for the adoption of a Labour Platform for the Americas, which consists of a range of actions for governments to create healthy economies based on full employment as well as social and economic justice for all (ORIT 2005).

Concrete proposals have also been developed to address the situation of regional migration and employment. ASEAN civil society proposes the creation of a regional mechanism to ensure 'mutual recognition and accreditation of skills by member States' and adoption of 'standard employment contracts that protect the well-being of native and migrant labour alike' (SAPA 2006a). Similarly, in Latin America, groups advocate a regional identity card that would allow free circulation and residence of people in the member countries, as well as a permanent regional commission for the defence of the human rights of migrants (HSA 2006g). In order to 'bring to an end the forced migration of millions of workers', SAPSN (2000) is promoting regional policies that 'develop holistic and integrated urban and rural programmes to enable people to create their own incomes or obtain employment incomes'.

Even though health is primarily a national concern, regional networks have highlighted the need to address some health policy issues in a regional manner. In ASEAN, SAPA (2006a) has proposed a regional coordination in terms of 'research and manufacture of generic drugs … to respond to pandemics and illnesses'. Similarly, Latin American groups have advocated the establishment of a South American plan to guarantee the universality of access to public health (HSA 2006j). And in Southern Africa, SAPSN (2007) has gone even further, proposing the creation and implementation of a regional fund where 15 per cent of national budgets is allocated to the provision of essential drugs including antiretrovirals (SAPSN 2007).

In Latin America, civil society has presented strong proposals regarding the need to address the issue of access to water as a regional concern. The HSA (2006b) and the Bolivian government have called for the drafting of a South

American convention on water, or a similar legal instrument, that declares access to water as a human right and forbids its privatization (not only drinking water but also water as a means of life for communities) by excluding the issue of water from all trade negotiations and rejecting the intensive use of water for extractive activities (mainly mining and oil). It is envisaged that this convention would take precedence over free trade agreements and investment treaties. An additional proposal had also been put forward for the creation of a South American tribunal on water or a similar instrument that deals with the violations of people's and communities, right to water (HSA 2006b). Finally, proposals and initiatives are being developed for putting in place regional policies that protect the main water sources in the continent (such as wetlands, glaciers, subterranean water, etc.), and setting up regional mechanisms to facilitate exchange of experience and capacities among public water companies (public–public partnerships), ensuring the social responsibility of the state (HSA 2006b).

Asymmetries, both among and within the countries of each region, are a key issue, and concrete proposals have been put forward to try to address them. In ASEAN, SAPA (2006a) has proposed the establishment of a regional redistribution mechanism, for example an ASEAN development fund geared to support local initiatives and countries with balance of payments deficit or unsustainable debts. In Latin America, a proposal has been made for the creation of a compensation fund for the least developed countries, its resources to be allocated to develop sectors of the popular economy, cooperatives and offer projects in agreement with the decisions of the peoples of these countries (HSA 2006j).

The right to food is intimately linked to social development, and the regional networks have strongly advocated a regional approach to food and agriculture. In ASEAN, SAPA (2006a) has proposed the creation of support mechanisms for small-scale producers (including farmers, fisherfolk and indigenous people), including 'policies ensuring equitable access to and ownership of markets and productive resources such as land, water, seeds, capital and appropriate technology'. They also proposed the development of a regional mechanism to protect citizens' human rights to food, water and a livelihood, including regional regulations of trade-sensitive products, in order to ensure food security and protection for the livelihoods of small-scale producers (SAPA 2006a). Similarly, in Latin America, groups have advocated regional policies that promote, support and encourage agrarian activities, driven by the principle of food sovereignty, understood in the sense of the 'right of the people to produce their own food in an independent, diverse and healthy manner'. Regional policies promoting food sovereignty would include: land reform, free and universal technical assistance, credits to small farmers and artisanal fisherfolk and, access to water and home-grown seeds without constraints (HSA 2006a). These issues have also been emphasized in Southern Africa, where the SAPSN (2007) highlighted the need for regional policies that 'prioritize the sustainable livelihoods of the rural communities, and equity in the land reform processes' in contrast with the current trend towards 'eviction of people from their ancestral land, land privatization, and capitalization of land'.

A range of other issues and concerns (such as the environment, energy, infrastructure, financing mechanisms, security and conflict) are also on the agenda of the regional social movements and civil society alliances. Besides the creation of a regional mechanism for the advancement of women (SAPA 2006b), other proposals include: cross-border mechanisms to address issues like 'smuggling, dumping of toxic wastes, trans-boundary pollution, transnational territorial waters, trafficking, etc.' (SAPA 2006a); publicly funded regional support mechanisms to promote 'science and technology for the regional collective good' (SAPA 2006a); establishment of 'regional sustainability plans and environmental policies and programmes' which include 'efforts for the rehabilitation of the environment' to 'restore the biological biodiversity of the region, and stabilisation of global climate', etc. (SAPA 2006b).

In addition, proposals have been made calling for new mechanisms of solidarity finance between the countries in the region, including the proposal for a solidarity bank of the south (banco del Sur) and a common reserve fund (HSA 2006e), as well as a regional mechanism which includes 'provisions for the disciplining and regulation of the financial markets' and regional mechanisms that regulate the operation of transnational corporations (SAPA 2006a).

Future perspectives and challenges

In quite diverse geopolitical contexts, the HSA, SAPSN and ACSC/SAPA have emerged as key regional actors confronting the neo-liberal paradigm as it impacts on the regions of Latin America, Southern Africa and South East Asia, respectively.

These regional social movement and civil society networks have effectively mobilized the resistance of people in these regions both to the instruments of neo-liberal globalization (the WTO, IMF and WB) and to the liberalization and privatization demands of the free trade agreements (FTAs) and bilateral investment treaties (BITs) being imposed by the US and the EU on the South. As part of the 'alterglobalization movement', these strategies of resistance have given social movement alliances a profile as main trans-national social actors at both the global and the regional levels. Besides, within the framework of their respective regions, these social movement alliances have broken new ground as oppositional movements, initiating substantive theoretical and practical work in articulating proposals for an alternative form of regional integration. In this way, the new concrete regional proposals articulated by these alliances are laying the basis for the emergence of a third wave of regional integration processes which can be called 'alternative regionalism'.

However, if these regional alliances of social movements and CSOs are to sustain the momentum of their struggles and strengthen their capacity as key protagonists shaping a different regional integration, they must face a number of key challenges: combining strategies of resistance and alternatives; steering the movements and alliance networks on a course that avoids both co-optation and repression by governments; and making real advances that impact positively and effectively on people's lives and their struggle against poverty.

Some commentators have focused on the material as well as the political difficulties of sustaining trans-national collective action – for instance, Scholte (2004) in terms of resources, networking, official attitudes, mass media, political culture and the democratic accountability of the civil society organizations themselves. Others have identified the challenge of trans-national networks to remain rooted in national processes, and have also addressed the risk of co-optation by governments (Grugel 2006: 214). The main challenge that has been identified, however, is not so much that of resources, but that of achieving sufficient leverage to change the configuration of power in order to create the political space necessary to reclaim regional integration from the institutions and forces of neo-liberalism.

Notes

1 For further reading on the differences between old and new regionalisms, see: Väyrynen (2003), Wilfred (1998), Mansfield and Milner (1999), and Breslin and Higgott (2003).
2 For an analysis of the concept of 'open regionalism' and its application to regional integration in Latin America, see Gudynas (2005).
3 Some examples of research addressing this issue are: Söderbaum (2007), Podesta *et al.* (2000), Grugel (2005, 2006), Acharya (2003), Keck and Sikkink (1999), Keet (2007), Serbin (1997).
4 In December 2006 in Cochabamba, Bolivia, the presidents of South America held the Summit of the South American Community of Nations (SACN) while social movements and civil society organizations from all over Latin America gathered for the Social Summit for the Integration of the Peoples.
5 There have been earlier people's regional initiatives at the Asia level such as: People's Plan for the 21st Century (PP21) initiated in Japan in 1989 and the Working Group for an ASEAN Human Rights Mechanism formed in 1994.
6 To see details of SAPA's working mechanisms visit its website: www.asiasapa.org/.
7 The draft charter was published online by Prachatai, an alternative Thai media organization, and is available at: www.prachatai.com/english/news.php?id=362.

Part II

The social policy dimensions of regional integration

Case studies from four continents

5 Social policies and rights in the European Union and the Council of Europe

Exhortation, regulation and enforcement

Monica Threlfall

Introduction

The main social challenges faced by European societies are said to be similar to those that confront all industrial societies, at least at the macro-level: the new labour order, the ageing of populations, the trend towards migration and multi-ethnicity, new social risks, regional differentiation and the demands on people of the knowledge-based economy (Maydell *et al.* 2006: 50). In such a context, regional associations can find an appropriate role in helping to bring nations together to confront these social challenges. This is the case of the European Union (EU), which is increasingly projecting itself both as the forum where discussion of common problems should take place and as the venue where solutions will be found – through the reform of the European Social Model (Lisbon Council 2008) and through streamlining and consolidating social policies into the heart of integration policy (Maydell *et al.* 2006: 285–95). For its part, the second major European regional body, the Council of Europe, has been credited for its role in opening up discussion of social and human rights issues to the countries of Eastern Europe (Huber 1999). Its aims include social goals such as 'to find common solutions to the challenges facing European society: such as discrimination against minorities, xenophobia, intolerance, bioethics and cloning, terrorism, trafficking in human beings, organized crime and corruption, cyber crime, violence against children' (Council of Europe 2008a). In other words, both organizations see themselves as part of the solution.

With the repeated adherence of new member states – the total is currently twenty-seven – and the continuing queue for membership from Eastern and Southern European states, the European Union is the most advanced of the world's regional socio-economic and political integration projects. And with its ever-evolving Treaties – most recently the 2007 Treaty of Lisbon – and the repeated extension of powers accorded to its central supra-national body, the European Commission, it is also the world's most developed case of nation-states pooling their sovereignty. Of the many facets of this integration project –

its single market, Central Bank and single currency, common foreign policy and extensive development aid, to name the main ones – the social dimension is one of the least well known. This is partly because in 1957, at the time of the founding of the European Economic Community through the Treaty of Rome, Western European states were already welfare states with well-developed public health and education services and a commitment to expenditure on social benefits reaching 15–20 per cent of their respective gross domestic products (GDP), much of it channelled through regional and local administrations. The notion of creating a single, pan-European welfare system with harmonized levels of expenditure was therefore daunting to policy-makers, given the idiosyncrasies of the member states' social protection systems. For this and other reasons, the social provisions in the original Treaty of Rome were few, and their development tardy. While scholars favourable to welfare integration tended to stress this lack of integration, sceptics merely ignored it, leading to a common consensus that social policy integration was severely restrained by national governments on the grounds that they were eager to retain control over welfare provision and social expenditure budgets in their ongoing bids to gain and retain the support of their electorates. Needless to say, this powerful rationale leads to lowered expectations of any kind of sharing of sovereignty in the social field, which in turn promotes the belief that social integration must by its very nature lag in comparison to other fields: it must display scarce delegation of decisions and standards to the supra-national level, and little removal of barriers between countries.

In the mid-1990s this view began to change with the work of Leibfried and Pierson (1995) and Hantrais (1995), who had perceived just how much European-level social policy had developed in the interim. The following decade saw liberal circles in the EU engaged in much hand-wringing about the supposedly outmoded state of Europe's social model and the need to restructure rather than expand it, followed by a spate of counter-arguments attesting to its good health, proposals on how it could be preserved with reforms, claims that it was being energetically defended by social forces, and affirmations that it was in any case essential to Europe's future (see Bieler and Morton 2001, Sakellaropoulos and Bergman 2004, Adnett and Hardy 2005, Jepsen and Serrano Pascual 2006, Giddens *et al.* 2006, Maydell v. *et al.* 2006, Bieler 2006). On the other hand, the less well-known Council of Europe, founded in 1949 in London, presently with forty-seven member states stretching from Portugal to Turkey and Russia to Iceland, is sometimes seen as having more advanced social rights, mainly on two grounds: first, because of its historic achievement of a European Convention on Human Rights in 1950 (even though this does *not* cover social rights at all), and second on account of its European Social Charter of 1961, which gained considerable international recognition. By contrast, the European Union did not adopt a social charter until 1989, and then only as a declaration of principles, which the UK refused to sign anyway. Therefore the Council of Europe's earlier European Social Charter remained memorable, a symbol of advanced democracies' social progress, their protective state and inclusive social values. Third, the Council of Europe's ability to receive many Eastern European states as members at an early stage of their post-communist democratization processes showed that countries with different socio-political traditions could share the values of the older democracies. This gave the European Social Charter the patina of authority in a pan-European context. By contrast, the European Union only relaunched the project of agreeing a common social charter in 1999, ten years after its first attempt, and again only managed to get it approved as a non-binding commitment (something of a contradiction in terms) at the Nice Summit of Heads of European States and Governments in 2000. Named the Charter of Fundamental Rights of the European Union, it was finally incorporated into the draft Constitution for Europe, only for that to run aground on the rocks of the French and Dutch referenda of 2005. This occurred even though it was not the Charter the voters mainly objected to – on the contrary, for the French, the social provisions of the draft Constitution were considered too weak.

The Constitution for Europe, amended and redrafted as the Reform Treaty, was relaunched in 2007 under a German presidency of the EU. At the end of the year, the Charter of Fundamental Rights became an intrinsic part of the new version of the EU's grounding legal text, now called the Treaty of Lisbon, signed on 13 December 2007. Though it was proclaimed as binding, Britain and Poland managed to secure an ambiguous opt-out from it. Its ratification by each member state was scheduled to continue at least until the 2009 elections to the European Parliament. Even now, the justiciability or enforceability of this charter – the power of the text to have effect as a legal rule – is in some doubt, at least in terms of the ability of citizens to use it before a court of law to force their member state to grant them a right spelled out in an article of the text. For instance, could the right to have access to vocational and continuing training (Art. 15) actually force states to design and run such courses? Doubts arise from the ambivalent meanings of Article 51 'Scope' in Chapter VII on General Provisions (European Communities 2000). Yet it would be a mistake to pass judgement on the European Union's social policy domain simply on the basis of a comparison between its social charters and ones of the Council of Europe, since the former represents only a small part of the European Union's social dimension, while the latter is the only social policy domain the Council of Europe has – given over as it is to the promotion of democracy and the protection of wider human rights. Furthermore, it is key to bear in mind that the EU is a supranational project of advancing legally binding integration between states, while the Council of Europe can only be described as a 'significant presence in European integration' (Macmullen 2004), as it remains fundamentally intergovernmental, as will be seen in this chapter's examination of its weak enforcement of social norms. The aim of this chapter is to argue, first, that the social dimension of European integration is a highly complex array of policies, which is in many fields more advanced than is often supposed, due precisely to the complexity that makes it hard to grasp in its entirety. Second, the chapter argues that the European Union is also a more effective body for implementing cross-national social policies than the Council of Europe. Therefore, the second section of this chapter is devoted to assessing the European Union's multifaceted social dimension; this is followed in the third section by a thematic discussion on the EU's regional social redistribution apparatus; its social regulation; EU-wide procedures that give citizens a voice to challenge rights abuse; and dialogue and cooperation between social groups around regional institutions. In the fourth section the Council of Europe's work is addressed separately, in order to avoid comparing like with unlike until the last part of the section where the case of gender equality policy in both institutions is compared, ending with an exploration of the advantages and drawbacks of the policy options of exhortation versus regulation. This soft versus hard law crossroad reflects the crucial difference between the Council of Europe and the European Union as regional bodies that seek integration, convergence and common ground in different measure; and it represents a key dilemma for regional associations generally.

The European Union's social dimension in perspective

The European Union's social policy dimension is complex for it consists of all Treaty articles on broadly social matters; all binding social and labour directives and regulations – what is called the social 'acquis communautaire', the list of adopted social and labour law that all new member states must transpose into their own legislation and implement before they can join; and also encompasses all non-binding exhortative measures such as declarations of principle and aims; Recommendations, Commission Action Plans, Year of Action events, and guidelines on goals and standards, European Council joint strategies, and social policy convergence decisions made by member states under the Open Method of Coordination – much of which is referred to as 'soft' law, meaning non-regulatory and non-binding. Then there are financial support programmes of the structural funds, which have certain redistributive social effects such as on employment creation and training. And there is also the unique pooled social security system that supports the free movement of EU workers, employees and self-employed entrepreneurs by aggregating their contributions and entitlements from country to country. Yet another dimension is the way the EU, in addition to granting freedom of residence and establishment for all its citizens in any member state, whether working or retired, also offers entitlements to students, consumers and health patients who cross and re-cross borders. Overarching all this, there is the general commitment to the mainstreaming of gender equality, which means that all the above-mentioned policy areas have to include women and pay attention to gendered effects. Yet despite the above, EU member states are still free to decide on social expenditure budgets and the types and amounts of benefits, and to impose cuts to social services, as they wish. Thus spending on welfare benefits, for instance, continued to vary between member states from 8 to 18 per cent of their GDP over the last decade (Eurostat website 2008a), as did the overall social expenditure of governments on social protection, even when adjusted for population and purchasing power: Norway, Switzerland, Austria, Sweden, the Netherlands and Denmark spent over 8,000 euro per person in 2004, while Greece, Portugal and Spain spent under 5,000, and some of the new members spent less than 2,000 euro per capita (Eurostat website 2008b). Governments also remain free to set the content of education, housing and health policies, although the desirable outcomes of these are discussed and even coordinated at EU level with a view to achieving a convergence of national trends. Looking back over nearly five decades, a number of critics recognize that there has been a fundamental expansion of the social dimension of European integration (e.g. Springer 1994, Hantrais 1995, 2000, Geyer 2000, Falkner (2003: especially Figs 17.1 and 17.3), amongst others). A significant set of powers have been transferred to the supra-national level (Leibfried and Pierson 1995), particularly with regard to the physical working environment of employees and the equal treatment at work of different categories of workers. As to workers having a say in the management of their companies, both labour and business actors are involved in a 'corporatist policy community' (Falkner 1998). By the late 1990s, a lasting consensus between member states had been achieved around a fairly extensive corpus of shared employment-focused regulation. Furthermore, the EU's 'workerist' focus had become more 'welfarist' (Threlfall 2002) as by the new millennium a welfare space had opened up, containing a 'patchwork of interventions' (de Bùrca 2005: 7). In particular, with the launch of the 'Open Method of Coordination' procedures between member states in 1998, they engage in an array of simultaneous and interlocking cooperation and mutual surveillance processes (Goetschy 2002), covering poverty reduction (social inclusion), education, training, pensions, and job creation, amongst others. Through all these, the European Union is building a 'still fragmented' but 'distinctive EU welfare dimension' (de Bùrca 2005: 1). In addition, some actual *social integration of member states* has taken place through the convergence of policies, policy outcomes and social trends, as well as through harmonization and approximation of laws, to the point where a series of 'single social areas' have been created in which EU nationals experience living or working in the EU as if they were living in a single country (Threlfall 2003). Yet Moravcsik (2005: 365) contends that social *welfare*, viewed in terms of citizen–state relations, has been left 'essentially untouched [by] direct EU policy-making', and that 'the EU policy pays a subordinate role' in social policy compared to the national state. And Goetschy (2006: 48, 58) still believes that employment, social protection, and industrial relations policies are 'essentially' matters of national responsibility, with EU dispositions remaining a 'fragmentary corpus' of measures. In a context of such complexity, 2008 represented a moment of uncertainty and also of great possibility for the social dimension of the EU. The recently agreed Lisbon Treaty states that the EU will be devoted to the 'well-being of its citizens' (Art. 3.1), as opposed to just improving working conditions, and will aim 'at full employment and social progress'. It states that it 'shall combat social exclusion and discrimination, and shall promote social justice and protection, equality between women and men, solidarity between generations, and protection of children's rights', all based on a 'social market economy' (Art. 3.3). Children's rights are an example of yet another new field of EU concerns. When finally ratified by all members, the treaty will establish a stronger social philosophy at the heart of Europe. A

Charter of Fundamental Rights made justiciable would open the way for new rights for workers and women. The very broad new anti-discrimination laws of 2001, presently coming into force, could have an enormous impact on countless citizens in each state, and almost a dozen cooperation processes over employment and social policies still hold quite some potential. Echoing the more detailed assessment made in Threlfall (2007), what is most striking about the EU's social dimension is the steady growth of social fields in which the Commission has gained a role to play and the member states have agreed to Europeanize either their legal practice, their policy priorities, or their discourse and debates. Every time the Treaty is amended, the EU's social concerns and competencies are enhanced, and never more so than in the Constitutional text, revised as the Lisbon Treaty. Clearly, the social dimension has what could be termed an 'organic spreading habit' of developing common policies through supranationalization and intergovernmentalism, involving a repeated widening of the categories of citizens affected by the measures adopted, and the increasing participation of non-state actors such as representatives of business and trade unions, and to a lesser extent, women's organizations, disability and race groups, as well as experts and service providers. This view was strikingly illustrated, showing a steep rise in new directives, reforms and extensions of existing ones and growth of spending on social and structural funds.

Overall, the EU has become more concerned with the general welfare of its citizens than it was even a decade ago, moving from deciding on the supranational regulation of working conditions to taking responsibility for *living* conditions. The social protection and freedom from discrimination required to ensure a better quality of life for citizens and residents is now a fundamental mandate of the Union – even when it does not always deliver clear improvements. For it is correct to say that recent years have seen a slowing of social regulation in favour of improving existing legislation or the alternative standard-setting and exhortative approaches. But since the potential for strengthening social policy is there in the framework, what is mainly lacking is the political will to advance further. This is not insuperable, given the greater variety of social groups who are becoming stakeholders in the European Union through the treaties' social messages and commitments. Greater social integration of one kind or another is likely to be attempted, and conversely, it is unlikely that all fronts will fail, though some may disappoint. Further incremental developments of an uneven kind, on a variety of policy fronts, leading to different types of social integration, are therefore to be expected. But as this brief presentation shows, the fundamental characteristic of the social policy dimensions of European integration is its complexity. This marks it out as different from the Council of Europe, together with the two institutions' dedication to fundamentally different kinds of convergence between member states. The sections that follow will illustrate this in greater depth.

Thematic analysis of key facets of the EU's social dimension

As Deacon (2007) proposed, the key facets of the social policy edifice in any country can be identified as social redistribution, social regulation and the promulgation of social rights. Let us see then how these key facets are constituted in the case of the European Union.

Regional social redistribution mechanisms

It is sometimes forgotten that the EU already contained a distribution mechanism when it was first set up. In other words, it was already considered that redistribution could not be left till after the benefits of a customs union and market integration had been felt in the member states. Instead, the Treaty of Rome planned a form of redistribution targeted at depressed areas of the six member states in the form of a European Social Fund (Arts 123–8), finally set up in 1958, to help retrain workers made redundant by the shrinking of the old coal and iron and steel industries. In 1962 the creation of the European Agricultural Guidance and Guarantee Fund (EAGGF) took place, devoted as its name implies to supporting farming and agricultural prices. And a genuinely redistributive fund, the European Regional Development Fund, was created in 1975, specifically targeted at reducing regional disparities and redressing inequalities. Richer member states contributed a greater share of the budget than poorer ones, and also received fewer disbursements as their regions often did not qualify for aid – the key goal being economic convergence between member states and regions. All member states are divided into regions and budget lines are allocated to commonly agreed objectives under a series of agreed programmes. For instance, Objective 1 is for regions where the GDP per head is at or below 75 per cent of the Community average; Objective 2 aims to revitalize all areas facing structural difficulties, whether industrial, rural, urban or dependent on fisheries, even though these may be situated in regions whose development level is close (up to 90 per cent) to the Community average. In addition, to help lower GDP countries prepare for monetary union, a special Cohesion Fund was set up in 1993 to co-finance major environmental and transport projects in the four least prosperous member states, then Greece, Portugal, Ireland, and Spain. After May 2004, all ten 'accession' countries (Cyprus, Czech Republic, Estonia, Hungary, Latvia, Lithuania, Malta, Poland, Slovakia and Slovenia) became eligible for regional funding, as their gross national product (GNP) per capita was below 90 per cent of the EU average. They also benefit from the Cohesion Fund (European Commission Regional Policy website 2006). There is some evidence that these structural funds have indeed reduced disparities: between 1988 and 1998, the lag in income per head in the Objective 1 regions (compared with the Community average) was reduced by a sixth, and their GDP per head rose from 63 per cent to 70 per cent of the EU-15 average. By 2004 Ireland was no longer eligible for any Cohesion Funds at all, and Spain was due to be excluded as it had overtaken Italy in per capita GDP, but was reprieved by negotiations to soften what would have been an abrupt loss of funds. However, such national progress disguised great differences in regional performances, which were associated with the general economic framework in which they developed, according to the Commission, with Ireland demonstrating a good balance between the benefits of suitable structural assistance from the EU and a healthy and stable macroeconomic policy (European Commission Regional Policy website 2006). Meanwhile the older European Social Fund (ESF) has continued its work in support of job training and employment creation, describing itself as 'a key element of the EU's strategy for Growth and Jobs targeted at improving the lives of EU citizens by giving them better skills and better job prospects' (European Commission European Social Fund website 2004). A much more modest undertaking than the other funds, it is due to distribute some 75 billion euro to the member states and regions to achieve its goals over the period 2007–13. But the co-financing mechanism is 'responsive', meaning that non-governmental and community organizations can apply for funding on their own initiative with projects they design or co-design at the national level. It remains redistributive in the sense that regions receiving disbursements do so on the basis of need according to four criteria based on GDP. It is tempting to consider that the EU has also attempted redistribution through its 'Poverty' programmes. These began in a small way well before the Commission had gained a competence to act in this field, and consisted mainly of pilot programmes (Room 1993). After these were suspended for a period in the mid-1990s, issues of social inclusion were debated again at EU level through the Open Method of Coordination that brought together government ministers and officials from the member states. In 2000, EU leaders established the 'Social Inclusion Process' to make a decisive impact on eradicating poverty by 2010. However, this was not strictly speaking a form of redistribution, as it does not involve a central EU fund receiving its income in proportion to the wealth of each member state and disbursing it according to need. Instead, taking the period 2006–8 as an example, member states drew up 'national action plans' to step up efforts to: tackle child poverty; promote 'active inclusion' of the most disadvantaged in society; ensure adequate and sustainable pensions; and ensure equal access to health and long-term care. But the financial means to tackle such goals have to be provided by the member states themselves. They do not receive additional monies for the social inclusion process in addition to what they already receive through the much larger structural funds that support agriculture and industry.

Social regulation

Regulation remains a key characteristic of the European Union's social policy, and takes the form of binding directives, binding regulations (statements declaring how approved policies are to be deployed), and non-binding recommendations to introduce new policies, as well as surveillance methods to monitor implementation by member states, and procedural 'toolkits' to aid compliance. Regulation also varies as to the types of effects it pursues. Some of it aims to establish defined standards, or minimum/maximum thresholds, across the EU, such as scientifically defined health and safety levels in European workplaces; or a minimum number of weeks of maternity leave for women employees. Others aim to eradicate discrimination between categories of workers within member states rather than across frontiers. The most telling example of this is paying unequal rates for the work of men and women, which is illegal in every state, whereas paying the same low wage to both sexes is legal. No wage standard-setting is intended since wage-bargaining is outside the purview of the European Union and the level of pay is regulated by national collective bargaining agreements and responds to local market perceptions of what the going rate is. Much regulation also involves ensuring that no workers moving to work in another EU state lose out on any social security and pensions entitlements that they may have accumulated in one country before transferring to another. As to the aims of regulation, right from its origins as an economic community, the EU professed social aims, particularly the improvement of working and living conditions. Yet it is not idle to consider the less lofty purposes that might account for long-term regulatory developments. One is the avoidance of unfair competition. This is a formal rule for the functioning of the internal market in the EU, and the Directorate-General for Competition is devoted to making sure that governments and businesses stick to European rules on 'fair play' in goods and services. While their main activity covers control of antitrust measures, cartels, mergers, market liberalization and state aid (European Commission Competition policies website 2007), the concept of fair play has also been applied to social issues. It was argued that equal pay for men and women in the Treaty of Rome was introduced to prevent a 'distortion of competition' for French employers who were already bound by domestic law to equal pay. Similarly, the rationale for developing social policy in the form of EU-wide employment rules was claimed to be the prevention of 'social dumping' from the 1970s to the 1990s. It was only the weak evidence about the actual occurrence of social dumping (Adnett 1996) that led to a change of vocabulary, with the Commission moving towards making 'the business case' for social policies, presenting them as good for productivity and labour quality. But the notion of maintaining fair competition between member states remains.

Regional mechanisms that give citizens a voice to challenge rights abuse

The third arm of global social policy is rights, not only in the sense of the regulations already mentioned above, but in terms of citizens' access to those rights and to mechanisms of redress if they are either not implemented or subsequently flouted. Social charters or international social conventions may be considered one such tool for safeguarding rights. However, the two European Union charters, the 1989 Community Charter of Fundamental Rights of Workers and the 2000 Charter of Fundamental Rights of the European Union, should be classed primarily as declarations of principle because they did not make the rights contained in them justiciable – citizens cannot go to court brandishing the Charter to claim a right (see Threlfall 2007). This may change with the adoption of the Lisbon Treaty after which the 2000 Charter may open the way to Commission proposals for new regulations despite the legal ambiguities mentioned previously.

Much more important from the point of view of European citizens is the legal doctrine of 'direct effect' applied since 1962, which holds that the citizen is able to enforce the right(s) contained in European treaties, directives, regulations and decisions via their national courts. This interpretation of EU law has been enormously influential in so far as it has put the onus on states to implement the laws they have agreed to, under the threat of citizens taking their case to the European Court of Justice (ECJ). And judging by the long list of cases that have come before this court, the doctrine has been applied to a range of specific circumstances within the area of social policy and citizen rights, and has increased the impact of treaty law.

Since national authorities are responsible for applying European law properly, it is national courts who have, in the first instance, the duty of ensuring that they actually do so. If they fail, citizens are backed up by European action. In the area of free movement rights, this process has been facilitated by the Commission's online advice service Europe Direct, and specifically by its Citizen Signpost Service, which answers queries about cross-border problems (European Commission 2005: 3). More recently, SOLVIT, a new online service for smaller problems of rights, was created to help to enforce rights without recourse to legal proceedings. There is a SOLVIT centre in every European Union member state, which handles complaints from both citizens and businesses. SOLVIT centres are, in fact, part of a member state's national administration and therefore reflect the fact that a certain amount of devolution of problem-solving to the national level has taken place. SOLVIT gives advice on taxation, motor vehicle tax, social security, access to employment, health care, recognition of diplomas, and voting rights in European elections (European Commission, Enforcing Your Rights website 2005). In this sense, SOLVIT mainly supports the rights of free movers within the EU. It also explains how citizens can seek *non-judicial* redress in each member state, such as from the National Ombudsman (Defender of the People) in the UK, Austria, Spain and the Czech Republic; from the Parliamentary Ombudsman in Denmark, Sweden, Greece and Finland; from the Chancellor of Justice in Sweden and Estonia; and from the (federal) Parliamentary Petitions Offices in Germany, Portugal and Greece. Notably, there appears to be no *non-judicial* redress in France or in Slovenia, or at least not one the government is willing to advertise under SOLVIT. Apart from these procedures to enforce individual rights, there are also strong legal mechanisms to ensure enforcement by member states of their treaty and other legal obligations. Most of the monitoring and enforcement work is carried out by the Commission itself, using its own facilities (see their Monitoring Reports). The Commission issues a 'reasoned opinion' to the member state that has been challenged, which will set out clearly the grounds of the alleged infringement and will call on the member state to comply with European law within a prescribed deadline. Most cases are resolved via a dialogue with the member state in this way (European Commission Enforcing Your Rights website 2005). However, if the member state is observed to continue with the infringement, the Commission will refer it to the European Court of Justice. If after the latter's decision the infringement still continues, the Commission will refer a member state back to the ECJ and ask it to impose a fine. At the same time, any person or business can lodge a complaint with the Commission about an alleged violation of European law by a member state (European Commission 2005: 9). The procedure is free of charge and straightforward, consisting of a written statement posted, e-mailed or entered on a standard form. The Commission is committed to deciding within one year whether to follow up the complaint on behalf of the complainant who cannot him/herself present the case in court. People can also lodge a complaint with the European Parliament (EP) on a matter related to the EU that directly affects the complainant. The EP's Committee on Petitions will scrutinize it, but this procedure does not create legal obligations on the member state (European Commission 2005: 10). Instead, it merely puts pressure on those concerned. However, the EP can recommend to the Commission to take out infringement proceedings against this member state before the ECJ, as mentioned above. ECJ rulings do not *directly* affect an individual's rights, and cannot, as such, annul decisions taken by national authorities, or directly award damages to a complainant. But they have an indirect effect: once the procedure has succeeded, these rulings are legally binding on the member state and can be invoked before any national court of administration, by *any* citizen or business, not just the original complainant (European Commission 2005: 9). Thus it is presumed that the member state will amend its laws or procedures and that any new complaint made to the national court after such an ECJ ruling will be much more likely to be successful. In this sense, although citizens do not obtain justice at the supra-national level, or use the ECJ to overrule national law, they can make the ECJ oblige their own member state to comply, and thereby they indirectly obtain redress for their grievance and win their case at home. Furthermore any such case will be path breaking, since all persons or businesses in the country will benefit from the ruling.

Dialogue and cooperation between social groups around regional institutions: towards empowerment?

Another point of interest for regional integration associations is the extent to which they provide opportunities, parallel to those of governments and public administrations, for civil society organizations to cooperate and engage in mutual policy learning. In the EU, these opportunities take the shape of a variety of different forums, designed to encourage such groups both to move closer together in a lasting fashion and to commit to agreements on policies, and also designed to simply allow them to engage in dialogue and exchanges over good practices that have worked at the national or local level. These forums are often referred to in EU publications as the 'Social Dialogue' and the 'Civil Dialogue' (European Economic and Social Committee 2003). The question is whether such forums actually empower the organizations involved in them, or are merely another tool of integration useful to the Commission and Council. For social policy-making there are several institutionalized and non-institutionalized forms of dialogue between organizations from different countries, from different policy fields, and from representatives of different social interests. As to the *institutionalized* forums, these are, first, the Social Dialogue between the EU-wide business confederation UNICE (Union of Industrial and Employers' Confederations of Europe) and the European Trade Union Confederation (ETUC). Each confederation not only has a consultative status with the main EU bodies but together they also have a legislative role through the mechanism known as the Social Partners' Agreement – a procedure that allows any agreement these partners make on a proposal for a directive from the Commission to go directly for adoption to the Council of Ministers (see Art. III-106 of the Treaty establishing a Constitution for Europe 2003). Three directives were adopted as a result of this Social Partner Agreement: Parental Leave (96/34/EC), Part-Time Workers (1997/81/EC), and Working Time of Seafarers (1999/63/EC). In the latter case the Social Partners were sectoral: European Community Shipowners' Associations and Federation of Transport Workers' Unions. The second institutionalized Social Dialogue within the EU takes place in the European Economic and Social Committee (EESC). This is the consultation body that issues formal opinions before legislation is passed. One-third of it is composed of representatives of trade unions, one-third of business organizations, and the remaining third is a mixed Various Interests Group. The three groups are supposed to represent the three main types of interest organizations in civil society in each member state; however 'Various Interests' do not stretch beyond farmers, small and medium enterprises, social economy groups such as cooperatives, foundations and social non-governmental organizations (NGOs), and consumers and environmentalists groups (see EESC website 2008). They come together to debate EU policy and to reach a joint point of view – their published Opinions. Although this body was established as 'a point of access to the policy process for socio-economic groups' (Wallace 2005: 74) who have to be consulted, most analysts see it as a body lacking in influence, which has struggled to find a significant role (Allen 2005: 219, citing Jeffery 2002). Some believe it has been 'focused and vocal' around the turn of the century, maintaining that it is the institutional 'home' for civil society within the EU (Curtin 2003). Providing such a home may still be one of its current goals (see EESC 2006), but there is no denying that in the meantime socio-economic groups have found more direct forms of access through various types of European-level federated organizations (Wallace 2005: 75). To this should be added the fact that the non-institutional forums, mentioned above, are generated by their organizations and rest on their membership base. By contrast, the EESC, while having a corporatist structure that in theory does not exclude mass membership organizations, is composed of people who are in fact appointed by member state governments. Furthermore, an analysis of the members of the Various Interests Group, using the 2007 membership lists from the EERC (Economic Education and Research Consortium) website, reveals that these so-called representatives cannot be said to represent any organizations at all, nor do they claim to do so. Thus, the official forum for participation of civil society (other than business and trade union organizations) does not, in practice, fulfil its function. The Civic Dialogue, on the other hand, takes place outside the EU institutions, as a result of the *intra-sectoral* dialogue and cooperation between similar organizations from different countries, such as disability, environmental or women's groups. The latter are organized in an independent confederation of women's organizations, the European Women's Lobby (EWL), which in the case of the United Kingdom includes the National Alliance of Women's Organizations (NAWO). In addition to the inter-sectoral dialogue, an active non-institutional *cross-sectoral* dialogue takes place between the European confederations of different lobbies, for instance between all those which are members of the Platform of European Social NGOs. This body brings together a wide range of less powerful organizations than the big trade unions and business lobbies – those who could be members of the Various Interests Group of the official consultation body EESC, but are not nominated by their governments. The Platform of Social NGOs advocates on behalf of large and small social groups and interests, including, by way of examples: consumer organizations, the European Anti-Poverty Network, the European Older People's Platform (AGE), the European Region of the International Lesbian and Gay Association (ILGA–Europe), the European Confederation of Workers' Cooperatives, Social Cooperatives and Participative Enterprises (CECOP), the European Disability Forum (EDF), the European Network Against Racism (ENAR), the European Federation of Unpaid Parents and Carers at Home (FEFAF), the European Roma Information Office (ERIO) and organizations advocating children's rights such as Eurochild (Platform of European Social NGOs 2006: 11–17). This Civic Dialogue is a new form of cooperation that was not envisaged by the original European Economic Community when it started, but was recognized as legitimate in the new Constitution and Reform Treaty. In fact, the Commission even supports the Platform and the European Women's Lobby financially because it wants more feedback from civil society in order to increase the legitimacy of EU institutions and balance out in some small way the policy pressure coming from the very well-organized business lobbies with their private sources of finance. An interesting point to note is that, despite representing a variety of country-based organizations (a few have as many as 500 members), these European-level NGOs have been able to adopt a common position on key policy areas from migration to flexicurity. This is an indication of a policy convergence, arguably facilitated by the opportunities for exchanges and cooperation provided by the European Union's openness to dialogue with external civil society policy advocates and lobbies. What this analysis shows is that any regional integration institution will need to have at the very least a platform for dialogue with non-governmental bodies, because otherwise, although NGOs and social lobby groups will try and exercise pressure of their own accord, they will be outgunned by the resources of corporate interests and their industrial and commercial lobby groups. Regional integration bodies thus face a dilemma: if they become closely associated with corporate elites, they will lose any legitimacy in the eyes of their wider publics. If they face elections or referenda, on the other hand, they will become acutely aware of the need to justify integration in ways that will elicit popular support from the social interest groups and NGOs. The lesson of history is that while in the post-war era it was enough to set up a social dialogue between trade unions and employer groups, since the 1970s the new social movements have shown that there are many more social constituencies demanding to be taken into account. It is not unfair to say that, so far, the EU has become institutionally fossilized around the 'two sides of industry' – the two Social Partners, the EESC – and has no *institutional* auditorium for women's, disability or ethnic minority voices. The best the European Union has been able to do is to contribute (via funding the joint Platform of NGOs), to maintain their ability to make themselves heard. Who hears them and who learns from their voices is another question.

The Council of Europe

Many observers of developments in human rights will be even more familiar with the Council of Europe than with the European Union. The Council of Europe has a much longer tradition of work defending human rights – starting with the 1950 Convention on the Protection of Human Rights and Fundamental Freedoms – and was the first to adopt a social charter in 1961, in force since 1965. The discussion on the Council in this chapter will be brief for the reason that the Council of Europe neither is, nor was, fundamentally a regional *integration* project. Despite mentioning 'unity' in Article 1: 'The aim of the Council of Europe is to achieve a greater unity between its members', this is for the purpose of 'safeguarding and realizing the ideals and principles which are their common heritage and facilitating their economic and social progress' (Council of Europe 1949). The 1949 Statute made no mention of pooling national sovereignty or of applying joint policies in order to achieve economic and political union, despite the fact that delegates to the 1948 pre-foundational congress in The Hague had called for this. The Council ended up having only two institutions, a Committee of Ministers composed of Ministers of Foreign Affairs of the member countries, and a Consultative Assembly. This was a structure suited to intergovernmental cooperation, not supra-national integration. It was the Committee of Ministers that had the power of initiative; the Consultative Assembly started life as a body without powers, as its name suggests. The Council's history is peppered with tensions between the two organs, with the Assembly trying to increase its powers (see Council of Europe 2007a), with some success. The renamed *Parliamentary* (as opposed to 'Consultative') Assembly may now make proposals to the Committee of Ministers, but little has changed: the latter only recently confirmed that it would be consulting (i.e. only consulting) the Parliamentary Assembly before the adoption of decisions. It is worth noting that the Council of Europe has attracted little attention from scholars (Lovecy 2002, Macmullen 2004), so its internal workings, achievements and failures are not well researched. Two aspects of the Council remain of major interest in debates about social policies in regional integration processes. The first concerns its 1961 European Social Charter and, in the light of this, the Council's powers of enforcement, if any; and the second concerns the breadth of its remit in social and human rights matters, which has been much broader than the EU's, at least before the appearance the European Constitution and the Reform Treaty of Lisbon. A third important aspect is the Council of Europe's ability to integrate members from all over the European geography including Russia. However, this has ceased to be a significant achievement since the 2004 and 2007 eastward enlargements of the European Union. Nonetheless, there are still thirteen Eastern European countries that are members of the Council but do *not* belong to the EU (Council of Europe 1949, Art. 26 last amended May 2007).

The European Social Charter

Ever since its launch in 1961, the Council of Europe's European Social Charter has set out the rights of citizens and workers much more clearly than the European Community and Union treaties. But with the EU's 2000 Charter of Fundamental Rights, the gap has narrowed. The Council of Europe's Charter remains more specific in listing thirty-one types of rights, and also supports more extensive rights in many areas such as children's rights, housing, protection of workers' representatives and workers with family responsibilities. It also provides in Article 14 the right to benefit from social welfare services, while the European Union's Charter and Constitution texts contain no mention of welfare or of the kinds of services that community social workers provide. And by far the greatest differences between the two lie in the fields where the EU has traditionally refrained from activity: the right of employees to organize into trade unions, to bargain collectively, to take strike action, and to receive a fair wage, as well as job protection from dismissal and termination of employment. Only the EU's 2000 Charter addressed these areas for the first time (mainly in Arts II-12, II-28, II-30), yet their wording remains weaker than in the Council of Europe's older Charter. So in effect the Council of Europe continues to be the organization that offers the broadest defence of workers' rights, since the EU remains reticent in most of this area. In addition, the Council of Europe is much more elaborate in its protection of migrant workers and their families from outside Europe (Art. 19) in comparison to the EU, which has tended to concern itself mainly with migrant nationals from its own member states.

Impact, implementation and enforcement

The key difference in terms of overall impact between the two institutions is that the EU is supra-national and the Council intergovernmental. This gives the EU institutions enormously more power because their member states agreed from the start to subordinate their immediate interests to a longer-term goal by giving the Commission and the ECJ certain powers to lead member states into policy integration and force them into policy implementation. In this context, can the Council of Europe's Social Charter even be considered a force for integration in the sense of getting member states to adopt the same social goals and standards for social policies? Both hard and soft common standards should be assessed in considering this question. To judge 'hard' standards, it is worth remembering that the EU's (then European Community (EC)) 1989 Charter of Fundamental Rights was recognized as a mere declaration of principles that was unlikely to be implemented unless turned into a set of laws and regulations, which is why its adoption was accompanied by the European Commission Social Action Programme foreseeing no less than sixteen new draft directives. But it took close to two decades for these sixteen to be developed into law. Therefore, if the gap between principles and practice can be considerable in an international organization with a supra-national policy-initiating body such as the Commission, any expectations that an intergovernmental body such as the Council of Europe would be able to fully implement its Social Charter should be moderate. Furthermore, in the case of the EU any violation of the social provisions on the part of member states can be appealed, with citizens taking their case to the European Court of Justice. But any violation of the Council of Europe's Social Charter provisions *cannot* be taken to the European Court of Human Rights because this court is designed to enforce only the Convention for the Protection of Human Rights and Fundamental Freedoms, better known as the European Convention on Human Rights (see European Court of Human Rights website 2008). This makes a significant difference, as a reading of this Convention's contents shows that it protects neither rights *at work* nor *social* rights generally. In addition, the European Court of Human Rights' own categorization of the subject matters of its jurisprudence in its list of nearly 2,000 case titles, reviewed for this study, does *not* include social rights as a category (see European Court of Human Rights 2004, 2005). Therefore it is no wonder that the Council's Social Charter – being legally unenforceable and carrying only light administrative penalties – did not become a strong instrument to ensure member states applied the rights they had subscribed to. Many failed to live up to their commitments. Although they officially called themselves 'contracting parties', no binding contract existed.

This problem of the implementation of policies by member states was eventually recognized by the Council itself, in so far as it galvanized its members into adopting the 1995 Additional Protocol to the European Social Charter, which states that it was 'Resolved to take new measures to improve the effective enforcement of the social rights guaranteed by the Charter'. But by then it had already been in operation for thirty years, three decades during which the contracting parties had suffered no real penalties. Article 9 of the new Protocol now provides for a system in which outside organizations have the right to submit complaints alleging unsatisfactory application of the European Social Charter. When a complaint is found to be justified, the Committee of Ministers issues a

Recommendation to the member state concerned, and in return the latter has to provide information explaining the measures taken to give effect to the Recommendation (Council of Europe 1995, Preamble and Arts 1–10). Little is known about how effective the new procedure is. For the period 1998–2003, Churchill and Khaliq (2004) studied its likely utility and effectiveness, in the light of the fact that it had been introduced to revitalize the Council's charter. They found there had only been twenty-three complaints over five years, and concluded that the new system was unlikely to have achieved its objectives.

For this chapter, a re-examination was carried out of the full list of complaints recorded by the Council of Europe (2008b) after the introduction of its new procedure. A rather different picture emerges. First, there were only fifty-three complaints between 1998 and 2008, with the annual number being so low as to be insignificant for a large multi-country organization: 1, 5, 4, 1, 2, 10, 5, 4, 7, 7, 7. Examined by target, it was found that: seventeen of these were directed against France, nine against Portugal, seven against Greece, six against Bulgaria, three against Italy, two each against Belgium, Ireland, Finland and Croatia, one each against the Netherlands, Sweden and Slovenia. In all, only twelve out of the Council's thirty-seven contracting parties were targeted. There is so far no explanation of why only a few countries are the butt of complaints. As to which organizations raise the most complaints, French public sector unions were in the lead, but had several of their cases rejected by the Council. Children's human rights organizations have also complained about the way France deals with the education of autistic children. The Council of Europe's annual Statutory Report described the measures taken by the French government in response to this case, and found these to be insufficient because of France's narrow definition of the term 'autism'. But it also lists the other extensive measures taken by the French government, which clearly showed that the complaint had been taken seriously. As to the other organizations, the most frequent complainants were, unsurprisingly, trade union federations, especially of public sector employees, followed by the World Organization against Torture (six complaints on the failure to prohibit corporal punishment of children) and the European Roma Rights Centre with four cases (yearly Council of Europe Statutory Reports for all years 2003–7). On the basis of the data presented above, it is possible to reach some preliminary conclusions. A handful of complaints per year is simply too few to consider that a system is functioning as a safeguard against the disregard of a convention voluntarily entered into by its thirty-seven contracting countries. Indeed, the system seems to be used in an oddly concentrated way: a limited number of organizations present complaints about a limited number of countries and a limited number of rights, despite the Council's long list of organizations which are registered as having a formal right to lodge complaints, including the international and national trade union and business confederations, and many national NGOs and no less than seventy international ones (Council of Europe 2008c). Given these imbalances, doubts can be raised not so much about the complaints procedure itself – since the responsible committee gives its responses within a short time period and mostly upholds the complaints (Council of Europe Statutory Reports for 2003 to

2007) – but about the fact that the procedure is used very infrequently, perhaps reflecting the perceived effectiveness of other channels such as national mechanisms for enforcing social rights, especially employment and labour tribunals.

By comparison, one should look at the social case law of the European Union's European Court of Justice. This is difficult to do over a broad spectrum of rights. Suffice to say that counting only recorded cases on sex equality from 1971 to 2006, there were 188 complaints of violations of EU laws that reached the stage where they were heard at court, an average of five per year for one topic alone. The total list of cases heard under the rubrics 'Social Policy', 'Social Security of Migrants', 'Workers', 'Equality and Non-discrimination' and 'Fundamental rights' covers sixty-three tightly packed pages, running to several thousand cases for 1985–2001 alone (European Court of Justice website 2007).

Thus only one conclusion can be drawn, namely that in matters of social law, the European Union, despite its more restricted formulation of social rights than that contained in the Council of Europe's European Social Charter, is by far the stronger player in the rights enforcement field, and the one which is much more likely to deliver social policies and rights to citizens. Such a conclusion suggests that there is a trade-off between binding regulations and exhortative declarations, or 'hard' versus 'soft' power: namely, the one delivers specific protection on a narrow basis, the other opens up awareness and a world of possibilities on a wide front, maybe even setting international political agendas, yet is unable to enforce compliance against defaulters and therefore fails to ensure consistent delivery.

'Soft' power and the breadth and depth of social concerns

The analysis above raised the important questions of the advantages and drawbacks of regulation versus exhortation in social policy fields. It also demands that the link between human rights and social policies be questioned: does an organization such as the Council of Europe, designed around human rights, aid the development of common social policies among its members? In contrast to the European Union, the Council of Europe is not bound by its Statute to only deal with certain rights formulated in a certain way (as they are in the European treaties). Instead, it exists to safeguard 'ideals and principles' and the 'further realization of human rights and fundamental freedoms' (Art. 1). Indeed, the distinction between human and social rights becomes eroded when one looks at the Council of Europe's concerns. To consider this question, it is best to look at a category of person, and it is particularly revealing to focus on women and men, since the goal of gender equality covers women's social *and* human rights. For instance, it is revealing to compare the range of gender issues covered by the Council of Europe and the European Union, as seen in the wordings used in their respective constitutive documents and in their policy reports. These show that the Council of Europe has been able to defend and promote measures to overcome all forms of gender discrimination in greater breadth and depth than the EU has. The chief reason is arguably because the Council of Europe has not been hamstrung by the EU's limited remit to address employment-related equality questions. Instead, the Council has addressed women's *human* rights, mainly those that are most frequently infringed through physical violence based on the different physiology of the two genders. It is interesting to note how the two organizations have reflected two strands of feminist thought in this respect. The first, traditionally socialist and socialist-feminist theory, has been more concerned with women as unequal workers, and the barriers that maintain that lack of equity in thc labour market; the second, originally termed radical feminism, has focused more on the body as the site where gendered power struggles are played out, which have historically reduced women to subordinate positions through their lack of control over their reproductive capacities and their continued exposure to threats and acts of physical violence.

For instance, in the Beijing Declaration of 1995, governments, at the instigation of the United Nations (UN), took the major step of recognizing that in respect of physical or bodily integrity, women lacked the basic human right of protection from violence. Yet the European Union as an entity has not been able to respond to this holistic understanding of gender inequality (see the work of Elman 1996 in this respect). One line says it all: in the EU's 2000 Charter of Fundamental Rights, the chapter 'Equality' merely states that 'Equality between women and men must be ensured in all areas, including employment, work and pay', without suggesting anywhere that 'all areas' might really mean women's equality beyond the world of employment, such as in reproductive rights and freedom from violence. The proposed European Constitution (2004 text, Art. III-271: 208) took only a small step further by mentioning the 'sexual exploitation of women' as one of many areas of crime containing a cross-border dimension where there is a 'special need to combat them on a common basis' (retained in the Lisbon Treaty as Art. 69B: 65). In other words, the EU is still trapped by the legacy of its mission to integrate markets and market conditions, and by the greater difficulty it encounters in introducing new priorities. It is clear by the simple absence of specific proposals that the EU's member states have not been willing to 'supra-nationalize' or even merely 'europeanize' women's human rights, such as by agreeing on the policies and legal treatments needed to address violence against women and to ensure their reproductive rights. Some of the reluctance, especially over human reproduction, can be related to strong anti-abortion stances by member states such as Ireland, Poland, Malta and Lithuania, yet other aspects of reproductive health have not been brought into line across the EU either (see Wikström 2008). By contrast, the Council of Europe's Parliamentary Assembly passed a resolution on 16 April 2008 that abortion should be legal and accessible for all women in Europe: 'The Assembly takes the view that abortion should not be banned within reasonable gestational limits' (paragraph 4 of the Resolution, Council of Europe Parliamentary Assembly 2008). It deplores the difficulties of access to safe services even in the countries where it is legal, and endorses the reproductive health and rights strategies and policies that contribute to reducing illegal abortions. Though this is a recent development, Lovecy (2002) does in fact credit the Council with making a distinctive contribution to the framing of women's rights over the last two decades. Lovecy also believes that elements of congruence with the major mobilizing themes of second-wave feminism can be found in the Council's work; in other words, it has been permeable to the evolving language and concepts of women's policy advocates. It has also taken the bold step of adopting much of the feminist perspective on equality, namely the demand for *substantive* equality. At its 1011th meeting on 21 November 2007, the Committee of Ministers adopted a Recommendation on Gender Equality Standards and Mechanisms. Article A.2 of the Recommendation states that:

> Acceptance of these [gender equality] principles implies not only the elimination of all forms of discrimination, legal or otherwise, on the basis of sex, but also the fulfilment of a number of other requirements that must be seen as qualitative indicators of political will to achieve substantive gender equality or de facto equality.
>
> (Council of Europe 2007b)

It goes on to detail such requirements which the contracting parties have to commit themselves to, which include such steps as: the elimination of sexism from language and promotion of language that reflects the principle of gender equality; wide-ranging equality in private and family life; equality in political and public life, in sexual and reproductive health, in the media; and, most importantly given how great a barrier it is to the enjoyment of rights already gained: ensuring that women are freed from male and societal violence. To return to the issue of the power of soft exhortation versus the power of hard regulation, the discussion above shows how regional associations using the first approach can merge human and social policies in a way that can address a major worldwide problem of abuse in greater depth than is possible for a regional integration body that uses a regulatory approach. There is no space in this chapter to study what happens when integration institutions adopt advanced feminist discourses and social policies. But the importance of *naming* something in order to be able to problematize it, whether 'sexual harassment' or 'rape within marriage', has been a constant refrain in feminist thought since Betty Friedan (1963) talked about the 'problem that had no name' when she tried to pinpoint the inexplicable discontent of women confined to being homemakers. The naming tactic and the exhortative approach are both 'soft', yet lastingly awareness-creating. For instance, an issue such as domestic violence, which policy-makers thought was entirely private, and which police forces believed they were impotent to deal with, is now discussed as an important social cost to public agencies and the government purse (see Hagemann-White 2006). Regulation can follow from this, being by definition downstream in the social policy process, as 'hard' laws reflect only the existing understanding of an issue in a given society. Yet much of social policy is concerned with bringing to the fore the unseen needs of ordinary people, for which new vocabularies and radical shifts in perspectives are required before public intervention can be perceived as necessary and policies be designed to alleviate a problem. Thus policy advocacy and promotion of public understanding of issues of the exhortative kind, which the Council of Europe engages in as illustrated here with the case of gender, is also a key part of the work that regional integration bodies can do. Indeed, it suggests that, while the European Union's mechanisms are undoubtedly more efficient in the legal sense than the Council of Europe's, nonetheless an incremental approach, in which finding common ground around principles and normative ideas may be seen as a first stage, with integration through supra-national regulation being a second stage, may also be appropriate for regional integration bodies. In fact, it is possible to conceptualize a third stage, post-regulation, in which civil society actors complement the process of enforcement. As the Council's Access To Social Rights Department website states:

> legal instruments are not always sufficient to ensure full access to social rights by European citizens. These rights become more accessible to a wide range of people, if they are also actively promoted and supported by sound public policies and involvement of the civil society,

reflecting the contents of its report on the topic of access (Daly 2002). So, instead of regional organizations having to make a simple choice between the regulatory and the exhortative approach, it is possible for them to tackle social policies through a circular, iterative process in which exhortation is followed by social and political support, then regulation; a return to exhortation in order to gain sufficient social and political support to achieve implementation; another return to exhortation to galvanize social and political support for enforcement; and again exhortation to gain social and political support for a new extension or improvement of the regulation; and so on successively. An example might be the UK Sex Discrimination Act passed in 1975 after pressure from feminist advocates, which has gone through a series of enforcement drives, amendments, additions, extensions, more pressures, improved enforcement measures, consolidations and changes of name, ending up in 2006 as a Sex Equality Act that imposes a duty on public bodies to achieve substantive equality outcomes, for which they need to draw up action plans, in other words a repeated combination of exhortation and regulation.

Conclusions

The European Union and the Council of Europe are quite different institutions, despite the possible confusion induced by the similar names of their charters of social rights. First and foremost the difference arises because the EU is led by a supra-national Commission charged with driving the socio-economic integration of its member states, backed by a supra-national court with the power to enforce the European laws that have been adopted by the member states. The Council of Europe is an intergovernmental body devoted to the promotion of democracy and human rights without a centripetal institution at its centre to act as an inward-pulling force to integrate the members' economies into a single regional one. In this sense, the Council of Europe is not even a *regional integration* body in the most frequent sense of the word, since it does not seek the physical breakdown of frontiers and economic barriers, and therefore does not fit De Lombaerde and Van Langenhove's (2007) selection of the functions of regional integration associations, four out of eight of which are economic.

While fundamentally non-comparable, the EU and the Council of Europe can nonetheless be compared over their social policies on the basis of their charters, and particularly in areas where social rights merge with human rights, such as over policies on the treatment of women. To simplify, Table 5.1 shows up key similarities and differences between the two organizations in social policies and their application, as discussed in this chapter.

Table 5.1 shows that although there is overlap between the two organizations, the crucial differences are mainly two: first, the strength of regulation and enforcement, which is stronger in the European Union; and second, the notion of 'portability' of rights, which is absent from the Council of Europe's provisions. This is inherent in the European Union's key goal of free movement of persons based on the removal of frontiers through the creation of single markets and single social areas, as well as *cross-border* rights in education, health care and consumer protection of a kind that do not require people to move their place of residence. Nonetheless, both institutions are dynamic in their continuous

Table 5.1 Comparing the European Union's and the Council of Europe's toolkits

Social policies	*European Union*	*Council of Europe*
Population covered	500 million	800 million
Main thrust of policy content	Working conditions, employment-related social protection, sex equality, free movement	Human, civil and social rights
Overall reach	Narrow	Wide
Ongoing or frozen policymaking?	Ongoing, regulatory + exhortative	Ongoing, exhortative only
Regulatory policies	Yes	No
Redistributive policies	Yes	No
Cross-border application and enjoyment	Yes	No
Exhortative policies	Yes	Yes
Rights promotion	Yes	Yes
Grievance procedure	Yes	Yes
Grievance procedure enforceable on member states or contracting parties	Yes	No
Court of Justice for social rights	Yes, European Court of Justice (Luxembourg)	No, European Court of Human Rights (The Hague) does not cover social rights

Source: drawn up by Monica Threlfall.

engagement with key social challenges, which has seen the Council of Europe develop policy on migration, for instance. Yet the EU renews its legal basis with a certain regularity, while the Council of Europe mainly does not: it has not updated the contents of its European Social Charter since 1960 and it has strengthened its complaints procedure only once since 1949. Lastly, this chapter has reviewed the fundamental question for regional integration, which is whether to proceed through regulation or through exhortation and persuasion. It suggests that the constitutions of international or regional organizations can force such a stark choice upon them, which has the effect of constraining their progress towards their ultimate goals. In this case both the EU and the Council were found to have attempted to overcome such limitations, the former by engaging in greater exhortation and persuasion on social affairs, the latter by attempting to strengthen the regulatory aspects of their work, for instance by introducing a right to collective grievances against infringements to the European Social Charter in 1996. The chapter ended by pointing out that the diffusion of policies into societies probably works best through an iterative process that moves in repeated cycles of exhortation and regulation. In consequence, regional associations will work best if they can combine both, which means that they must confront and succeed at the more difficult challenge of setting up regulatory frameworks and institutions, even at the cost of narrowing the ambit of these to cover fewer common policies, in order to forge consensus between member states more easily – at least as a first stage – and then hope to expand later, as the European Union has done.

6 Regional social policies in Latin America

Binding material for a young giant?[1]

Manuel Riesco[2]

Diverse times along the same tectonic fault

Emerging after a century of tectonic change from its traditional agrarian identity, Latin America (LA) still seems to be in full transition. According to a CELADE (Centro Latinoamericano de Demografía)[3] classification of demographic transition, about 10 per cent of the Latin American population are still at the early or moderate stage, while 75 per cent are in full transition. Only the remaining 15 per cent have already achieved an advanced level in this process (CELADE 1998). Moreover, when many other indicators are displayed alongside population data, they seem to suggest that this classification captures much more than demographic transition. In most cases, it may well be a quite precise indicator of the current state of evolution of the overarching socio-economic transformation process. Countries in the full transition group, for example, show levels of per capita productivity, and public social expenditure, which are five times and fourteen times higher, respectively, than those observed in the early stage. In the case of public expenditure on social security, this ratio rises to over thirty times (see Tables 6.1–6.6). The region harbours two of the four largest urban centres in the world, each of them approaching twenty million inhabitants, and it also has several in the ten million range. However, over 42 per cent of the population are still peasants, according to the most recent World Bank (WB) estimates (World Bank 2004).

Every day in Latin America sees people living and working in ways that present a microcosm of almost every social formation recorded in history. They range from the high-qualified professionals employed by large LA private multinationals, one of which is owned by the second richest man in the world, to indigenous American peasants tending their *alpacas* in the magnificent Andean highlands, and even aboriginals deep in the Amazonian rain forests. The vast majority, however, will descend before sunrise by the tens of millions into packed metros, or ride for hours in noisy buses that inch through the tortuous traffic of congested streets, on their way to salaried jobs somewhere in the huge factories that bustling LA cities have become. They will work long, strenuous hours, even on Saturdays, Sundays and *fiestas de guardar*,[4] mostly in small or medium-sized private shops and firms, increasingly in the service sector.

Moreover, their jobs are extremely short term and they are constantly forced to cross the quite porous boundaries between formal and informal employment – no wall of China stands between the two categories – with periods of unemployment in the meantime. In Chile, for example, excellent statistics constantly track the individual job histories of the entire workforce, this being perhaps the only undisputedly positive outcome of the renowned Administradoras de Fondos de Pensiones (AFP) pension system. Of salaried workers, 96.5 per cent are in the system and make compulsory contributions to it while they are working. However, only 11 per cent contribute regularly every month. Two-thirds contribute less than one month in every two, a third less than one in five, and one-fifth less than one in ten, on average. In the case of women, the frequency of contributions is even less.

Many roads lead to Rome

Seen from the outside, or even from the inside of each country, LA seems to present one single, easily identifiable face. However, a careful listener will distinguish a rich variety of tonalities in the Iberic tongues spoken by all – a variety which popular continent-wide TV soap operas have not yet been able to erase. In the same way, its peoples have traversed quite diverse historical paths – *huellas y chaquiñañes*, as Andean trails are called – towards their rather astoundingly different modernities (Therborn 1995). The fertile valleys and highlands of the Andes, from Mexico to Peru and Bolivia, have harboured most of the indigenous American population down the millennia, and they still vastly predominate there. Their hands forged the golden magnificence of the ancient American empires, as well as the classical colonial and *latifundia* periods. The architectural remains of all these epochs bear witness to the greatness of each one (Lipschutz 1955). It seems not at all improbable that when these regions finally complete their ongoing, massive, rapid, painful and sometimes chaotic transition to the contemporary age, their deep roots, rich cultures and complex structures (Anderson 1974) may perhaps also cradle the distinctive richness of authentic American modernity. However, that is yet to come, perhaps some decades into the twenty-first century, although some signs of it may already be apparent in modern Mexico.

On the opposite side, the rich shores of Rio de la Plata witnessed the massive immigration that flooded the area by 1900 and created the twin cities of Buenos Aires and Montevideo, one of the very few million-strong metropolises in the world at the time. Railways and the army expanded into the *pampas* as far south as Patagonia, in a pincer movement that virtually exterminated the sparse and nomadic indigenous population – in a way not at all dissimilar to what was taking place in the conquest of the North American West around the same time. These early developers created what was then and still is the most advanced LA social formation, although other zones are catching up quickly.

Brazil is unique in its sheer size, which encompasses 42 per cent of the surface of LA, and about one-third of the population, GDP and practically everything else therein. Slavery played a predominant role in this country, as in Cuba. Brazil accounted for about 40 per cent of total imports of slaves from Africa for four centuries, and both countries held almost all those remaining in the world by the last decades of the nineteenth century (Blackburn 1997).

Finally, countries that lay on the fringes of the ancient American empires, such as Costa Rica and Chile, were never in the past able to sustain anything more than peasants and very modest lordships. The poor Spanish settlers established there since the sixteenth century could well have passed, even in the mid-twentieth century, for the butlers of their seigniorial counterparts in the richer regions, as the remaining mansions and churches from the colonial and *latifundia* periods may still witness. Nevertheless, they comprised tight-knit elites that built relatively strong states quite early. Even today, after several mutations, these families form the core of the aggressive emergent bourgeoisies that have grown up in their respective countries (Jocelyn-Holt 1999).

It is interesting to note that these transition categories and historical patterns not only seem to predominate in a given country but also appears to be present within all. This is quite evident in the larger countries, which harbour all levels and patterns within themselves. However, the small country of Ecuador, for example, seems to comprise three different countries – the Pacific coast, the Andes, and Amazonia to the east – none of which is like those described above (Draibe and Riesco 2007).

States guided by with two successive strategies: developmentalism and the Washington Consensus

LA states were guided by their transition by two successive development strategies during the past century. Starting around the mid-1920s, but especially after the Great Depression, many of them explicitly assumed the twin challenge of bringing both economic and social progress to their then quite backward agrarian societies. State-led developmentalism was forced to replicate what had already happened in advanced countries by the early emergence there of the social actors that LA then lacked, and to develop such actors in the process.

Developmentalism gave rise to quite impressive achievements on both counts, at least in the main countries. By the end of the period, many had built basic institutions, infrastructure and industries, and achieved significant and sometimes spectacular economic growth. Most importantly, they were remarkably active in changing the region's social structures, teaching millions of peasants to read and write, improving their health, and accommodating their massive migration to the cities. Social policies played an essential role in this process. This has frequently been overlooked (UNRISD 2003), and seems to justify the usefulness of the concept of the developmental welfare state in LA (Draibe and Riesco 2007, Kwon 2005).

The power elite or valuing bloc was led by state bureaucracies – in which the military played a central role in many countries – and they were supported by the urban middle classes, including the nascent bourgeoisies, workers and the poor, as well as peasants in the final phase. However, there were many forms of developmentalism. Many started through progressive military coups, although two of them had epic revolutionary origins. Some started decades before others. More than one reached their developmental climax under conservative military rule, for example Brazil. In others such as Chile, democratic governments of all flavours steadfastly pursued a developmental strategy, after being primed by the military. In the remarkable case of Mexico, the civil bureaucracy consolidated through revolution and civil war presided throughout this period, in a lasting alliance with entrepreneurs, peasants and workers. Moreover, it also led the phase that would follow.

Everywhere, this bloc increasingly confronted the traditional LA landed elites, sometimes quite violently, especially as developmentalism reached its climax towards the middle part of the second half of the century. In certain countries, it climaxed in full-blown revolutions that rapidly, drastically, massively[5] and irreversibly wiped out old agrarian relations. It does not seem at all surprising that – based on the progressive legacy of developmentalism – these some countries seemed to miraculously leap ahead of the pack during the period that was to follow.

By the last two decades of the twentieth century, throughout the region, states adopted what would later be known as the Washington Consensus. As a strategy, it was little more than a short list of simple rules, emphasizing the importance of markets in the framework of openness to globalization (Williamson 2002). In practice, the rules were applied unilaterally in the interest of emergent local capitalists, and especially foreign investors, together with their small high-income entourage. Many times, this resulted in a vigorous process of dismantling state institutions, especially in the realm of social policy, as a frenzy of privatization and tariff reduction took hold of LA elites. Some benefited considerably from it, especially foreign multinationals but local capital as well, as they grabbed many privatized state companies for themselves at bargain prices. New segmented private services, including social services, were made available to those who could afford to pay. Everybody more or less enjoyed the flood of better-quality and lower-priced imported goods – except those who had lost their jobs, often when their companies closed down after hasty import tariff reductions.

On average, the most affluent 10 per cent secured for themselves over 40 per cent of national income. They were the happy few. Meanwhile, the poorest 40 per cent had to survive on no more than 10 per cent of the income. The middle 50 per cent got their corresponding share of income, but about half of it went to the upper 10 per cent within this segment. Some countries, such as Brazil, Chile and Colombia, had even greater disparities. Meanwhile, three constituted notable and commendable exceptions in this respect: Cuba, Uruguay and Costa Rica (Draibe and Riesco 2007). Furthermore, the dismantling of public social policy affected the middle sectors most seriously, as they were left largely unprotected at the same time as their jobs became precarious and their lives more insecure in the face of globalization. Meanwhile, reduced public social spending was targeted at the extreme poor, slightly alleviating their horrible conditions or at least keeping them from deteriorating further (UNDP 2002b).

However, the degree of unilateralism varied widely, mainly depending on the kind of government that implemented the 'reforms' and their timing. A first wave was pioneered in a few countries during the late 1970s and 1980s, in the midst of a severe economic crisis a decade or more before consensus was reached in Washington.[6] It was imposed by murderous military dictatorships which seemed to plague the region at around that time and which were sponsored by local elites and the US in the name of counter-revolution or counter-insurgency. In some countries young emergent entrepreneurial classes vehemently supported neo-liberal 'reforms', inspired by hatred of the successful state-led reforms of the previous period, most of which had been to the detriment of their landowner forefathers. In countries that had not experienced significant developmentalism, this wave of 'reforms' was reluctantly pushed through by decadent and terrified landed oligarchies, sometimes in the midst of civil war.

The second wave of 'structural reforms' was implemented during the period of general economic expansion in the 1990s by the democratic governments that replaced dictatorships almost everywhere. They were quite moderate in some countries, and took place against the backdrop of an expansion in per capita public social spending that averaged 40 per cent during the decade (UNDP 2002a). Nevertheless, some degree of more or less severe state dismantling took place anyway, although now under the influence of 'third wave' ideologues, who made damaging efforts to transform public institutions into service providers to citizens whom they conceptualized as consumers (Suleiman 2004).

The massive and rapid social transformation that had been taking place in LA under developmentalism continued its momentum during the neo-liberal period. It even reached new heights, although this time in a rather ruthless manner. Education and agrarian reform had been the main instruments of social change under developmentalism. During the neo-liberal period, such reform was replaced in some countries such as Chile by the violent culmination of agrarian reform processes that did not re-establish *latifundia* but forcibly expelled hundreds of thousands of peasants. In others this effect was the result of cruel, open and protracted civil war, which resulted in massive peasant migration to the cities, and to the North, especially in Central America and Colombia. Massive economic displacements induced by severe economic crisis and globalization also played a significant role everywhere.

As a result, peasant migration peaked during the height of developmentalism, averaging 0.8 per cent of the overall population per year from 1960 to 1985 in Latin America. It slowed down to an average of 0.5 per cent of the overall population per year from 1985 to 2005 in the region as whole, but accelerated in the countries in the early and moderate stages of transition (see Table 6.4). This means that during the 2000s, almost three million immigrants arrived in LA cities every year, almost twice the number arriving into the EU-25 countries in the same period (*Financial Times* 2007).

On the other hand, neo-liberal privatization of state enterprises, social services and pension funds replaced the tariffs and credit policies used by developmentalism as the main ways to promote local capitalists. Through these policies some companies developed into huge conglomerates. In some cases, local capitalists attained their status without disbursing, or needing to possess, any money of their own; as functionaries in charge of privatizing public enterprises and utilities, they kept them for themselves (Illanes and Riesco 2007).

Why did the Washington Consensus replace developmentalist strategies in LA? A sober, data-supported assessment will probably contradict the usual slogans. The Washington Consensus does not seem to have been improved because of stagnant growth, because the developmentalist period shows an unparalleled record here, especially as it approached its climax. The 1980s crisis had affected the extreme neo-liberal Chile the most, and pragmatic or 'unorthodox' Costa Rica the least. Nor was it due to the 'big state', because public expenditures have always been very low in LA by international developed country standards, especially on social policies, and regulations have always been rather slack. It also seems difficult to blame 'populist monetary irresponsibility' (Dornbusch and Sebastian 1991) because although developmentalism was generally expansive, the worst episodes of hyperinflation in fact took place under neoliberal ministers. Conspiracy theories blaming the Bretton Woods institutions do not offer a convincing explanation of this wide and overarching phenomenon, although they clearly promoted the Washington Consensus with all their might.

Perhaps it was just the success of developmentalism in modernizing social structures that made it redundant. In the end, it became a hurdle, especially some of its economic aspects. State developmentalism put in place the initial conditions, the essential although rarely mentioned premise for the take-off of modern markets: the existence of large numbers of fairly well-educated and healthy workers, mostly urban but in any case freed from the bondage of traditional peasantry. Maybe it created its own gravediggers.

Another turn of the rudder? Latin America: a new developmental welfare state model in the making?

An unambiguous shift of direction away from neo-liberalism – as formulated by *The Economist*'s (2002) assessment of Lula's election – has been taking place in LA since the 1997 economic crisis. Throughout the region, wide coalitions have appeared, sometimes unexpectedly, and have gained access to political power in many countries, and narrowly missed doing so in others. Neo-liberal thinking is still strong and dominates within academia and government circles, holding its own in the still mostly impregnable citadels of finance ministries and central banks. However, it seems clearly on the defensive and even right-wing parties no longer campaign under its slogans. The current world crisis has reinforced this tendency considerably.

A new development strategy seems to be in the making, which repositions the state as the leading actor, although this time it may rely on the modern actors of civil society who came of age in the two previous periods. Social policy once again moves centre stage, as the new strategy offers an explicit Rooseveltian New Deal to the massive urban *salariat* that is emerging in the region's booming cities, and renews its commitment both to the urban poor and to the peasants who continue their migration in huge numbers.

Although subject to serious criticism from the left, and certainly controversial, the case may be argued that President Lula is the pioneer of the new LA development. Based on the Partido dos Trabalhadores (PT), Lula has managed to assemble an impressive alliance based upon a highly structured and experienced mass worker-based party and movement while still maintaining unprecedented popular support. President Kirchner and his wife Cristina have been able to reshuffle the Peronist party once again in Argentina. Through decisive state intervention they rescued the economy from the catastrophic collapse of neoliberal policies in 2002 and continued to push for a version of the emerging model. As in the case of Lula, their popular support remains overwhelming, even though they have faced strong opposition from the powerful Argentine conservatives. Even in neo-liberal Chile, President Michelle Bachelet has expressed a desire for change, and although her government has not made significant breaks with the prevailing model, she is partially overhauling the privatized pension and education systems.

A good example of how the current crisis has empowered the new tendencies is the current renationalization of privatized pensions by the Argentine government, on the grounds that those funds were making massive losses. The probable outcome is that all privatized pension systems will be renationalized throughout Latin America before the crisis is over.

All the above-mentioned events are taking place in South American countries that have attained advanced stages in the transition process, including the giant Brazil. In a different scenario, major events are taking place in Bolivia, and change is also on the way in Nicaragua and other countries that are still in early or moderate stages of socio-economic transition, as well as in Venezuela and Ecuador which are still in full transition. In all these countries, movements have surged to power which question the neo-liberal model in a generally radical manner. Their achievements are considerable, especially as regards recovering revenues from natural resources[7] and improving the incomes and participation of the poor, which in turn have voted for them overwhelmingly in successive democratic elections.

It must be emphasized that although both versions of the emerging strategy coalesce under the same ‘change the model’ slogan, the processes in the less advanced countries are different in nature from the ones described above in the relatively more advanced countries. Perhaps the best illustration of this difference is the fact that the main social actors in the less advanced countries are peasants or recent rural immigrants, a social group reduced to a relatively small number in the more advanced countries, especially Argentina.

In this sense, the two versions of the emerging strategy are not competitive but complementary. If President Lula were to change places with President Morales, for example, each would probably broadly continue the policy of the other. For this reason, Brazil and Argentina, and even Chile, have consistently supported what has been happening in the less developed countries, despite aggressive intervention against them by the Bush administration, which has been extremely irresponsible in promoting regional separatism in countries whose governments it does not like. This could easily create havoc throughout the region. Europeans have also shown a marked tendency to demonize the latter group of countries, especially those that have nationalized their multinationals.

In addition, both versions fully coincide in what seems to be the main feature of the emerging model: regional integration.

A young giant in the making: the Latin American region?

A new developmental welfare state model seems to be in the making in LA. Its outline design and underlining social structure bear strong resemblances to what Western Europe, the US and other developed countries experienced during the Golden Age of the twentieth century. Relevant questions seem to be: will the emerging strategy remain confined within the national borders of the different countries? Or will it evolve over the wider space of an increasingly integrated LA? If so, what might be the role of regional social policy in this construction?

Modern nation-building seems to be driven by an underlying tendency towards sovereign spaces of adequate dimensions. During the nineteenth century, these may have more or less coincided with the order of magnitude of Great Britain, the leader at the time. The emergence of the US during the twentieth century, a new leader with continental dimensions, opposed by Soviet Union, may have prompted the formation of the European Community. Strategic planners and informed public opinion have recently been assessing the consequences of the emergence of China and India, which may in the near future surpass the order of magnitude of the US. Certainly, this phenomenon weighs in the minds of those who have been seeking to elevate the status of the EU and enlarge it still further.

Rapidly modernizing LA faces challenges that seemingly greatly exceed the dimensions of its present republics, even the largest. Achieving a basic level of autonomy and competitiveness in science and technology, energy provision, territorial and information communications networks, complex industries such as aerospace and defence and many others does not seem possible for most countries within their current dimensions. Creating a market of the appropriate size and degree of sovereignty to compete in the twenty-first century seems to be the main challenge facing LA. Strategic planners should give thought to this matter, and some are doing so (Pinheiro Guimarães 2007).

The region appears a natural space over which such institutional construction may take place. The total area of Latin America is twice that of China, and its inhabitants number nearly 600 million today, and will reach 700 million within two decades, and near one billion by mid-century – well within the order of magnitude of the world's leading countries and regions. They will no longer be ignorant subservient peasants, as they were in their overwhelming majority at the turn of the nineteenth to twentieth century or even masses in full transition as they are at the turn of the twentieth to twenty-first century. In two or three decades at the most, the vast majority of the LA population will have achieved the status of citizens, with decent health standards, basic and secondary education of reasonable quality, and large numbers having completed the tertiary level as well. Even today, per capita GDP adjusted by purchasing power in LA is almost twice that of China, according to the 2007 ranking by the World Bank. These huge concentrations of market-oriented workers are bound to generate vast economic power in the region.[8] They seem to constitute a sound base for an economic market in the top league – if, in addition, LA manages to acquire some degree of sovereign power – certainly a big 'if' (CENDA 2004).

A long and winding road to regional integration

The idea of integration is as old as LA independence, which is why it is called Bolivar's dream. Frustrated, stagnant or ineffectual initiatives abound (French-Davis and Devlin 1998). However, the exhaustive list of successive integration initiatives, duly updated by the Inter-American Development Bank (IADB) (INTAL 2008, shows an impressively consistent, and rapidly accelerating, activity in the matter (see Figure 6.1 and Table 6.1).

The figure and table show that, despite the high profile of the projected Free Trade Area between the US and LA, it has been intra-regional trade and integration agreements which have been at the centre of LA foreign policy all along. Extra-regional schemes appeared in the 1990s and have been important in the 2000s. Meanwhile, LA integration efforts have been mounting consistently for half a century, and have vastly predominated during the last two decades.

The first integration initiative took place in 1951 in the Tratado de San Salvador, which inaugurated activity towards the Mercado Común Centroamericano-Sistema de la Integración Centroamericana, the scheme that is both the earliest and the longest standing. The start of trade agreement negotiations with the EU in October 2007 was the forty-fourth major agreement in five decades of consistent development, which includes a common market (1960s), a regional parliament (1980s) and a court of justice (1990s). The Caribbean countries have developed their own integration process in CARICOM (1968), reinforced by Asociación de Estados del Caribe (1994). Both schemes have been very active up to the present day.

The most ambitious project as promoted by developmentalism in its climax. The Treaty of Montevideo signed on 18 February 1960 created the Asociación Latinoamericana de Libre Comercio (ALALC). Later the Asociación Latinoamericana de Integración (ALADI), it embraced all the main countries of LA, enacted several barrier reductions, and built a secretariat following the EU model. ECLAC, inspired by Prebisch, and Chile, led by Frei Montalva and then by Allende, were active promoters of ALALC-ALADI, together with progressive governments throughout the region, certainly including Mexico. It is still the widest legal framework for LA integration. Cuba joined in 1999, and when MERCOSUR signed a pact in 2004 with Venezuela, Colombia and Ecuador, they asked ALADI to manage its protocols.

In 1966, after conservative military governments had taken power in Brazil and Argentina, progressive governments in Chile, Peru, Bolivia, Ecuador, Colombia and Venezuela started working towards the more advanced Acuerdo de Cartagena. Signed on 26 May 1969, it created the Comunidad Andina de Naciones (CAN) as a temporary second best, placed under the auspices of ALALC, as it still is. CAN institutions include the well-funded Corporación Andina de Fomento (1968) and the Banco Andino de Fomento (1969). CAN operates from large, modern headquarters in Lima, and created a regional parliament in 1979, among other institutions.

The evolution of CAN has certainly not been problem-free. Chile withdrew in 1976, after the Pinochet coup. Peru withdrew partially under Fujimori, but rejoined in 1997. Venezuela withdrew in 2006, in protest against the signing of an FTA with the US by Colombia and Peru, rightly denouncing such pacts as contrary to LA integration. In a quite evident countermove, Chile rejoined the pact one month later. However, at the same time, the newly elected governments of Presidents Morales and Correa in Bolivia and Ecuador two of the Andean Pact's longest-standing members, are signalling their adherence to the main integration strategy led by MERCOSUR, which Venezuela has already joined (INTAL 2008).

The creation of MERCOSUR by the treaty of Asunción, signed by Brazil, Argentine, Uruguay and Paraguay on 26 May 1991, was a major milestone in the LA integration process. MERCOSUR is the most advanced move towards Latin American integration so far. With the inclusion of Venezuela in April 2006, it now encompasses 256 million inhabitants (according to 2005 figures) and a GDP of almost $2 trillion (PPP, 2002), which represent 46 per cent and 50 per cent of the respective figures of the LA region as a whole. Not only has MERCOSUR advanced consistently on the economic front, surmounting severe economic and political crisis in its major members, but it also has complex and growing institutions. The latest addition is the Parlamento del Mercosur, officially inaugurated on 7 May 2007 and initially constituted by eighteen members from each member country, selected by their respective parliaments, which in 2010 will hold its first universal election. The countries with associate membership of MERCOSUR, Bolivia, Chile, Colombia, Ecuador and Peru, may send non-voting observers.

The MERCOSUR-led integration strategy is presently focused on the convergence of all South America in a common initiative (Pinheiro Guimarães 2007). The Comunidad Sudamericana de Naciones was created on 9 September 2005, signed by all LA countries, and coordinating the existing structures of both MERCOSUR and CAN, with the concurrence of the remaining structures of ALADI, as well as the sub-regional initiative that unites Caribbean nations, CARICOM. This process received an important boost during the presidential meeting of Cochabamba on 12 September 2006. The final declaration of this meeting created a coordinating secretariat for the Comunidad Sudamericana, and announced progress in integration projects, mainly in the area of energy.[9]

Mexico and Panama have signed up as observers to UNASUR, as the initiative is now called.[10] This certainly represents a real alternative for the other regional giant, Mexico, whereby it may decide to look more towards the south, as it did during the height of the developmentalist period. In parallel, Venezuela is leading a sub-regional effort that has a more ambitious timetable, the Acuerdo para la aplicación de la alternativa Bolivariana para los pueblos de nuestra América y el Tratado de Comercio de los Pueblos (ALBA), and the Tratado de Comercio de los Pueblos, which also includes Cuba, Bolivia, Ecuador and Nicaragua. The first three countries signed this pact on 29 April 2006, and the last joined in January 2007.

The highest symbolic expression of LA integration to date took place in December 2008, when President Lula organized a marathon of integration initiatives in a Brazilian resort near Salvador de Bahía. In four days, he successively chaired the presidential meetings of MERCOSUR, the Grupo de Río, UNASUR and the new Cumbre de Latinoamerica y el Caribe (CLAC). This new organization, CLAC, includes Mexico, Central America and the Caribbean states. It was the first time for 200 years that all LA states had met without the presence of either Spain or the US. Commenting on the meeting, Juan Emilio Cheyre, ex-Commander in Chief of the Chilean Army and currently Director of the Centre for Strategic Studies of the Universidad Católica de Chile, wrote: 'It could create an organization where for the first time Mexico and Brazil join efforts to lead the regional dialogue without the US' (*La Tercera* 2009).

Regional social policies in Latin America[11]

Social policy has not hitherto been a major component of LA integrations schemes. However, it has been present in all of them since their conception. MERCOSUR is probably the scheme that has advanced the most in this respect, and represents a good example of both the advances and the limitations of regional social policies in LA. In MERCOSUR it was only after trade union agitation, mainly from the Coordination of Trade Unions of the Southern Cone (CCSCS) that the working group (Subgroup 10) was set up in 1991 on 'Labour relations, employment and social security' (Newell and Tussie 2006: 48). This was done at the level of the Common Market Group, the executive organ of MERCOSUR. The subgroup provided a forum for discussion of labour issues and the development of recommendations to member states. For example, it recommended that governments ratify basic ILO conventions (Weeks 2000). In 1994, the inclusion of a social charter was rejected but the Economic and Social Consultation Forum (FCES) was created, a tripartite structure for labour, business and NGOs. Its recommendations, however, have no binding authority on the MERCOSUR governments.

In 1998, the Social-Labour Declaration created a tripartite MERCOSUR Social-Labour Commission, consisting of twelve government, labour and business members (da Motta Veiga and Lengyel 2003). Governments annually submit a report on changes in national labour law and practice. The declaration covers core labour rights including migrant workers' rights and commits the member countries to enforce their own labour laws. While these institutions conduct some useful work on minimum standard setting, they are advisory rather than enforcement institutions. Compared with the freedom of movement guaranteed to investors, this is not a very useful protection. The participatory and consultative mechanisms have given civil society actors a voice in the MERCOSUR integration process but there is no effective labour rights regime (Polanski 2004).

MERCOSUR adopted in 2002 an agreement on residence for nationals of MERCOSUR States, Bolivia and Chile, which grants temporary residence for a maximum of two years, then changing into permanent residence for citizens of member states. The regulation provided by the Protocol of Montevideo of MERCOSUR acknowledges the right of a member state to recognize the education, experience, licences, matriculation records or certificates obtained in the territory of another member or any country that is not a member of MERCOSUR without requiring an extension to other MERCOSUR members. However, the signatory parties commit themselves to encouraging the relevant bodies in their respective territories, including government bodies as well as professional associations and colleges, to develop mutually acceptable rules and criteria for the exercise of activities and to propose a recommendation on mutual recognition to the Common Market Group. The parties have mandated the Commission to review the recommendation, and each party is requested to encourage the competent authorities to implement it. In 1999 the Board of Architecture, Agronomy, Geology and Engineering Professional Entities for MERCOSUR Integration adopted a resolution on the temporary exercise of professional activities by foreign architects, agronomists, geologists and engineers. A cross-sector initiative was launched by the ministers responsible for education in 2000 when they adopted a Memorandum of Understanding on the implementation of an experimental accreditation mechanism for the recognition of university degrees in the countries of MERCOSUR (Movimiento Estudiantil Xicano de Aztlan (MEXA)). A Working Group of Specialists in Accreditation of Higher Education was charged with the elaboration of both principles and procedures for such recognition, based on quality assurance through evaluation and accreditation processes. Like the European Association for Quality Assurance in Higher Education) (ENQA) in the European context, a network for quality assurance agencies, the Iberoamerican Quality Network, has been established to facilitate the exchange of information and experiences amongst quality assurance and accreditation agencies.[12] A very interesting new development in higher education in MERCOSUR is the creation in 2008 of the Universidade Federal da Integração Latino-Americana (Federal University of Latin-American Integration) (UNILA). Its aim is to enrol 10,000 students in undergraduate and postgraduate courses, who will become specialists on Latin America and with a 'Latin-American conscience'.

At the 2004 Regional Employment Conference, political leadership emphasized the need to give the issue of employment generation a more central place in regional and national public policies. A Declaration of MERCOSUR Labour Ministers called for the drafting of a Strategy of Employment Growth for MERCOSUR. For that purpose, the Council of the Common Market (CMC) created a

High-Level Group (GANEmple) (CMC Decision 46/04). A draft proposal of such a strategy was approved at the presidential summit of Córdoba in July 2006, where the need to (re-)formulate and implement a social agenda for MERCOSUR was strongly emphasized. The strategy was based on two principles: (i) the generation of (decent) employment should be achieved through the articulation of macro-, meso- and micro-economic policies, on the one hand, and labour, social and educational policies, on the other; and (ii) all policies should be aimed at respecting and establishing labour rights and principles as contained in the Social-Labour Declaration and in the ILO declaration on fundamental rights. The decision-making process takes place on two interrelated levels: regional and national. Technical assistance was initially provided by the MERCOSUR Labour Market Observatory, but the creation of the Social Institute of MERCOSUR, with a broader mandate, was prepared by the working group Grupo para la Creación del Instituto Social (GISM) at the level of the CMC, the political organ of MERCOSUR. This institute is conceived as a body that should design, promote and implement regional social policies. The objectives of the institute also include the construction of a harmonized system of social indicators. It is further foreseen that the decision-making procedures of MERCOSUR in the area of social policy will be adjusted in order to convert the intentions expressed at the Córdoba Summit into reality.

Finally, through Decisions 45/04 and 18/05 of the CMC, the Fund for Structural Convergence of MERCOSUR (FOCEM) was created. This fund, which should particularly benefit the smaller member states (Uruguay and Paraguay), resembles in its objectives the European structural funds. FOCEM is still in its pilot phase, with the first projects approved in 2007.

The Andean Labour Advisory Council (ALAC) is an advisory institution of the Andean Integration System that is comprised of top-level delegates chosen directly by the representative organizations in the labour sectors of each of the member countries. ALAC expresses opinions on programmes or activities of the Andean sub-regional integration process that are relevant to it. Today, ALAC is governed by Decisions 441 and 464, approved by the Andean Community Commission pursuant to the Guideline of the Andean Presidential Council ordering the attainment of 'fuller participation' by this sector 'in the construction of an integration process leading to the creation of a common market'. In its first meeting, held on 3 December 1998, ALAC adopted by-laws which established its composition and functions. Another important participative body is the Andean Business Advisory Council (CCEA) that is governed by Decisions 442 and 464 and is made up of representatives of employers' organizations. In addition to the aforementioned participative forum, the Andean Community has other instruments at its disposal, such as the Simón Rodríguez Agreement, which consists of a tripartite forum for debate, participation and coordination between labour ministers, employers and employees. This agreement was one of the first instruments of Andean social integration but in 1983 it came to a standstill. On 24 June 2001, the agreement took on its current format with the Protocol of Substitution of the Simón Rodríguez Agreement.

The Labour Council is consulted on an ad hoc basis only and has relatively little influence on Andean Community decision-making. For some observers it 'is merely a forum for debate'.[13] Issues like safety and health in the workplace, labour migration, social security and capacity building are discussed but with little consequence. Labour rights are not covered, but there is a declaration regarding the protection of human rights. The Andean Community is currently working on the establishment of an Economic and Social Council (EESC 2006, ETUC 2006, Tizón 2004) and a Consultative Council of the Indigenous Peoples of the Andean Community.

In the context of Latin America, the Andean Pact has played a pioneering role with respect to intra-regional migration. Already in 1973, an Andean migration card was launched in principle following the adoption of Decision 397 of the Andean Group. Other decisions tending towards facilitating movement of persons have since been adopted by the Andean Community. In 2001, Decision 503 on 'recognition of national identification documents' recognized the possession of a national identification document as the only requirement for travel, and Decision 504 provided for the creation of an Andean passport by January 2005. Other instruments also deal with migration issues inside the region, such as the Andean labour migration instrument (Decision 545) and the social security instrument (Decisions 546 and 583), and other instruments facilitating procedures, such as Decision 526 on 'Airport incoming immigration formality booths for nationals and foreign residents of Member Countries'. Free movement of persons is also seen as a precondition for the further implementation of the Andean Common Market.

Decision 439 of the Andean Community of Nations on Services Trade, adopted in 1998, established a general framework of norms and standards with a view to liberalizing trade in services in the Andean Community region (Dangond 2000). The Community is currently drafting a decision that will establish norms and standards aiming at facilitating the recognition of academic degrees and national requirements, in addition to professional diplomas. In more general terms, a number of government-to-government agreements and conventions for cultural cooperation have been established in Central and Latin America, which provide for the recognition of higher education qualifications. One well-known example is the Convenio Andrés Bello signed or acceded to by ten countries of Central and Latin America, and Spain. This framework, established in 1970, has become an important platform designed to improve communication and facilitate agreement between education ministries. One important means is the list of equivalent degrees, designed to assist members in the comparison of higher education qualifications. In 2007, technical meetings were held to prepare for the introduction of the Andean labour card in 2008. This mechanism should help citizens of the Andean countries with respect to the mutual recognition of university qualifications, free movement of labour, labour rights, pensions and social security.

In the case of CARICOM, since 1997 the Charter of Civil Society has recognized fundamental labour rights. There is a mechanism for submitting complaints regarding labour rights violations but there are no sanctions. Consequently, as yet there have been no complaints (Human Rights Watch 2001). Trade unions are consulted on all trade matters through a formal mechanism and there is a policy of harmonization of labour rights, e.g. regarding health and safety.

The Caribbean Community Single Market and Economy (CSME) established a single open market and waived cross-border restrictions, as a way to facilitate the free movement of labour (articles 45 and 46). In January 2005, the CARICOM passport was launched, first by the Republic of Suriname. Following the launch of the CARICOM passport, another initiative, the OECS passport, was delayed and then abandoned. Another CARICOM measure related to less strict limitations on visa requirements to ensure hassle-free movement of visitors during the 2007 Cricket World Cup. Moreover, in January 2006, the Central American passport, designed and adopted by the four members of the C-4 Treaty (El Salvador, Guatemala, Honduras and Nicaragua), became effective. All these events reflect progress in cooperation between the countries of the region on the movement of persons.

CARICOM member states agreed to set up or employ appropriate mechanisms to establish common standards to determine equivalency or to accord accreditation to diplomas, certificates and other evidence of qualifications secured by nationals of the other member states. Currently, university graduates, artists and musicians, sportspersons, media workers, and managerial, supervisory and technical staff as well as the self-employed can move freely without work permits. In order to have their qualifications recognized, they must, however, obtain a Certificate of Recognition of CARICOM Skills Qualification, also called a CARICOM Skills Certificate, from their home or host country's ministry responsible for issuing skills certificates.[14] Since 2002 a competency-based education and training model for vocational training has been developed by the Council for Human and Social Development (COHSOD). The effort to coordinate vocational training and education culminated in the memorandum of agreement between the Community members establishing the Caribbean Association of National Training Agencies (CANTA) in November 2003. CANTA has been given a mandate to establish a regional qualification framework.[15] This framework covers five levels of skill, responsibility and autonomy, linked to typical entry requirements, credits and academic levels. To date, some 120 occupations have been recognized and certified under CANTA (CANTA Secretariat 2005: 37–8).

The Alianza para el Desarrollo Ostensible de Centroamérica (Alliance for the Sustainable Development of Central America) (ALIDES), signed in 1994 by the presidents of Central American republics, is probably the most comprehensive agreement signed in the region. It states that 'we have created a national and regional strategy that is integral, considering political, moral, economic, social and ecological aspects'. While that is true, a very wide distance seems to separate the stated intentions from their practical implications. This applies to LA regional social policies in particular, but also to the overall integration process.

Gravitational pull from the huge mass to the north: the demise of the FTAA?

The LA integration process, including regional social integration is very complex, subject to contradictory forces that push it through constant advances and retreats. It has more than enough obstacles to surmount, not least of which are the substantial differences in the socio-economic, historical and institutional evolution of the different countries and regions.

However, the key hurdle to LA integration is the attraction from its massive neighbour to the north. The imbalance of powers is huge. Just in economic terms, LA GDP (PPP) as a whole adds up to around 40 per cent of US GDP; Brazil, the largest country, is about a third of the LA total, meaning its economy is about 15 per cent of the size of the US economy at present. In other aspects, the difference between their relative power is today even more overwhelming. It seems out of the question that the US would even consider surrendering a minimal degree of sovereignty to benefit the construction of an integrated zone on more or less equal terms. Quite the contrary, explicit US state policy promotes the subordination of individual LA countries.

As is well known, in 2001 President George H. Bush launched the FTAA, 'an economic free zone extending all the way from Alaska to Tierra del Fuego'. However, the evidently imbalanced approach of the US to 'free trade', in favour of its own interests, has all but buried the FTAA for the time being. MERCOSUR, led by Brazil, did not accept unilateral opening to trade and investment, government procurements and intellectual property rights while among other things the US would not even consider lowering its farm subsidies or non-tariff barriers. Those LA countries – led by Mexico and Chile – that have been adhering to individual FTAs, have accepted the more restricted version of the FTAA which the US has been pushing throughout the region as their second best option, after the failure of the larger initiative (CENDA 2004, INTAL 2008).

Powerful godfathers of regional integration

Surmounting the difficulties confronting LA integration requires powerful, motivated and committed actors, operating under a more or less coordinated long-term state strategy. This is consistent with the requirement of a new ruling bloc that has been mentioned in reference to the emerging development strategy. Are these actors in place today? Are they authoritative enough? Do they have a strategy? Are they riding favourable winds and currents? In what follows, the conclusion is that there may be some grounds not to be overly pessimistic on this matter. Moreover, it will be argued that regional social policy could become a key factor to embed at least two of these potential actors firmly into the integrated development strategy.

Latin American state bureaucracies

Professional LA bureaucracies are important sponsors of LA integration. They have been a primary actor in the region for over a century, as has been highlighted above, and constitute by far the largest, best-structured, and stably employed group in any country, especially the branch that is most powerful, autonomous and strategically aware: the military. Even the Commander in Chief of the army of Chile – the country that under Pinochet notoriously withdrew from integration efforts – has recently declared that not only should Chile join MERCOSUR as a full member but this association should also advance rapidly from an economic to a political union.[16] The Chilean military also plays an active role in improving the country's relations with its neighbours, through what is called the 2+2 diplomacy which has been implemented for the last few years and officially includes both a diplomat and a soldier in most key meetings among LA countries, especially neighbouring ones.[17]

A similar kind of bureaucratic 2+2 has been a systematically consistent key driving force behind the LA integration process for at least a couple of decades. Itamarati (the Brazilian Foreign Office) has long assumed the leading role under governments of otherwise quite divergent political stances (Pinheiro Guimarães 2007). Moreover, they have made sure that they are not alone in this quest. Most of the region's professional diplomats have studied in Brasilia's highly regarded academies at some point in their careers, and all LA representations around the world officially constitute and operate as the Group of Latin America and Caribbean Countries (GRULAC) or Grupo Latinamericano. Members become friendly, and it is not unusual to catch them exchanging sardonic glances from opposite sides of negotiating tables when their usually less experienced foreign ministers and other political dignitaries say something they consider inappropriate, especially regarding LA integration.

The EU, Spanish capital and the business push to Latin American integration

The EU has been a driving force regarding LA integration on multiple planes. Quite probably it has its own strategic considerations that could reflect an aspect of its long-term rivalry with the US. The influence of the EU vis-à-vis the US seems to favour Latin American integration. The alternative is the subordination of individual countries to their northern neighbour or, even worse, their collective subordination in the framework of the FTAA.

However, a more pressing factor behind this EU interest is the quite extraordinary surge of Spanish direct investment in LA. EU countries other than Spain have also increased their investment, but much less significantly. Spanish capital has displaced all other direct foreign investors in LA, including the US, in just a few years. A virtual *armada* of modern Spanish conquerors landed in LA in the 1990s. Large private, recently privatized, and even public Spanish conglomerates spearheaded the process. Amazingly quickly, they acquired a dominant role throughout the whole region in banking, energy and telecommunications, as well as in public services under private concession, such as water and infrastructure. They have attained significant stakes in several other relevant industries as well.

This was stimulated by the simultaneous occurrence of Spain's first ever launch of FDI in general, on the one hand, and privatizations and market openings in LA, on the other. Both developments seem to be rooted in the late-coming but rapid socio-economic change that has been taking place in the one as well as the other. Spain appears to have a lead of perhaps no more than one or two decades at most over the more advanced regions of LA. It seems only natural that increasing Spanish FDI would look towards LA. Young capitalism has a long, complex, rich, creative and terribly disruptive history of similar expansions.

The long-term impact of this business invasion on LA integration may have been underestimated and is certainly under-researched. In the future, it will probably be considered a key detonator of the process, much as British capital was in the US 'conquest of the West' in the second part of the nineteenth century. Just as their ancestors did during the conquest of America, the Spaniards view the region as a whole as they move swiftly across it.

It has always been astonishing that *descubridores* and *conquistadores* covered the entire span of what today is LA in just a few years –on foot most of the time. Peoples coming from Asia across the Bering Strait achieved the same feat, of course, much earlier, but it took them thousands of years to reach the southern tip of the continent. The third wave of immigration, which was by far the most massive, took place by the turn of the twentieth century, but was confined to specific regions, mainly around Rio de la Plata and north of Rio Grande.

To be fair, under Spanish dominance LA retained a remarkable unity, which was projected to the independence movement that took place simultaneously throughout the region. In an impressive demonstration of continental span, Bolivar and San Martin finally embraced in Ayacucho, in the heart of South America, after leading the victorious march of their liberation armies, which started from what today are Venezuela and Argentina, respectively.

However, in the wake of independence, LA republics behaved in a way that was no different to the early indigenous inhabitants. After demonstrating an incredible drive to cover the whole continent, they established communities that returned to almost complete isolation, lasting centuries in one case, and millennia in the other. This is evident in the different intonations of the Iberic languages and the quite different structures of the Native American dialects.

The new *conquistadores*, however, behaved as latter-day Pizarros. The triumphant LA forays of Banco Santander and Banco Bilbao Vizcaya Argentaria (BBVA), Endesa and Repsol, or Telefonica during the 1990s are well known. These large Spanish *fragatas* were followed, or sometimes preceded, by a swarm of young, enthusiastic, small and medium entrepreneurs, who landed in LA for the first time during the 1990s, sometimes enticed by EU-sponsored joint venture programmes for *pequeña y mediana empresas* (PYMEs). Drawing fewer headlines, but exhibiting a sense of adventure and courage not unlike the heroism of old *descubridores*, they criss-crossed the region doing business, in a flash getting to know it much better than almost any native. Some were successful, others less so, and many ended up like old Cabeza de Vaca – the amazing Spaniard who literally walked from the Rio de la Plata to the Mississippi, whose bones lie somewhere in the as yet unexplored depths of America.

Evidently, foreign direct investors view the region as a whole, and operate accordingly, usually from headquarters located in one of the main LA capitals. They follow a comprehensive LA business plan, and use standardized procedures, centralized services and contract provision, outsourcing and publicity for the whole region. On the other hand, in order to be successful, they are obliged to rapidly master the subtleties of each country, experience that they share among the highly qualified professional cadres who manage their operations, flying from one capital to the other just as any EU or US executive does within his/her respective territory. Iberians have the great advantage of the common peninsular languages and cultural origins, so they move in LA like fish in water.

Many of these cadres are in fact native Latin Americans. In this way, Spanish capital is becoming an extraordinarily effective business school for those who, quite probably, will end up jumping ahead of them as the main economic unifying force of regional integration: LA business. One example of LA business pursuing the integration route is Chilean capital. Mainly since 1990, Chilean big business has started dispensing FDI for the first time ever. Large Chilean companies have directly invested around US$40 billion abroad – about a third of 2006 Chilean GDP – most of it in energy, forestry and retail, but in several other industries as well. Over half (52 per cent) of the accumulated total is concentrated in Argentina and most of the rest distributed among Brazil (16 per cent), Peru (16 per cent) and Bolivia (8 per cent). Practically all the remaining FDI is in other LA countries (CENDA 2004).

Intellectuals and artists: co-opted to liberalism or agents for regional integration?

Traditionally a very important part of LA bureaucracy, its intellectuals – who were mostly trained in universities and other public academic institutions – have always played a hugely progressive role in LA strategic development. The climactic moment of developmentalism may perhaps be dated to 29 November 1971, when President Fidel Castro – then the guest of President Salvador Allende – visited the new beautiful and imposing circular central auditorium of ECLAC in Santiago, to address one of the most illustrious gatherings of LA intellectuals ever, chaired by none other than Dr Raul Prebisch himself.

Fidel delivered a formidable speech, showing how revolutionary Cuba had implemented ECLAC's programme in nutrition, health, education, industrialization, energy, etc. He concluded with a vibrant statement in favour of LA integration. After mentioning the giants of the moment, the US, the Soviet Union and the European Union, and emphasizing how the EU had managed to unite the territory of 'ferocious warfare, which during the last five centuries has seen people killing each other systematically, and where each speaks his own very different language', he called for an end to

> balkanization, the weakened position of peoples who have as much in common as our LA peoples, who will have no chance to survive in the future except through the closest economic union and, consequently, also in the future the closest political union, constituting a new community that in thirty years' time could reach 600 million inhabitants [APPLAUSE]. However, even in that conjuncture we would need to make huge efforts to occupy a place in the world of tomorrow.

After each assertion, he paused and looked for approval from Raul Prebisch, seated beside him. 'Isn't it true, Dr Prebisch?' 'Yes, Mr President,' answered the founder of ECLAC and the main inspirational force behind LA developmentalism, 'it is true' (Castro 1971).

That twentieth-century LA's most formidable political figure came together with LA's most illustrious intellectual, in the site of perhaps its highest academic institutional creation, symbolizes Prebisch's importance in defining the region's autonomous strategy during the developmentalist period. However, nothing of the kind is happening today, at least as regards LA integration. Even ECLAC hardly studies integration any more, and certainly is not behind it as a driving force, as it was until three or even two decades ago. The little analysed privatization of LA intellectuals during recent decades, as well as the systematic co-optation of public universities and other academic institutions by neo-liberal ways of thinking, has probably played no small part in this decline.

The US strategy to block or delay LA integration and subordinate individual countries to its hegemony not only follows grand schemes such as NAFTA, the FTAA or FTAs. It must be noted that not a minor part of US strategy here has consisted in co-opting LA intellectuals, mainly its economists, to an abstract and non-strategic view of regional integration, such as is promoted by neo-liberalism, for which these considerations simply do not exist, as opening up markets is always beneficial in the long run. The US has played a subtle and intelligent game of networking these cadres, and promoting them through a long chain of institutions, at the top of which sit the Bretton Woods institutions (BWI), but with 'independent' central banks and semi-autonomous finance ministries playing a key role at the country level. Universities also play an important role in this kind of networking, as do other international organizations.

The BWI– and the complex network they have built and lead – may certainly take a lot of credit for this shift, as well as other US agencies such as those that sponsored the seminal agreement between the University of Chicago and the Catholic University of Chile (Pontificia Universidad Católica, PUC) in 1955, which produced the 'Chicago Boys'. Since the 1980s, PUC has implemented one- and two-year courses,[18] where governmental cadres from all over LA come to study the elementary concepts of the neo-liberal model, financed by their respective governments, which pay their salaries, and by the Banco Interamericano de Desarrollo (BID) and other BWI grants. The even less studied role of donor agencies – including prominent European donors – that assumed a significant role in financing intellectual activity in LA during the 1980s and 1990s, and in shaping their agenda in the process, has played a significant role as well in this shift.

Certainly, however, the main cause of the decline of LA intellectuals as a driving force behind LA integration and other strategic aspects of development should be sought within LA societies, mainly in the unilateral and in some cases extreme course followed by the second state strategy adopted during past decades, especially, when this took place under right-wing dictatorships, but also under the 'third wave'-influenced democratic governments that followed. As has been suggested, these are also the main culprits behind the privatizations and the dispersal of the distinguished traditional intellectual drive behind LA developmentalism. It is regrouping, mainly within the realm of a reconstructed and reinforced modern LA public university system. A process that probably needs seminal efforts modelled in a way on the PUC–University of Chicago 1955 agreement seems quite imperative today.

Even though this is not the appropriate place to treat the matter *in extenso*, a mention must be made of artists as one of the major forces behind this process. This is quite clear to anyone who listens to the beautiful 'Canción para todos', the real anthem of LA integration, which is usually sung by artists and the public at small and large musical events throughout the continent (Isella and Tejada Gómez Junio 1996).

Salaried workers, peasants and urban poor: regional social integration serves their needs

No integration process whatsoever will be possible if it is not able to seduce the region's emerging, overwhelmingly massive, social force: the new urban salaried middle classes. In the present social scenery of LA as a whole, and especially in the countries that are in the more advanced phases of transition, any progressive strategy, and certainly regional integration, must include this emerging force as a basic part of the power bloc required to make it successful.

In this sense, the situation of LA today is not entirely different to the one in the second part of the nineteenth century facing West European regions that were relative late-comers to the process of national unification. As then, the leading states were already in place and thriving, and in order to catch up, it seemed necessary to build sovereign spaces of a similar order of magnitude. On the other hand, the underlying socio-economic conditions within the late-coming regions had matured to a point where this ambition seemed possible to realize. Significantly, a new massive modern *salariat* had emerged, which then, as today, is a fundamental base of such a possibility. How to persuade it to support a political bloc that may achieve its ends? The Iron Chancellor found a way to do it. Perhaps, the driving agents behind today's process in LA should follow his lead.

The emerging progressive LA coalitions have already made an explicit revival in their political programmes of the other towering figure behind the building of progressive modern coalitions in this continent: the figure who offered a New Deal to the masses of American salaried workers in the wake of the Great Depression, and was advised by Lord Keynes. It then looks possible that with portraits of Roosevelt and Bismarck hanging as an incongruous pair in the background, Latin America will move ahead towards integration under the auspices of a New Deal in which regional social policy is the basic building block.

But it must be added, Latin American integration must accommodate its crucial peasant population, if it is to succeed – peasants represent almost half the overall population when recently immigrated urban poor are included in this category. If it is relatively easy to incite separatist, nationalistic, xenophobic, self-destructive sentiments among urban salaried workers, it is all the easier in the case of peasants and the urban petite bourgeoisie – as tragic historical experiences prove.

Huge and vital cross-border developmentalist projects and the sheer need to build a modern market of twenty-first-century dimensions could perhaps be enough to persuade business to allow frontiers to be opened to regional trade, investment and labour mobility. Maybe the strategically minded general staffs of LA bureaucracies are already convinced of the need to partially cede what is now rather ineffective national-level sovereignty in order to share a more effective regional stature. Nevertheless, it is unlikely that salaried workers will be enthusiastic about such a move if it is not associated with potent signals regarding their rights, and smaller-scale but more concrete measures of regional social policy for their direct benefit. Furthermore, concrete regional social policy measures seem indispensable to motivate the integration of the vast masses of LA peasants and urban poor.

Possible measures include regional minimum livelihood guarantees, which seem feasible from an economic or financial point of view. Lula's political success in Brazil seems to prove this point. This huge country is like a slightly reduced version of LA, and contains within itself almost everything that is present in the larger region – and in similar proportions. It has been noted that Lula's direct cash transfers to the poor have been a major element in his successful first term in office – and that those policies are indeed quite cheap. In the larger region, it seems possible to argue that similar policies associated with a regional integration process must incorporate peasants and the urban poor into the emerging political power blocs that are needed to promote the new LA developmentalist welfare states and the region that may be in the making.

Appendix

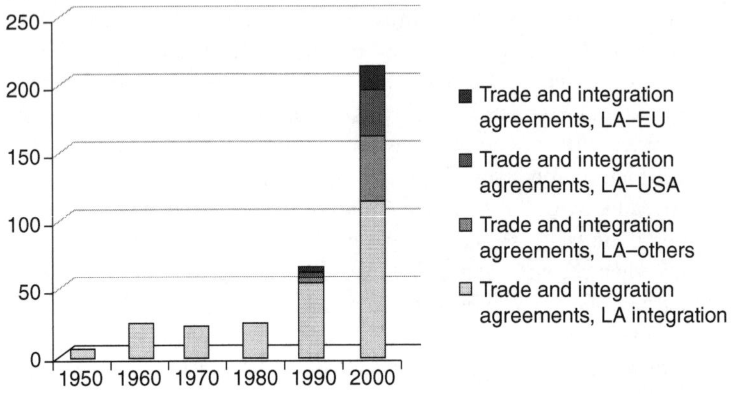

Figure 6.1 LA trade and integration agreements by decade (source: INTAL (2008: Table 9 in Appendix).

Table 6.1 Latin American integration initiatives, 1958–2008 – summary

Participants	*Decade started*	*New schemes*	*New agreements*
LA integration	1950	1	3
	1960	5	20
	1970	2	19
	1980	1	21
	1990	8	52
	2000	15	118
Total		32	233
LA–USA	1990	2	5
	2000	4	34
total		6	39
LA–Others	1990	1	3
	2000	18	45
Total		19	48
LA–EU	1990	1	2
	2000	4	15
Total		5	17
Grand total		62	337

Source: Table constructed by the author from data in INTAL (2008).

Table 6.2 Latin American and Caribbean countries according to group of demographic transition drawn up by CELADE

Groups of demographic transition: CELADE definition	*Countries*
Group I: Early transition Countries with high birth and mortality rates and moderate natural growth of around 2.5 per cent. Countries in this group have a very young age structure and a high dependency ratio.	Bolivia and Haiti
Group II: Moderate transition Countries with a high birth rate but moderate level of mortality, making their natural growth natural high, around 3 per cent. Reduction of the mortality rate, especially during the first year of life, has caused a rejuvenation of the age structure, which also causes a high dependency ratio.	El Salvador, Guatemala, Honduras, Nicaragua and Paraguay
Group III: Full transition Countries with moderate birth and low or moderate mortality rates, resulting in a moderate natural growth rate of around 2 per cent. As the reduction of fecundity is recent, the age structure is still relatively young, even though the dependency ratio has already decreased.	Brazil, Colombia, Costa Rica, Ecuador, Mexico, Panama, Peru, Dominican Republic, Venezuela, Guyana, Surinam and Trinidad and Tobago
Group IV: Advanced transition Countries with low birth rates and low or moderate mortality rates, which translates into low natural growth rates of around 1 per cent. Two sub-groups may be defined: • countries that have had low fecundity and mortality for a long time (Argentina, Uruguay and, to a lesser extent, Cuba) and consequently have growth and age structures that are similar to developed countries'; • countries that, although having recently attained very low fecundity and mortality rates, still have higher growth rates because their population is relatively young.	Argentina, Chile, Cuba and Uruguay; Bahamas, Barbados, Guadeloupe, Jamaica, Martinique and Puerto Rico

Source: Riesco (2007).

Table 6.3 Population and GDP in LA and the Caribbean, according to demographic transition groups

Groups of demographic transition	*Population (thousands) (2005)*	*Population growth (annual %, 2000–10)*	*GDP (PPP) (2002) (millions, international dollars)*	*Per-capita GDP (PPP) (2002) (international dollars per inhabitant)*	*Position in per capita GDP ranking (2002) (175 countries)*	*GDP growth (1960–2002) (average % per year)*
Group I: Early transition	18,361 (3.3%)	1.9	34,996 (0.9%)	2,081	145	1.6
Group II: Moderate transition	39,293 (7.1%)	2.3	138,102 (3.5%)	4,109	112	3.6
Group III: Full transition	418,623 (75.3%)	1.3	2,968,667 (75.7%)	7,164	73	4.2
Group IV: Advanced transition	79,926 (14.4%)	0.9	779,478 (19.9%)	10,262	61	2.6
Total Latin America and the Caribbean	556,203 (100.0%)	1.4	3,921,243 (100.0%)	7,050	73	3.8

Source: Riesco (2007).

Table 6.4 Urbanization and salaried workers in LA and the Caribbean, according to demographic transition group

Demographic transition classes	*Urban population (%)*		*Average urbanization rate (% of total population per year)*		*Economically active population in agriculture (%)*		*Non-farm occupational structure, 2000 (% of total occupied workforce)*		
	(1960)	*(2005)*	*(1960–85)*	*(1985–2005)*	*(1970)*	*(1990)*	*Total formal sector*	*Public sector*	*Private firms with over 5 workers*
Group I: Early transition	26.2	55.2	0.5	0.8	63.2	39.3	NA	NA	NA
Group II: Moderate transition	33.4	50.9	0.4	0.4	58.2	43.9	39.3	10.1	29.2
Group III: Full transition	47.4	78.4	0.9	0.5	43.3	23.1	52.4	13.2	39.3
Group IV: Advanced transition	69.3	86.5	0.6	0.3	20.5	12.4	54.2	12.4	41.7
Total Latin America and the Caribbean	48.9	76.7	0.8	0.5	41.8	23.6	53.1	13.0	40.1

Source: Riesco (2007).

Note
NA = not available.

Table 6.5 Public social expenditure in LA and the Caribbean, according to demographic transition group

Demographic transition group	*Public social expenditure 2000–1*								
	Total			*Education*		*Health*		*Social security*	
	1997 per capita dollars	*% of GDP*	*% of public budget*	*1997 per capita dollars*	*% of GDP*	*1997 per capita dollars*	*% of GDP*	*1997 per capita dollars*	*% of GDP*
Groups I and II: early and moderate transition	114	9.8	44.2	51	4.4	25	2.4	22	1.6
Group III: full transition	618	14.2	54.3	161	3.9	111	2.7	320	7.1
Group IV: advanced transition	1,445	20.2	65.1	335	4.7	308	4.3	653	9.2
Total Latin America and the Caribbean	686	14.8	55.1	175	4.1	130	2.9	338	6.8

Source: Riesco (2007).

Table 6.6 Human development and income distribution in LA and the Caribbean, according to demographic transition group

Demographic transition group	*Human development index (HDI) 2001*			*Share of total income (%)*		
	Relative position in HDI ranking of 175 countries	*Life expectancy at birth (years)*	*Adult literacy rate*	*Poorest 40%*	*Medium 50%*	*Richest 10%*
Group I: early transition	132	56.2	68.5	10.1	50.8	39.3
Group II: moderate transition	110	68.3	75.8	13.2	49.6	37.2
Group III: Full transition	65	70.3	89.6	12.4	47.5	40.1
Group IV: advanced transition	41	74.8	96.4	14.7	47.7	37.7
Total Latin America and the Caribbean	65	70.3	89.2	13	47.8	40

Source: Riesco (2007).

Table 6.7 Latin American integration initiatives 1958–2008 – intra-regional schemes

Schemes	*Types*	*Start date*
Mercado Común Centroaméricano-Sistema de la Integración Centroaméricana	LA integration	10 June 1958
Asociación Latinoamericana de Libre Comercio (ALALC)	LA integration	18 February 1960
Comunidad Andina	LA integration	16 August 1966
CARICOM	LA integration	1 May 1968
Cuenca del Plata	LA integration	23 April 1969
ALADI	LA integration	12 December 1969
SELA	LA integration	17 October 1975
Cooperación Amazónica	LA integration	3 July 1978
Programa de Integración Comercial Argentina–Brasil (PICAB)	LA integration	29 July 1986
MERCOSUR	LA integration	26 March 1991
Grupo de los Tres	LA integration	13 June 1994
Asociación de Estados del Caribe	LA integration	24 July 1994
MERCOSUR – Bolivia	LA integration	17 December 1996
Central America – Dominican Republic	LA integration	16 April 1998
MERCOSUR – Chile	LA integration	13 October 1998
Central America – Chile	LA integration	18 October 1999
Central America – Mexico	LA integration	29 June 2000
MERCOSUR – Colombia, Ecuador and Venezuela	LA integration	22 August 2001
Dominican Republic – CARICOM	LA integration	1 December 2001
Central America – Panama	LA integration	6 February 2002
Iniciativa para la Integración de la Infrastructura Regional Sudamericana (IIRSSA)	LA integration	27 May 2002
Central America – Panama	LA integration	11 April 2003
MERCOSUR – Peru	LA integration	25 August 2003
CARICOM – Costa Rica	LA integration	10 March 2004
Comunidad Sudamericana de Naciónes	LA integration	8 December 2004
Acuerdo para la Aplicación de la Alternativa Bolivariana para los Pueblos de Nuestra América y el Tratado de Comercio de los Pueblos	LA integration	29 April 2006
Chile – Panama		27 June 2006
Columbia – Triangulo Norte de Centroamérica	LA integration	16 March 2007
Panama– Costa Rica	LA integration	22 June 2007

Source: Table constructed by the author from material in INTAL (2008).

Table 6.7 Continued

Schemes	*Types*	*Start date*
NAFTA	LA – USA	17 December 1992
ALCA	LA – USA	4 November 1999
Chile – United States	LA – USA	6 June 2003
Central American Free Trade Agreement (CAFTA)	LA – USA	17 December 2003
United States – Colombia, Ecuador and Peru	LA – USA	19 May 2004
Panama – United States	LA – USA	18 December 2006
Canada – Chile	LA – others	18 November 1996
Mexico – Israel	LA – others	1 July 2000
Costa Rica – Canada	LA – others	23 April 2001
Chile – South Korea	LA – others	15 February 2003
Panama– Republic of China (Taiwan)	LA – others	21 August 2003
Peru – Thailand	LA – others	17 October 2003
MERCOSUR – India	LA – others	5 January 2004
Mexico – Japan	LA – others	12 March 2004
MERCOSUR – SACU	LA – others	15 April 2004
MERCOSUR – SACU	LA – others	15 April 2004
Acuerdo Estratégico Transpacífico de Asociación Económica (Brunei Darussalam – Chile – New Zealand – Singapore)	LA – others	25 April 2004
Chile – China	LA – others	25 January 2005
Chile – India	LA – others	6 April 2005
Central America – Republic of China (Taiwan)	LA – others	26 September 2005
Chile – Japan	LA – others	24 February 2006
Panama – Singapore	LA – others	1 March 2006
Guatemala – Republic of China (Taiwan)	LA – others	1 July 2006
MERCOSUR – Israel	LA – others	5 July 2006
Peru – Singapore	LA – others	28 September 2006
MERCOSUR – Gulf Cooperation Council	LA – others	10 October 2006
Chile – Malaysia	LA – others	5 June 2007
Chile – Australia	LA – others	9 August 2007
Peru and Columbia – Canada	LA – others	6 October 2007
Mexico – European Union	LA – EU	8 December 1997
Mexico – European Free Trade Association (EFTA)	LA – EU	1 July 2001
MERCOSUR – European Union	LA – EU	2 July 2001
Chile – European Union	LA – EU	1 February 2003
Chile – EFTA	LA – EU	26 June 2003
Colombia and Peru – EFTA	LA – EU	29 October 2007

Source: Table constructed by the author from material in INTAL (2008).

Notes

1 The first four sections of this chapter summarize some of the findings of the book *Latin America, A New Developmental Welfare State Model in the Making?*, edited by Manuel Riesco (London: Palgrave-Macmillan, 2007). The book is part of the UNRISD research project Social Policy in a Development Context. All data throughout this text, not specifically referenced, have this source.

2 The final version of this chapter has benefited from suggestions by this book's editors.

3 Centro Latinoamericano de Demografía, part of the United Nations (UN) Economic Commission for Latin America and the Caribbean (ECLAC).

4 Religious feast days.

5 Jacques Chonchol, Allende's Minister of Agriculture and father of the Chilean agrarian reform – a brilliant, serene and prudent person – argued that in order to minimize disruption it should be rapid, drastic and massive.

6 Much celebrated by some, the Washington Consensus emerged from a meeting in that city in 1992 (Williamson 2002).

7 President Morales, for example, has successfully renegotiated the terms under which foreign companies extract oil and gas. Meanwhile, neo-liberal Chile has not been able to do the same with international mining companies that from 2006 to 2008 withdrew earnings from copper exports – 70 per cent of which are under their control – of about US$20 billion per year. This is the equivalent of two-thirds of the overall annual Chilean state budget.

8 According to the now classic 2001 calculations of investment bank Goldman Sachs, for example, BRIC (Brazil, Russia, India and China) countries now represent 15 per cent of GDP of the G6 economies. By 2025 they will represent half of 96 and by 2040 will have overtaken them, in dollar terms (Wilson and Purushothaman 2003).

9 Wikipedia describes it quite correctly in the following way:

> The Union of South American Nations (Spanish: Unión de Naciones Suramericanas and Portuguese: União das Nações Sul-Americanas, abbreviated as Unasur and Unasul) is a fledgling supranational and intergovernmental union that will unite two existing free-trade organizations – Mercosur and the Andean Community – as part of a continuing process of South American integration. It is loosely modeled on the European Union. According to agreements made thus far, the Union's headquarters will be located in Quito, the capital of Ecuador, while its bank, the South American Bank, will be located in Brasilia, Brazil. The Union's former designation, the South American Community of Nations (Spanish: Comunidad Sudamericana de Naciones and Portuguese: Comunidade Sul-Americana de Nações, abbreviated as CSN; Dutch: Zuid-Amerikaanse Statengemeenschap) was dropped at the First South American Energy Summit on 16 April 2007. Complete integration of the Andean Community and Mercosur to create Unasur/Unasul is expected by the end of 2007.

10 See note 9.

11 This section was drafted by UNU-CRIS, which was commissioned by the ILO to deliver a report on the Social Dimension of Regional Integration (UNU-CRIS 2008).

12 The Spanish name is Red Iberoamericana para la Acreditación de la Calidad de la Educación Superior (RIACES).

13 Interview, Luciano Sanín, Director of the National Trade Union School in Medellín.

14 For more details see www.jis.gov.jm/special_sections/caricomnew/applyingforacaricom.html.

15 See Memorandum of Agreement establishing the Caribbean Association of National Training Agencies (CANTA) (www.cinterfor.org.uy/public/english/region/ampro/cinterfor/news/canta.doc).

16 General Juan Emilio Cheyre expressed this view at length in an interview with several

leftist political leaders in the course of the 2005 presidential and parliamentary campaign. The author was present at this interview.

17 The role of the military regarding integration efforts was confirmed by a front-page picture that appeared in April 2007 in the Chilean and Bolivian press, showing the Commander in Chief of the Chilean navy together with his Bolivian counterpart, at the helm of an Incan *piragua* in Lake Titicaca. Chile and Bolivia, of course, have had no formal ambassador-level diplomatic relations for decades, and tensions have been especially high recently.

18 The Curso Intensivo de Evaluación Económica de Proyectos Públicos (CIAPEPP), Facultad de Economía, Universidad Católica de Chile.

7 Regional social policies in Asia

Prospects and challenges from the ASEAN and SAARC experiences

Jenina Joy Chavez

This chapter examines in detail nascent regional social policy in two world regions in Asia – Southeast and South Asia – represented by two regional associations, the Association of Southeast Asian Nations (ASEAN) and the South Asian Association for Regional Cooperation (SAARC).

ASEAN was established in 1967, and counts as members ten countries: the big economies of the ASEAN five (Indonesia, Malaysia, Philippines, Singapore and Thailand) and the relatively smaller economies and/or newer members of the BCLMV (Brunei Darussalam, Cambodia, Lao PDR, Myanmar and Vietnam). It covers a land area of 4.5 million square kilometres, is home to 558 million people, and boasted a regional GDP of almost US$1 trillion in 2005. SAARC, on the other hand, is a younger initiative established in 1985, but boasts the largest of all regional groupings in terms of population, covering 1.5 billion people and eight countries: India, Pakistan, Bangladesh, Sri Lanka, Nepal, Maldives, Bhutan and Afghanistan. It sits on a land area of 5.1 million square kilometres and also had a regional GDP of US$1 trillion in 2005. Together, ASEAN and SAARC account for 30 per cent of the world's population. While their share of global output is modest (ASEAN and SAARC account for less than 1 per cent of world production), they count as members some of the most dynamic and fastest-growing countries in the world.

This chapter aims to shed light on the differences and similarities between ASEAN and SAARC in terms of the extent to which the two associations have been able to develop regional social policies in their particular contexts. The first section lays out the context for comparing the two associations, with a discussion of their origins, organization and governance. The second section elaborates on common regional social policy concerns and why strengthened regional social policy is needed in SAARC and ASEAN. The third section discusses the extant social policy dimensions in the two regional associations and analyses initial distinctions between them. The final section introduces the important elements of demand, people's access and participation as key components of successful regionalist projects.

ASEAN and SAARC: evolution, organization and governance

Many comparisons can be made between the way that ASEAN and SAARC have developed, and how they developed institutions and ways of working. This history is a vital context of how and to what extent regional social policies have already emerged in ASEAN and SAARC and how they might be further developed in the future.

Origins and evolution

As former colonies in Asia asserted their new-found independence at the end of The Second World War, the seeds of cooperation among them and other newly independent states were sown.[1] But the onset of the Cold War in the 1950s frustrated fledgling Asian unity and polarized countries into contradictory positions. New forms of foreign intervention, which Indonesian President Sukarno then called neo-colonialism, were observed in the region. The pressure was greatest in South Asia, where India and Pakistan had aligned themselves with opposing camps: Pakistan with the United States and India with the Soviet Union (Dash 1996, Solidum 2003, Inayat 2007). Emergent links between Southeast Asia and South Asia consequently weakened.

The regionalisms that eventually emerged diverged in their political orientations and concerns. Southeast Asia was mainly concerned about external threats, in particular that of communism (Narine 2002). In 1966, the Communist Party of Indonesia staged a failed coup, leading to a military takeover of the government and the ousting of then President Sukarno. Wary of communist advances in Indochina, Southeast Asian governments considered regional cooperation to be a necessary and acceptable response. This paved the way for the creation of the ASEAN in Bangkok on 8 August 1967. While ASEAN was carefully presented so as not to be a security platform or military alliance, the Bangkok Declaration nonetheless emphasized that members were 'determined to ensure their stability and security from external interference ... in order to preserve their national identities' (ASEAN 1967).

Meanwhile, the polarized foreign policy taken up by India and Pakistan impeded talks of regionalism in the South Asian sub-region. The situation was aggravated by various internal national and ethnic conflicts.[2] But the desire of smaller South Asian states for regional understanding, and to neutralize what was perceived as India's hegemonic rise, renewed interest in regionalism in the sub-region (Dash 1996, Bailes 2007, Inayat 2007). Regional cooperation was seen as a way for smaller states to deal with their fear of India by providing a forum giving everyone a semblance of equality. Between 1977 and 1980, then Bangladeshi President Ziaur Rahman discussed the creation of a South Asian regional cooperation framework with Nepal, India, Pakistan and Sri Lanka, which he followed up with a suggestion for a summit to sort out institutional arrangements, this time including Bhutan and the Maldives. In the following three years, preparatory meetings involving senior officials and foreign secretaries prepared the basic framework, addressing initial concerns by India and Pakistan over references to security issues. This framework led to the First South Asian Foreign Ministers' Conference (August 1983, New Delhi) that adopted the Declaration on South Asian Regional Cooperation, formally launching the Integrated Programme of Action (IPA) on the agreed areas of cooperation in agriculture, rural development, telecommunications, meteorology, and health and population. In December 1985, the First Leaders' Summit was held in Dhaka and the South Asian Association for Regional Cooperation (SAARC) was established (Dash 1996, Inayat 2007). SAARC at this time focused on social and technical cooperation, addressing issues of economic cooperation only much later.

Organizations and institutions[3]

Both ASEAN and SAARC adhere strictly to inter-governmentalism, thus precluding the development of broad EU-style supranational arrangements. ASEAN and SAARC share a similar organizational set-up. Most decisions are taken by governments at the Summit Meetings of Heads of State. Next to the Summit of the Heads of State is a Council of Ministers (called the Coordinating Council in ASEAN), composed of foreign ministers, which formulates and coordinates implementation of agreements and the work of different ASEAN and SAARC bodies. For SAARC, this is followed by the Standing Committee (foreign secretaries), the seven Technical Committees (sectoral representatives responsible for the SAARC IPA), and five Working Groups. SAARC has established several Regional Centres, each addressing specific areas of cooperation (e.g. human resource development, tuberculosis, agricultural information, etc.), hosted by different member countries. Specialized Ministerial Meetings form part of SAARC's consultative structure.

A major development in ASEAN was the signing in 2007 and entry into force on 15 December 2008 of the ASEAN Charter. It strengthened the role of the Secretariat, particularly in the implementation and monitoring of ASEAN agreements. The Secretary-General was given the rank of Minister and was officially made the Chief Administrative Officer of ASEAN. Supporting the three pillars of cooperation are the ASEAN community councils (ASEAN Political-Security Community Council, ASEAN Economic Community Council, and ASEAN Socio-Cultural Community Council), which coordinate the relevant ASEAN sectoral ministerial bodies in the implementation and coordination of community work plans.[4]

Both ASEAN and SAARC recognize non-governmental entities, usually professional or business bodies that have to go through a strict accreditation process. However, only ASEAN has held official interfaces with these organizations, first with business groups through the ASEAN Business Advisory Council and, more recently, with civil society through the ASEAN Civil Society Conference. Still, neither ASEAN nor SAARC has clear mechanisms for receiving unofficial input or feedback from constituents.

The ASEAN Charter also mandated the creation of other bodies to improve coordination within the ASEAN system, as well as opening up spaces for enhancing people's access to the association. A Committee of Permanent Representatives will be based in Jakarta to support the work of the ASEAN community councils and ASEAN sectoral ministerial bodies, and to coordinate and liaise with the Secretary-General on relevant work. The ASEAN Foundation will support the office of the Secretary-General and work with the relevant ASEAN bodies to support ASEAN community building through development of the ASEAN identity, people-to-people interaction, and collaboration with key stakeholders in ASEAN. Finally, the ASEAN Charter mandates the creation of an ASEAN human rights body. While all these bodies have yet to be defined, the hope is that they will enhance and facilitate access to ASEAN processes. So far, these bodies have no parallels in SAARC.

Governance

All decisions in ASEAN and SAARC are political, in the sense that nothing gets passed or recognized unless declared in the Summit Meetings of Leaders. Both SAARC and ASEAN follow a strict decision-making process and are known to avoid discussion of domestic issues. SAARC sticks to two general provisions: (i) discussions at all levels in SAARC are to be taken on the basis of unanimity; and (ii) bilateral and 'contentious' issues are to be excluded from the deliberations of the Association (SAARC Charter 1985), while ASEAN's explicit mandate is to make decisions based on 'consultation and consensus' and this decision-making follows the principle of 'non-interference in the internal affairs of ASEAN Member States' (ASEAN Charter 2007). The unanimity principle is cushioned in ASEAN by 'a formula for flexible participation'.[5]

ASEAN has also had more experience in deploying different tracks of diplomacy than has SAARC.[6] And with the ASEAN Charter, ASEAN's processes acquire a new formality. Mechanisms for dispute settlement are supposed to be instituted at various levels, whereas in SAARC these mechanisms are confined to trade agreements. However, the question of the extent to which new formal structures will strengthen regional programmes in ASEAN remains an open one. The biggest single obstacle in both SAARC and ASEAN remains the unwillingness of the leaders to relinquish even part of their control over policy-making.

Dealing with the impacts of economic integration

In terms of economic cooperation, both associations react to developments outside the region and to international agreements in much the same way. ASEAN and SAARC have embraced economic openness as a crucial strategy essential to regional integration, although some members are more cautious than others. Both have introduced – but failed to build on – preferential trading arrangements, and have in principle embraced 'free' trade agreements. The economic sphere is the most active area of discussion in the two sub-regions today.

Beyond the free trade agreements (ASEAN Free Trade Area (AFTA) and South Asian Free Trade Area (SAFTA)), ASEAN and SAARC have started discussions on services, investments and erstwhile taboo issues like the movement of persons. Developments in ASEAN are more advanced, with the professed aim of establishing an ASEAN Economic Community by 2015, entailing the creation of a single market and production base. In SAARC, where regional economic talks are slower, India has granted unilateral concessions to the least developed country (LDC) members, covering trade, investments and technical assistance, ostensibly to help appease fears about India's alleged predatory intentions. Although the pace by which ASEAN and SAARC advance economic integration differs, both have declared their commitment to pursue economic integration as a key basis for regional integration more generally.

Increased openness and integration of markets has exposed countries to different forms of volatility over the last decade. These include crises in the financial system (East Asia 1997, global 2008), in food prices (first half of 2008), and in fuel prices. While not confined to Asia, the insecurity these crises have generated is heightened by the way global developments impact upon the region and how the region itself is able to respond. Such volatility is expected to increase as ASEAN and SAARC members sign free trade agreements left and right. The penchant for signing bilateral agreements (see Table 7.1) not only potentially harms regional agreements, but also opens the sub-regions to other problems (see Chapter 9 below for further discussion of this issue).

Economic agreements are the most binding and legalistic in ASEAN and SAARC. While concerns ultimately refer to the social ramifications of potential economic displacement when borders are opened up, rarely do ASEAN and SAARC negotiate economic agreements that contains a social agenda. Importantly, though, the economic and the social were most closely linked in ASEAN's Vientiane Action Programme, where the 'profound social impact' of 'domestic policy adjustments and emerging regional production arrangements' was recognized. Such connections as have been made are, however, confined to the labour market and to the health sector, mainly for reasons of the liberalization processes being instituted (ASEAN Secretariat 2003).

The need for regional social policy in ASEAN and SAARC

A limited focus on economic integration has failed to substantially increase intra-regional trade and investments in both ASEAN and SAARC. If anything, trade and economic agreements have been highly contentious, and constituencies are divided over their benefit and relevance in particular country contexts. On the other hand, sensitive political-security issues have been shunned by the two associations, although there has been high demand for their resolution. It can be argued, then, that ASEAN and SAARC have avoided discussing political conflicts whose resolution would be popular, yet dwell on agreements for which public reception has been ambivalent. Thus the question raised by critics and supporters alike is: how can ASEAN and SAARC be more relevant?

Table 7.1 Status of free trade agreements in ASEAN and SAARC member countries as of June 2008

	Under negotiation				*Concluded*			
Country	*Proposed*[a]	*FA Signed/Under negotiation*[b]	*Under negotiation*[c]	*TOTAL*	*Signed*[d]	*Under implementation*[e]	*TOTAL*	*TOTAL*
Brunei	4	1	2	7	2	4	6	*13*
Cambodia	2	1	2	5	1	3	4	*9*
Indonesia	6	2	2	10	2	4	6	*16*
Lao PDR	2	1	2	5	1	5	6	*11*
Malaysia	4	2	6	12	2	5	7	*19*
Myanmar	2	2	2	6	1	3	4	*10*
Philippines	4	1	2	7	2	3	5	*12*
Singapore	5	1	11	17	2	13	15	*32*
Thailand	6	5	4	15	1	8	9	*24*
Vietnam	2	1	4	7	1	3	*4*	*11*
Sub-total	37	17	37	91	15	51	66	157
Afghanistan	1	0	0	*1*	2	0	*2*	*3*
Bangladesh	0	2	1	*3*	1	2	*3*	*6*
Bhutan	0	1	0	*1*	1	1	*2*	*3*
India	11	5	6	*22*	4	5	*9*	*31*
Maldives	0	0	0	*0*	0	1	*1*	*1*
Nepal	0	1	0	*1*	0	2	*2*	*3*
Pakistan	8	5	3	*16*	2	6	*8*	*24*
Sri Lanka	2	1	0	*3*	1	4	*5*	*8*
Sub-total	22	15	10	47	11	21	32	79
Total	59	32	47	*138*	26	72	*98*	*236*

Source: Asian Regional Integration Centre Database (2008).

Notes

a Parties are considering a free trade agreement, establishing joint study groups or joint task forces, and conducting feasibility studies to determine the desirability of entering into an FTA.

b Parties initially negotiate the contents of a framework agreement (FA), which serves as a framework for future negotiations.

c Parties begin negotiations without a framework agreement.

d Parties sign the agreement after negotiations have been completed; some FTAs would require legislative or executive ratification.

e The provisions of an FTA become effective, e.g. tariff cuts begin.

Asia's diversity is not limited to its politics, culture and economy. The region also offers many areas where some regional intervention would be necessary and desirable. These include health, labour mobility, social protection, education, natural disasters and regional development. Not only do these areas demonstrate the similarity of concerns among countries in the region, they also offer the opportunities for tangible cooperation around less controversial issues.

In addition to the reasons for regional cooperation in social policy set out by Yeates and Deacon (Chapter 2 above), for ASEAN and SAARC such cooperation offers two additional distinct advantages. First, it would contextualize, give deeper motivation to and potentially alter the direction and nature of economic integration. Instead of the narrow focus on managing competition, regional social policy changes the terms of economic agreements if designed in conjunction with them. To the extent that regional social policy relates to peoples and communities in a different way from economic policy, it would have more popular resonance, relevance and acceptability. Second, well-planned and carefully implemented regional social policy can address both the root causes and the results of inter-state conflict. ASEAN and SAARC's adamant refusal to discuss internal conflicts is regrettable, especially since most of these conflicts can be traced to historical processes of political and social marginalization that need urgent remedy. Regional social policy can deal with some of the social issues generative of these conflicts. In the end, it is the vision of regional associations that will define how much of the social aspect is integrated into the economic and political agenda. Regional social policy, however, can broaden the constituency for regionalism. In time it can lead to more democratic access to regional association's processes, and the possibility of redefining regional agendas on the basis of meeting social needs. In the next part of this section, five key areas of possible cooperation are outlined.

Health

The threat incidence of infectious diseases like HIV/AIDS, avian flu and severe acute respiratory syndrome (SARS) continues to increase in Asia. In 2007, an estimated 33.2 million people were living with HIV globally, of whom an estimated four million were in South and Southeast Asia. While the epidemic seems to be declining in Cambodia, Myanmar and Thailand (lower prevalence), it is growing fast in Indonesia, Pakistan and Vietnam. Vietnam and Bangladesh are of particular concern, where HIV infections are growing rapidly, with those in Vietnam doubling between 2000 and 2005 (UNAIDS 2007). As regards avian flu, 72 per cent of the 387 confirmed human cases are accounted for by Southeast Asia (WHO 2008). While only four cases have been reported for South Asia, the higher population density and the relatively weaker health infrastructure in the region give cause for concern; and while only Bangladesh and Pakistan reported human infections, avian flu in poultry has also been reported by Afghanistan and India. The continuing outbreaks of highly pathogenic avian influenza in several Southeast Asian countries that began in 2003–4 have been disastrous to the poultry industry in the region, threatening livelihoods and welfare, and have raised serious global public health concerns.[7] Various measures have been taken (particularly in Vietnam and Thailand) to stem the spread of the disease, but the risk of its reappearance remains; and while these success stories provide some encouragement that coordinated efforts can help in the control of avian influenza, they also clearly point to the high level of investment required to support an integrated control strategy, not always available to countries less endowed with the necessary human or physical resources. Finally, the SARS epidemic hit the region in late 2002 to 2003. South and Southeast Asia only accounted for 4 per cent of infections and less than 6 per cent of all deaths due to SARS, but the outbreak hit the region's tourism industry hard.[8]

Various initiatives have been taken in ASEAN and SAARC to address these health issues. In ASEAN, the ASEAN Work Programme on HIV/AIDS is already on its Third Phase (2005–10), and Phase I of the Emerging Infectious Diseases (EID) Programme will soon be completed and Phase II started. In 2005, ASEAN endorsed a Regional Framework for Control and Eradication of Highly Pathogenic Avian Influenza. Many of these are in collaboration with external partners and international institutions. ASEAN works with the Plus Three (Japan, South Korea and China) countries on the EID, and with a variety of donors including the United Nations Development Programme, World Health Organization and United Nations Programme on HIV/AIDS and USAID on HIV/AIDS, and with the Food and Agriculture Organization and various UN bodies avian flu. SAARC has a Tuberculosis (TB) and HIV/AIDS Centre based in Kathmandu. It has developed regional strategies for HIV/AIDS as well as for TB/HIV co-infection. These strategies focus on education and awareness, surveillance and monitoring, research and advocacy, information exchange and communications, and coordination of various health programmes. These efforts are supported by external partners such as the Canadian International Development Agency.

Despite these various initiatives, the need for further regional cooperation in health issues cannot be overemphasized. The opening up of borders for both trade and tourism, common elements in regionalist projects, has increased the risk of spread of infectious diseases in the sub-regions and in Asia as a whole. Health risks affect regionalist projects both in terms of the negative effect on trade and tourism (e.g. trade declines due to production losses and tourism due to bad publicity) and in terms of increasing adjustment and mitigation costs as a result of integration projects (e.g. greater exposure to infections increases the need for specialized facilities and trained health care personnel to deal with them). It is therefore important to have programmes in health not just for the general welfare of regional populations, but also to protect the more ambitious integration agenda that regions are pursuing.

Labour mobility and social protection

Overseas remittances constitute a significant part of household income in both regions. Five of the top twenty remittance-recipient countries in 2004 are from the region (India, the Philippines, Pakistan, Bangladesh and Vietnam), capturing US$43.8 billion or more than a quarter of total formal remittances worldwide. Such remittances are most significant for Bangladesh, India and the Philippines, which could see their headcount poverty deteriorate by as much as 5–13, 3–23, and 3–10 percentage points respectively (World Bank 2006). This makes migration a very important concern for the region. South and Southeast Asia are home to two of the three biggest migrant-sending countries in the world (the Philippines and India supply 13.5 per cent of international migrants). The economic changes in the last two decades, and long-standing internal conflicts in some countries, prompt the continuous rise of intra-regional migration. India alone hosts 6.3 million migrants (GCIM 2005), mostly from within South Asia. Asian migration is characterized by high levels of irregular migration, mostly by unskilled and semi-skilled labour going to favourite destinations like the Middle East and other developing Asian countries (IOM 2008, Waddington 2003). Southeast Asia, Malaysia and Thailand host as many as 3 million undocumented migrants between them, while India is a major destination for undocumented migrants from South Asia. Additionally, human trafficking, especially in women and children, is high.

The movement of labour poses challenges to both sending and receiving countries. In some Asian countries (e.g. the Philippines) migration has evolved as an outlet for 'surplus' labour for which there is no local employment, so the quality and security of employment abroad are important issues. Receiving countries need to manage potential conflicts with local labour as well as the actual flows of workers. Reports abound about discrimination against migrant labour, involving violation of labour standards. Undocumented migrants face even harsher treatment. Aside from the obvious economic and human rights dimensions, high levels of migration also punctuate the regional health concerns discussed above (Chavez 2007).

While some Asian countries have proactively pursued access to international markets for their migrant labour (Waddington 2003), this is done on a bilateral basis. Undocumented migration is usually only raised in the context of trafficking as a security concern. Neither ASEAN nor SAARC has to date signed regional labour mobility or social protection pacts.[9] As regional integration progresses, however, the need to do so will increase as well as enhance social protection standards. Raising migration as a regional agenda will create spaces for the diffusion of social policy, making it possible to elevate, say, social protection to the level of the more advanced migrant labour-receiving countries.

Education

Various studies have pointed to the important contribution of education to economic development. Asian countries have made the expansion of primary and secondary education a priority by devoting substantial portion of national budgets to the sector. As a result, Asia's achievement in education was credited with both creating incomes and enhancing well-being in the region (Sen 1999, Ahuja *et al.* 1997). The lessons of past successes make a good case for regional cooperation in education, yet the level of investment in education of ASEAN and SAARC members varies widely, with corresponding differences in adult literacy.[10]

Unlike in other areas, cooperation in education can be done with minimal cost and controversy. Current efforts to link institutions of higher learning can be complemented with cooperation in curriculum development for basic education. Some Asian countries rank among the top achievers in primary science and mathematics (e.g. Singapore) (Mullis *et al.* 2008, Martin *et al.* 2008), and are high achievers in elementary reading (e.g. Indonesia, Malaysia and Thailand) (Mullis *et al.* 2007). Cooperation in software projects like teacher training and design of standard regional curricula for core courses would cost less than would cooperation in hardware projects like school building. In any case, both ASEAN and SAARC have been active in capacity building and information exchange projects. It is just a matter of giving focus to such initiatives to maximize results.

Disaster management

The two regions have been hard hit by a number of natural and social disasters in recent years. First, the effects of the December 2004 tsunami heavily affected Indonesia and Thailand in Southeast Asia, and Sri Lanka, India and the Maldives in South Asia. It resulted in 350,000 deaths and hundreds of thousands more injuries. Second, decades-old logging in the Sumatra and Kalimantan forests in Indonesia has caused unabated haze that affects Southeast Asia. In 1997, the issue caught international attention when Malaysia and Singapore openly expressed dismay over Indonesia's inability to contain the haze pollution, creating economic and health problems for them (Giam 2006). Third, in 2008, increases in world demand for rice combined with increases in fuel prices led to sharp increases in the price of rice. Being top rice consumers and producers, South and Southeast Asia were particularly hard hit. In reaction to soaring prices and increased pressure to export, and to safeguard domestic stocks, several countries imposed temporary bans on the export of rice, worsening already precarious price and supply situations (FAO 2008).

The Asia region shares a common environment and therefore experiences the same vulnerabilities throughout. Haze knows no state borders, and Asia Pacific witnessed the largest number of tsunamis in the last century. Asia is the biggest consumer of rice and only 7 per cent of the commodity is traded worldwide. The added importance of rice is that food security becomes a bigger issue in times of natural disaster, and food insecurity is a disaster in itself. In times of disasters and extreme food shortages, conflict areas are doubly imperilled as political contexts complicate responses, further marginalizing people caught in conflict. These are but some of the reasons why regional cooperation in disaster responses should be placed high on the agenda of ASEAN and SAARC. Much more can be accomplished when countries share information and technical knowledge and skills, pool scant resources, and agree to mutual emergency response arrangements. The provision of support and aid from outside would also be better channelled to regional bodies coordinating these responses.

Development gaps

Huge disparities within and among member countries exist in ASEAN and SAARC. ASEAN is characterized by different stages of development and variable economic structures, ranging from the most open economy, Singapore, to predominantly agricultural Laos and petroleum-based Brunei. Per capita income ranges between US$750 (PPP[11]) for Myanmar and US$49,370 (PPP) for Brunei, while unemployment can be as low as 1.4 per cent (Thailand) and as high as 9.8 per cent (Indonesia). Disparities also exist in SAARC but to a lesser extent than in ASEAN. Whereas in ASEAN the highest per capita income is 66 times that of the lowest per capita income, in SAARC it is only six-fold. Per capita income is lowest in Afghanistan at US$881 (PPP) and highest in the Maldives at US$5,027 (PPP). Bhutan has the best employment record with an unemployment rate of only 1.4 per cent versus the Maldives' worst at 14.4 per cent. The incidence and depth of poverty is much higher in SAARC and its members generally rank

Table 7.2 Comparative poverty and inequality measures: ASEAN and SAARC countries

Country	*HDI rank, 2005*	*GDP per capita, 2006 (PPP/current $)*	*Unemployment rate (%), 2007*	*Poverty rate($2/day), latest year*	*Income ratio of highest 20% to lowest 20%, latest year*
ASEAN					
Brunei	*30*	49,370	3.4	–	–
Cambodia	*131*	1,633	1.8 (2001)	61.7 (2004)	7.0 (2004)
Indonesia	*107*	3,471	9.8	40.0 (2005)	6.6 (2005)
Lao PDR	*130*	2,032	1.4 (2005)	74.4 (2002)	5.4 (2002)
Malaysia	*63*	12,314	3.2	9.8 (2004)	7.7 (2004)
Myanmar	*132*	750 (2004)	4.0 (2003)	–	–
Philippines	*90*	3,127	6.3	45.2 (2006)	9.0 (2006)
Singapore	*25*	47,065	2.9	–	–
Thailand	*78*	7,403	1.4	25.8 (2002)	7.7 (2002)
Vietnam	*105*	2,363	2.0	43.2 (2004)	6.2 (2004)
SAARC					
Afghanistan		881	3.0 (1990)	–	–
Bangladesh	*140*	1,298	4.2 (2006)	81.7 (2005)	5.0 (2005)
Bhutan	*133*	4,022	1.4 (1999)	–	–
India	*128*	2,463	3.1 (2005)	79.6 (2004)	5.5 (2004)
Maldives	*100*	5,027	14.4 (2006)	–	–
Nepal	*142*	1,079	8.8 (2001)	64.3 (2003)	9.5 (2003)
Pakistan[a]	*136*	2,370		73.6	4.3 (2002)
Sri Lanka	*99*	3,930	6.0	41.5 (2002)	6.8 (2002)

Sources: UNDP (2007), ADB Key Indicators 2008.

Note

a Data for Pakistan are from UNDP (2007), using World Bank estimates. The rest use Asian Development Bank data.

lower in terms of human development. Both regional formations share sharp income inequalities (see Table 7.2).

Such economic disparities have political consequences. They may create apprehension among smaller or poorer country members that their weaker position makes them vulnerable to predatory behaviour by the bigger and richer members of regional associations.[12] This makes it more difficult to negotiate economic agreements, not only because of unequal negotiating strengths, but also because economic agreements will be received differently by different countries. Not surprisingly, their popularity would be diminished in contexts where potential economic displacement is huge. Smaller and poorer countries also tend to perform lower in social development. Whereas economic integration implies some dislocation, some deterioration in social indicators can also occur, adding to apprehensions about the implications of regionalist integration projects.

The success of regional associations depends in large part on whether significant members see them as a way of improving domestic economic and social conditions and ameliorating development disparities among members. In the cases of ASEAN and SAARC, the regional development gap can be addressed using both economic and social policy responses. In economic agreements, this may be in the form of special and differential treatment or unilateral concessions for newer or smaller members. It may also come in the form of redistributive funds, similar to the EU's Structural and Cohesion Funds (see Chapter 5). Addressing these concerns would also help towards closing the regional development gap. Economic growth and development give countries confidence to meet the challenges of political integration. But for this to be sustainable, improved social development is crucial: better performance in the social sectors (health, education, poverty) is as critical to improving productivity and growth as are improvements in infrastructure and capital base (Hasan 2001).

Nascent regional social policy in ASEAN and SAARC

The absence of any supranationalist elements to ASEAN and SAARC has resulted in minimal progress in regional social policy. The two associations have instead developed along the lines of inter-governmentalism and their brand of functionalism, where cooperation tends to be piecemeal and specific rather than covering broad clusters of issues or policy areas. Instead of binding policies, regional social policy development has proceeded through declarations and statements which outline intentions, visions or guidelines for members to make operational in their own way. These are complemented by discrete and practical activities, normally involving information sharing, studies, exchanges and capacity building, undertaken under the auspices of various technical working groups, task forces, committees, expert groups or regional centres. This functional approach to regional cooperation has been somewhat mediated by the adoption of medium-term programming. In 1999 ASEAN adopted medium-term programming with the Hanoi Plan of Action, followed up by the Vientiane Action

Programme (VAP) in 2004 (Chavez 2007). SAARC has had an Integrated Programme of Action since its establishment, but it was only with the adoption of the SAARC Development Goals (SDGs), contained in 'a comprehensive and realistic blueprint … in the areas of poverty alleviation, education, health and environment' (ISACPA 2004), that programmes have adopted time targets.

Functional cooperation does not require the institution of regional policy, nor does it imply changes in a member's national policy or process. Members are, however, required to commit funding for projects, devote human resources for their implementation, and coordinate with other members on their progress and implementation. Often these discrete projects receive support from non-regional partners and international organizations (for example, the health projects mentioned in the previous section). Some projects yield guidelines that can be adopted by members as common protocols (e.g. common protocol for travel in conjunction with infectious diseases). The role of international partners is crucial in securing regional responses to these health issues. Not only are these regional health initiatives largely externally funded, the priority given to them globally exerts constructive pressure for regional associations to act more decisively. The nature of infectious diseases prompts this global support (and pressure), ensuring global public health security as a main motivation. It can be argued that the area of health is where regional cooperation would most likely emerge as it is one of the most developed areas of global social policy.

Though slow to emerge, some form of regional social policy has developed in Asia, not only as a result of changing needs but also prompted by new ambitions and a growing trans-border/regional identity. In 1997, *ASEAN Vision 2020* conceived of an ASEAN Economic Region, 'an ASEAN community conscious of its ties of history, aware of its cultural heritage and bound by a common regional identity', and dreamed of evolving 'agreed rules of behaviour and cooperative measures to deal with problems that can be met only on a regional scale' (ASEAN Leaders 1997). This was sealed in 2003 with the establishment of an ASEAN Community comprising three pillars – political and security cooperation, economic cooperation, and socio-cultural cooperation. It gave birth to the ASEAN Socio-Cultural Community (ASCC) that looks for 'a Southeast Asia bonded together in partnership as a community of caring societies' (ASEAN Leaders 2003). The ASCC consolidates all the functional forms of social cooperation in ASEAN, and lays the foundation for deeper regional social policy. It has been recently backed by a Blueprint which was signed in the Fourteenth ASEAN Summit in February 2009.

The SAARC counterpart is the signing in January 2004 of the Social Charter, which ascribes to member states accountability for social rights and entitlements. While implementation remains in the control of national bodies, the Social Charter provides strong guiding language: 'State Parties agree that the obligations under the Social Charter shall be respected, protected and fulfilled without reservation and that the enforcement thereof at the national level shall be continuously reviewed through agreed regional arrangements and mechanisms' (SAARC Charter 2004a).

SAARC members agreed to each set up a National Coordination Committee to monitor and devise programmes to implement the goals of the SAARC Social Charter, and to issue regular status reports on members' compliance.

Overall, ASEAN has generated a fuller set of instruments and mechanisms for social policy than has SAARC, despite social issues being on SAARC's agenda at an earlier stage. This is partly explained by the longer period that ASEAN has been in existence compared to SAARC, but a more important reason has been the inability of SAARC to hold annual meetings, especially during the height of the conflict between India and Pakistan which prevented it from meeting, let alone moving forward coherently with a social policy agenda. The absence of inter-state conflicts has made it possible for ASEAN to focus on areas beyond security concerns, something that has not been possible in SAARC for a long time. The greater engagement of Track one (policy community) and Track two (civil society) in ASEAN also bolstered support for the social agenda within the sub-region. Overall, though, regional social policy in ASEAN and SAARC remains rudimentary. The next part of this section outlines the progress made in regional social policy in the two formations under consideration, as summarized in Table 7.3.

Social rights

The question of rights has always been sensitive in the two sub-regions. The idea of collectively recognizing rights did not make any headway in ASEAN until as recently as six years ago. The term 'human rights' was first introduced in an official ASEAN document with the VAP, despite a broad-based human rights campaign and lobby since the early 1990s. The most significant development to date is the mandate given by the newly signed ASEAN Charter for an ASEAN Human Rights Body, the terms of reference for which has been left to a High Level Panel to draft by 2009. In SAARC, the Social Charter consolidates the different social commitments. Its language is progressive, with access to basic services guaranteed, and provisions on women are strong. However, it has limited scope, omitting labour, social security and environment. Aside from the Social Charter, SAARC has a strongly worded Convention on Regional Arrangements for the Promotion of Child Welfare in South Asia. Despite the strategic importance of migration and labour mobility, both associations have come late to the issue. Only ASEAN has a Declaration on the Protection and Promotion of the Rights of Migrant Workers, though this does not yet have mechanisms to operationalize the regional instrument or make it binding. In SAARC, the issue is not being discussed at all, as border dispute remains one of the most contentious issues within the sub-region.

Social redistribution

ASEAN's main vehicle to address the development gap is the Initiative for ASEAN Integration (IAI). While the initiative is available to all members, special focus is given to the newer members, Cambodia, Laos, Myanmar and Vietnam (CLMV). The initiative covers seven areas: energy, human resource development, information and communications technology, regional economic integration, tourism, poverty reduction, and projects of general coverage. As of May 2007, ninety-six projects had been completed under the IAI (ASEAN Secretariat 2007). ASEAN also established a common resource pool, the ASEAN Development Fund (ADF), to support projects under the VAP, which includes the IAI. The ADF was established in 2005 using funds (US$10 million) converted from the earlier ASEAN Fund and another US$1 million from equal contributions from the ten members. Aside from the mandatory contribution, Malaysia made an additional voluntary contribution of US$500,000 to the Fund. Other contributors to the ADF include: Australia (AUS$1.3 million), China (US$1 million) and India (US$700,000) (ASEAN Secretariat 2006, 2007). The IAI and the ADF are not specifically designed for redistribution per se, as their purpose is to equip newer ASEAN members with technical and other resources to help them maximize the benefits from, and address the negative impacts of, regional integration.

SAARC has the SAARC Development Fund (SDF) which was also a product of reconsolidating earlier SAARC funds. It has three windows (social, economic and infrastructure) and three sources of funds (grant contributions, assessed contributions, and funds mobilized by donors and international organizations). Total assessed contributions reach US$300 million, shared by members based on a formula (not equal contribution); the SDF still operates on a one-member one-vote principle. India is said to have declared that it will not draw money from the SDF for its own use, and has pledged an additional US$100 million on top of its assessed contributions (interviews: Shifau 2008, Kwatra 2008). Given the different contribution formula and a substantial top-up contribution from India, the SDF can be said to have stronger redistributive elements than does the ADF.

The Food Security Reserve schemes in ASEAN and SAARC may also be considered instruments for regional social redistribution. A regional food security reserve has been designed to aid members in time of food emergencies, by providing access to a regional stockpile to which the entire association is supposed to contribute. ASEAN's Food Security Reserve (AFSR) was established in 1979, while SAARC's SFSR was established in 1987. Unfortunately, despite episodes of rice shortages in the past, both schemes have not been utilized and have had to be reviewed and reactivated. The AFSR was augmented with the cooperation of the Plus Three partners (Japan, China and Korea), and was revived as the East Asian Emergency Rice Reserve (EAERR) in 2003 (Daño and Peria 2008). The SFSR did not manage to build a stockpile and the scheme was reactivated with the creation of the SAARC Food Bank in 2007. The EAERR was used for the first time when the Philippines tapped it during the rice price crisis in March 2008. Critics are, however, sceptical about the relief function of food security reserves, given the heavy focus on trade of the revitalized schemes, away from the original intent of building up the region's capacity to feed itself (Daño and Peria 2008).

Social regulation

The current scope of regional social regulation in ASEAN and SAARC is even more limited, but what there is shows some encouraging signs. For instance, both formations have instruments on trafficking in women and children, with clear definitions of offences, and SAARC even allows for extradition for certain offences. Both conventions have yet to be tested.

ASEAN has completed Mutual Recognition Arrangements in nursing and engineering services, making the movement of people in these professions within the region easier. Other than this, ASEAN has yet to develop common standards and regulation in other areas like social protection. Worse, attempts at binding agreements in certain areas are impeded by a lack of cooperation amongst members. An example is the ASEAN Agreement on the Conservation of Nature and Natural Resources signed in 1985 which, after more than twenty years, has been ratified only by Indonesia, Thailand and the Philippines – a stark reminder of ASEAN members' lack of readiness to develop regional norms. A more recent example is the ASEAN Agreement on Trans-boundary Haze Pollution signed in 2002, which Indonesia refuses to ratify.

Clearly, ASEAN and SAARC share many similarities in the conduct of social policy. First, both employ a functional mode of social cooperation, where initiatives are dominated by concrete projects and technical assistance, rather than policy or statute-based standards and regulation. The origins of this mode lie in adherence to the principle of non-interference in the internal affairs of members and in aversion to supranationality. The heavy emphasis on sovereignty necessitates that cooperation is dominated by time-bound and sector-specific research, training and public information. While important, most of these projects are 'invisible' and lack a clear regional focus. Second, both ASEAN and SAARC have embarked on medium-term planning and the adoption of plans of actions allowing for projects with a long gestation period. Third, both have established regional funds, have reviewed such funds for broader use, and rely on non-regional partners and international institutions for resources to fund regional initiatives. In the case of ASEAN, external contributions far outpace the contributions of its members. SAARC receives external funds too, but members are relatively more cautious and selective about what funds they receive from outside (interview: Ghimire 2008). Fourth, both have different levels of diplomacy, complementing the official track with the non-official and even the people track, albeit on a limited scale. Fifth, both have a level of formality – they have Charters that define the political and institutional aspects of the Association. Sixth, as yet, both have unclear regional dispute and redress mechanisms, with the exception of mechanisms defined under economic agreements. Unfortunately, while there has been some progress over the years, regional social policy in ASEAN and SAARC as it is presently constituted is not enough to confront the formidable regional challenges outlined earlier.

Table 7.3 Regional social policy[i] in ASEAN and SAARC

	ASEAN (est. 1967)		*SAARC (est. 1985)*	
	Instrument[a]	*Mechanism*[b]	*Instrument*[a]	*Mechanism*[b]
Rights[c]	• ASEAN Charter – mandate to establish an ASEAN Human Rights Body • ASEAN Declaration on the Protection and Promotion of the Rights of Migrant Workers (2007)	• High Level Panel (HLP) on the drafting of the *TOR* for the *AHRB*[ii] (mandate until 2009) • ASEAN Socio-Cultural Community Council (mandated) • ASEAN Socio-Cultural Community Blueprint (draft, expected to be signed by in 2009)	• SAARC Convention on Regional Arrangements for the Promotion of Child Welfare in South Asia (2002) • Social Charter of the SAARC (2004)	
Redistribution[d]	• Initiative for ASEAN Integration (IAI) • Agreement on the ASEAN Food Security Reserve (1979)	• ASEAN Development Fund (ADF)	• SAARC Agreement on Food Security Reserve	• SAARC Development Fund • SAARC Food Bank
Regulation[e]	• Agreement on Trans-boundary Haze Pollution (2002) • ASEAN Declaration Against Trafficking in Persons Particularly Women and Children (2004) • Mutual Recognition Arrangements in Skilled Professions (nursing, engineering) *		• SAARC Convention on Preventing and Combating Trafficking in Women and Children for Prostitution (2002)	

Technical cooperation/capacity building; functional cooperation in social sectors[f]	• Various declarations and statements of commitment on various issues (e.g. Agreement on the Establishment of the ASEAN University Network in 1995; Declaration on ASEAN Unity in Health Emergencies in 2006) • Various work programmes initiated to support the declarations and statements (e.g. on HIV/AIDS) • Vientiane Action Programme (2004–10)	• Various Working Groups, Task Forces (e.g. on AIDS; on Highly Pathogenic Avian Influenza) and Expert Groups • Various Coordinating Centres (e.g. for Trans-boundary Haze Pollution; for Humanitarian Assistance on Disaster Management; for Biodiversity) • Other initiatives (e.g. ASEAN University Network; ASEAN Occupational Safety and Health Network)	• SAARC Integrated Programme of Action	• Various Technical Committees (e.g. Agriculture and Rural Development; Health and Population Activities; Women, Youth and Children; Environment and Forestry; Human Resource Development) • Various regional centres (e.g. SAARC Tuberculosis and HIV/AIDS Centre, Kathmandu; Dhaka; SAARC Human Resource Development Centre, Islamabad; SAARC Coastal Zone Management Centre, Male)

Sources: SAARC Secretariat (2002a, 2002b, 2004a, 2004b), ASEAN (2007a), ASEAN Secretariat (2007), ASEAN website: www.aseansec.org, SAARC website: http://saarc-sec.org.

Notes

i The framework used for classifying regional social policy into rights, redistribution and regulation is developed by Yeates and Deacon (Chapter 2 above). The concept of technical cooperation/capacity building as an additional aspect of social policy is from `Deacon *et al.* (2007).

ii TOR = terms of reference; AHRB = ASCAN Human Rights Body.

a ‘Instrument’ includes official declarations, treaties or conventions. It does not include pronouncements that have not been formalized by at least an official declaration.

b ‘Mechanism’ means activities, processes or funds created to operationalize the instrument. Mechanisms only include discrete processes or bodies created by agreement, and exclude ministerial and senior officials’ meetings related to social policy.

c Rights refer to social rights (e.g. human rights, rights of women and children, etc.), officially recognized by the regional associations.

d Redistribution refers to instruments or mechanisms that seek to promote sharing of resources or access to resources.

e Regulation refers to instruments or mechanisms that establish standards or benchmarks for certain sectors or activities.

f Technical cooperation/capacity building refers to discrete initiatives that address particular concerns. They form bulk of the functional cooperation schemes in ASEAN and SAARC, usually involving studies, workshops, information exchange, monitoring, and other projects along these lines.

* Some of the instruments are themselves mechanisms (e.g. the Initiative for ASEAN Integration) or cover broad areas of concern (e.g. Social Charter of the SAARC), while some mechanisms are mandated by agreements (e.g. the Funds)

Prospects and challenges: people making regional cooperation work

A major weakness in the mode of regionalism practised by ASEAN and SAARC is that it is underlined by competition as a framework. In the case of ASEAN, it is a competition of who can attract more investments and generate more trade. For SAARC, it is political competition. It has been shown, though, that reasons abound for countries in these regions to come together. But for this to be successful, they would need to adopt substantive and meaningful cooperation. Regional social policy, I suggest, is an ideal terrain for such cooperation.

Both ASEAN and SAARC have strong bases on which to build: ASEAN countries have a strong tradition of developmentalism, while SAARC members have strong socialist influences. SAARC started with cooperation in the social sectors, long before it considered economic integration. SAARC can be said to be as committed, if not more, to the social dimension as ASEAN. Note that even after more than forty years, social policy in ASEAN is also still rudimentary. The signing of the ASEAN Charter advances institutional formalization (procedures, mechanisms), but it does not have a strong rights-based approach or deep commitment to social policy, as the SAARC Social Charter does. South Asia also has a stronger tradition of developing its internal markets and relying on its own capital, quite in contrast with ASEAN's outward-looking development. ASEAN's experience has been that members 'do not like to pay', making cooperative funds hard to come by. In contrast, SAARC members make bigger contributions to the SDF, and are more selective in receiving donations from non-regional partners. External funding has been generally positive for regional social policy. However, unless regions increase their own contributions, regional social policy will be constrained to follow initiatives that have global support or the priority of the external partners, instead of what the regions require the most.

Why then can ASEAN and SAARC not give the needed attention to the social dimension of regionalism? The biggest stumbling block to successful regionalism is the lack of democracy – the distance of regionalist initiatives from the people – together with the lack of progress in taking regionalism outside the realms of an elite project located in official diplomacy. Without popular support, indeed unless popularly demanded, regional initiatives will require a long socialization process.

On a positive note, recent experiences show that there is increased openness to regionalism. The holding of official summits in parallel with people's events or civil society processes is evidence of this. These parallel events are not confined to condemning the official meetings; rather, they focus on reclaiming and redefining a regional agenda based on long-standing advocacies. In ASEAN, civil society groups participated in the Charter-drafting process, making submissions on economic, political-security and socio-cultural cooperation, as well as on institutional reform. There are also efforts to make similar submissions for the Political-Security Community and the Socio-Cultural Community Blueprints, and the Terms of Reference for the ASEAN Human Rights Body. Migrant rights advocacy groups also continue to push for the passage of a binding regional instrument on migration to operationalize the Declaration on the Protection of Migrant Workers. Peace groups advocate alternative dispute settlement mechanisms, especially in areas of armed conflict. These groups come together in the ASEAN Civil Society Conference convened yearly since 2005, and in the many other regional gatherings of civil society and social movements in Southeast Asia. In South Asia, the People's SAARC is held parallel to or very close to the official SAARC Summit. Regional groups have been advocating peace and disarmament, poverty eradication and social development. An advanced notion of regionalism, a People's Union of South Asia, was also proposed in the People's SAARC of July 2008. Imagination is rich in the People Track, despite the lack or absence of mechanisms for people's access, transparency and participation in both ASEAN and SAARC.

If ASEAN and SAARC were more open to inputs from these groups and movements, they would be able to respond to the most pressing needs in the two sub-regions. Specifically, the Secretariats of the two Associations should have the ability to officially receive inputs from citizens; groups and direct such inputs to relevant bodies. More importantly, ASEAN and SAARC should open up regional deliberations to civil society participation. The official interface between the ASEAN leaders and representatives from civil society is significant, but is largely symbolic in nature. To be meaningful, there also needs to be greater access to committees, working groups, senior officials and ministerial meetings where the details of programmes are discussed and finalized. To enable this type of participation, it is imperative that mechanisms for access to information, accountability and redress are institutionalized in both ASEAN and SAARC.

To reiterate, based on identified common concerns in the two sub-regions, a good regional social policy should be able to:

1 promote regional standards and cooperation in social services, particularly in health and education;
2 address the practical concern of labour mobility, and contextualize this within general social protection issues as well as regional health standards;
3 respond to vulnerabilities due to emergencies and natural disasters by enhancing members' capacity to deal with, and developing defences against, disasters and emergencies through regional pooling of resources and know-how and mechanisms for coordinated response; and
4 address social and economic disparities among members by cooperating in catch-up programmes, and recognizing differential levels of endowments and development when designing agreements.

For maximum impact, these elements of regional social policy should be reflected, defended and further promoted in multilateral fora. ASEAN and SAARC are not known to carry common positions in international negotiations. India, Pakistan and Bangladesh are known to have each carried strong positions in international trade talks, while Indonesia and the Philippines have allied together in defence of special and differential treatment and special products in the WTO. However, neither SAARC nor ASEAN has held a strong position as a bloc in the WTO or elsewhere; members sometimes even carry conflicting positions.[13] ASEAN and SAARC should be able to bring to the regional discussion matters that are also being discussed in multilateral agreements and, if possible, forge unities around them. After all, if and how members are able to identify and concur on common agendas is another measure of their confidence in a regional association. The creation of clear constituencies for regional cooperation is a key to its success. The challenge is in prying open erstwhile closed regional processes and giving more democratic space for people to help define a regional social development agenda that is relevant to them.

Notes

1 The Asian Relations Conference in New Delhi in March/April 1947 introduced the idea of Asian unity. This was successful in promoting Asian studies and the idea of regional cooperation. In January 1949, the New Delhi Conference was convened on the initiative of India to discuss the Dutch occupation of Indonesia. This resulted in the united call by Asian governments that Indonesia be given complete control of its territory by January 1950. In July 1949, the Philippines attempted to introduce but failed to get support for a stronger pact through the Asia-Pacific Union as a third force in international affairs. Undaunted, it convened the anti-communist Baguio Conference in May 1950, the first ever gathering of fully independent states in Asia and Western Pacific. In April/May 1954, the Colombo Powers Conference discussed closer ties between African and Asian countries. This Conference and their subsequent meetings paved the way for the Asian–African Conference and the creation of the Bandung Movement (later becoming the Non-Aligned Movement or NAM) in April 1955 (Dash 1996, Solidum 2003, Inayat 2007).

2 These included: disputes over territories (Kashmir, affecting India and Pakistan, and China); domestic insurgencies driven by ethnic conflicts (Tamil Eelam insurgency affecting Sri Lanka, and implicating India as an unreliable mediator because of its posture on the conflict as well as pressure from local Indian Tamil population); political conflicts (e.g. Maoist insurgency in Nepal, coups in the Maldives); and other domestic violence.

3 Basic information on the institutional set-up is drawn from *SAARC – A Profile* (SAARC Secretariat 2004b) and the *Charter of the Association of Southeast Asian Nations* (ASEAN 2007a). Additional information is available online at www.aseansec.org and www.saarc-sec.org.

4 The term 'community' first appeared in the ASEAN Concord I (ASEAN Leaders 1976) but it was not until 2003 in the ASEAN Concord II (ASEAN Leaders 2003) that the three ASEAN Communities were formalized. The three communities were established to serve as a foundation for the ASEAN Community aspired to in *ASEAN Vision 2020* (ASEAN Leaders 1997).

5 This flexible participation has three general expressions: the ASEAN-X, where an initiative is passed even if not all members join it; sub-regionalism, which differs from ASEAN-X in that participation by national or sub-national territories is allowed (e.g. the Greater Mekong Subregion/GMS Programme); and ASEAN+X, sometimes deployed in conjunction with the ASEAN-X formula, which is used for cooperation with external partners (e.g. with Japan, South Korea and China or ASEAN+3). This flexibility is best seen in the areas of economic cooperation but is of limited use in other areas (Chavez 2007). There is yet no equivalent in SAARC.

6 The official track (Track One) is complemented by gatherings of public intellectuals, academics and other non-state actors to provide expert advice and inputs to official processes (Track Two). ASEAN-recognized Track Two actors include: the ASEAN Inter-Parliamentary Organization (AIPO), the ASEAN Institutes of Strategic and International Studies (ASEAN-ISIS), and the ASEAN University Network – most of their interventions involve political and security issues. ASEAN recently recognized the business sector as Track Two, and established the ASEAN Business Advisory Council (ABAC). Some form of Track Three, or a people's track (via official interfaces with the ASEAN Civil Society Conference), has emerged recently but has yet to be institutionalized (Chavez 2007). Roughly approximating the non-official Track in SAARC would be the recognition of the Association of SAARC Speakers and Parliamentarians, and the recognition of professional bodies: three SAARC Apex Bodies – SAARC Chamber of Commerce and Industry (SCCI), the South Asian Association for Regional Cooperation in Law (SAARCLAW), and the South Asian Federation of Accountants (SAFA); and thirteen SAARC Recognized Bodies – architects; management development institutions; university women; town planners; cardiac society; engineers; teachers; state insurance organizations; radiological society; surgical care; dermatologists, venereologists and leprologists; and free media association. However, the interface with them is unclear (SAARC Secretariat 2004a).

7 Economic losses to the Asian poultry sector are estimated at around US$10 billion. The livelihoods of the rural poor are particularly threatened, with avian flu affecting their income and food security.

8 In South Asia, only India reported SARS cases, but tourism in the region was badly damaged nonetheless, first because of lack of knowledge about the disease, and second, because most tourists going to South Asia pass through Southeast Asia.

9 ASEAN has Mutual Recognition Arrangements (MRAs), and a Declaration on the Protection and Promotion of the Rights of Migrant Workers. These initiatives, however, are limited. The MRA to date only covers the skilled professions of nursing and engineering, while the Declaration on the Protection and Promotion of the Rights of Migrant Workers has yet to evolve regional mechanisms to make it operational.

10 SAARC members spend more on education than do ASEAN members, the highest spenders being the Maldives (7.1 per cent of GDP) and Malaysia (6.1 per cent), while Indonesia (0.9 per cent) and Mynamar (1.3 per cent) are the lowest. Adult literacy is highest in the Maldives (97 per cent) and Brunei (94.9 per cent) (ADB 2008, UNDP 2007).

11 Purchasing power parity based on current US dollars.

12 This apprehension tends to be stronger in SAARC than in ASEAN. The economic successes of the original ASEAN members serve as inspiration to newer members who use membership in the association to signal their readiness to join the global stage. In SAARC, however, the sheer size of India intimidates much smaller members and stokes fears of Indian economic hegemonic designs.

13 Indonesia and the Philippines were on the opposite side to Thailand and Malaysia on the Special Differential Treatment and Special Products issues in the WTO.

8 Regional social policies in Africa

Declarations abound

Bob Deacon[1]

This chapter first reviews the recent history of regional integration attempts on the African continent. It then focuses on the drivers for injecting a social dimension into the regional integration process. The issue of whether the European Union's attempts to negotiate Economic Partnership Agreements (EPAs) with Africa are helping or hindering the process of regional social integration is discussed here. Using the examples of ECOWAS in West Africa and the SADC in South Africa, a more detailed account is then provided of the emergence of sub-regional social policies. The chapter ends with a report on the most recent developments at the continental level, with the agreement in January 2009 of the Africa Union to a Framework for African Social Policy. The place of regional and sub-regional social policy within that framework is reported.

African regional integration agreements[2]

Pre-independence patterns of regional integration shaped by the colonial management of Africa in terms of trans-frontier integration (monetary, administrative, fiscal and social provisioning) provide the backcloth of regional integration arrangements in Africa today (Adesina 2007). Thus 'French' West Africa and Central Africa, 'British' West Africa, Southern Africa, and 'Portuguese' Africa continue to cast their shadows. There was a social dimension to colonial trans-frontier integration involving trade, fiscal and monetary policies, common currency zones, and education and labour markets. There was trans-frontier education provisioning even in the context of non-unified educational systems and also trans-frontier social security systems – often racially structured but existent nonetheless, although the situation in North Africa was significantly more differentiated (Adesina 2007). Most of the currently active regional organizations in Africa are shaped by this colonial legacy.

In West Africa, the most comprehensive regional initiative is the Economic Community of West African States (ECOWAS), created in 1975. Nigeria, accounting for more than half the region's population and an equally significant proportion of its GDP, has been one of the driving forces behind ECOWAS.

Another track of the West African regional integration scene is linked to the aftermath of French colonization. Following their independence most of the

French colonies maintained their monetary union with France. In 1994 the Union Economique et Monétaire Ouest Africaine (UEMOA) was established with its own common currency. It established the customs union in 2000.

In Central Africa regional integration has also been affected by the colonial legacy. Already in 1964 the five French ex-colonies in the region had formed the Union Douanière et Economique de l'Afrique Centrale (UDEAC). But unlike in West Africa, Central African integration is hampered by the limited cross-border infrastructure. The countries in the Central African region have also formed a wider body known as the Economic Community of Central African States (ECCAS). ECCAS has not made much progress towards economic integration.

Eastern and Southern Africa are the regions with the most complex institutional structures. The Southern African Development Coordination Conference (SADCC) was founded in 1980. The SADCC was initially conceived to reduce dependence on apartheid South Africa. It was later transformed into a regional integration arrangement, the Southern African Development Community (SADC). Following its first democratic elections in 2004, South Africa joined the SADC which therefore became the economic integration block with the largest combined GDP in Africa.

In 1994 the Common Market for Eastern and Southern Africa (COMESA) was formed with overlapping membership with the SADC. At the end of 2006, there remained a sizeable overlap between COMESA and the SADC as the following seven countries are members of both: the Democratic Republic of Congo (DRC), Madagascar, Malawi, Mauritius, Swaziland, Zambia and Zimbabwe.

There are a number of other important integration initiatives in Eastern and Southern Africa, which operate at the sub-regional level – the Intergovernmental Authority for Development (IGAD), the East African Community (EAC), the Southern African Customs Union (SACU) and the Indian Ocean Commission (IOC). We mention here only the EAC and SACU.

The EAC, comprising Kenya, Uganda and Tanzania, can trace its origins to the era of the British colonies of Kenya and Uganda and the protectorate of Tanganyika. It established a customs union comprising the three countries, together with a common currency, and an organ for the management of common services for ports, railways and air transport. This community broke up under political strains in the 1970s but was reconstituted by the signing of a new treaty establishing the East African Community, which came into force in July 2000. The treaty provided for the formation of a customs union followed by a common market. Burundi and Rwanda joined the EAC during 2007. The EAC is considered by some as a pace setter for COMESA – an application of variable geometry or allowing countries to move at different speeds. However, the practicality of this became questionable when Tanzania also became a member of SADC while the other two countries are in COMESA.

The formation of the Southern African Customs Union (SACU), sometimes referred to as the oldest on-going customs union in the world, goes back to an agreement in 1910 between South Africa and Britain, representing at that time the three British protectorates that would much later become the independent states of Botswana, Lesotho and Swaziland. At its independence in 1990, Namibia became a member. South Africa dominates SACU, with the other four members – Botswana, Lesotho, Namibia and Swaziland – representing only 15 per cent of its total population and less than 10 per cent of its GNP. The deep integration aspect of SACU is partly reflected in the mechanism of pooling all tariff and excise revenue together with a formula to share the revenue in a manner that provides compensation for the polarization effects within SACU. All the SACU members are also in the SADC. In other words, SACU is an example of variable geometry within the wider SADC.

All the North African countries – except for Egypt but including Mauritania – established the Arab Maghreb Union (AMU) in 1989. More recently another grouping, the Community of Sahel–Saharan States (CENSAD), actively promoted by Libya, has been created. It comprises a large number of countries from North Africa and even parts of Central Africa, the West African coast and the Horn of Africa. CENSAD is the largest African sub-regional body. Most members of AMU and ECOWAS as well as several CEMAC (Communauté Economique et Monétaire de l'Afrique Centrale) and COMESA countries have joined CENSAD. According to Dinka and Kennes (2007), 'it has been mostly active as a political dialogue forum and not that much as an economic integration body'. In terms of the African continent as a whole there has always been a vision of African unity. This vision was behind the creation of the Organization of African Unity (OAU) in 1963.

In 1991 this idea became the central feature of the Abuja Treaty establishing the African Economic Community (AEC). The Abuja Treaty introduced the notion of Regional Economic Communities (RECs) as building blocks of the AEC. This led to the designation of AMU, ECOWAS, ECCAS, COMESA and the SADC as RECs. Subsequently, ECA, IGAD and CENSAD have been recognized as RECs. The pan-African ideal was further reaffirmed by the reconstitution of the OAU into the African Union (AU) in 2002. The AU Act foresaw the creation of a stronger institutional framework, in some respects similar to the EU's. The New Partnership for Africa's Development (NEPAD), an initiative promoted by a number of African countries including South Africa, is now considered a programme of the AU. A related initiative, developed in the NEPAD context, is the African Peer Review Mechanism, a voluntary mechanism for mutual monitoring of governance and accountability.

In terms of the social dimension of regional and sub-regional integration this chapter will focus on ECOWAS, UEMOA, the SADC, SACU and the AU. The achievements in the social dimensions of regional integration in the other sub-regions will therefore be under-reported. The achievements of the ECA and the possible new initiatives stemming from Libya's creation of CENSAD need further documentation.

The drivers of the social dimension of regional integration in Africa

This section reviews the recent views and actions concerning the social dimension of regional integration at pan-African and at sub-regional levels by several regional and sub-regional actors including the AU, ILO, NEPAD, UNDESA, UNESCO and civil society organizations. In keeping with the subsequent section's focus on West and South Africa, mention is also made of the views of the tripartite stakeholders on the social and labour dimensions of regional integration in both South and West Africa.

The African Union, the Ouagadougou Summit and Livingstone

Several important initiatives call attention to the importance of integration of employment and decent work into the African political and civil agendas. A first step was made at the 37th Ordinary Session of the Assembly of Heads of State and Government of the OAU, which was organized in Lusaka, Zambia, in July 2001, when it was decided that a Ministerial Meeting on Employment Promotion and Poverty Reduction in Africa would be organized.[3] Consequently, in April 2002 in Burkina Faso, a meeting of the OAU's tripartite Labour and Social Affairs Commission was organized, where member states acknowledged the importance of job creation in Africa. Moreover, at the Second Summit in July 2003, in Maputo, Mozambique, the Assembly of African Heads of State and Government decided[4] to organize an Extraordinary Summit on Employment and Poverty Alleviation in 2004. All the AU member states were invited to attend the Summit and the AU Commission was asked to organize it, in collaboration with the Regional Economic Communities (RECs), the ILO and other partners and stakeholders. The Summit took place in September 2004 in Ouagadougou, Burkina Faso, and the result was a Declaration, a Plan of Action, and a Follow-up Mechanism for the promotion of employment and poverty alleviation.

The topic of the Extraordinary Summit on Employment and Poverty Alleviation in Africa was Strategies for Employment Creation and Enhancing Sustainable Livelihoods. One of the most important meetings was the African Social Partners' Forum, on the theme Decent Work: a Driving Force for Africa's Development, which represented the first assembly of the representatives of African workers and employers' organizations as social partners. The promotion of a tripartite social dialogue and decent work were the main topics on the agenda.

The background paper prepared by the AU Commission highlighted that the main objectives of the Summit should be to: (i) significantly raise the level and increase the growth rate of productive employment in all sectors of the economy; (ii) promote increased and decent employment opportunities throughout the economy with adequate social protection and respect for core labour standards; and (iii) strengthen participation and voice. On the same lines, the expected outcomes of the Summit were, among others: (i) better institutional arrangements and capacity for delivering employment programmes and poverty alleviation interventions; (ii) partnership and greater participation by all stakeholders; and (iii) an integrated approach in designing and implementing programmes to combat poverty and unemployment (AU 2004a).

In the Declaration on Employment and Poverty Alleviation in Africa, the heads of state and government of the AU acknowledged the importance of strengthening 'social dialogue mechanisms and institutions as a means of realizing participatory democracy involving the social partners and civil society in policy making, implementation, evaluation, and monitoring' (AU 2004b). In order to promote productive employment and poverty alleviation, the Economic, Social and Cultural Council (ECOSOCC) and the Labour and Social Affairs Commission of the AU have become the principal fora for discussion and partnership between governments, social partners and civil society. Additionally, they are devoted to support the ongoing efforts of the governments, social partners and civil society organizations to promote the decent work development agenda of the ILO. Furthermore, the heads of state and government committed themselves to boost the role of RECs in their attempt to promote a productive employment dimension into the regional and inter-regional cooperation agenda. An important asset is the designation of the member states and RECs[5] as main implementation bodies of the Plan of Action and Declaration, and the AU Labour and Social Affairs Commission is delegated to coordinate the implementing mechanisms. The first comprehensive Evaluation Reports are expected to be presented in 2009 and 2014.

The Plan of Action adopted by heads of state in Africa committed the AU to develop strategies for generating decent and productive work, and to explicitly address employment generation issues in national poverty reduction strategies. This plan has as its fundamental objective the reversal of the trend towards persistent unemployment, underemployment and poverty. Among priority objectives, areas and strategies to ensure this fundamental objective is met are 'promoting and harmonizing regional initiatives on poverty alleviation' (2.3.iii), 'harmonizing and coordinating labour legislation' (2.3.iv), 'strengthening regional cooperation ... through harmonization of labour laws and regulations, establishing mutual recognition of training and skills' (2.9) (AU 2004c).

Subsequently the AU organized a series of five sub-regional meetings in 2006 aimed at supporting capacity building in the regional economic communities. Regional frameworks in integrated employment strategies were agreed at each of these. The workshops were held in Khartoum for East Africa, in Yaoundé for Central Africa, in Abuja for West Africa, in Algiers for North Africa and in Windhoek for Southern Africa. The papers presented at those workshops covered elements and strategies that would form part of the Integrated Regional Employment Policy. The ILO also signed memoranda of understanding with ECOWAS in 2005 and CEEAC in 2006.

However, the concept note for an AU consultative meeting on employment policies and programmes held on 28–29 November 2007 notes the obstacles to progress in this area. Thus, it comments:

> The purpose of this meeting is two-fold. First, the meeting will review the progress that has been made and challenges that have been encountered implementation of the Ouagadougou Summit. Chief among the challenges has been lack of feedback from some RECs and member states in relation to implementation of the recommendations of the Summit including failure to reply to questionnaires from the AU Commission. For instance, at the time of April 2006, only 28 member states and two RECs had responded to questionnaires as to what they were doing as part of the follow-up process. It would be necessary to have an update on the responses but also a review of this process including a consideration of the challenges and how to overcome these challenges to improve the feedback flow and response rate and improve generally the progress reporting system. What national and REC follow-up institutions have been set up and what are their compositions? What have been their core functions, priority tasks and outputs to date?
>
> (AU 2007: 3)

Issues of the institutional capacity of the RECs clearly arise here.

Also of note is the fact that at the 2005 UN World Summit, the African governments reaffirmed their commitment to support 'full employment and decent work for all ... as a central objective of our ... national development strategies'. The decent work agenda is officially supported by UN agencies and by major financiers like the EU. The decent work agenda involves:

1 social pacts for employment-generating economic policies;
2 labour standards and fair income;
3 skills development for enhanced productivity; and
4 social protection for all.

Furthermore, at the Third Ordinary Session of the Labour and Social Affairs Commission of the African Union held on 18–23 April 2005 a *Draft Social Policy Framework for Africa* was tabled (AU 2005). It envisaged that regional (pan-African), sub-regional (e.g. SADC), and national programmes would be developed by the AU Social Affairs Department working with the UN, ADB and ECA. It continued: 'However, one vital condition for meaningful ownership by the countries is their full involvement in the formulation of the programmes' (para. 117). A revised version of this draft was adopted by African Ministers of Social Development in late 2008 and subsequently adopted by the heads of state in early 2009. This final document is reviewed in the last section of this chapter in terms of its contribution to the issue of cross-border regional cooperation in social policy.

In terms of specific social protection measures, it is to be noted that in March 2006, the AU and its development partners in collaboration with the government of the Republic of Zambia organized an inter-ministerial conference in Livingstone, Zambia. The key outcome of the conference was the Livingstone Call for Action which stated that social protection and social transfers have played and do play a key role in 'reducing poverty and promoting growth' in African countries. It also acknowledged that they are 'affordable within current resources', and that they should be a 'more utilized policy option in Africa to reach vulnerable children, older people and persons with disabilities'. The Call for Action asked governments to develop plans within three years and to engage in capacity building and experience sharing to support this work. A bi-annual conference under the auspices of the AU (2008a) was explicitly called for to ensure that follow-up dialogue takes place. In September 2006, the Yaoundé Call for Action was agreed at an Africa-wide workshop hosted by the government of Cameroon and supported by the AU and its partners. The Yaoundé Call for Action explicitly calls on governments to implement the Livingstone Call for Action. The African Union, in collaboration with HelpAge International, has been working on a programme to follow up the Livingstone Call for Action and the Yaoundé Call for Action. The programme aims to inform and build up an African constituency on national social protection programmes. The AU has declared its commitment to these Calls for Action and has commissioned a review of its social policy framework to make explicit the linkages with social protection. (This framework as just mentioned will be reviewed at the end of the chapter.) To support this ministerial conference, six national consultations and three regional experts meetings were convened in 2008 to review the progress on social protection action in Africa and feed the findings into the ministerial debate. It is expected that this process will help to develop an AU-led Africa-wide social protection 'network group' and activities with core regional and international stakeholders (AU 2008).

ILO: regional integration and decent work

Since the report of the World Commission on the Social Dimension of Globalization (WCSDG 2004), the issue of regional social integration has received increasing attention within the ILO. The social dimension of regional integration is largely dealt with through a mixture of projects and research whenever subregional developments correspond to ILO policy priorities (e.g. regional labour migration protocols, poverty reduction and related development plans, skills and social security portability, regional labour law harmonization or regional social dialogue). Among the projects in Africa are: (i) the promotion of Social Dialogue in Francophone Africa (PRODIAF) (reviewed later in this section); (ii) labour migration for integration and development in the Euromed context and West and East Africa; (iii) strengthening the capacity of the SADC to promote social dialogue and corporate social responsibility; (iv) support to the (AU) Ouagadougou Summit on employment and poverty alleviation; and (v) the secondment to Gaborone in 2008 of a Senior Programme Manager (Employment, Productivity, Labour, and Social Security) whose function is to coordinate labour and employment programmes within the SADC Secretariat.

In Africa the ILO regional office is conveniently located in Addis Ababa which is home to both the AU and the UN's ECA. This enabled close cooperation between the ILO and African governments at the Summit of Heads of State and Governments in Ouagadougou in 2004 on Poverty Alleviation and Employment. The ILO signed memoranda of understanding with ECOWAS in 2005 and CEEAC in 2006. And the ILO International Training Centre secured funds in 2007, from the French and Flemish governments, to provide. in association with UNU-CRIS, capacity-building activities in regional employment and social protection policies for ECOWAS and the SADC.

In terms of the follow-up to the Ouagadougou Summit the Eleventh African Regional Meeting of the ILO held on 24–27 April 2007 in Addis Ababa focused on defining the steps that member states, the ILO and its development partners need to take in the coming years to make decent work a reality in the region and thus provide an effective way to reduce poverty in a sustainable fashion. Debate at the meeting centred on two reports presented by the ILO's director-general. The first report described how the ILO had worked with its member states and development partners, particularly the African Union Commission and the Regional Economic Communities, to implement the Plan of Action adopted by the Ouagadougou Summit. The second report identified a number of policies and practical actions that are necessary to implement the decent work agenda in the different areas of the ILO's mandate: international labour standards and fundamental rights at work, employment, social protection, and social dialogue. The report focused on linking the decent work agenda to the MDGs and on work to strengthen the ILO's tripartite constituents across Africa.[6] The meeting agreed a large number of targets[7] that three-quarters of Africa countries would try to achieve, including targets relating to investment in decent work, closing the skills gap, investing in basic social protection, implementing labour standards at the workplace, getting children into school, and escaping the informal employment trap. The International Institute of Labour Studies (IILS) followed this up with a meeting in September 2007 bringing together researchers in Africa to strengthen research on labour issues in Africa. A further consequential follow-up event was the first Africa–EU trade union meeting held on 26–27 October which generated a joint statement to the AU–EU summit.

NEPAD and the limitations of its social dimension

The New Partnership for Africa's Development, the socio-economic programme of the African Union, had also become an increasingly important driver of development on the continent. The NEPAD strategic framework document[8] arose from a mandate given to the five initiating heads of state (Algeria, Egypt, Nigeria, Senegal, South Africa) by the OAU to develop an integrated socio-economic development framework for Africa. The 37th Summit of the OAU in July 2001 formally adopted the strategic framework document. NEPAD was very much driven by the US, EU and other donors, and was designed to address the current challenges facing the African continent. Issues such as escalating poverty levels and the continued marginalization of Africa needed a new radical vision and new plans, championed by African leaders, to guarantee Africa's renewal.

NEPAD's primary objectives are: (i) to eradicate poverty; (ii) to place African countries, both individually and collectively, on a path of sustainable growth and development; (iii) to halt the marginalization of Africa in the globalization process and enhance its full and beneficial integration into the global economy; and (iv) to accelerate the empowerment of women. In that sense it was designed within assumptions, dominant at the time, of the Washington Consensus. NEPAD works with regional Action Plans but, despite its objectives, these have mostly focused on economic and governance topics, leaving social development lagging behind. Until now NEPAD Action Plans have dealt with social development only in its human development or human capital aspects of education and health. This is insufficient for achieving NEPAD's objectives. Social policies to promote equity, decent employment and social integration are necessary to ensure social development. The broader thrust of numerous NEPAD documents clearly demonstrate a greater awareness of the need for comprehensive social policy at the national, regional and continental level but these were not converted into specific donor-funded projects.

A number of African governments recognized these gaps and suggested that the emerging African Regional Social Policy become part of NEPAD Action Plans. The United Nations Commission for Social Development and the 2005 United Nations World Summit had welcomed NEPAD and urged African countries to better incorporate social dimensions among the priorities of the New Partnership.

In the next section we report how SADC partners took the initiative to elaborate a more operational regional social policy for Africa, commencing within the SADC sub-region, and suggested that these deliberations be fed into the NEPAD process to strengthen its social dimension with a view to proposing specific programmes to be implemented using various funding options, including possible use of donor funds. Because NEPAD already has some programmes in education and health, this SADC document paid less attention to these sectors and more to employment and social protection. However in the formulation of education and health policy the SADC meeting (discussed below) stressed the importance of addressing the impact of any user charges on the standard of living of poor users. Issues of equitable access through free services or the establishment of funds to cover the cost to poor people become important.

UNDESA and the Johannesburg Declaration on Regional Social Policy

In recognition of the slow progress being made by the AU in finalizing an African social policy framework and in recognition of the limitations of the social dimension of NEPAD, the South African government requested the help of the UN Department of Economic and Social Affairs (UNDESA) to convene a workshop of SADC Ministers of Social Development to pursue the issue. The meeting in Johannesburg on 24 November 2006 gave rise to the Johannesburg Declaration in Support of an African Regional Social Policy. It resolved to endorse the principles of the Johannesburg draft document 'Towards an African Regional Policy', dated 24 November 2006, and to commit members to expedite the process of finalizing the draft document and facilitate its adoption as an SADC sub-regional social policy.

The draft document drawn up with UNDESA advice and reflecting the principles of the UNDESA Social Policy Guidance Notes (Ortiz 2007) covered the following issues with *specific regional social policy* recommendations in each topic:

1 employment and decent work;
2 social protection;
3 cross-border aspects of health;
4 higher education and regional research;
5 housing;
6 social regulation of services and water, electricity and other utilities;
7 disaster prevention, management and mitigation;
8 gender;
9 children, youth, older persons, persons with disabilities, refugees and minorities; and
10 human rights, social and economic empowerment.

In terms of the first of these, employment and decent work, the draft principles envisaged a number of capacity-building and regional funded projects to enhance SADC regional labour markets. These included the following.

Capacity-building activities

- to ensure policy-makers understand the links between economic and social policies;
- to enhance inter-ministerial cooperation (economic and social sectors) to ensure that economic policies are employment-generating;
- to promote sharing of experiences and best practices in the areas of employment, sustainable livelihoods and labour standards to combat Africa's race to the bottom;
- to develop appropriate legislative frameworks that strike a balance between economic efficiency and labour protection, and create disincentives for migration;
- to strengthen capacity of labour market institutions in areas such as employment statistics and labour inspections, to better inform social dialogue for evidence-based and employment-sensitive economic policies.

Regional funds

- for programmes for employment generation and for promoting formalization of informal work (promoting small and medium enterprises, coopera-

tives, wage subsidies, public works, guaranteed job schemes, and special employment programmes for women, youth, and persons with disabilities);
- for skills development programmes (training and retraining of labour to enhance employability and productivity).

Similar detailed recommendations were made in other social policy fields. This proposal for a regional social policy is now being considered by the SADC Ministers of Labour and their social partners.

UNESCO and the Cape Verde Regional Research Centre

Rather separate but not unimportant has been the work of UNESCO on regional social policy in Africa. As mentioned in the Introduction above, UNESCO convened in February 2004 in Uruguay a High-Level Symposium on the Social Dimension of Regionalism within the context of its International Social Sciences – Policy Nexus event. UNESCO through its Management of Social Transformations (MOST) programme has subsequently organized regional meetings of Ministers of Social Development. Zola S. Skweyiya, Minister of Social Development in South Africa and chair of MOST, has ensured that the focus of such meetings in Africa has been on regional integration. The MOST programme's initiative emphasizes some very important aspects of this new dynamic in Africa's regional integration processes, notably: promoting awareness of the added value that social sciences can bring to this process of regional integration, and fostering the dialogue between decision-makers and social scientists. It is within this perspective that MOST organizes a series of seminars on regional integration policies in the ECOWAS region, called Nation-states and the Challenges of Regional Integration in West Africa, which has now ended with a call to establish a regional integration studies centre in Cape Verde (Barry 2008).

Stakeholders in the SADC and ECOWAS

Within the SADC sub-region the social partner organizations and broader civil society organizations have articulated their views on the issue of regional integration, inter-regional trade arrangements and the relationship to employment, decent work, and labour and social policy.

The Southern Africa Trade Union Coordination Council (SATUCC) has recently resolved its position on the regional integration process and on the EU EPA process and published these in the form of both a long (Kanyenze *et al.* 2006) and short (ANSA 2007) text, both entitled *The Search for Sustainable Human Development in Southern Africa.* The view is taken that the SADC has not achieved regional economic, let alone social, integration on its own terms. It should focus on a 'home-grown' development strategy to increase cross-border investment to enhance industrialization and regional trade and labour mobility rather than let its development be dictated by outside pressures. The development of the Southern African regional market should take precedence over international trade deals. In this context SATUCC perceives the current EU EPAs as both divisive of the region and serving the needs of the EU at the expense of the Southern African economy and society. They need to be renegotiated. The orientation is to return to a state-led developmental import substitution regime in the region which is seen as having served regional development in East Asia and Latin America in the past. Of note is the membership of SATUCC on the Council of SADC NGOs which are consulted on some aspects of SADC affairs.

The Business Unity of South Africa (BUSA), on the other hand, representing the Southern African Employers Group (SEG) tries to strike a balance between trade liberalization and development issues (ILO 2008: 5). Moreover, it envisaged the need to place the decent work agenda at the heart of the EPAs, since it provides a concrete basis for both economic and social development, social protection and social dialogue. The conference restated demands from trade unions of Africa and Europe that regional integration should include 'a real social dimension' (ILO 2008: 7). The main achievement of the regional conference was the deliberation of a generic social charter to be included in the EPAs. This will include binding commitments on the promotion of the decent work agenda, and should also address the unforeseen social impacts 'likely to be engendered by the implementation of the EPAs' (ILO 2008: 8), especially on vulnerable groups. Another noteworthy result of the conference is the 'Kampala Trade Union Declaration on Social Agenda and Economic Partnership Agreements'. In its recommendations the Declaration highlights, among others: (i) the EU–ACP countries, need to include a social chapter in all EPAs; (ii) the need to strengthen the assessment of social and labour impacts of trade policy and to promote labour standards; (iii) the need for the trade unions to campaign for a social dimension of EPAs and to raise awareness at the governmental levels of the impacts of EPAs; and (iv) the need for the ILO and the EU to mobilize resources for capacity building of trade unions and negotiators (ILO 2008: 18).

PRODIAF and social dialogue

The Regional Programme for the Promotion of Social Dialogue in Francophone Africa of the ILO has strengthened the capacities of governments, employers and unions in various countries of Southern and West Africa, including Senegal, Togo, Mali, Burkina Faso and Congo. Social dialogue has been actively promoted through PRODIAF initiatives and interactive workshops debating social negotiation and mediation techniques.

A social charter in Senegal, a social pact in Mali and other initiatives came out of the PRODIAF efforts. Moreover, the programme contributed to the creation of the Tripartite Social Dialogue Committee (CEMAC) and the Labour and Social Dialogue Council (UEMOA).

The ILO–PRODIAF programme started in 1998, financed by the Belgian government. During the first phase (1998–2003), PRODIAF activities included twenty-one national studies on the state of social dialogue and tripartite cooperation, as well as assistance in four sub-regional tripartite meetings. The adoption of the declaration of Ouagadougou regarding the strengthening of social dialogue at the sub-regional level of the UEMOA in 1999 and the tripartite meetings of CEMAC are considerable results of the PRODIAF programme. Consequently, in its second phase, PRODIAF encouraged the creation of a network of social dialogue experts for the French-speaking countries of Central Africa and the Great Lakes region. The meeting held in Kigali in May 2005 was attended by numerous participants and they expressed the need to strengthen the capacity of government officials as well as of social partners to mediate in labour disputes.

PRODIAF is an example of the broad efforts in Western and Southern Africa, coordinated and/or implemented by the ILO, to support at national levels social dialogue, tripartite negotiations, labour codes and employment programmes. These efforts go well beyond the Francophone zone: indeed Ghana and Liberia, among other countries in the West African zone, have also benefited from support for improvements of labour conditions. Similar efforts took place in Southern Africa.

Civil society organizations, the social dimension of regional integration and the role of EPAs

Some civil society organizations[9] on the African continent and within Europe which are in favour of strengthening the social dimension of regional integration have been in the forefront of the criticisms of the emerging EPAs. The Alternative Regionalisms Project of the Trans National Institute, which is in favour of strengthened regionalism within Africa, has set the terms of the debate. Keet (2007a) sets out the problems as they see them for developing countries. The EPAs, she argues, are a means for the EU to gain (i) preferential investment liberalization agreements; (ii) protection of EU corporate intellectual property; and (iii) preferential EU company access to service liberalization and government procurements. Being set up as the basis for EPAs, however, the artificially constructed groupings of countries cut across, in some cases, organic and actually existing regional groupings. In sum, according to the TNI (Keet 2007a: 7) 'ACP governments must be persuaded not to sacrifice long-term development co-operation among themselves by making highly questionable compromises with the EU in EPAs under pressure.' Keet notes further that the US has continued its preferential trading deal with Africa under the Economic Opportunities Act until 2015 without incurring WTO reaction on the grounds of discrimination. The EU should be persuaded to continue its preferential deals in the same way and not capitulate to the WTO official position that such deals must end by 2008. In order to review the latest developments in the EPA negotiations, at the meeting in Cape Town, South Africa (20–23 February 2008), under the umbrella of the Africa Trade Network, this organization reaffirmed its opposition to these agreements.[10] It is to be noted within this context that the report of the UN's Economic Commission for Africa on EPAs states that regional economic integration should always be given priority over EPAs; it is critical of the artificial groupings of countries set up by the EU in the context of the EPA process (ECA 2006).

At the annual meeting held in December 2006, the Africa Trade Network of civil society organizations reiterated opposition to the EPAs, calling for 'changes in the EC negotiating directives and more coherence to African negotiators' approaches to reconciling the architecture of EPAs with underlying development concerns'.[11] The statement issued at the end of the meeting calls for a new approach based on 'non-reciprocity, protection of ACP producers and regional markets, exclusion of trade-in-services issues'.

The Africa Trade Network (ATN) in collaboration with the Economic Justice Network (EJN)[12] hosted in June 2007 a pan-African Stop EPA Peoples' Forum. The main focus areas of debate were: (i) EPAs, African unity and regional integration; (ii) EPAs in Africa: social and human rights; (iii) EPAs and HIV/AIDS; and (iv) EPAs as anti-development and anti-democratic. The two-day meeting concluded that the EPAs, as currently formulated will jeopardize local African businesses, farmers and social services. Furthermore, the EPAs will open up the market to European imports to the detriment of local products and the well-being of Africans.[13]

In November 2007, the Southern African civil society organizations campaigning on the EPAs held a meeting in Gaborone, Botswana, to review the EPA negotiations. In the statement issued after the meeting it is declared that 'the proposals on market access contained in the interim agreement still reflect the offensive interests of the EU and are not comprehensively linked to addressing supply-constraints in the region'.[14] Furthermore, it is stated that civil society organizations are not involved in the EPA negotiations process and that the governments do not consult the stakeholders in the negotiations. The current EPAs/FTAs are 'anti-developmental and will have tremendous potential to destroy the economies' of Southern African countries.[15]

Regional social policy in West and Southern Africa

We now turn to the review of the extent to which regional social policies have actually been developed as distinct from argued for in two sub-regions of Africa, namely the South and the West.

The Southern African Development Community and the Southern African Customs Union

As we noted earlier, the SADC was created in 1994, as a result of the transformation of the former SADCC, which started in 1980 as a common front for political and economic liberation from the dominant neighbouring apartheid regime in South Africa. The member states of SADC are Angola, Botswana, Democratic Republic of Congo, Lesotho, Malawi, Mauritius, Mozambique, Namibia, South Africa, Seychelles, Swaziland, Tanzania, Zambia and Zimbabwe. The main objectives of the SADC are to achieve development and economic growth, alleviate poverty, enhance the standard and quality of life of the people of Southern Africa and support the socially disadvantaged through regional integration; to realize complementarities between national and regional strategies and programmes; to promote and maximize productive employment and utilization of resources in the region; to develop policies facilitating the free movement of trade, labour and capital; and to strengthen and consolidate the long-standing historical, social and cultural affinities and links among the people of the region (ECA 2006).

The SADC Programme of Action (SPA) represents the cornerstone of its development and integration agenda. It is guided by two key instruments, the Regional Indicative Strategic Plan (RISDP) and the Strategic Indicative Plan for the Organ (SIPO). Under the SPA framework, SADC launched a Trade Protocol in 2000, aiming at the creation of an FTA area amongst the member countries by 2008 and a Customs Union by 2010. The SADC FTA came into effect from August 2008 when South Africa took over the presidency of SADC. This means most goods produced in the region will then enter member countries free of custom duties. However, some SADC states are concerned that South Africa will benefit most as it is the region's powerhouse, exporting more to SADC countries than it imports from them. The products will now move freely among member states, but other countries will still continue with tariffs as they feel there is a need to protect some of their infant industries. There are fears that goods from large exporters like South Africa could swamp the markets of small countries and therefore result in the collapse of industries, but the South African government says inter-state dialogue will be maintained to ensure that the declaration of the SADC as an FTA area benefits all players.

The SADC has developed an infrastructure and capacity for the implementation of sub-regional social policy. It has established Directorates of Food; Agriculture and Natural Resources; Trade, Industry, Finance and Investment; Infrastructure and Services; Social and Human Development and Special Programmes; and HIV and AIDS. The SADC 2000 Health Policy included cooperation in terms of communicable diseases and the referral of patients between member states. Sub-regional education policy was the focus of a needs assessment in 1998. The SADC NGO Forum is long established, providing a sub-regional civil society voice in SADC affairs.

In particular, the Social and Human Development Directorate already had responsibility for an SADC Social Charter which included among its objectives in Article , 'the harmonization of social policies which … contribute to productive employment … facilitate labour mobility … and … ensure regional cooperation in collection of labour market data', and in Article 5 asserted that 'member states shall ratify and implement the ILO core labour standards … and that member states shall establish regional mechanisms to assist member states'. Additionally, it has elaborated codes of conduct on HIV and AIDS and employment, on child labour, on safe use of chemicals and on social security (Chitambo 2007).

Concerning the free movement of persons, the SADC Windhoek Treaty of 1992 also contains provisions for the movement of people across borders. In the

SADC region in 1994 visa requirements were abolished for travel by SADC citizens inside the region, and then, in 1997, negotiations were launched on a draft protocol on the facilitation of movement of persons in the SADC. The protocol was finally signed in Gaborone in August 2005. However, because of the huge inequities in development between some countries the issue of the free movement of peoples remains controversial.

A Memorandum of Understanding between the SADC and the ILO was signed in April 2007. The ILO has provided support to the SADC to facilitate the engagement for a period of one year (2008) of a Senior Programme Manager (Employment, Productivity, Labour, and Social Security) whose function is to coordinate labour and employment programmes within the SADC Secretariat. The following are the planned activities and areas in which assistance will be provided to the SADC:

1 the development of a monitoring and evaluation mechanism/instrument of the SADC standards on employment and labour;
2 technical assistance in the implementation of the SADC programme on productivity which involves the establishment of the SADC Productivity Organization;
3 the setting up of a regional labour market information system;
4 development of monitoring and evaluation mechanisms in the implementation of the Declaration and Plan of Action for Promotion of Employment and Poverty Alleviation in Africa and of the SADC Policies, Priorities and Strategies on Employment and Labour;
5 capacity building to enhance gender mainstreaming in employment policies and promotion of women in the sub-region; and
6 popularization of the provision of the newly adopted Code on Social Security in the SADC and promotion of compliance with the provisions of Convention 102 on social security in the sub-region.

In addition, through the newly approved ILO Project on Harnessing Corporate Social Responsibility and Social Dialogue to realize Decent Work Objectives (CSR/SD Project), the following actions are envisaged:

1 enhancement of the capacity of the SADC Secretariat and the umbrella employers' and workers' organizations to implement the SADC Social Charter on Fundamental Social Rights through dialogue and consultative mechanisms; and
2 promotion of the provisions of the Social Charter and the Tripartite Declaration of Principles concerning Multinational Enterprises and Social Policy with a view to enabling social partners and SADC Investment Promotion agencies to formulate an integrated regional policy framework for promoting flows of foreign direct investment which will avoid the 'beggar-thy-neighbour' syndrome.

Regional labour policy is overseen by the annual meetings of the Ministers of Labour. The latest took place in March 2008 and resolved to establish a task force (involving South Africa, Botswana, Zambia and Lesotho as well as social partners) which will oversee the setting up of two SADC technical subcommittees on Social Protection and Employment and Labour. The task force met in May 2008 and included issues of capacity building and training on its agenda.

The Ministers of Labour also considered the Draft Regional Social Policy document and the Johannesburg Declaration resulting from the 2006 meeting of SADC Ministers of Development. The document will now be considered by the tripartite process in each member country before returning in 2009 for agreement.

Despite this recent reinvigoration of the labour and social agenda of the SADC it should be noted that no dialogue is currently taking place between the SADC Department for Trade and Investment and the Labour Directorate. The Task Force on Regional Economic Integration does not meet with the Task Force on Labour. Furthermore the trade meetings between the SADC and the EU on EPAs do not involve the Labour Ministers.

In addition, as we saw on p. 163, in the same region is the Southern African Customs Union (SACU), a regional integration arrangement which has been in existence since 1910 as a free trade area and a customs union with a common external tariff and a common revenue pool between Botswana, Lesotho, Namibia, South Africa and Swaziland, all members of the SADC as well. Exception in the case of Botswana, SACU is not only a customs union, but also a monetary area for the member states. When the apartheid period in South Africa came to an end, the SACU agreements were renegotiated and the current SACU 2002 agreement came into force on 15 July 2004. SACU is managed by a Council of Ministers and on a daily basis by a secretariat, based in Windhoek, Namibia. SACU does not have a labour or social charter but in the view of the Ministry of Labour of South Africa, 'it is assumed that the SADC charter applies to SACU as well'. The relationship and division of labour between SACU and the SADC will become increasingly important as SADC evolves its free trade area in 2008 and it own customs union by 2010. At present the envisaged SADC FTA does not make provision for customs duties sharing, an issue objected to by other SACU partners within the SADC.

The Economic Community of West African States

ECOWAS was established in 1975; the member states are Benin, Burkina Faso, Cape Verde, Côte d'Ivoire, Gambia, Ghana, Guinea, Guinea Bissau, Liberia, Mali, Niger, Nigeria, Senegal, Sierra Leone and Togo. In 1993, ECOWAS revised its original treaty in order to speed up and strengthen its process of full integration. The objectives of ECOWAS, among others, are to improve the living standards of its citizens; to promote sustainable and stable economic growth and development; to contribute towards the development of the continent and an eventual establishment of a continent-wide economic union.

Since 1990, ECOWAS has been pursuing a programme under the framework of its Trade Liberalization Scheme (TLS), which calls for the creation of a free trade area and the complete elimination of tariff and non-tariff barriers. This work is on-going although effective implementation of an FTA was announced in 2004. Beyond trade, ECOWAS is heavily involved in peace and security in the region and its interventions in Côte d'Ivoire, Liberia and Sierra Leone have been key to preserving stability in the region.

ECOWAS has been reorganized into a commission-type executive organization based in Abuja, Nigeria. Beyond the headquarters, ECOWAS also has specialized institutions:

- the West African Health organization, based in Ouagadougou;
- the Community Court of Justice in Abuja;
- the ECOWAS Bank for Investment and Development in Lomé, Togo.

Moreover, ECOWAS has adopted a Protocol on Inter-State Road Transit and a transit guarantee bond. It has also introduced a common certificate of origin for goods crossing the borders, a uniform and simplified customs declaration form. This last customs document was jointly developed with UEMOA as a replacement for different forms used by their member states.

Furthermore, ECOWAS is working on the creation of a West African Monetary Zone, with a common currency and a common central bank. Travellers from an ECOWAS state can use local currency in lieu of foreign exchange; all countries adopted this programme, with the exception of Liberia and Sierra Leone (ECA 2006).

The movement of persons and the rights of residence and establishment within UEMOA are fully harmonized with ECOWAS, including the introduction of a common passport. Since 1975 one of the aims of this regional organization has been the removal of obstacles to the free movement of people (Preamble and Art. 27). This idea was further pursued in 1979 with the ECOWAS Protocol on Free Movement of Persons and the Right of Residence and Establishment, but also, in 1992, with the revision of the treaty. ECOWAS launched an ECOWAS passport in 2000, to be used alongside the Travel Certificate.

In 2001, ECOWAS adopted a Political Declaration and an Action Plan against Trafficking. The Plan of Action commits ECOWAS countries to urgent action against trafficking of persons. It calls for countries to ratify and fully implement crucial international instruments of ECOWAS and the United Nations that strengthen laws against human trafficking and protect victims of trafficking, especially women and children. The Action Plan calls for new special police units to combat trafficking of persons. Training for police, customs and immigration officials, prosecutors and judges is also an important aim. This training will focus on the methods used in preventing such trafficking, prosecuting the traffickers, and protecting the rights of victims, including protecting the victims from the traffickers. It will take into account human rights and child- and gender-sensitive issues, and encourage cooperation with non-governmental organizations and other elements of civil society. Under the Plan, ECOWAS states will set up direct communication between their border control agencies and expand efforts to gather data on human trafficking. The information gathered will be shared between all ECOWAS countries and the United Nations. States will create a task force or agency on trafficking in persons, as a focal point to direct and monitor the on-going implementation of this Plan of Action at the national level, and report, on a bi-annual basis, to the ECOWAS coordination structure set up within the ECOWAS Secretariat.

After a recent (2007) reorganization, ECOWAS labour and social affairs are now the responsibility of the Commission for Human Development and Gender within which there is a Department of Humanitarian and Social Affairs. This Department focuses upon labour policy, health policy and social service reform. There is a joint ECOWAS/ECCAS Plan of Action on Trafficking in Persons and an ECOWAS Child Protection Programme.

The treaty of ECOWAS permitted the establishment under Article 14 of an Economic and Social Council, although this has yet to be established. There is, however, a Forum for Associations Recognized by ECOWAS (FARE) which is made up of NGOs with no apparent links with the regional trade unions. Within the projected work programme of the Humanitarian and Social Affairs Department there is a plan to establish a Social Dialogue Forum in 2009. This initiative derives from a joint ECOWAS–ILO meeting in December 2007 which was part of the implementation of the ECOWAS–ILO Memorandum of Understanding signed in 2005. The meeting initially had the aspiration of establishing an Economic, Labour and Social Affairs Commission of ECOWAS to 'replace' the Human Development Technical Committee but it retreated to the idea of this Social Dialogue Forum.

Under the ECOWAS Treaty, Article 61 encourages the harmonization of labour laws and social security legislation. A meeting of ECOWAS experts on labour was held in Abuja from 19 to 20 September 2005. Six member states (Benin, Côte d'Ivoire, Guinea, Mali, Nigeria and Togo) and six organizations were represented at this meeting. One of its outcomes was a proposed framework for the implementation of the ECOWAS priority programmes on labour matters. Furthermore, the meeting recommended, among other actions, the 'commissioning of a study on issues involved in the formulation of a labour policy for ECOWAS Region'. This study was commissioned. A subsequent ECOWAS experts meeting in March 2008, convened to develop an ECOWAS Labour Policy and Strategic Plan, received a report on the study from the Lagos consultant who recommended a labour policy. The final report of the consultant was delivered on 12 July 2008. It was the intention of the Social Affairs Department of ECOWAS to take it to a meeting of ECOWAS Ministers of Labour in late 2008. The draft report (and presumably the final report) comprises an exhaustive and comprehensive set of recommendations for an ECOWAS labour policy in line with ILO policy and based on consultations with ILO colleagues in Geneva. It also calls for a Regional Social Fund. It makes a strong case that the Organisation pour l'Harmonisation en Afrique du Droit des Affairs

(OHADA) draft labour law might be a possible model for parts of an ECOWAS labour policy.

The first meeting of the ECOWAS Ministers of Social Development took place in 2007 and called for the drafting of an ECOWAS Social Charter (cf. the SADC). This too is in the 2009 projected work programme of the Social Affairs Department of ECOWAS.

Among other aspects of the work of the Social Affairs Department of ECOWAS are: (i) work on an ECOWAS Social Security Convention. This was initiated in 1993, picked up again in 2003, adopted by the ECOWAS Ministers of Labour in June 2006, discussed at experts meetings in 2006 and 2008, and is intended to be popularized and disseminated in 2009; (ii) following the ECOWAS Protocol on Education and Training in 2001, work is taking place on the harmonization of education certificates across the three language groups; and (iii) endorsement of the recent establishment of the UNESCO-sponsored Cape Verde Regional Studies Centre.

At the meeting of the heads of state and government of ECOWAS in Ouagadougou in January 2008, participants demonstrated their determination to address the pervasive poverty in the region with the adoption of a poverty reduction strategy document, which proposes a mix of initiatives and programmes to be undertaken at various levels. Concretely it resolved to:

1 Adopt the ECOWAS Common Approach on Migration, a multi-sectoral regional mechanism for addressing the challenges of intra-community mobility and migration to third countries. The mechanism incorporates the regional development dimensions of migration, especially the development of points of departure of migrants as well as the formulation of a regional territorial planning strategy. Furthermore, the meeting set up an ad hoc ministerial committee with responsibility for migration and urged member states to take necessary measures to remove all existing obstacles to intra-community movement of the citizens of the region;
2 on the issue of the EPAs being negotiated with the European Union, to continue to negotiate as a bloc. Participants directed the ECOWAS Commission to convene a meeting of member states to agree an appropriate regional framework on the EPA. The meeting will also make proposals on the outstanding issues in connection with the introduction of a region-wide Common External Tariff (CET). They further said the agreement should contribute to the realization of its integration objectives, enhances regional development, reduce poverty, contribute to employment and take cognizance of the development concerns of the region;
3 approve the creation of a West African Institute on Regional Integration which will be based in Cape Verde and charged with promoting research on regional integration and social dialogue.

ECOWAS also has established a Court of Justice in Abuja, initially to resolve disputes between states although it now receives individual complaints. Indeed

90 per cent of cases now submitted to the Court are human rights cases. Significantly, a case brought before the Court in April 2007 concerned a former slave in Niger. The case is being brought before the ECOWAS Court of Justice on the grounds that Niger has violated its obligations under the Treaty of ECOWAS, the African Charter of Human and People's Rights, the International Covenant of Civil and Political Rights, the Convention for the Elimination of All Forms of Discrimination Against Women, the African Charter on the Rights and Welfare of the Child, the Slavery Convention and the Supplementary Convention on the Abolition of Slavery, the Slave Trade, and Institutions and Practices Similar to Slavery. Niger has ratified all of these conventions. The Court criticized Niger for the enslavement and upheld the complaint.

The Union Economique et Monétaire Ouest Africaine (West African Economic and Monetary Union)

UEMOA was established in 1994 and its member states are Benin, Burkina Faso, Côte d'Ivoire, Guinea Bissau, Mali, Niger, Senegal and Togo. It is based in Ouagadougou, Burkina Faso. It was preceded by several agreements on customs and monetary issues, also involving France. The aim of UEMOA is to create an enabling environment and to attain full economic and financial integration based on the pre-existing monetary union (the CFA franc zone) and a customs union (CU). All member states are also members of ECOWAS. The main objectives are to harmonize the legal environment, to convert the economic policies of the member states and to coordinate the policies on human resources, transport and communication, environment, agriculture, energy, industry and mines.

In 1996, the member states of UEMOA adopted the Community Preferential Tariff Agreement. In accordance with this document, internal tariffs have been fully eliminated on agricultural commodities and traditional handicrafts in the region. In 1998, the Community Compensation and Solidarity Fund was established, pooling 1 per cent of external duties in order to compensate some of the member states for the loss of customs revenue arising from the reduction of tariffs on intra-community trade and to 'provide a cohesion mechanism aimed at reducing disparities within the region' (Dinka and Kennes 2007: 74).

In addition, UEMOA started to harmonize its policies on other areas like agriculture and industry and adopted a convergence agenda in the areas of sector and macro-economic policy coordination and harmonization, all conducive to a regional common market (ECA 2006).

Reflections on regional social policy in West and Southern Africa

The UNU-CRIS Report commissioned by the International Training Centre of the ILO (Deacon *et al.* 2008), upon which much of section is based, reflected that strong political will at the highest levels and strong adherence by civil society at the base are very much needed in order to build regional integration with a social dimension successfully. The actual role played by regional organizations, beyond the declarations and intentions, is in practice limited in scope and implementation because the technical human resource capacity is insufficiently available. A major condition for deep regional integration, beyond political will, is available expertise and institutional capacity. Both major organizations, ECOWAS and the SADC certainly have a highly qualified core team but this is a very small group of leading experts and managers in key areas such as political affairs, health, education, macro-economic policies and labour issues.

When it comes to institutional capacity, the same limitation is valid for the social partners in the tripartite set-up. Neither labour unions nor employers' organizations dispose as yet of strong regional representations. The most important structural lack of capacity is in the informal sectors, which are large and predominant in most member states. Informal sectors lack institutional fora for negotiations and representation by suitable leaders as they are reluctant to take time off for fear of losing income. The need for stronger regional representation and intensive capability efforts at regional level are obvious. There are some more positive signs in terms of a broader civil society organized across borders, especially in South Africa. Migration is also a huge challenge but could be part of the solution, as stated in the ECOWAS approach to migration. As there is not yet a strong supranational enforcing authority for migration issues, migration needs specific well-designed strategies and policy-making at regional level and this should be well monitored.

African Union social policy framework

The Commissioner for Labour and Social Affairs of the African Union had been keen for some time to develop a focus for political discussion of social development and hence social policy issues in Africa separately from the ongoing tripartite-based Labour Ministers' meetings. This was partly because of the non-acceptance by the tripartite Labour Ministers' meetings of earlier drafts of the social policy framework for Africa. Therefore, in 2008 the Commissioner commissioned a draft to be presented to the first ever meeting of Ministers of Social Development held in Windhoek, Namibia, in October 2008. The process leading to the draft tabled at the meeting was interesting for the tension it embodied between a wish on the part of the Commissioner to draft an African social policy as distinct from an ILO or UNICEF or EU social policy on the one hand and the actual involvement of some of these Northern-based players in the drafting process on the other.

Before the conference the DfID, GTZ and SIDA had been instrumental in funding Help Age International to run a two-year campaign for social protection and universal social pensions in Africa with a series of six sub-regional meetings. Help Age, UNICEF, UNU-CRIS in the shape of the author of this chapter, and several Northern social policy scholars were invited to a pre-meeting in Windhoek to comment upon the draft social policy framework and feed recommendations into the ministers' meeting. At the same time at the actual meeting of ministers, Brazil, Venezuela and other Southern countries were present arguing for the relevance of South–South exchange based on the Latin America conditional cash transfers experience. The issue of how to inject policies on social protection and on regional and sub-regional social policy into the draft became a matter of some controversy involving North–South and South–South dialogues.

The main purpose of the Social Policy Framework for Africa (SPF) as agreed at the 2008 meeting,

> is to provide an overarching policy structure to assist AU Member States in the development of their national social policies to promote human empowerment and development in their ongoing quest to address the multiple social issues facing their societies. The SPF moves away from treating social development as subordinate to economic growth. Rather, the framework justifies social development as a goal in its own right. It acknowledges that while economic growth is a necessary condition of social development, it is not exclusively or sufficiently able to address the challenges posed by the multi-faceted socio-economic and political forces that together generate the continent's social development challenges.
>
> (AU 2008b: Para. 15)

The theme of cross-border cooperation in social policy was inserted into the SPF at the suggestion of the delegate from UNU-CRIS who was invited to the pre-meeting of global experts held the days before the main Ministerial Conference. On the floor of the Ministerial Conference an UNDESA official lent further support to this approach, as did the UNESCO delegation. All of these interventions at this event flowed from the earlier involvement by UNDESA, UNESCO and UNU-CRIS in discussions about African regional social policy.

The relevant part of the agreed text addresses the social consequences of free trade agreements in the context of globalization. It reads:

> There are social consequences of this economic and trade driven process including: (a) job loss as well as creation, (b) the erosion of the power of national bargaining rights, (c) the possible lowering of labour and social standards, and (d) the variable impact on the prices of food and [goods of] basic necessity. While economic integration is essential, it will not respond to Africa's development challenges without corresponding social integration. Hence, Ministers of Social Development must engage in the process of regional trade negotiations with the EU and other trading partners in order to ensure these social consequences of regional trade are addressed in the negotiating process. Thus, Continental and Regional social policies need to be developed at the same time.
>
> These policies, led by the AU and the Regional Economic Communities (RECs), can support the process of socio-economic integration by enhancing the productivity of the African labour force, providing regional social cohesion and peace, and enabling the integration of the regional labour

> markets through the portability of social security rights and benefits. Regional social policies can also benefit from economies of scale by facilitating in cross-border investments and sharing of regional health and education specialist resources.
>
> Indeed, the adoption of the Abuja Treaty, the Sirte Declaration and the Constitutive Act of the African Union reflect the considerable importance which African Leaders attach to regional integration as a strategy for meeting the challenges of development in the twenty-first century. The adoption of the Social Policy Framework by the AU and the Johannesburg Declaration towards an African Regional Social Policy by the SADC, bears testimony to that fact.
>
> (AU 2008b: Section 2.2.17, Paras 23, 24 and 25)

Among the associated recommendations to countries are the following:

> a Provide basic social security, retrain workers for growing sectors and improve access to market orientated skills and credit for entrepreneurs to effectively respond to challenges of globalization;
> b Increase inter-governmental cross border cooperation in sector investments and programmes in the fields of employment, education, health, social protection, housing and utilities;
> c Increase inter-governmental cross-border co-operation on policies, which address *social issues and social problems* such as poverty and social exclusion. Such policies should promote regional social justice and equity, social solidarity and social integration (e.g. establishment of regional social funds or regional disaster mitigation funds, and the development of regional regulations of labour markets and utilities and health and education services);
> d Member States to increase cooperation to protect human rights and fundamental freedoms (e.g. by establishing sub-regional charters of human and social rights and regional observatories to monitor progress).
>
> (AU 2008b: Para. 2.2.17)

The Regional Economic Communities within Africa are then charged to:

> a Establish a regional Coordinating Mechanism to promote follow up, monitoring, evaluation and reporting on the implementation of the SPF and all regional social issues.
> b Establish, where they do not exist, social development desks to disseminate and popularize the SPF, and lead the agenda for social policy in the region.
> c Work closely with Member States and other stakeholders to adopt and implement the key recommendations of the SPF.
> d Leverage resource mobilization to meet additional needs identified by Member States in implementing the key recommendations of the SPF.

e Collaborate and exchange information with the African Union Commission on all matters related to social issues and policies in the region.
f Establish a process for best practice learning and cross-border mechanisms in the sector of social policy.

(AU 2008b: Para. 3.3.2)

Conclusions

In sum, there is no shortage of players both within Africa and outside placing the issue of regional social policy on the agendas of governments and regional economic commissions. The continent now abounds with declarations on the theme that sometimes go far beyond the actual achievements. However, there are some significant advances in the development of regional and sub-regional social policies that are remarkable for their development in unpropitious circumstances. Among these may be listed:

- agreements on the free cross-border movements of labour in ECOWAS and UEMOA and moves towards this in the SADC;
- the Regional Court of Justice in ECOWAS adjudicating on national labour rights;
- Charters of Social Rights in the sub-regions;
- cross-border cooperation in health in terms of both disease control and service;
- cross-border cooperation in education and agreements on skills portability;
- the use by UEMOA of customs duties to address regional disparities;
- cross-border social security conventions on portability of rights;
- meetings of Ministers of Social Development at sub-regional level to compare national practices;
- effective sub-regional social dialogue mechanisms and processes in place especially in Southern Africa.

This chapter has focused only on South and West Africa. Similar arrangements exist in East and North Africa but have not been documented here.

Thus, whether it is regional or sub-regional redistribution, regional or sub-regional social regulation, regional or sub-regional social rights or simply cross-border cooperation in social sector investments or cross-border lesson learning, Africa exhibits examples of each type of regional social policy.

The problem remains, however, one of overcoming low national and regional capacity in the social sectors, combined with the difficulty, particularly in Southern Africa, of confronting the very real cross-border problems of labour migration between countries of very different living standards. It is also an open question whether external players (the EU in particular) seeking to direct, in their own interests, regional integration on the African continent have the best interests of regional social development of Africa at heart.

Notes

1 The author originally commissioned to write this chapter was unable to fulfil the commitment. It has been compiled by me from a number of sources that are referenced as appropriate. A major part of the chapter is a reproduction of a section of the UNU-CRIS Working Paper 2008/13 by Bob Deacon, Karel Van Hoestenberghe, Philippe De Lombaerde and Maria Cristina Macovei (2008) *Regional Integration, Decent Work, and Labour and Social Policies in West and Southern Africa.* This paper was prepared as part of the UNU-CRIS/ITC-ILO project on regional integration, economic partnership agreements and their impact on employment and labour market policies – an awareness and capacity development project.

2 This section is heavily based on 'Africa's Regional Integration Arrangements: History and Challenges' (Dinka and Kennes 2007).

3 Decision: AHG/Dec.166 (XXXVII).

4 Decision: Assembly/AU/Dec.20 (II).

5 Eight RECs are accredited to the AU: ECOWAS, COMESA, ECCAS, SADC, AMU, IGAD, CEN-SAD, EAC (First Conference of African Ministers of Economic Integration in March 2006, Ouagadougou, Burkina Faso, CAMEI/Consol. Report (I)).

6 www.ilo.org/public/english/standards/relm/rgmeet/africa.htm.

7 ILO: AfRM/XI/D.3 (Rev).

8 See NEPAD website: www.nepad.org.

9 http://www.stopepa.org.

10 http://www.tni.org.

11 http://agritrade.cta.int/en/content/view/full/3081.

12 ATN is a coalition of pan-African civil society groups involved in trade issues and EJN is a coalition of civil society groups in Ghana.

13 http://www.bilaterals.org/article.php3?id_article=881.

14 http://www.europeafrica.info/eu/documents/epa-interim-agreement-a-dangerous-trojan-horse.

15 http://www.europeafrica.info/eu/documents/epa-interim-agreement-a-dangerous-trojan-horse.

Part III

Regional social integration and global social governance

9 The evolving context of world-regional social policy

Nicola Yeates, Maria Cristina Macovei and Luk Van Langenhove

Introduction

This chapter addresses a number of issues that have a bearing upon the prospects for the development of regional formations with a strong social agenda and effective social policies but which were not the focus of attention in the earlier chapters in this book. These issues include those developments which might *undermine* such regional social policy – e.g. the inter-regional open trading formations such as the Asia Pacific Economic Cooperation (APEC), the Free Trade Area of the Americas (FTAA), and the bilateral trading arrangements made between the United States of America, the European Union (EU), China and Japan and individual countries. Such issues also include the inter-regional dialogues and support processes which might *reinforce* such regional social policies, taking place on a North–South basis as between, for example, the EU and MERCOSUR, the EU and ASEAN+3, the Asia–Europe Meeting (ASEM), the EU and the African Union (AU), the Southern African Development Community (SADC), and the Maghreb. The EU Economic Partnership Agreements (EPAs) with the group of African, Caribbean and Pacific countries (ACP) are also discussed as both *reinforcing* and, in the view of critics, *undermining* regional social policies.

The chapter is framed around two questions. The first question concerns the social policy content of these processes: what social welfare and development concerns are raised by these processes and how are such concerns being addressed? The second question concerns the relationship between these trade formations and world-regional social policy: how do these formations impact on the prospects for the emergence of world-regional social policy supportive of social development?

Discussion of these cross-cutting developments in relation to world-regional social policy formation unfolds across three main sections. The chapter opens by reviewing the different forms of trading formations at the regional and inter-regional level, together with bilateral trade pacts and regimes that bear upon the prospects for world-regional social policy. Here we review arguments and evidence suggesting they may have detrimental effects on the development of world-regional social policy. The chapter then proceeds to examine the social dimensions of North–South inter-regional dialogues. Its focus in particular lies with such dialogues involving the EU, especially those involving EPAs with developing countries. The chapter then turns to three trans-regional agreements – APEC, Forum for East Asia Latin America Cooperation (FEALAC) and ASEM. There, we outline the extent of their engagement with social policy issues, and come to a preliminary assessment of whether they are supportive of injecting a social dimension into regionalism or an obstacle to such a development. The conclusion returns to the two key questions we set out above in the light of the chapter discussion.

The evolving context of world-regionalism

Any evaluation of the prospects of world-regions becoming sites of developmental social policies needs to take account of the range of ways in which state and non-state actors are mobilizing through regionalist and other fora. It needs to consider the extent to which these alternatives are complementary to or competing with the pursuance of social and other policy objectives through world-regional formations. Here we briefly review two sets of key developments that directly bear on this assessment: first, a trend towards world-regions and inter-regional cooperation, and second, the increasing use of bilateral preferential trade agreements as a means of achieving trade liberalization.

Emergent trends in regionalism

First, regional formations are expanding their membership, leading to the emergence of world-regions encompassing dozens of member countries and hundreds of millions of people. Examples here include the EU, whose membership has doubled over the last three decades and whose fifth and most recent round of expansion swelled the numbers of member states to twenty-seven and inhabitants to 500 million; it is set to further expand within the next few years. Another example is APEC, a multilateral economic and trade forum, which currently encompasses twenty-one Pacific Ocean countries and more than one-third of the world's population (2.6 billion) and which is also set to expand further in 2010. Smaller (in terms of member states) organizations are also expanding: SAARC, for example, recently (2007) expanded to eight member states when Afghanistan joined, and proposals are afoot to include China; such a move would double SAARC's population to three billion people. In 2005 the Greater Arab Free Trade Area (GAFTA) came into existence. It was set up by the Arab League as part of a vision to establish a Euro-Mediterranean free trade area encompassing EU member states, Arab Maghreb states and Middle East states. Alongside the expansion of extant regional formations are proposals to establish new and bigger regional trade blocs, the best known of which is the US-led FTAA which, if it had been realized, would have spanned thirty-four North, Central and South American nations and 750 million people.

Second, a new category of regional cooperation has emerged, involving formal cooperation ties among distinct regional formations acting as single powers. It is a development in which the EU has been especially active. Relations between regional groupings occur on a North–South basis (e.g. EU–ASEAN, EU–Gulf Cooperation Council, EU–MERCOSUR, SAARC–EU, EU–CARICOM and EU–SADC) and on a South–South basis (e.g. MERCOSUR–SACU, SAARC–ASEAN and MERCOSUR–ASEAN). Modes of cooperation vary, with some based on framework cooperation agreements (e.g. EU–ASEAN, EU–MERCOSUR), while others involve meetings at ministerial and senior official level and collaboration around activities and programmes focused on specific issues (Hänggi 2000, Söderbaum and Van Langenhove 2005).[1]

A third trend is the emergence of trans-regional formations. The business of these large formations proceeds through summits and ministerial meetings, joint projects and programmes. Trans-regional formations differ from relations between regional groupings in that membership is more diffuse, may not coincide with regional formations in terms of membership, and may involve participants from more than two regions; also, states participate in an individual capacity (though there may be some regional coordination). The emergence of this category of regionalism began in the context of cooperation amongst the Triad (Western Europe, the US, Japan and the 'dragon communities' of Asia) but has spread to other regions in recent years. Five trans-regional linkages can be identified: APEC (1989), ASEM (1996), Europe–Latin America Rio Summit (1999), Africa–Europe Cairo Summit (2000), and FEALAC (2001) (Hänggi 2000, Olivet 2005).[2] Only APEC has a dedicated (if modest) secretariat. Fitting with regionalisms, the main axis of cooperation closely revolves around economic (trade) concerns, with two provisos. First, EU participation in such fora involves a political dialogue and elements of socio-cultural and development cooperation. Second, APEC, which otherwise has a firm identity as a multilateral economic and trade forum, has recently begun explicitly discussing social policy issues facing its 'member economies'. For example, in 2007 it committed to a three-year Initiative on Ageing Issues.[3]

These three developments present a number of challenges for regional social policy. In particular, to what extent are institutionalized regions that currently have, or which might develop, a social dimension cut across by regional trade arrangements that exist essentially as trading blocs and which downplay social equity and development dimensions? In the case of the EU, competition with more open trading arrangements (such as APEC) is putting a strain on its social dimension, with some EU countries restricting access to labour markets and social services by legal intra-EU migrant workers (Yeates and Deacon 2006). In the Latin American context, this was played out as concerns over whether regional regimes with relatively developed social dimensions, such as MERCOSUR, would survive the FTAA which was only committed to liberalization. The concerns were not only about the different models of economic integration (MERCOSUR aims at the free movement of production factors, while the FTAA is based on the North American Free Trade Agreement (NAFTA) and concerned with market access) but also about the absence of a positive social agenda in the FTAA and the detrimental social effects of a model of liberalization premised solely on market access. From the vantage point of 2009 such predictions seem somewhat outdated due to the serious stalling of the FTAA process, due to the mobilization of multilateralist social forces 'from below' to oppose it, combined with the resurgence of social democratic leftist governments in the region – forces that are articulating alternative regionalist visions there as well as in other regions (see Chapter 4 above).[4] This is not to say, however, that the concerns have no relevance or that the challenges to regional social policy have disappeared: the use of bilateral agreements as a means of pursuing free trade liberalization strategies on the part of the US in the region are a particular cause for concern.

Finally, progress in the development of strengthened regionalism with a social dimension will be influenced by two kinds of inter-regional dialogue: a North–South one and a South–South one. One question here is whether Northern regions such as the EU are putting their narrow trade interests ahead of their responsibility to promote positive social policy in Southern formations. Another question is how South–South dialogues are being used to strengthen the development of stronger regional social policies. The discussion picks up the questions relating to the EU on pp. 197–202. Regrettably, South–South issues lie outside the scope of this chapter.

The rise of bilateralism

Alongside these trends in regionalism must be situated the resurgence of bilateral free (preferential) trade agreements[5] in recent years. In common with trade agreements more generally, the present generation of bilateral negotiations and agreements go beyond issues of tariffs and trade of goods alone. They encompass trade-related issues, notably trade in services, investment, intellectual property, trade facilitation and competition. Although the use of bilateral trade agreements never completely disappeared in the post-Second World War period (e.g. it has been part of the established practice of the EU since the 1950s), a major driver behind the increasing use of bilateral agreements in recent years is the failure of progress at the multilateral/WTO trade talks in Cancun in September 2003. The US has been a key actor here, using bilaterals to promote trade liberalization across the Middle East, Asia, South America and Africa.[6]

In the context of such relative lack of progress in multilateral trade negotiations, bilateral agreements offer many advantages to negotiating parties. In a way not totally dissimilar to regional trade agreements, bilateral agreements offer greater flexibility in the sense that they are easier and quicker to conclude simply because a smaller number of countries are involved. As Choudry (2008) argues, 'Governments have preferred bilateral labour agreements (BLAs), usually sectoral, giving them more flexibility, control and regulatory discretion over multilateral agreements'. Finally, of course, not to be discounted is the balance of power among negotiating parties changes in bilateral negotiations, enabling the stronger party to exercise power over its negotiating counterpart; in particular, bilateral negotiations mean that governments can bypass the kinds of political alliances that emerge in multilateral negotiations (as among Southern governments against Northern ones at the WTO) (Choudry 2008).

In principle, there is no reason why bilateral agreements cannot be instruments to improve social standards. As they are not part of multilateral/WTO agreements they can go further than anything such agreements could have offered. In this regard, the Global Union Research Network (GURN) (2008) comments positively on recent US free trade agreements with Panama and Peru, agreements that include a commitment to international (ILO) standards in terms of respect for these standards and labour law and enforcement mechanisms. These agreements stand out, however, among an otherwise bad lot. Different regional powers' approaches to bilateral negotiations can also potentially drive up standards and lead to a broader developmental approach not recognized within multilateral agreements.

While both the US and EU have included labour protection in their bilateral agreements they have taken very different approaches. The US has focused on core labour standards in its FTAs but the mechanism has been different from one agreement to another. The EU has varied in its approach, with older agreements focusing on core standards, and newer agreements including a 'sustainable development approach that includes but goes beyond core labour standards' (GURN 2008).

With this flexibility comes variability, then, and the problem of course is that bilateral agreements have the potential of driving down standards as much as they can uplift them. The potential of bilateral agreements to undercut multilateral (global or regional) social and trade agreements is noticed by defenders of multilateralism. For advocates of liberalized free trade, bilateral agreements pose a serious threat to multilateral liberalization based on the Most Favoured Nation (MFN) principle, and create what Bhagwati (2008) calls the 'spaghetti bowl problem': fragmented, criss-crossing agreements that create a chaotic system of discriminatory tariffs. They also pose distinct technical and political problems in the event of an attempt to consolidate bilateral agreements into a region-wide free trade agreement. Far from being building blocks to regional or global agreements, bilaterals are, from this perspective, a road block.

The proliferation of bilateral agreements signals the introduction of variable standards and the possibility of undercutting global pacts. Individual country deals allow governments to selectively invoke aspects of multilateral trade agreements in ways that favour the more powerful party involved. Since bilateral free trade agreements are about market access for the more powerful country, its potential to negotiate deals to its own advantage is accentuated. As Choudry (2008) notes in the context of the labour dimensions of trade in services, although US FTAs (such as the ones concluded with Singapore and Chile) allow temporary entry of business professionals from other parties to facilitate trade in services, the US approaches each trade deal individually to determine if a temporary entry chapter will benefit US trade in services. In addition, as the International Confederation of Free Trade Unions (ICFTU) (2008: 5) notes, 'Public services are not excluded from bilateral trade negotiations. Given the "negative list" approach in bilaterals, they will therefore be included automatically, unless provisions are made in specific bilaterals for them to be exempted'. An example worth noting in this regard is the Australia–US Free Trade Agreement: this included water, a service deemed to be excludable from the WTO's General Agreement on Trade in Services (GATS) due to its public goods properties (Hawthorne 2007). In the health context, the US–Peru bilateral agreement includes a provision on data exclusivity that effectively more than doubles the cost of generic medicines and potentially reduces access to such medicines, a development about which both the Special Rapporteur for the UN on the Right to Health and a WHO commission have expressed concern, while the US–Thailand Free Trade Agreement is cited as an example of how developing countries are being persuaded 'to barter away their patent-breaking rights [confirmed by the 2001 Doha Declaration] in exchange for lucrative trade benefits' (Cheng 2007). On the role of the US in particular, Sinclair and Traynor (2004) note in relation to the US government's post-2003 strategy of 'competitive liberalization':

> The U.S. administration employs bilaterals to set legal precedents that it can then replicate and expand in succeeding negotiations. Moreover, once a government has signed a bilateral deal based with the US, there is little point in it opposing similar provisions and commitments in the FTAA talks or in multilateral negotiations, including the WTO Doha round.
>
> (Sinclair and Traynor 2004: xiii)

It is not just global (and regional) trade agreements and the social gains negotiated within them that are undercut by bilateral agreements: adherence to established international social law is by no means a feature of all bilateral agreements purportedly 'protecting' labour standards. Indeed, many only require participating governments to protect labour to domestic standards that do not otherwise fully conform with international law (here the US–Jordan bilateral can be cited as a case in point[7]), many also include a commitment not to weaken labour protection in a way that affects international trade and investment between the two signatories (KFTU 2008).

North–South inter-regional dialogues

The North–South dialogue comprises two strands. The first strand is the United States (US)–South 'dialogue' which is being driven by the US to open up all world regions to either broader trading blocs that involve the US (APEC, FTAA) or to bilateral trade deals with the US. This strand, we suggest, spells disaster for regional social protectionism in the South. The second strand is the EU–Southern Regionalism dialogue that is a little more complex. On the one hand, it contains features present in the US–South dialogue where a Southern regionalism is being encouraged to open up trade links with the EU to its advantage (Keet and Bello 2004); on the other hand, it involves an inter-regional policy dialogue that seems to be motivated to spread the message of the importance of developing a social dimension to regional trading arrangements.

Among the North–South processes is the European Union's engagement via the EU–Gulf Cooperation Council, EU–MERCOSUR, EU–SAARC, EU–CARICOM and EU–SACU (Southern African Customs Union). The EU also engages with Asian countries (ASEAN 7 (Brunei, Indonesia, Malaysia, the Philippines, Singapore, Thailand and Vietnam) plus China, Japan and South Korea) through ASEM.

At the level of inter-regionalism, collaboration around social policy issues is mostly confined to information exchange, though there are occasional notable examples of more substantial collaboration relating to the development of institutional capacity. While Asia has resisted European advice (Rüland 2002), other regional formations have been more receptive. The EU has funded a training centre for regional integration in MERCOSUR and has helped strengthen the secretariats of MERCOSUR and the SADC (Deacon 2001). The EU–CARICOM health partnership entails the provision of services and technical assistance by the EU to strengthen institutional responses to HIV/AIDS amongst CARICOM member states (Yeates 2005). Similarly, the EU missions inside the SADC and MERCOSUR have capacity-building and training elements to them that do not seem primarily motivated by protecting the trading interests of the EU (Farrell 2004).

In part, this conundrum reflects the ambiguity of the role of the EU on the world stage in relation to globalization. Is it possible to characterize the response of the EU as a whole as a reaction to the pressures of a liberalizing globalization? To what extent has the EU used its position as a globally powerful player to push for socially responsible globalization? The response of the EU to neo-liberal globalization in terms of both its internal and its external social policy has been variable over time and between component parts of the EU system (Deacon 1999, 2007, Orbie and Tortell 2009). Certainly if the EU wishes to extend its influence to help construct a world of regions with a strong social dimension in order to counter global neo-liberalism then it will have to put its social development policy before its trade interests and it will have to match its moralizing about rights with resource transfers to enable these rights to be realized in practice. The tension between EU trade interests and the EU interest in promoting universal labour and social standards is illustrated in the case of the EU EPAs with the ACP countries discussed below.

North–South regional social policy dialogues: the case of the EU[8]

During the last decade, there has been an increasing emphasis within the EU on inter-regionalism (region-to-region relations) as a foundation for its external policies. This foreign policy 'doctrine' is deeply rooted in the European Commission and has become a key feature of the relations between the EU and other regions in many parts of the world. The EU recognizes that the incorporation of labour standards into FTAs with third countries or regional groupings is politically sensitive because developing countries fear that such provisions could be used as a form of protectionism (Dasgupta 2000). Since 1992, the EU has included a human rights clause in all agreements with third countries. The clause defines respect for human rights and democracy (as laid out in the Universal Declaration on Human Rights) as an 'essential element'. A violation of human rights permits the EU to terminate the agreement or suspend its operation in whole or in part.

Regarding non-core labour standards, the EU takes a more flexible approach and encourages countries to adopt those standards according to their socio-economic level of development. Many countries have already adopted multilateral obligations concerning ILO labour standards but frequently fall short of proper implementation in their domestic economies. To encourage better implementation and monitoring, the EU offers special incentives through its unilateral Generalized System of Preferences (GSP). The Community GSP scheme provides market access on a preferential basis to developing countries. As stated in the European Commission (2001) communication, *Promoting Core Labour Standards and Improving Social Governance in the Context of Globalization*, the GSP mechanism addresses the issue of core labour standards by 'providing a positive incentive scheme. Within this scheme, effective compliance with core labour standards qualifies for additional trade preferences – the ILO Conventions on freedom of association and the right to collective bargaining and those on child labour – and 'allowing for a withdrawal, in whole or part, where beneficiary countries practise any form of slavery or forced labour' (European Commission 2001). Moreover, the Communication states that in a future review of the GSP scheme, a priority would be to enhance the possibilities to use the GSP incentives to promote core labour standards. The revised GSP scheme (GSP+) came into force in 2004, when the Commission issued the Communication *Developing Countries, International Trade and Sustainable Development: the Function of the Community's GSP for the Ten-year Period from 2006 to 2015* (European Communication 2004). The novelty is that the Commission proposes a new incentive for sustainable development and good management of public affairs by replacing the separate drugs, social and environment special arrangements with a single new category: GSP+. The new scheme will provide special incentives for countries which have signed up to the main international agreements on social rights, environmental protection, governance, and combating the production of and trafficking in illegal drugs.[9] The developing country willing to apply to GSP+ has to comply with the international labour rights conventions, including the core labour standards endorsed in the 1998 ILO Declaration of Fundamental Principles and Rights at Work.

The promotion of core labour standards and social dialogue are foreseen in all the EU's most recent bilateral and regional trade agreements with the developing countries. The agreements signed with Chile, and the Africa, Caribbean and Pacific (ACP) countries are examples in this sense. The fact that these agreements make the ILO's standards a point of reference is not a matter of dispute (Granger and Siroën 2006). The EU–South Africa agreement of 1999 refers to the ILO standards as the point of reference for the development of social rights. However, the negotiations with ACP countries have become an issue of dispute, as discussed below.

In Asia, the EU is engaged in strong inter-regional relations with ASEAN, and additionally offers support for SAARC, focused on trade integration among South Asian countries. The EU's exchanges with ASEAN gave birth to a new institutional framework of inter-regional multidimensional relations in the form of ASEM in 1996. The historic ASEM 5 Summit held in Hanoi in October 2004 marked the enlargement of ASEM from twenty-six to thirty-nine partners through the accession of the ten new EU member states and three new countries from ASEAN that were not yet part of the process: Cambodia, Laos and Burma/ Myanmar (discussion of the social policy dimensions of ASEM is given on pp. 206–9 below).

Regarding Latin-America, the EU has developed two levels of inter-regionalism: namely the EU and Latin America and the Caribbean countries (EU–LAC), and the EU and Latin America (the Rio Group),[10] and bi-regional agreements that the EU has with MERCOSUR, the Andean Community and CARICOM. The most developed relationship is with MERCOSUR through the EU–MERCOSUR Interregional Framework Cooperation Agreement and the EU has prepared the ground towards the opening of negotiations on Association Agreements with Central America and the Andean Community.

The relations between the EU and Latin America and the Caribbean were entrenched in 1999, during the first official Summit held at Rio de Janeiro that ended with a declaration of the intention to create a bi-regional strategic partnership. The Summit in 2004 at Guadalajara in Mexico focused mainly on issues concerning combining economic growth with social justice and poverty reduction. Social cohesion became the common policy objective and an important feature of the EU–LAC relationship. Moreover, the final declaration claims that the partners should 'prioritize social cohesion as one of the main elements of the bi-regional strategic partnership and have committed ourselves to cooperate to eradicate poverty, inequality and social exclusion' (European Commission 2007b: 22). This statement was reinforced at the Vienna Summit in 2006 when the partners committed themselves to 'continue to give social cohesion a high priority in our bi-regional cooperation and assistance programmes'. Following the EU–LAC Summit in Guadalajara in 2004, the Andean Community (CAN) adopted a new Integrated Social Development Plan, which addresses social cohesion. It is important to underline that the bottom-up approach with inputs of national monitoring 'mirrors the open method of coordination applied by the EU in the social field' (European Commission 2007b: 16).

In 2004, the EU set up an assistance programme to implement social policies – EUROsociAL – among other objectives. The five-year programme costing 30 million euro foresees assistance from the European Commission to Latin America to develop and implement social policies (UNU-CRIS 2008). The programme is designed to strengthen social cohesion via education, employment, justice and taxation policies (European Commission 2007b). The measures foreseen

> should be considered under the regional partnership to underpin civil society's participation, social dialogue and integration of marginalized sections of the population on the basis of a policy dialogue, based, for example, on the coordination approach of the Lisbon Strategy which incorporates a number of instruments.
>
> (European Commission 2007b: 16)

Additionally, the EU has historically clearly acknowledged the link between regional integration and development in its policy towards the ACP countries by including regional integration among the three focal priorities for poverty reduction given in the Cotonou Agreement.[11] Since the ACP framework comprises countries widely dispersed geographically, the EU has also developed more specific inter-regional partnerships – the Economic Partnership Agreements (EPAs) with Central Africa, Eastern Africa, Southern Africa, the Caribbean, and the Indian Ocean. The relations between the European Union and the ACP countries represent an essential aspect of EU trade and development cooperation policies, and an important step forward in that they include the promotion of core labour standards (CLS). In 2000, the member states of the European Union and the African, Caribbean and Pacific states signed the Cotonou Agreement to replace the Yaoundé Agreements and Lomé Conventions. The main aims of the Agreement are poverty eradication, sustainable development and the gradual integration of the ACP countries into the world economy. The Cotonou Agreement refers to internationally recognized social rights and labour standards as defined by the ILO and UN Conventions.

Article 50 of the Agreement, 'Trade and labour standards', makes explicit the commitment to internationally recognized core labour standards defined by the ILO. There is clear reference to the Conventions regarding the freedom of association and the right to collective bargaining, the abolition of forced labour, the elimination of the worst forms of child labour and non-discrimination in respect to employment. Nevertheless, the Agreement stipulates that the CLS should not be used for protectionist trade purposes. Moreover, it establishes the areas of cooperation, which include among others exchange of information on legislation and work regulation and the formulation of national labour legislation and strengthening of existing legislation. Regarding the endorsement of social dialogue, Article 25 reaffirms the commitment of both parties to encourage 'the promotion of participatory methods of social dialogue as well as respect for basic social rights'. The European Commission considers the Cotonou Agreement 'an important step forward in promoting core labour standards in bilateral agreements' and a model for further trade cooperation agreements (European Commission 2001). The Cotonou Agreement, under Article 25, places the development objective in a social context that aims to fight poverty, to improve the level of education and training, to strengthen labour policies, and to promote participatory social dialogue and human and social rights. Social dialogue has a key role to play in improving conditions for development in ACP countries at the local, national and regional levels.

The institutions and bodies involved in EU–ACP cooperation are the ACP–EU Council of Ministers, the ACP–EU Joint Parliamentary Assembly, the European Commission, the European Economic and Social Committee's ACP–EU Follow-up Committee, the ACP Secretariat, the European Investment Bank and the Centre for the Development of Enterprise.

The Cotonou Agreement established a framework for cooperation between the EU and ACP countries until 2020. However, the trade chapter, Articles 36 and 37, of the Cotonou Agreement are a violation of Article 1 of the WTO: the Most Favoured Nation principle (MFN) favours some countries, selected on the basis of their colonial past at the cost of other developing countries. The EU's EPAs with ACP countries were designed to be compatible with the WTO MFN rules. The main cooperation areas of the EPAs are: economic development; social and human development; regional cooperation; trade cooperation; and financial cooperation through development funds (Gonzales 2007). The EPAs, according to some analysts, represent a major turning point in EU–ACP relations (Van Langenhove and Costea 2007).

The social aspects of the EPAs are highlighted in Chapter 5 of the Cotonou Agreement, endorsing the commitment of both parties to the internationally recognized ILO core labour standards. Cooperation between the EU and ACP is indeed considered to be a tool for achieving the social and labour objectives of the agreement. This cooperation is planned to take the form of exchanging information on social and labour legislation as well as other measures deemed necessary. Support from the EC in the formulation of national social and labour legislation, including measures aimed at promoting the Decent Work Agenda of the ILO, is also envisaged. Nonetheless, there is no clear specification of how these measures should be accomplished or of the explicit role of the EU in these matters. Greven (2005) argues that no clear action on labour standards has been taken and highlights that labour movements are demanding more labour provisions in the EPAs.

The EPA negotiations started in 2004 when the EU launched discussions with six ACP sub-regions, namely West Africa, the East and Southern African states, Central Africa, the Caribbean, the Southern African Development Community and the Pacific islands. The intention was to conclude negotiations by the end of 2007. For various reasons, some of which are discussed below, the EC and the ACP representatives in most cases did not reach a common agreement and approach on issues concerning the key principles of EPAs (ODI/ECDPM 2008).

The problems today are related to the actual implementation of the Cotonou Agreement. The EPAs have been fiercely criticized by some international NGOs and some countries within the ACP groups for being imposed unilaterally by the EU and for potentially undermining developing countries' economies. Thus 'the EPAs are a means of the EU gaining (a) preferential investment liberalization agreements, (b) protection of EU corporate intellectual property, and (c) preferential EU company access to service liberalization and government procurements' (Keet 2007a).

Certainly the promise given in Cotonou, that the EPA process would support African regional integration, was not going to be realized. On the contrary, both in West and Southern Africa the interim agreements are seen more as a threat to existing Regional Economic Communities than as positive steps towards regional integration. In their present format EPAs are unacceptable for some member states in the region. Senegal, for example, has suggested replacing the EPA by a Development Partnership Agreement (DPA).

> According to this view the extreme vulnerability and structural weakness of the economies of developing countries and LDCs in particular make reciprocal trade agreements unequal. Consequently, Senegal does not accept EPA as long as the supply side of the economy is not substantially enforced. The basic difference between an EPA and a DPA is timing: for a DPA, structural improvements must come first, and then the economy can open for reciprocity in trade agreements.
>
> (Deacon *et al.* 2008: 48)

Nevertheless, in the only signed EPA, the one between the EU and the Caribbean Forum of African, Caribbean and Pacific States (CARIFORUM), Article 5 makes explicit references to social aspects. An important aspect is the commitment of both parties to the internationally recognized core labour standards[12] and

> the beneficial role that core labour standards and decent work can have on economic efficiency, innovation and productivity, and they highlight the value of greater policy coherence between trade policies, on the one hand, and employment and social policies on the other.
>
> (European Union 2008: 66)

The ILO plays the role of an advisory body and there is no clear specification of how these measures should be accomplished, or what the role of the EU is in this regard.

Despite the 'sprawling variety' (Gilson 2005: 307–26) across regions and sectors in this policy of inter-regional relations, the EU is becoming the 'hub' of inter-regional arrangements, which, in turn, are strengthening its own regionalist ideology (Söderbaum and Van Langenhove 2005). Promoting regional and inter-regional relations not only justifies and enhances the EU's own existence and efficiency as a global actor, the strategy also promotes the legitimacy and status of other regions. This, in turn, promotes further cross-cutting regionalism and inter-regionalism around the world. Most of these EU-promoted inter-regional arrangements encompass not only trade and economic relations but also political dialogue, development cooperation, cultural relations and security cooperation. The proponents of this approach even speak of a European model or doctrine of global policy based on inter-regionalism. According to Hettne (2001), this foreign policy strategy of the EU based on inter-regionalism has the potential to counteract and offer an alternative model of world order to the unipolar Pax Americana.[13] Critics, however, see it differently and point to the ways in which EU trade interests; despite all EU efforts to the contrary might be an obstacle to the realization of the social dimension of regionalism elsewhere.

Trans-regional social policy

We turn now to three trans-regional agreements – APEC, FEALAC and ASEM – in order to assess the nature of their engagement with social policy issues and whether they are supportive of injecting a social dimension into regionalism or are an obstacle to that development.

APEC

The Asia-Pacific Economic Cooperation was established in 1989 in order to further boost the economic growth and welfare of the region and to reinforce the Asia-Pacific community. APEC has twenty-one member economies,[14] working to reduce tariffs and other trade barriers across the Asia-Pacific region. One of the main goals of APEC is 'to create an environment for the safe and efficient movement of goods, services and people across borders in the region through policy alignment and economic and technical cooperation' (APEC website).

In order to achieve the Bogor Goals, endorsed in 1994 in the APEC Economic Leaders' Declaration of Common Resolve, at Bogor, Indonesia, on free and open trade and investment in the Asia-Pacific by 2010 for developed economies and 2020 for developing economies, the Forum mainly focuses on three key areas, also known as the 'Three Pillars': (i) trade and investment liberalization; (ii) business facilitation; and (iii) economical and technical cooperation.

Social issues are encompassed under the third pillar – economic and technical cooperation (ECOTECH). In 1996, the Ministers of APEC adopted the APEC Framework for Strengthening Economic Cooperation and Development, for better guidance in implementing the Osaka Action Agenda, approved the previous year. The Steering Committee on Economical and Technical Cooperation (SCE) coordinates the ECOTECH agenda, which prioritizes, among other things, the development of human capital, integration in the global economy, and the social dimension of globalization. Of relevance also is that the Human Resources Development Working Group (HRDWG) of ECOTECH addresses social issues via the Education Network and the Labour and Social Protection Network (LSPN). The rationale of the LSPN is

> to foster strong and flexible labour markets and strengthen social protection including social safety nets through evidence-based interventions, collaboration, technical cooperation and the provision of labour market and social protection information and analysis to address sustainable human resource development across APEC member economies.
>
> (APEC website)

The Group was set up during the twenty-first HRDWG meeting in 1999 in Japan, and met for the first time in Brunei in May 2000. At the HRDWG meeting in Bohol, Philippines, in April 2008, the LSPN revised its objectives and agreed to focus on issues and activities in the following areas:

> (i) foster economic development to enhance growth and employment creation and alleviate poverty through effective labour market policies, including such measures as enhancing productivity, labour force participation and skills development, (ii) maximizing the opportunities afforded by globalization through the development of improved workplace conditions and practices through the adoption of new technologies, effective labour–management relations, improved workplace health and safety practices and labour market adjustment measures to assist workers affected by globalization, and (iii) building capacity to strengthen social protection in APEC member economies through an appropriate combination of active and passive labour market measures, empowering individuals and mitigating dependence through the dissemination and information exchange of effective practices for better social safety net delivery.
>
> (APEC website)

Furthermore, in addressing the social dimension of labour, the Group emphasized the need to tackle issues like youth unemployment, labour mobility, brain drain, ageing population and industrial relations policies as key areas of policy development.

In addition, the meeting provided the opportunity to propose endorsement of the project proposal Seminar/Workshop on Good Practices in Social Safety Nets in APEC Member Economies for APEC funding. Other self-funded proposals from Japan – (i) the APEC Forum on Human Resources Development 2008: the Role of Technical and Vocational Education and Training Providers in Training for Employees; (ii) APEC Human Resources Development Seminar/Training Programme on the Adoption of IT Skills; and (iii) APEC Vocational Training Project in Cooperation with Enterprises – were also approved.

In addressing the social dimension of globalization, the Senior Officials' Meeting Report on Economic and Technical Cooperation in 2008 highlights the new HRDWG project Capitalizing Information Technology for Greater Equity and Access Among Poor and Rural Communities. The main focus of the project is the development of a set of materials to be used by policy-makers and other state and non-state actors to support poor people from rural areas 'in acquiring skills and knowledge to access information and data resources related to their vocation and allow them to participate in a globalized economy' (APEC 2008: 19).

FEALAC

The Forum for East Asia–Latin America Cooperation was established in 1999 to enhance dialogue and cooperation between the two regions. The Forum is an association of thirty-three countries from East Asia and Latin America aiming at: (i) increasing mutual understanding and political dialogue among the member states; (ii) boosting the potential of multidisciplinary cooperation, inter alia in economics, trade, investment, finance, culture, and education; and (iii) expanding 'common ground on important international political and economic issues with a view to working together in different international fora in order to safeguard common interests' (FEALAC website). FEALAC organization comprises three working groups, namely: Politics, Culture and Education; Economy and Society; and Science and Technology. It also has a Foreign Ministers' Meeting and a Senior Officials' Meeting. Different from APEC, the stated raison d'être of FEALAC is the accomplishment of regional integration of the countries from Latin America, as well as those of East Asia with the objective of achieving political and economic dialogue, and cooperation in all the areas of common interest.[15] A key difference between the Forum and ASEM is that most of the FEALAC members are developing countries (FEALAC 2002).

Several meetings tackling social issues were organized under the Politics, Culture and Education, and the Economy and Society Working Groups. Five meetings were organized under the Politics, Culture and Education Working Group – in 2002, 2003, 2004, 2006 and 2008. Most of the meetings included on their agenda an assessment of the proposed and on-going projects on politics, culture and education undertaken by the Working Group. It is relevant to mention the Training Course for FEALAC Cooperation on Poverty Reduction project initiated by Thailand, organized in July 2005 and July 2006. However, at the 2006 meeting in Bogota, Colombia, it was suggested that this project should be presented under the Economy and Society Working Group. Consequently, the Economy and Society Working Group, which met in Tokyo, Japan, in 2006, included a special cluster discussion dealing with social issues. During this meeting Thailand presented the details of the workshop on poverty reduction held in 2006. The workshop consisted of a seminar and country reports aiming to provide an opportunity for the countries to share the different strategies they had put in place. FEALAC member states participating in the workshop acknowledged the relevance of the seminar, notably 'the aspect of alternatives crops, and proposed that priority in trade be given to alternative crops to promote and facilitate their merchandizing' (FEALAC 2006: 4). Prior to this, the Final Report of the second meeting of the Economy and Society Working Group in 2003 included a special section on Socio-Economic Development and Poverty Reduction. It was reiterated there that the challenge of 'overcoming poverty' should be 'one of the highest priorities of FEALAC process' (FEALAC 2003: 2). Furthermore, the FEALAC governments committed themselves 'to the Millennium Development Goals, mutual support and assistance in pursuit of national strategies for poverty reduction, human rights approach to poverty matters, as possible means of increasing FEALAC value-addends' (FEALAC 2003: 2). In addition to these statements, the Group welcomed the initiative of Chile to share its experience of the 'Chile Solidario' project, which developed a social protection system, including social assistance programmes tackling poverty in an integral manner, aiming to support those living in extreme poverty. Moreover, it was proposed that Chile should organize a seminar or an exchange programme enhancing mutual learning on social protection issues. At the last meeting held in Quito, Ecuador, in November 2008, the Group welcomed a new project initiated by Thailand on Income Generation and Poverty Reduction for Development.

Earlier that year, Thailand had also hosted a training course on Income Generation and Poverty Reduction for Development in collaboration with the Mekong Institute, with the participation of Brazil (FEALAC 2008).

At the Fifth Economy and Society Working Group Meeting of FEALAC, held in October 2007 in Seoul, Korea, Chile proposed the project 'Institutional Strengthening and Human Resources Training for the Making of Social Policies Oriented to the Reception and Insertion of Migrants in Chile and in Other Member Countries of FEALAC', which is intended to train 'technical human resources able to formulate public policies that help vulnerable immigrants' (FEALAC 2007: 2). The novelty of this project is the creation of social policies for the establishment of integration mechanisms for migrants; it will also 'encourage the formation of a migrants' association as an effective instrument for exercising their rights, and … make use of international cooperation with FEALAC member countries that had success in insertion policies' (FEALAC 2007: 2). The project was subject to evaluation for the Korean Fund for Poverty Reduction, for a budget of US$129,600,000.

Additionally, during the seminar on social policies, Venezuela designed a project on Social Justice and Equality within the framework of bi-regional integration, aiming to promote exchanges of experience among the member countries of FEALAC regarding the implementation of social inclusion policies, focusing particularly on education and health issues. The main idea is to create a platform for cooperation between the specialized institutions of FEALAC members for the reduction of social differences and the promotion of inclusion and social justice.

In all these projects and initiatives FEALAC's stated aim is to tackle poverty and promote equal opportunities for the disadvantaged and marginalized people of the member countries, thereby contributing to socio-economic development.

ASEM[16]

The Asia–Europe Meeting began in 1996 as an informal multilateral process involving twenty-five countries of Western Europe and Asia.[17] Envisaged in part as a bulwark against US dominance of Asia through APEC, it cements institutions of global economic governance among the Triad (Richards and Kirkpatrick 1999, Rüland 2002). Unlike APEC, the ASEM process extends beyond trade and investment to a range of issues relating to the maintenance of peace, security and stability. Social policy questions are addressed in the two most institutionalized aspects of ASEM.

First, through its economic/business pillar it addresses questions of trade in services, health, education and social security. For example, at the Seoul ASEM Summit, the promotion of long-term savings for pensioners and diversification of pension schemes were discussed. Second, the ASEM Trust Fund was established in response to the 1997 Asian financial crisis to provide technical advice and training on policy issues in the financial, corporate and social sectors. Located in the Economic and Financial Pillar, half the Trust funds were allocated to projects in the social sector, defined as interventions to mitigate the adverse social effects of the 1997 financial crisis. Phase I (1998–2001) became operational in 1998, commanded a budget of US$44 million and was specifically focused on addressing the immediate effects of the financial crisis. Phase II (2002–5) commanded a budget of US$38 million and prioritized the provision of technical assistance and training to governments to help them design and implement institutional and policy reforms aimed at poverty reduction over the longer term.

The Fund is essentially a mechanism for channelling development assistance from governments in Europe to governments in Asia; it is one of the more institutionalized expressions of transnational social policy. Consistent with ASEM's role of providing a forum for mutual education, analysis and debate, the Fund operates to shape Asian social policy reforms. For the Europeans, it was a means of securing influence over East Asian policy reforms, both through the export of technical assistance (the conditions for the use of funds required that the technical assistance and expertise provided had to be from Europe) and through support for intellectual networks of experts and policy-makers on issues arising from the financial crisis. One such project was a seminar programme involving European and East Asian policy-makers and experts engaged in exploring European lessons for East Asia (Marshall and Butzbach 2003).

The Trust Fund was managed by the World Bank (East Asia and Pacific Region). The involvement of the World Bank (WB) was designed 'to ensure that the activities under the [ASEM] partnership would link tightly to the overall international effort to support East Asia's recovery, in which the World Bank played a leadership role' (Marshall and Butzbach 2003: 3). In particular, the condition that Trust Funds would be used to support policy reforms agreed upon with international financial institutions meant that it became a de facto mechanism to promote WB-approved policy prescriptions. Although the Europeans resourced the Fund, the WB could use its powers of financial leverage to promote its favoured social policy reforms in Asian nations – funding social safety net and poverty alleviation approaches to social policy, including projects monitoring the health and education impacts of the crisis in relation to low-income households and exploring the possibilities of a greater role for private pension funds and private sector involvement in training schemes for the unemployed. As such, critics have argued that ASEM has become a vehicle through which to promote East Asian subservience to Western principles of social liberal regulation promoted by the EU in alliance with the US-dominated WB.

A third way in which social policy features within ASEM lies outside the ASEM process itself. European and Asian NGOs and trade unions have repeatedly complained about their exclusion from the ASEM process and the exclusion of social development issues from the official agenda. Like other regional summits, ASEM meetings have generated popular fora that meet at the same time as ASEM but outside the official ASEM process (civil society meetings taking place through the Asia Europe People's Forum (AEPF). In effect, popular movements and NGOs have organized their own trans-regional dialogues in tandem with the official one, focusing on issues of democratic governance in such fora.

In terms of the declared aims of the NGOs, a decade of attempts by non-elite civil society organizations to gain access to the main ASEM meetings has proved to be a dismal failure. Participating governments (in particular Asian ones) have been unwilling to engage in a formal process of dialogue with CSOs. The organizing effects of civil society have not been without any results. In June 2004 the Asia Europe Foundation (the official ASEM pillar for cultural matters) hosted an informal consultation with civil society in Barcelona. The resulting Barcelona Report (2004) recommended creating a social pillar within the ASEM process and increasing transparency and accountability through the inclusion of civil society as a partner in the ASEM process. In what amounted to a rejection of attempts to extend the European partnership model to the ASEM process, the Hanoi ASEM Summit did not accede to these demands. While the NGOs failed in their attempt to push social policy into the core of the ASEM meetings, their constant efforts have resulted in small, incremental gains on the margins of the process. Under the auspices of ASEM, the WB, the Italian National Institute of Public Administration and the Italian Ministry of the Economy and Finance, government officials, administrators and academics attended a seminar on social policy-making in Europe and East Asia which dealt with social security, pension reform, labour market and health insurance policies and new ventures in social policy.[18] The participants in this official meeting expressed some of the same frustrations as the NGOs, with the concluding report emphasizing that

> in this seminar, as in virtually all others under this projects, the importance, and persistent difficulty, of linking economic and social policy was highlighted ... Some European examples suggested that indeed social policy makers are taking their seats firmly at the policy table, along with the powerful finance minister, but this theme was much less clear among Asian participants. From many, there remains a nagging sense that social policy is not the main driver it should be as yet...
>
> (ASEM *et al.* 2002)

The double effect of this civil society organizing is apparent. On the one hand, the demand advanced by civil society groups is for the integration of a social forum within the ASEM process. On the other hand, these groups are busily constructing their own social forum while they demand an ‘official’ social forum. In doing so they have laid out an agenda which they wish the eventual ‘official’ forum to take up. Finally it is no small achievement that, while they have failed to achieve their main aims, the Asian and European civil society organizations and networks have succeeded in running a sustained, decade-long campaign in both regions which, combined with lobbying at national and regional levels, again and again brought the ‘social question’ to the notice of the participant governments in the ASEM process.

This focus on ASEM has also highlighted the importance of the non-institutionalized aspects of trans-regionalism. Regionalism gives an impetus, not only to the state, but also to non-state actors to organize and act on trans-national scales. In the ASEM context, civil society networks have continued to press for the inclusion of social issues in the political process initiated by state and business elites, and have conducted a trans-regional social policy campaign, but they have been less successful in respect of forging policy channels in the ASEM process. That said, these organizations' activism is laying the foundations for a more inclusive, democratic and developmental social policy, and despite the resistance by ASEM governments to this social agenda the Asia–Europe Foundation is showing signs of recognizing the need to include non-business CSOs in the ASEM process.

Across these three formations we can see the emergence of a rudimentary trans-regional social policy dimension. Although their concerns did not originate in such matters, APEC, FEALAC and ASEM are now each engaging *to an extent* with such issues. Governments and non-governmental actors are using these fora to construct a political platform that is beginning to engage with issues of social development (FEALAC), labour market, ageing and health (APEC) and poverty reduction (ASEM). Admittedly, such dialogues and cooperation that do exist are framed by economic governance and business and trade concerns, as is consistent with their origins as elite projects, and in all fora there is a disappointing lack of institutionalized commitment to trans-regional social regulation, social redistribution and social rights. It remains to be seen whether they prove to be effective vehicles and catalysts for strengthened world-regional social policy over the longer term, but the arguments and experiences of CSOs in relation to ASEM at least suggest that without substantial democratization, ambitions for these fora to become key drivers of regional social policy may remain limited to the level of ideals. In terms, then, of whether trans-regional agreements are supportive of or undermining of regional social policy, both tendencies are at work: social issues are being raised, but the terms of debate are limited and largely confined to trade, economic governance and development issues. Further research is needed into how these fora are in practice influencing the development of social policy discourse and practice of smaller regional formations.

Conclusions

This chapter has for the first time presented and discussed a range of developments and issues that bear upon the development of regional formations with a strong social agenda and effective social policies. These include, on the one hand, the increased use of bilateral agreements as means by which governments pursue national policy objectives and, on the other hand, the emergence of inter-regional and trans-regional platforms and agreements. We have presented an overview analysis of the ways in which these developments are imbued with social policy agendas and have considered to what extent they may be seen as complementary to and supportive of strengthened regional social policy or whether they undermine and obstruct it. We need to emphasize that this chapter reviews and brings together for the first time a social policy analysis of these cross-cutting and diverse developments, and that given the absence of comprehensive research into these matters a conclusive analysis is not possible at this stage. Some preliminary conclusions can, however, be stated.

First, recent uses of bilateral agreements are probably overall more undermining than supportive of both regional and multilateral agreements. This does not deny the positive aspects of bilateral agreements, in particular the fact that they can be used to support global social regulations, such as core labour standards, but it is also clear that their popularity in recent years is related to difficulties in forging multilateral (global or regional) agreements. Indeed, they are instruments whereby particular governments can achieve domestic foreign policy objectives 'flexibly' and as such indicate a retreat from a commitment to global or regional collective action.

Second, inter-regional agreements, in particular those concluded between the EU and developing countries that we examined here, can be a means of promoting regional social policy by virtue of their promotion of regionalism more generally. In the case of the EU, the inter-regional arrangements it has entered into have gone beyond issues of trade and economic relations; such arrangements are also vehicles for promoting wider political dialogue that already has been and could continue to be a catalyst for the development of strengthened regional social policy. However, one of the issues is the perceived conflict between trade/economic objectives and interests and social policy ones. Here, the EU has been sharply criticized for putting its trade interests ahead of wider (including regional) social ones. In this respect, while the EPAs it is negotiating are an advance on the moralizing about human rights that it engaged in not so long ago, there are concerns that its new approach may not ultimately be conducive to a strengthened regional social policy. Our discussion was confined to North–South inter-regional dialogues and more research needs to be undertaken on South–South dialogues to situate the EU's experience as a global social policy actor. Similarly, this chapter did not address (for reasons of space) inter-regional arrangements between Southern regional formations, and this is an area that needs further attention in future.

Third, trans-regional formations are showing signs of beginning to engage with social agendas and are becoming fora in and around which debates over global and regional social governance are increasingly conducted. To date, though, progress on this front, in terms of institutional enactments of social policy measures of redistribution, rights and regulation, has been slow to materialize. As such, at the moment these formations do not appear to be key drivers of a strengthened regional social policy.

Notes

1 A hybrid version concerns the relations between regional groupings and single powers, for example between the EU and the US, the US and ASEAN, ASEAN and Russia, the European Free Trade Association and Mexico. It comes close to inter-regionalism in the sense that the single power has a dominant position in its own region (the US in North America, India in South Asia), and such relations can also be

seen as constituting an important component of trans-regional arrangements (e.g. EU–China/EU–Japan and ASEM) (Hänggi 2000). This is discussed in the next paragraph.

2 See Note 1 above.

3 The three-year Initiative on Ageing Issues in APEC (2007–9) is divided into two primary parts: 'Financial Markets and Ageing' and 'Public Finance and Others in Ageing'. The first part, implemented under the theme of 'Financial Markets and Ageing' (2007–8), consisted of three workshops and a high-level seminar. China, Korea, New Zealand, the United States, Chinese Taipei and Thailand, and ABAC, the IMF and the OECD participated in this initiative to formulate policy recommendations for the region. The results will be combined with the outcome of the second part of the initiative, 'Public Finance and Others in Ageing', which was launched in November 2008. The final result, including policy recommendations regarding financial markets, public finance and others in ageing issues in the APEC region, will be presented to the Finance Ministers at their 2009 meeting (see http://www.apec.org/apec/ministerial_statements/sectoral_ministerial/finance/2008_finance/annex.html (accessed 28 March 2009).

4 The People's Dialogue on Alternatives for Regional Integration, arising out of/inspired by the World Social Forum commitment to proposing alternative solutions for sustainable human development and democracy, works within regions and across them (e.g. South–South: Latin America–Asia–Africa; South–North focusing on EU policy towards the South) and with the Hemispheric Social Alliance (HSA) to fight the FTAA. In relation to labour, regionalist movements within Latin America and South Africa are emerging, for example 'Labour's Platform for the Americas' in Latin America.

5 Bilaterals is a term used in some circles to refer to regional trade agreements as well as bilateral trade agreements. While recognizing the usefulness of this broader use of the term (as it captures, for example, EU agreements with other single countries, an established practice of the EU since the 1950s), for the purpose of this chapter, the term bilateral refers to agreements involving just two signatory governments.

6 Since 1985, the US has completed ten such agreements, secured agreement from Congress for four further deals, and is waiting for Congress approval on three others; it is holding discussions with eleven more countries for preferential trade agreements, either bilateral or regional. The US has also expressed interest in bilateral trade agreements with all ten members of ASEAN (MacMahon 2008).

7 Indeed, it has been noted that workers' rights represent a major issue in US FTAs in the Middle East:

> the Agreements themselves do little to raise standards, as they basically commit the parties to implement their own policies of minimalist rights. Yet a huge part of the private sector labour force in the Middle East, especially the Gulf states, is composed of mostly Asian workers who are denied fundamental rights.
>
> (http://www.bilaterals.org/article.php3?id_article=6206 (accessed 15 December 2008))

8 This section is based on M.C. Macovei, 'The Role of the EU in Promoting Social Dialogue and Core Labour Standards in Inter-regional Agreements', paper presented at the ESPANET conference, *The European Social Model in a Global Perspective*, Luxembourg, March 2009.

9 http://europa.eu/scadplus/leg/en/lvb/r11016.htm.

10 The Rio Group was established in 1986 with an initial membership of six, and now comprises twenty-three countries: all the Latin American countries plus the Dominican Republic, Jamaica, Belize, Guyana, Haiti and Cuba (which joined the Rio Group in November 2008). The other Caribbean countries are represented by one of the full Caribbean members (presently Jamaica). It is administered by a rotating and temporary secretariat. Mexico is the current pro tempore secretary of the Rio Group. More on http://ec.europa.eu/external_relations/la/riogroup_en.htm.

As stated in Article 28 of the Agreement: 'Cooperation shall provide effective assistance to achieve the objectives and priorities which the ACP States have set themselves in the context of regional and sub-regional cooperation and integration, including inter-regional and intra-ACP cooperation' (European Commission Development DG, The Cotonou Agreement. Part 3, Title I, Chapter 2. Available at: http://europa.eu.int/comm/development/ body/cotonou/agreement/agr14_en. htm (accessed 23 February 2005)).

11 For the Cotonou Agreement, see http://europa.eu//development/geographical/cotonouintro_eu.cfm.

12 Labour standards should not be used for protectionist trade purposes.

13 For more detailed information see Van Langenhove and Costea (2005).

14 Australia, Brunei Darussalam, Canada, Chile, People's Republic of China, Hong Kong, China, Indonesia, Japan, Republic of Korea, Malaysia, Mexico, New Zealand, Papua New Guinea, Peru, Republic of the Philippines, Russian Federation, Singapore, Chinese Taipei, Thailand, United States of America and Vietnam.

15 See FEALAC website: http://www.focalae.org/.

16 This sub-section is an extensively edited version of Yeates (2007).

17 ASEAN 7 (Brunei, Indonesia, Malaysia, the Philippines, Singapore, Thailand and Vietnam) plus Japan, China and South Korea.

18 Summary proceedings of this meeting can be found at www.worldbank.org/asemsocial/rome_summary.pdf.

10 Global social governance and world-regional social policy

Bob Deacon, Maria Cristina Macovei, Luk Van Langenhove and Nicola Yeates

This book has constituted:

- an *argument* as to why a regional approach to ensuring there is a social dimension to globalization is important;
- an *exposition* of what a regional social policy might ideally look like within the several world regions;
- an *empirical review* and *assessment* of the extent to which a social dimension to regional integration is emerging in Africa, Latin America, South and East Asia and Europe;
- an *analysis* of the drivers for and obstacles to the further development of regional social policies.

In this final chapter we recapitulate what has been written in the earlier chapters under these headings. We then proceed to set out:

- the *global governance implications* for the United Nations and for other global actors and agencies;
- the *gaps* in our review in terms of world-regional coverage and the *research and capacity-building agenda* that now opens up if the work in this book is to be built upon.

The argument for world-regional social policy restated

Critics who warned, long before the global economic crisis of the end of 2008, of the negative social consequences of neo-liberal globalization had sought to propose reforms to globalization that would ensure that these negative social consequences were addressed. Alternative global social policies had been argued for that would ensure more *trans-national redistribution* (via global taxes and increased ODA) to create greater global equity. Calls were made for more *global social regulation* (via agreed international labour standards) to prevent what was perceived as a race to the bottom. A strengthened *global social rights regime* (with international courts of justice with a mandate to address social rights) had been suggested to ensure global citizens could take their government to court

(Deacon 2007, Held 2004, Yeates 2001, 2008). Some progress had taken place in some of these global social policy fields. There is an airline ticket tax and global funds to address many health problems. There is the global social compact and there are moves to improve the UN social rights system. Progress was slow, however, and, moreover, many of these proposed global social policies had become a matter of contestation between some in the Global North and some in the Global South.

A source of this North–South contestation was the wish of many in the Global South to escape from Northern-driven globalization. The negative experience of structural adjustment has led to many countries to seek to articulate their own social policies. They are therefore resistant to new Northern-driven social policies even if these were now progressive ones concerned to implant universal social protection measures and improve social governance. At the same time even as some countries in the Global South might still need increased ODA to top up weakened government health and education budgets, the over-riding wish was to be independent of aid. In the area of labour and social standards and social rights, there remained a suspicion that the self-interest of the Global North might be pushing these onto the global agenda in trade and other deals.

This led us to the conclusion that an alternative route to a socially just globalization might lie through a decentred globalization based on a federation of world regions. Each region would address trans-national social policies at the regional level (Deacon 2001, Deacon 2007, Deacon *et al.* 2007, Yeates 2005, Yeates and Deacon 2006, UNU-CRIS 2008).

These ideas about the importance of the social dimension of regions have also featured in many UN publications, as we outlined in Chapters 1 and 2. The report *A Fair Globalization: Creating Opportunities for All* by the World Commission on the Social Dimension of Globalization claimed that regional integration can contribute to a more equitable pattern of globalization, but only if it has a strong social dimension (WCSDG 2004). In the July 2006 session of ECOSOC the UN Secretary-General declared that 'multi-stakeholder policy dialogues at the national and regional level have to be developed with the objective of building national and regional capacity to develop a multi-disciplinary approach to economic and social issues' (UNSG 2006). Earlier that year, UNESCO organized a High-Level Symposium on the Social Policy Dimension of Regionalism in Montevideo in the context of the UNESCO International Social Sciences Policy Nexus Forum (Deacon *et al.* 2006). The resulting Buenos Aires Declaration called upon 'the regional organizations such as MERCOSUR and the African Union, in association with social scientists and civil society, to further develop the social dimension of regional integration and [called] upon the UN to facilitate inter-regional dialogues'.

The global economic crisis of 2008–9 combined with the ecological crisis caused in part by the carbon-fuelled global trade regime has only strengthened the case for rethinking how to manage world interconnectedness. The case for some degree of retreat to conservation and development of more sustainable local and regionally based forms of production and consumption has become stronger. This implies a greater focus upon regional trade arrangements that in turn implies a new urgency in addressing regional social policies to complement regional economic policies.

The exposition of world-regional social policy restated

As we outlined in Chapter 2 these regional social policies could include:

- *regional social redistribution* mechanisms: these could take several forms ranging from intra-regional transfers to development aid (ODA) and could be used to target depressed areas or to redress inequalities within regions;
- *regional social regulations*: these could include health and labour standards to combat an intra-regional 'race to the bottom', as well as the regulation of private social services and utilities (water, electricity);
- *regional social rights* mechanisms: these give citizens a voice to challenge rights abuse: the European Union's European Court of Justice or the Council of Europe's Court of Human Rights might serve as useful models of mechanisms by which citizens can be empowered to challenge the perceived failures of national governments to fulfil their social rights;
- *regional cross-border social sector investments*: these could address various common social policy priorities, for instance the production of cheaper generic pharmaceuticals at regional level to benefit from economies of scale, or common programmes to avoid cross-border transmission of diseases (e.g. malaria) or the sharing of higher education facilities within a region;
- *cross-border lesson* learning in social policy: this could provide an opportunity to learn from good practices that have worked at a local level within the same region and to develop innovative local solutions.

This book has addressed this issue of regional social policy in a number of ways. It asked in Chapter 3 whether UN social agencies, regional development banks and the UN regional economic and social commissions were arguing for and driving such regional social policies. In Chapter 4 it asked whether regional social movements more more important as drivers for these policies from below. We then turned in Chapters 5–8 to a region-by-region review of the extent to which regional social policies were evident in practice in Europe, Latin America, Asia and Africa. Chapter 9 examined some of the obstacles to the development of such regional social policies arising from inter-regional open free trade agreements and bilateral trade deals.

Overview and assessment of world-regional social policies in practice

This book has brought together for the first time a detailed review and assessment of developments in regional social policy in Africa, Latin America, East and South Asia and Europe. The social dimension of regional integration within

Europe is very well known and the subject of much detailed assessment and debate. The European Union represents the most advanced form of regional integration. In terms of regional social policy, the EU has made major advances in the three fields of social redistribution, social regulation and social rights. The Structural Fund/Social Cohesion Fund is the mechanism whereby the EU's funds (which are contributed approximately according to country GNP and population size) are allocated to the development of impoverished or economically underdeveloped areas within the EU member states. A range of regulations cover the fields of occupational health and safety, health services, equal opportunities, labour law, and social security and pensions schemes, together with social dialogue mechanisms that apply to all countries. In terms of regional social rights, the Community Charter of Fundamental Social Rights of Workers was established at an earlier stage and was added to in 2000 with the adoption of the Charter of Fundamental Rights. Harmonization of national social regulations and standards is a precondition for membership of the EU and for access to its internal market and regional transfers. Additionally, the Open Method of Coordination (OMC) is a mechanism whereby national civil servants are encouraged to coordinate their policies with agreed EU-wide benchmarks and engage in policy learning processes (de la Porte and Pochet 2002, Chalmers and Lodge 2003). The OMC was introduced in the fight against social exclusion in March 2000; in the area of pensions it was introduced in March 2001 and in the area of health care it was introduced in June 2001.

Chapter 5 above focuses on a comparison of the social dimension of the European Union and its Commission and agencies on the one hand and the less-known Council of Europe, covering a wider group of countries, on the other. The European Union and the Council of Europe are quite different institutions. This is because the EU is led by a supranational Commission charged with driving the socio-economic integration of its member states, backed by a supranational court with the power to enforce European laws, while the Council of Europe is an intergovernmental body devoted to the promotion of democracy and human rights without a strong institution at its centre. However, Chapter 5 compared their 'regional' social policies and concluded that the EU does operate regional redistribution mechanisms and regional social regulation procedures, and enforced certain social rights of citizens through the European Court of Justice. At the same time there is extensive cross-border cooperation involving the rights to access services abroad and established methods for cross-border social policy lesson learning. The Council of Europe, on the other hand, is not concerned with redistribution and regulation and its European Court of Human Rights does not encompass the social rights articulated within its own Social Charter. The Council of Europe, however, is an important player in exhorting countries to improve their social rights. As Monica Threlfall concludes, in matters of social law, the European Union, despite its more restricted formulation of social rights than the Council's European Social Charter, is by far the stronger player and the one which is much more likely to deliver social policies and rights to citizens. She suggested that there is a trade-off between binding regulations and exhortatory declarations.

The one delivers specific protection on a narrow basis, the other opens up awareness and a world of possibilities on a wide front, maybe even setting international political agendas, yet is unable to enforce compliance against defaulters and therefore fails to ensure consistent delivery.

In Africa, we noted some remarkable achievements in the development of regional and sub-regional social policies despite the context of weak economies and weak institutions. Many of these remained at the level of exhortation and declaration but others were very real. Among these were agreements on the free cross-border movement of labour in ECOWAS and UEMOA and moves towards this in the SADC. A Regional Court of Justice in ECOWAS adjudicates on national labour rights. In addition there are charters of social rights in the sub-regions and cross-border cooperation in health in terms of both disease control and service delivery. Cross-border cooperation in education and agreements on skills portability exist. UEMOA uses customs duties to address regional disparities. There are examples of cross-border social security conventions on the portability of rights. Ministers of Social Development meet at sub-regional level to compare national practices and effective sub-regional social dialogue mechanisms and processes are in place, especially in Southern Africa. The Africa chapter focused only on South and West Africa. Similar sub-regional arrangements exist in East and North Africa but have not been documented. Thus whether in *regional or sub-regional redistribution, regional or sub-regional social regulation, regional or sub-regional social rights* or simply cross-border cooperation in social sector investments or cross-border lesson learning, Africa exhibits examples of each type of regional social policy.

In terms of Latin America social policy has not been a major component of LA integration schemes until now but debate on these issues is now taking place with renewed urgency since the collapse of the FTAA strategy. However, it has been present to some degree in all of them since their initial conception. MERCOSUR is probably the scheme that has advanced the most. In 1998, the Social-Labour Declaration created a tripartite MERCOSUR Social-Labour Commission to which governments annually submit a report on changes in national labour law and practice. The declaration covers core labour rights including migrant workers' rights and commits the member countries to enforce their own labour laws. While there is a useful process of social dialogue, there is not strictly a supranational labour rights regime. A Working Group of Specialists in Accreditation of Higher Education is elaborating principles and procedures for the mutual recognition of courses. A Fund for Structural Convergence (FOCEM) of MERCOSUR was created which resembles in its objectives the European structural funds. The first funds were distributed in 2007. Safety and health in the workplace, labour migration, social security and capacity building are also discussed in the Andean Communities tripartite forum but with little consequence. However, decisions tending towards facilitating movement of persons have been adopted in preparation for the introduction of the Andean labour card in 2008. This mechanism will help the citizens of the Andean countries with respect to the mutual recognition of university degrees, free movement of labour, labour rights, pensions and social security. In the case of CARICOM the Charter of Civil Society recognizes fundamental labour rights. There is a mechanism for submitting complaints regarding labour rights violations but there are no sanctions. The new regional body ALBA, under the influence of Venezuela, redistributes funds for poverty relief to neighbouring countries and collaborates with Cuba in the regional use of health professionals and teachers. Elements of *sub-regional social policies of redistribution, very soft regulation and the articulation of social rights* exist on the continent but are as yet underdeveloped.

In South and East Asia, the general absence of supra-nationalist elements to ASEAN and SAARC has resulted in minimal progress in regional social policy. Instead of binding policies, ASEAN and SAARC issue declarations and statements, outlining intentions, visions or guidelines for members to operationalize in their own way. Overall, ASEAN has generated a fuller set of instruments and mechanisms for social policy than has SAARC. In terms of *social rights*, the most significant development to date is the mandate given by the newly signed ASEAN Charter for an ASEAN Human Rights Body, the terms of reference for which has been left to a High-Level Panel to draft by 2009. In SAARC, the Social Charter consolidates the different social commitments. Its language is progressive, with access to basic services guaranteed, and provisions for women are strong. However, it has limited scope, not covering labour or social security. In terms of *redistribution*, ASEAN's main vehicle to address the development gap is the Initiative for ASEAN Integration (IAI), which covers seven areas: energy, human resource development, information and communications technology, regional economic integration, tourism, poverty reduction, and projects of general coverage. Under the IAI, ASEAN also established a common resource pool, the ASEAN Development Fund (ADF). SAARC has the SAARC Development Fund (SDF), which has three windows: social, economic and infrastructure; and three sources of funds: grant contributions, assessed contributions and funds from donors and international organizations. The Food Security Reserve schemes in ASEAN and SAARC are also instruments for social redistribution. The current scope of *social regulation* in ASEAN and SAARC is limited, but there are some encouraging areas. For instance, both have instruments to combat trafficking in women and children, with clear definition of offences, and SAARC even allows extradition for certain offences. ASEAN has completed Mutual Recognition Arrangements in nursing and engineering services, making easier the movement of people in these professions within the region. Other than this, ASEAN has yet to develop common standards and regulation in other areas like social protection. In SAARC, the issue of labour migration is not discussed at all, as border dispute remain one of the most contentious issues within the sub-region.

We have captured these developments in matrix form, as shown in Table 10.1.

Table 10.1 Regional social policies in practice on the four continents

Regional association	*Redistribution*	*Social regulation*	*Social rights*	*Cooperation in social sectors*	*Cross-border lesson learning*
EUROPE					
EU	Yes	Yes	Yes	Yes	Yes
Council of Europe	No	No	Yes but not force of law	No	Yes
LATIN AMERICA					
MERCOSUR	Yes	Soft law*	Yes but not force of law	Yes	Yes
Andean Community	Yes	Soft law	Yes but not force of law	Yes	Yes
CARICOM	No?	Soft law	Yes but not force of law	Yes	Yes
ALBA	Yes	No	No	Yes	Yes
ASIA					
ASEAN	Yes	Soft law	Yes but not force of law	Yes	Yes
SAARC	Yes	No except trafficking of women and children	Yes but not force of law	Yes	Yes
AFRICA					
AU	No	Soft law	Yes but not force of law	Yes via sub-regions	Yes
ECOWAS	No?	Soft law	Yes	Yes	Yes
UEMOA	Yes	Covered by ECOWAS	As ECOWAS	As ECOWAS	As ECOWAS
SADC	No	Soft law	Yes but not force of law	Yes	Yes
SACU	Yes	Covered by ECOWAS	As SADC	As SADC	As SADC

Source: edition based on Chapters 5, 6, 7 and 8.

Note

* Soft law means that regional declarations/agreements on standards etc. are left up to countries to implement with exhortation from the region.

Drivers for and obstacles to world-regional social policy

What do our various chapters tell us about the drivers helping the development of a regional social policy strategy? What do they tell us about the obstacles to further development? Here we review the role of global players from above, trans-national social movements from below, the specific conditions and players in countries and regions themselves and the contribution of inter-regional dialogues, allied inter-regional trade processes and bilateral trade agreements.

In terms of global players, Chapter 3 above addressed the role of the 'players' from above: regional development banks, regional economic commissions and regional branches of the UN social agencies and their role in addressing aspects of regional social policies and regional social integration. It was found that much of the analytical work and policy prescriptive work of these players was focused on the region defined merely as a collection of individual countries that happen to occupy a particular regional territory rather than as actually existing regional associations of countries. In other words, what was observed was first the continued focus of the agencies *on advice to countries within regions rather than advice to regional associations of countries.* Second, where there was advice to regional associations *the advice often neglects the social policy dimension of regional social integrations.* However, where the genuinely regional dimension comes in it is in the useful form of *lesson learning across borders* from countries within the region. It was the exceptional intervention which was designed to contribute to *the building of the capacities of the regional associations of countries* in the field of social policy.

Where there is a focus on cross-border supra-national regional and sub-regional social policy issues by the agencies surveyed these tend to be in the following fields: (i) economic and labour migration management; (ii) communicable diseases monitoring; (iii) measures against trafficking of women and children; (iv) social protection and social security portability and commonality; (v) capacity building of the secretariats of regional and sub-regional associations of governments; and (vi) support to social dialogue mechanisms at sub-regional institutional level.

Explanations for this limited focus on regional social policy on the part of these actors from above lie in a combination of three factors: first, the constitutionally driven focus of the UN system on individual countries; second, the general ideological drift towards global free trade in the latter part of the twentieth century which refused any kind of regional protectionism; and third, the absence of calls from regional associations of countries for such a focus. Where more effort in the direction of fostering regional social policies was evident it could be attributed to the purchase within some parts of and among certain individuals in the ILO, UNESCO, UNICEF and UNDESA of the 'idea' of regional social policy as an alternative to neo-liberal globalization. The drive to foster regional social policy in these organizations was an ideological one motivated by a desire to attend to the negative social consequences of globalization. There was no systematic coherent planned approach to this work even within the ILO, the organization which has done most and has itself argued for the social dimension of regional integration to be taken seriously in its World Report on a Fair Globalization (WCSDG 2004). Nonetheless, where initiatives were taken, significant regional social policy developments were influenced positively by such players, as noted in Chapter 4 and for Africa in Chapter 8 and for Asia in Chapter 7.

Rather in contrast to the absence of a focus on regional social issues and regional social policy found among the global actors from above, Chapter 4 revealed a new constellation of regional social movements from below all arguing and campaigning for a new 'alternative regionalism' within which regional social policies should find a central place. As the authors of that chapter argue, the new generation of social movements and CSOs in Latin America, Southern Africa, and Southeast and South Asia, shaped in particular over the past ten years by their strong resistance to trade liberalization and privatization, have become key agents and players in regional integration processes. They are shaping regional integration processes that are responsive to the interests of the people. Thus in Latin America the Hemispheric Social Alliance (HSA) was created in 1997, with the purpose of resisting the negotiations towards a Free Trade Area of the Americas (FTAA) promoted by the United States. In this project they were successful. However, it is less clear exactly what are the precise forms the movement wishes the regional integration of Latin America to take and what precise regional social policies they would wish to see put in place. In the case of Southern Africa, the Southern African Peoples' Solidarity Network (SAPSN) was formed in 1999 to challenge the interlinked issues of debt, structural adjustment and globalization. The core of its strategy lies in the organization of a series of SADC People's Summits in parallel to the Intergovernmental and Heads of the State SADC Summit. In East Asia on the eve of the Eleventh Official ASEAN Summit the first ASEAN Civil Society Conference (ACSC) was organized in Kuala Lumpur in December 2005. Similar social movements have emerged in South Asia. Cecilia Olivet and Brid Brennan make a strong case that these movements are influential in the shaping of the new regionalism, arguing that the 'demands' of these movements embrace regional social rights, issues of migration and common labour practices, and cross-border health issues including collaboration to produce or purchase cheap drugs. Water supply and access to water have been a key focus, as have the asymmetries within regions and the associated need to develop regional funds to compensate for these.

The region-specific Chapters 5, 6, 7 and 8 draw attention to particular social forces and political processes that have lent support to and been more important in developing the social dimension of the regional integration efforts. For Monica Threlfall, the focus was on the use by regional bodies of exhortation to improve country/regional social policies or of legally binding regulations to compel adherence to regional norms. She concluded that regional associations will work best if they can combine both. However, they do have to confront and succeed in the more difficult challenge of setting up regulatory frameworks and institutions, even at the cost of narrowing the ambit of these to cover fewer common social policies as a way of obtaining consensus between member states, at least as a first stage.

For Africa, the argument ran that strong political will at the highest levels and strong adherence by civil society at the base are very much needed in order to build successfully regional integration with a social dimension. The actual role played by regional organizations, beyond the declarations and intentions, depends on overcoming the limited technical and human resource capacity available. A major condition for deep regional integration, beyond political will, is available expertise and institutional capacity. When it comes to institutional capacity, the same capacity limitation is valid for the social partners in the tripartite set-up. Neither labour unions nor employers' organizations in most African sub-regions dispose of strong regional representations. In addition therefore to strong regional leadership from above is the requirement of effective regional organization from below.

For Latin America (LA) Manuel Riesco argues that the future regional social policy that still needs to be developed requires 'powerful, motivated and committed actors, operating under a more or less coordinated long-term state strategy'. He therefore includes among the key players the professional LA bureaucracies. They have been a primary actor in the region for more than a century and will be central to any advance. He draws attention also to the EU, Spanish capital and the business push to LA regional integration. But equally important is the role of intellectuals. They unfortunately became the main culprits behind the privatization and dissipation of the previously distinguished traditional intellectual drive behind LA developmentalism and regionalism. Its regrouping, mainly within the realm of a reconstructed and reinforced modern LA public university system, would aid the push to regional social integration. No integration process whatsoever will be possible, he insists,

> if it is not able to seduce the region's emerging, overwhelmingly massive social force: the new urban salaried middle classes. In the present social scenery of LA as a whole, and especially in the countries that are in the more advanced phases of transition, any progressive strategy, and certainly regional integration, must include this emerging force as a basic part of the power bloc required to make is successful.

Its interests have to be accommodated in any regional social policy. In other words, he rather turns the argument on its head and does not consider who will drive the regional social integration project but rather asks whose interests need to be recognized and met by the regional integration process for it to succeed. Thus salaried workers will be enthusiastic about such a move (only) if it is associated with potent signals regarding their rights, and smaller-scale but more concrete measures of regional social policy to their direct benefit. Furthermore, in the case of the still vast masses of LA peasants and urban poor, concrete regional social policy measures seem indispensable to motivate their own integration.

For East and South Asia, the issue for Jenina Joy Chavez is one of building upon the strong bases that exist, which are different in each region, by the current economically orientated (ASEAN) and politically orientated (SAARC) leaderships opening themselves up to the influence of the growing cross-border social movements that exist in each region. ASEAN countries have a strong tradition of developmentalism, while SAARC members have strong socialist influences. SAARC started with cooperation in the social sectors, long before it entertained economic integration. SAARC can be said to be as committed, if not more committed, to the social dimension as ASEAN. The signing of the ASEAN Charter advances institutional formalization (procedures, mechanisms), but it does not have the strong rights-based approach or deep commitment to social policy that the SAARC Social Charter has. South Asia also has a stronger tradition of developing its internal markets and relying on its own capital, in sharp contrast with ASEAN's outward-looking development. ASEAN's experience has been that members 'do not like to pay', making cooperative funds hard to come by. In contrast, SAARC members make bigger contributions to the SDF, and are more selective in receiving donations from non-regional partners. The biggest stumbling block to successful regionalism is the distance of regionalist initiatives from the people and the lack of progress in taking regionalism outside the realms of an elite project in the hands of official diplomacy. Without popular support, indeed unless popularly demanded, regional initiatives will require a long socialization process. In these terms there is room for optimism. The paralleling of official summits by people's events or civil society processes is evidence of this. In ASEAN, civil society groups participated in the drafting of the Charter. In South Asia, the People's SAARC is held in parallel with or very close to the official SAARC Summit. Regional groups have been advocating peace and disarmament, poverty eradication and social development. An advanced notion of regionalism, a People's Union of South Asia, was also proposed in the People's SAARC of July 2008. If ASEAN and SAARC were more open to inputs from these groups and movements, they would be able to confirm the most pressing need in the two sub-regions. The Secretariats of the two Associations should have the specific ability to officially receive inputs from citizens' groups and direct such inputs to relevant bodies.

In terms of identifying the drivers for and obstacles to enhanced regional social integration, we also need to take account of the review in Chapter 9 of the large trans-regional processes such as APEC, the array of inter-regional dialogue and negotiating processes such as ASEM, and the plethora of bilateral trade deals that often cut across regional formations. Moves towards enhanced regional social integration and very real obstacles to its advance are to be located within these processes. The chapter concluded, first, that bilateral agreements are probably overall more undermining than supportive of both regional and multilateral agreements. This does not deny the positive uses of bilateral agreements, in particular the fact that they can be used to support global social policy regulations such as core labour standards, but it is also clear that their popularity in recent years is related to difficulties in forging multilateral (global or regional) agreements. Indeed, they are instruments for particular governments to achieve domestic foreign policy objectives 'flexibly' and as such indicate a retreat from a commitment to global or regional collective action.

Second, inter-regional agreements, in particular those entered into by the EU with developing countries that we examined here, can be a means of promoting regional social policy. In the case of the EU, the inter-regional arrangements it has entered into have gone further than issues of trade and economic relations and such arrangements are also vehicles for promoting wider political dialogue that already has been and could continue to be a catalyst for the development of strengthened regional social policy. However, one of the issues is the perceived conflict between trade/economic objectives and interests and social policy ones. Here, the EU has been sharply criticized for putting its trade interests ahead of social considerations. In this respect, while the EPAs it is negotiating are an advance on its moralizing about human rights, there are concerns that its new approach may not ultimately be conducive to a strengthened regional social policy.

Third, trans-regional formations are showing signs of beginning to engage with social agendas and having become fora in and around which debates over global and regional social governance are increasingly conducted. To date, though, progress on this front, in terms of institutional enactments of social policy measures of redistribution, rights and regulation, have been slow to materialize. As such, these formations do not at the moment appear to be key drivers of a strengthened regional social policy.

The global governance implications for the United Nations and for other global actors and agencies

The *argument* of this book has been that a strengthened system of world-regional governance, with each region adopting a social dimension to its regional integration project, is the best way of securing a socially responsible globalization. The *exposition, empirical evidence and assessment* in this book suggest that developments along these lines are slowly taking place within regional associations of governments on four continents. The *analysis* has suggested that there are huge obstacles to the further development of this agenda in practice. These include (i) low capacity in some underdeveloped regional associations of government; (ii) national sovereignty concerns that resist supra-nationalism; (iii) continued elite focus in regions upon issues of regional trade; and (iv) external interventions that are as often undermining as they are supportive of regional social development. We have also shown that there are sound reasons for advancing regionalism with a strong social dimension and that increasingly influential cross-border social movements are seeking to advance that agenda. Here we address the one rather negative finding in this book from Chapter 4 that with notable exceptions UN social agencies, UN Economic and Social Commissions and regional development banks are not giving much attention to this agenda. That is to say, we turn to the *global governance implications* for the United Nations and for other global actors and agencies if the UN system, and other elements of global social governance are to become a force for the further development of the social dimension of regionalism. These reforms are necessary to elevate regional associations of governments and, within them the Social and Labour and/or Social Development commissions and secretariats of regional associations, to a more prominent place in world social governance.

ECOSOC has been strengthened recently although it is still regarded by many as a weak body. The creation of the Bi-annual Development Cooperation Forum which had its first meeting in July 2008 and the instigation of High-Level Annual Ministerial Reviews by Ministers of Social Development have added to its credibility. To bring the regional dimension into this process we suggest that ECOSOC convenes on a regular basis high-level meetings of the commissioners and secretariats of actually existing *regional associations of governments* responsible for social development and social and labour policy. These meetings would review best practice in the development of regional social policies of redistribution, regulation and rights and cross-border cooperation and lesson learning in the fields of health, education, social protection, food security and allied policy fields. These deliberations can then be fed into the Development Cooperation Forum and the Annual Ministerial Reviews.

For the UN economic and social commissions, this means devoting considerably more resources to working not with governments in a region but with the regional associations of governments of a region. It also means giving equal priority in work focused on regional associations to social policy issues alongside economic issues.

For the UN social agencies (ILO, WHO, UNICEF, UNESCO, etc.) it means that the World Health Assembly, World Labour Conference and other annual assemblies must create a more prominent space within their deliberations and decision-making processes for representatives of the relevant Social Policy Commissioners of regional associations of countries. It also means fashioning a coherent strategy for working on health, labour, education or any other social policy topic at the level of regional associations of countries. It also means that the regional offices of the UN agencies must devote a far greater part of their analytical and technical capacity to working with the secretariats of the regional associations of governments within their territory. This might also mean relocating regional UN social agency offices to the city hosting these secretariats.

Given that in each world region the exact configuration of regional associations of governments is different and the relationship between regional and sub-regional associations of countries varies too, and given also that the ministries and secretariats with responsibility for social policy use varied terminology, it is not possible to give precise institutional and location reform proposals. Taking Africa as an illustrative example of a region and the case of the SADC as one of several sub-regions, what is proposed is that:

1 The AU Commissioner for Social and Labour Affairs together with the Secretariat dealing with Social Policy in the SADC and the other Africa sub-regional RECs attend the proposed ECOSOC-convened high-level regional association meetings periodically.
2 The ECA focuses its support efforts on the AU, the SADC and the other sub-regional REC offices and pays more attention to the social dimension of regional and sub-regional integration.
3 If not already so located, the WHO, ILO, UNICEF, UNESCO and UNDP establish their head regional office in Addis Ababa and establish their sub-regional offices in Gaborone (for the SADC), Abuja (for ECOWAS) and similarly for the other sub-regions.

The governance, policy and operational reforms will permit appropriate attention to be paid to the development of effective regional and sub-regional social policies by *regional associations of governments* that are important building blocks of a global integration project that puts human need and inclusive social development first.

These reform suggestions build upon the case already being made for regions to become a more important element of global governance within the UN system more generally. The human security dimension has driven this approach. Thus, the UNDP 1993 *Human Development Report* triggered the security dimension debate over the need to change the traditional perspective (i) from an exclusive interest on national security to focus on the security of the individual and of people; (ii) from security based on armaments to a security based on human development; and (iii) from territorial security to food, environmental and employment security. The following *Report* in 1994 set the scene for the human security concept as one intending to embrace freedom from fear, meaning freedom from violence, freedom from want and poverty alleviation. By including new security dimensions – economic, environmental, political and social – human security becomes 'a transversal concept that affects every sector that can impact upon people's welfare and that requires the adoption of cross-sectoral policies to respond to a range of human security vulnerabilities in societies' (UNDP/UNU-CRIS 2009: 7).

Thus in the case of human security a regional dimension of governance has emerged within the UN. As discussed in Chapter 1, this is built upon the UN Charter, which envisages in Chapter VIII the possibility of cooperation between the UN and regional organizations. In recent years several non-permanent members of the Security Council have taken initiatives to strengthen this relationship. In the period 1994–2006, several high-level meetings between the UN and regional organizations took place and former Secretary-General Kofi Annan repeatedly called for a 'regional-global' security mechanism (Van Langenhove 2009). Today, that process of formal consultations has unfortunately been stopped. Ad hoc cooperation is still continuing, however, and it is hoped that this regional-global process of policy-making in the human security field might be revitalized.

The UN system generally has welcomed regional integration processes as it needs regional organizations, 'and particularly the EU, to share the burden of global governance' (Van Langenhove and Marchesi 2008: 484). Unfortunately, and here is another example of the EU being both an agent for regional integration and an obstacle to it, the EU, however, does not see itself conforming entirely to the vision a Chapter VIII organization in the UN Charter of Regional Arrangements. It has the global ambition to go beyond Europe, specifically for third-generation regionalism.

Finally, we need to note that there are competing visions or at least steps being taken in practice to reform global governance arrangements that do not focus only on the strategy of strengthening the UN. The G20 may become a more important forum for world leaders to debate global economic and social governance and address development issues (ODI 2009). It is regarded as effective at dealing quickly with issues whereas the more representative ECOSOC is slow and ineffective. A twin-track approach is suggested (ODI 2009: 27) whereby a G20 with a permanent secretariat addresses matters which are on the UN agenda but handles them in ways which do not undermine the UN; at the same time efforts should be made to streamline further the work of ECOSOC, maybe by creating an Economic Security Council. In this scenario the implication of our argument in this book is that the G20 should be seen as a body which brings together not key global *national* players such as Brazil, China, South Africa, Indonesia and India but countries which are *representatives of regional associations of governments.* Then, when G20 agendas include development issues and global social policy, the regional dimension would be built into the process. The EU attends already but so should MERCOSUR, ASEAN, the AU, and other regional groupings. To advance the reform of the G20 to make it a body that represents regions, the EU would need to replace the national European governments. This is unlikely in the near future –once again underlining the fact that in terms of the further development of world regionalism with a social dimension the EU is both a model and an obstacle.

Gaps and a future research and capacity-building agenda

Finally, we turn to the *gaps* in our review in terms of world-regional coverage and the *research and capacity-building agenda* that now opens up if the work in this book is to be built upon. In choosing Europe, Africa, Latin America and South and Southeast Asia to illustrate progress towards regionalism with a social dimension we have chosen in some ways the most propitious examples. Middle Eastern regionalism, post-Soviet Union regionalism, Black Sea regionalism and even Southeast European regionalism are still in the making. There are examples of cross-border cooperation in social policy in all of those formations, though we would probably not find there the more institutionalized manifestations of regional social policy, such as social development secretariats, that were located in the case studies covered in this book. China, Japan, South Korea and the ASEAN+3 processes further complicate the global scene. Nor did we pay attention to regional social policy in North America, in particular NAFTA. Equally, there are many sub-regions, development corridors and a variety of contested regional spaces that cut across and overlap with even those more defined regional associations of governments we have researched (Söderbaum and Taylor 2008).

The first item on our suggested research agenda is therefore to build on and extend knowledge about the social policy dimensions of regional integration in a wider range of regionalisms around the world. This is in part a mapping exercise, given that none have previously been undertaken in any comprehensive way. It is also an evaluative exercise, assessing the extent to which the formations in question are moving in the direction of a genuinely regional dimension of social redistribution, social regulation and social rights.

Beyond this there is a need to examine in more detail the workings in practice of regional social policy arrangements. While we have been able to suggest some of the key drivers for and obstacles to the furtherance of regionalism with a social dimension, further research which examines the forces and processes leading to specific regional social policy agreements is needed. It would be useful to evaluate success stories of regional social policy innovation in terms, for example, of whether pressure for change was more effective when directed at the regional officials and regional summit events or at leading national governments who then in turn won support from other countries. This would lead to a better understanding of the opportunities for regional social movements to advance the regional social policy agenda. Furthermore, this research would be necessarily comparative in nature. Historicizing further the processes, policies and practices of regional integration with a social dimension that we have begun to map in this book would contextualize their emergence and deepen our understanding of the social, political, economic and cultural conditions, forces and dynamics. Comparisons of sectoral areas would extend understanding of regional formations' social policy responses. Comparisons of the effectiveness of particular models and modes of regional social governance in terms of the key policy issues identified as needing to be addressed would also be valuable. All of these indicative kinds of comparisons could be undertaken on an intra-regional basis and ideally on a cross-regional basis.

Here, the integration of insights of 'traditional' comparative social policy analysis and transnational studies would be productive. Doing so would mean that regional formation processes would no longer be treated as 'external' to domestically oriented studies of social policy change, and the policies and politics of 'domestic' regimes would be integrated into analyses of and theoretical explanations of the development of regional social policy. Equally, the integration of multilateral forces and agencies (the UN, WB, etc.) and other flanking organizations (regional development banks, trans-regional formations) into analytical frameworks would also be possible. These need to take account of the co-determining forces operating at complementary levels of governance. Such a move would, amongst other things, enable a more developed account of social policy formation generally, including the interaction of global, regional and domestic forces, policy actors and institutions, policy instruments and practices.

One of the issues in any such future research is the need to develop a set of comparable social (policy) indicators for each of the regions involved. At present, such data are not only lacking but not routinely collected. A key component of a future research agenda (as well as capacity-building agenda – see below) would therefore need to envisage and eventually develop a set of socio-economic 'baseline' data, including expenditure, transfers, etc. and a set of appropriate indicators to capture the progression towards tangible and effective regional social policies.

Of equal importance to the research agenda is the translation of this into capacity-building and knowledge-transfer agendas. For the many secretariats of regional associations which are struggling to advance the social dimension of regionalism, these elements would be vital. It is clear that while the labour and social dimensions of regional integration are on the agenda in many regional associations of governments, the exact ways in which and the exact policies by which these aspects of regional integration are to be strengthened is only partly understood by the secretariats and other actors involved. There is a need for more detailed debate of alternative forms of regional social policies which cover specific options for policy sectors such as labour, social protection, health and education, as well as cross-cutting issues of migration, corporate governance, financial regulation and the social dimensions of trade and production. As part of a strategy to strengthen regional labour and social policies, more dialogue between (for example) regional Ministers of Social Development who are normally concerned with poverty issues and regional Ministers of Labour who are normally concerned with employment issues is probably needed and both should collaborate to give more attention to regional social policy.

Training within regions should aim to enhance some or all of the following skills of officials, social and labour movement representatives and other actors/stakeholders. Analytical skills could be enhanced to facilitate a better understanding of regional integration processes and their different components and regional social policy development and implementation. This could be extended to include the trade–labour–social policy relations, trade impact assessment methods, and policy options for integration and sustainable development. The training could enhance capacity for more effective representation of labour and social interests at a regional level and their participation in decision- and policy-making. It would also improve the negotiation and ultimately the effectiveness of intra- and inter-regional trade and other deals by addressing labour and social concerns from the outset. Finally, there needs to be structured opportunities for all parties involved to reflect on experiences of and lessons learned from regional social policy development, together with an opportunity to disseminate them within and among regions. To this end, knowledge transfer opportunities would be a key element of the forging of epistemic and actual communities of stakeholders in regional social policy around the world.

We have offered this book as a contribution to the debate about how in a post-economic crisis world global and regional policies and institutions might be reformed and improved upon to ensure a fairer and more just system. If our analysis and conclusions are even partly on the right track then there is a UN and G20 global and regional governance reform agenda, a research agenda and a capacity- building agenda to be urgently attended to.

Bibliography

Acharya, A. (2002) *Regionalism and Multilateralism: Essays on Cooperative Security in the Asia-Pacific*, Singapore: Times Academic Press.

—— (2003) 'Democratisation and the Prospects for Participatory Regionalism in Southeast Asia', *Third World Quarterly*, 24(2): 375–90.

ACSC (2005) 'Civil Society Presentation to ASEAN Heads of State and Government', First ASEAN Civil Society Conference, Building a Common Future Together, Kuala Lumpur, Malaysia, 12 December.

—— (2006) 'Statement ASEAN for the People', Second ASEAN Civil Society Conference (ACSC II), Creating a Caring and Sharing Community – Enhancing People's Participation in Governance and Development, Cebu, Philippines, 10–12 December. Online: www.seaca.net/viewArticle.php?aID=959 (accessed 30 March 2008).

—— (2007) 'Singapore Declaration', Third ASEAN+ Civil Society Conference (ACSC III), Moving Forward – Building an ASEAN+ People's Agenda, Singapore, 2–4 November. Online: www.seaca.net/viewArticle.php?aID=1022 (accessed 30 March 2008).

—— (2007a) *Engaging the ASEAN: Proceeding of the 2nd ASEAN Civil Society Conference – 10–12 December 2006*, Philippines: SEACA.

ADB (2006a) *Regional Cooperation and Integration Strategy*, Manila: ADB. Online: www.adb.org/documents/policies/RCI-strategy/final-RCI-strategy-paper.pdf (accessed April 2007).

—— (2006b) *Regional Co-operation Strategy: South Asia 2006–2008*, Manila: ADB. Online: www.adb.org/Documents/CSPs/South-Asia/2006/CSP-SA-2006.pdf (accessed November 2007).

—— (2007a) *Strengthening Capacity of the ASEAN Secretariat in Regional Economic Integration and Policy Dialogue*, Manila: ADB. Online: www.adb.org/Documents/TARs/REG/40566-REG-TAR.pdf (accessed 16 April 2007).

—— (2007b) *Enhancing the Efficiency of Overseas Workers' Remittances*, Manila: ADB.

—— (2008) *Key Indicators 2008*, Manila, ADB.

Adesina, J.O. (ed.) (2007) *Social Policy in Sub-Saharan Context: In Search of Inclusive Development*, Basingstoke: UNRISD/Palgrave Macmillan.

Adnett, N. (1996) *The European Labour Markets: Analysis and Policy*, 2nd edn, London: Prentice Hall/Financial Times.

Adnett, N. and Hardy, S. (2005) *The European Social Model: Modernisation or Evolution?*, Cheltenham: Edward Elgar.

AfDB (2008) *Board of Governors. Annual Report 2007*, ADB-ADF/BG/AR/2007, Mozambique. Online: http://www.afdb.org/fileadmin/uploads/afdb/Documents/

Publications/30726071-EN-ENGLISH-ANNUAL-REPORT-2007 PDJ (accessed May 2008).

Ahearne, A., Pisany-Ferry, J., Sapir, A. and Véron, N. (2006) 'Global Governance: an Agenda for Europe', *Breughel Policy Brief*, Brussels.

Ahuja, V., Bidani, B., Ferreira, F. and Walton, M. (1997) *Everyone's Miracle? Revisiting Poverty and Inequality in East Asia*, Washington, DC: The World Bank.

—— (2008) *Annual Report*, ADB-ADF/BG/AR/2007. Online: www.afdb.org/fileadmin/uploads/afdb/Documents/Publications/30726071-EN-ENGLISH-ANNUAL-REPORT-2007.PDF (accessed October 2008).

Allen, D. (2005) 'Cohesion and Structural Funds', in H. Wallace, W. Wallace and M. Pollack (eds) *Policy-making in the European Union*, Oxford: Oxford University Press, pp. 213–42.

Anderson, P. (1974) *Lineages of the Absolutist State*, London: Verso.

Anner, M. and Evans, P. (2004) 'Building Bridges across a Double Divide: Alliances between US and Latin American Labour and NGOs', *Development in Practice*, 14(1): 34–47.

ANSA (2007) *The Search for Sustainable Human Development in Southern Africa*, Harare: ANSA Secretariat.

APA (2001) *An ASEAN of the People, for the People: Report of the First ASEAN People's Assembly*, Jakarta: CSIS.

ASEAN (1967) *ASEAN Declaration Bangkok*. Online: www.aseansec.org (accessed 28 September 2008).

—— (1985) *Charter of the South Asian Association for Regional Cooperation*, Dhaka. Online: www.saarc-sec.org (accessed 4 October 2008).

—— (2007a) *Charter of the Association of Southeast Asian Nations*, Singapore. Online: www.aseansec.org/AC.htm (accessed 28 September 2008).

—— (2007b) *ASEAN Economic Community Blueprint*. Online: www.13thaseansummit.sg/asean/index.php/web/documents/documents/asean_economic_blueprint.

ASEAN Leaders (1976) *Declaration of ASEAN Concord (Bali Concord I)*, Singapore: ASEAN Secretariat.

—— (1997) *ASEAN Vision 2020*, Jakarta: ASEAN Secretariat.

—— (2003) *Declaration of ASEAN Concord II (Bali Concord II)*, Jakarta: ASEAN Secretariat.

ASEAN Secretariat (1998) *Hanoi Action Programme 1999–2004*, Jakarta: ASEAN Secretariat.

—— (2003) *Vientiane Action Programme 2004–2010*, Jakarta: ASEAN Secretariat.

—— (2006) *Annual Report 2005–2006: ASEAN at the Centre*, Jakarta: ASEAN Secretariat.

—— (2007) *Annual Report 2006–2007: Becoming One ASEAN*, Jakarta: ASEAN Secretariat.

—— (2008) *Key Indicators 2008*, Manila: ADB.

ASEM, World Bank and National Public Administration Institute (SSPA) (2002) *Summary of Proceedings*. Seminar on Social Policy Making in Europe and East Asia, February 21–23, Rome-Caserta. Online: www.worldbank.org/eapsocial/asemsocial/rome_summary.pdf (accessed 15 November 2003).

Asian Regional Integration Centre Database (2009) *FTA Status by Country*. Online: http://aric.adb.org/10.php (accessed 20 September 2008).

Atkinson, A.B. (2005) *New Sources of Development Finance*, Oxford: OUP.

AU (2004a) *Strategies for Employment Creation/Promotion and Enhancing Sustainable Livelihoods*, African Union Commission, Third Extraordinary Session on Employment and Poverty Alleviation, Ouagadougou, Burkina Faso: EXT/ASSEMBLY/AU/2(III).

—— (2004b) *Declaration on Employment and Poverty Alleviation in Africa*, Third Extraordinary Session on Employment and Poverty Alleviation, Ouagadougou, Burkina Faso: EXT/ASSEMBLY/AU 3(III).

—— (2004c) *Plan of Action for Promotion of Employment and Poverty Alleviation*, EXT/ASSEMBLY/AU/4(iii)rev.3, Addis Ababa: African Union.

—— (2005) *Draft Social Policy Framework for Africa*, LSC/EXP/5(III), Addis Ababa: African Union.

—— (2007) *Concept Note*, Consultative Meeting on Employment and Policies and Programmes, Addis Ababa: African Union.

—— (2008) *Press Release: African Ministers of Social Development Committed to Implement the Social Policy Framework for Africa.* Online: www.africa-union.org/root/AU/Conferences/2008/october/sa/sd/press/final%20PR%20END%20FIRST%20MEETING%20AU%20MINISTERS%20SOCIAL%20DEVELOPMENT%2031–10–08.doc (accessed May 2008).

—— (2008a) *Concept Note: Investing in Social Protection in Africa*, Addis Ababa: African Union.

—— (2008b) *Social Policy Framework for Africa*, CAMSD/EXP/4(i), Addis Ababa: African Union.

Bailes, A.J.K. (2007) 'Regionalism and Security Building', in A.J.K. Bailes *et al. Regionalism in South Asian Diplomacy*, SIPRI Policy Paper No. 15, Stockholm: SIPRI, pp. 1–11.

Bailes, A.J.K., Gooneratne, J., Inayat, M., Khan, J.A. and Singh, S. (2007a) *Regionalism in South Asian Diplomacy*, SIPRI Policy Paper No. 15, Stockholm: SIPRI.

Baldwin, R. (2007) *Managing the Noodle Bowl: The Fragility of East Asian Regionalism*, Working Paper Series on Regional Economic Integration No. 7, Manila: ADB.

Baral, L.R. (2006) 'Cooperation with Realism: The Future of South Asian Regionalism', *South Asian Survey*, 13(2): 265–75.

Barcelona Report (2004) 'Recommendations from Civil Society on Asia–Europe Relations Addressed to the ASEM Leaders', prepared at Connecting Civil Society from Asia & Europe: An Informal Consultation, 16–18 June 2008, Barcelona.

Barua, P. (2006) 'Economic Diplomacy in South Asia: Priorities and Stakeholders in the New Economy', *South Asian Survey*, 13(1): 18–33.

Barry, B. (2008) 'MOST Seminar Series in West Africa Draws to a Close, SHS views', *UNESCO Social and Human Sciences Magazine*, January–March). Online: http://unesdoc.unesco.org/images/0015/001567/156781E.pdf#6 (accessed September 2007).

Bello, W. (2004) *Deglobalization: Ideas for a New World Economy*, London: Zed.

—— (2007) 'Globalization in Retreat', *New Labor Forum*, 16(3): 109–15.

Bergsten, C.F. (1997) 'Open Regionalism', *The World Economy*, 20(5): 545–65.

Berrón, G. (2007) 'De la Lucha contra el ALCA a la "Integración de los Pueblos": Movimientos Sociales y los Procesos de Integración', *Res Diplomática (RD), Segunda Época*, 1: 6–23. Online: www.isen.gov.ar/rd_pdf/1b.pdf (accessed 18 March 2008).

Bhagwati, J. (2008) *Termites in the Trade System: How Preferential Agreement Undermine Free Trade*, Oxford and New York: Oxford University Press.

Bieler, A. (2006) *The Struggle for Social Europe: Trade Unions and EMU in Times of Global Restructuring*, Manchester: Manchester University Press.

Bieler, A. and Morton, A.D. (eds) (2001) *Social Forces in the Making of the New Europe: The Restructuring of European Social Relations in the Global Political Economy*, Basingstoke: Palgrave.

Birdsall, N. (2006) 'Overcoming Coordination and Attribution Problems: Meeting the

Challenge of Underfunded Regionalism', in I. Kaul and P. Conceicao (eds) *The New Public Finance: Responding to Global Challenges*, New York: Oxford University Press, pp. 529–648.

Blackburn, R. (1997) *The Making of New World Slavery*. London: Verso.

Bowles, P. (1997) 'ASEAN, AFTA and the "New Regionalism" ', *Pacific Affairs*, 70(2): 219–33.

Brennan, B. and Olivet, C. (2007) 'Regionalisms Futures: The Challenge for Civil Society', *Global Social Policy*, 7(3): 267–70. Online: http://gsp.sagepub.com/cgi/reprint/7/3/267?etoc.

Breslin, S. and Higgott, R. (2003) 'New Regionalism(s) in the Global Political Economy. Conceptual Understanding in Historical Perspective', *Asia Europe Journal*, 1: 167–82.

Caballero-Anthony, M. (2004) 'Non-state Regional Governance Mechanism for Economic Security: The Case of the ASEAN Peoples' Assembly', *The Pacific Review*, 17(4): 567–85.

Castro, F. (1971) *Discurso Pronunciado por El Comandante Fidel Castro Ruz, Primer Secretario del Comite Central del Partido Comunista de Cuba y Primer Ministro del Gobierno Revolucionario. En Santiago de Chile: En la Sede de la Comision Economica Para la America Latina*. Online: www.cuba.cu/gobierno/discursos/1971/esp/d291171e.html (accessed 10 April 2008).

—— (1996) 'Impacto de las tendencias demográficas sobre los sectores sociales en América Latina; contribución al diseño de políticas y programas', *Serie E (45)*, Santiago de Chile: CELADE.

CELADE (1998) 'América Latina: proyecciones de población, 1970–2050', *Boletín Demográfico*, 31(62).

CENDA (2004) *Propuesta para una Nueva Política de Integración Regional*, Centro de Estudios Nacionales de Desarrollo Alternativo. Online: http://cep.cl/CENDA/Proyectos/Minsegpres/Propuesta_Integracion.doc (accessed 17 November 2004).

Chalmers, D. and Lodge, M. (2003) *The Open Method of Coordination and the European Welfare State*, London: ESRC Centre for Analysis of Risk and Regulation, LSE.

Chandra, A.C. (2006) 'The Role of Non-state Actors in ASEAN', in *Revisiting South East Asian Regionalisms*, Bangkok: Focus on the Global South, pp. 71–82. Online: http://focusweb.org/revisiting-southeast-asian-regionalism.html (accessed 20 March 2008).

Chavez, J. (2005) *Civil Society Meets ASEAN, Finally?*. Online: http://focusweb.org/civil-society-meets-asean-finally.html (accessed 12 March 2008).

—— (2007) 'Social Policy in ASEAN: The Prospects for Integrating Migrant Labour Rights and Protection', *Global Social Policy* 7(3): 356–76. Online: http://dx.doi.org/10.1177/1468018107082239.

—— (2007a) 'New Asean Charter Lacks Vision', *Bangkok Post*, 20 November.

Cheng, E. (2007) 'Big Pharma's New Offensive against World Poor', *Green Left*. Online: www.greenleft.org.au/2007/703/36494 (accessed 16 September 2008).

Chitambo, A. (2007) *An Introduction to SADC and SADC Tripartite Structures*, Gaborone: SADC.

Choudry, A. (2008) 'Free Trade, Neoliberal Immigration and the Globalization of Guest-worker Programs'. Online: www.bilaterals.org/article.php3?id_article=12431 (accessed 17 September 2008).

Churchill, R.R. and Khaliq, U. (2004) 'The Collective Complaints System of the European Social Charter: An Effective Mechanism for Ensuring Compliance with Economic and Social Rights?', *European Journal of International Law*, 15(3): 417–56.

Cisse, A.B. (2008) 'Tackling Poverty Reduction – The Role of the Islamic Development Bank', *UN Chronicle: A magazine for the United Nations*. Online: www.un.org/Pubs/chronicle/2008/issue1/0108p21.html (accessed April 2007).

Council of Europe (1949) *Statute of the Council of Europe*, London. Online: http://conventions.coe.int/Treaty/en/Treaties/Html/001.htm (accessed March 2008).

—— (1995) *Additional Protocol to the European Social Charter Providing for a System of Collective Complaints*, Strasbourg. Online: http://conventions.coe.int/Treaty/en/Treaties/Html/158.htm (accessed March 2008).

—— (2003–7) *Statutory Reports – Sections on European Social Charter Complaints*. Online: www.coe.int/T/CM/system/WCDdoc.asp?Ref=StatRep00&Ver=2008&Sector=CM&Lang=en# (accessed March 2008).

—— (2007a) *The Committee of Ministers of the Council of Europe: Working Methods and Procedures: Recent Developments. Chapter 10: Relations with the Parliamentary Assembly*. Online: https://wcd.coe.int/ViewDoc.jsp?id=1166413&BackColorInternet=9999CC&BackColorIntranet=FFBB55&BackColorLogged=FFAC75 (accessed November 2007).

—— (2007b) *Recommendation CM/Rec(2007)17 of the Committee of Ministers to Member States on Gender Equality Standards and Mechanisms*. Online: https://wcd.coe.int/ViewDoc.jsp?Ref=CM/Rec(2007)17&Language=lanEnglish&Ver=original&Site=CM&BackColorInternet=9999CC&BackColorIntranet=FFBB55&BackColorLogged=FFAC75 (accessed November 2007).

—— (2008a) *About the Council of Europe*: *Aims*. Online: www.coe.int/T/e/Com/about_coe/ (accessed 23 May 2008).

—— (2008b) *European Social Charter: List of Complaints and State of Procedure*. Online: www.coe.int/t/dghl/monitoring/socialcharter/Complaints/Complaints_en.asp (accessed 16 December 2008).

—— (2008c) *List of International Non-Governmental Organisations Entitled to Submit Collective Complaints*. Online: www.coe.int/t/dghl/monitoring/socialcharter/OrganisationsEntitled/INGOList_en.pdf (accessed 1 July 2008).

Council of Europe Parliamentary Assembly (2008) *Access to Safe and Legal Abortion in Europe, Resolution 1607*. Online: http://assembly.coe.int/Main.asp?link=/Documents/AdoptedText/ta08/ERES1607.htm (accessed November 2008).

Curtin, D. (2003) 'Private Interest Representation or Civil Society Deliberation? A Contemporary Dilemma for European Governance', *Social & Legal Studies*, 12(1): 55–75.

Daly, M. (2002) *Access to Social Rights in Europe*, adopted by the Council of Europe. Online: www.coe.int/t/dg3/socialpolicies/SocialRights/source/MaryDaly_en.pdf.

Daño, E. and Peria, E. (2008) *Emergency or Expediency? A Study of Emergency Rice Reserve Schemes in Asia*, Quezon City: Asiadhrra and AFA.

Dasgupta, A. (2000) 'Labour Standards and WTO: A New Form of Protectionism', *South Asia Economic Journal*, 1(2): 113–29.

Dash, K. (1996) 'The Political Economy of Regional Cooperation in South Asia', *Pacific Affairs*, 69(2): 1–24.

Deacon, Bob (1999) *Socially Responsible Globalization: A Challenge for the European Union*, Helsinki: Ministry for Social Affairs and Health.

—— (2001) *The Social Dimension of Regionalism, GASPP*, Occasional Paper No. STAKES. Helsinki.

—— (2007) *Global Social Policy and Governance*, London: Sage.

—— (2008) 'Global and Regional Social Governance', in N. Yeates (ed.) *Understanding Global Social Policy*, Bristol: The Policy Press, pp. 25–48.

Deacon, B., Yeates, N. and Van Langenhove, L. (2006) *Social Dimensions of Regional Integration – A High Level Symposium: Conclusions*, UNU-CRIS Occasional Paper, O-2006/13. Online: www.cris.unu.edu/fileadmin/workingpapers/20060607105556.O-2006–13.pdf (September 2008).

Deacon, B., Ortiz, I. and Zelenev, Z. (2007) *Regional Social Policy*, DESA Working Paper No. 37, ST/ESA/2007/DWP/37, New York: UNDESA.

Deacon, B., Van Hoestenberghe, K., De Lombaerde, P. and Macovei, M.C. (2008) *Regional Integration, Decent Work, and Labour and Social Policies in West and Southern Africa*, UNU-CRIS Report for the ITC-ILO, UNU-CRIS Working Papers (W-2008/13). Online: www.cris.unu.edu/UNU-CRIS-Working-Papers.19.0.html?&tx_ttnews[tt_news]=553&cHash=2612d7378c (accessed 10 March 2009).

De Bùrca (2005) *EU Law and the Welfare State: In Search of Solidarity*, Oxford: OUP.

de la Porte, C. and Pochet, P. (2002) *Building Social Europe through the Open Method of Coordination*, Brussels. Presses Interuniversitaires Européennes.

Delarue, R. (2006) 'ILO–EU Cooperation on Employment and Social Affairs', in J. Wouters, F. Hoffmeister and T. Ruys (eds) *The United Nations and the European Union: An Ever Stronger Partnership*, The Hague: T.M.C. Asser Press.

De Lombaerde, P. and Van Langenhove, L. (2007) 'Regional Integration, Poverty and Social Policy', *Global Social Policy*, 7(3): 377–83.

Dinka, T. and Kennes, W. (2007) *Africa's Regional Integration Arrangements: History and Challenges*, European Centre for Development Management Discussion Paper No. 74. Online: http://www.ecdpm.org (accessed 10 March 2009).

Dornbusch, R. and Sebastian, E. (eds) (1991) *The Macroeconomics of Populism in Latin America*, National Bureau of Economic Research (NBER) Conference Report, Cambridge, Mass: NBER.

Draibe, S. and Riesco, M. (2007) 'Latin America, A New Developmental Welfare State in the Making?', in M. Riesco (ed.) *Latin America, A New Developmental Welfare State in the Making?*, London: Palgrave-Macmillan.

Draibe, S. and Riesco, M. (2007a) 'Introduction', in M. Riesco (ed.) *Latin America, A New Developmental Welfare State in the Making?*, London: Palgrave Macmillan.

ECA (2006) *Assessing Regional Integration in Africa*, Addis Ababa: UNECA and African Union.

—— (2007) *Assessment of Progress on Regional Integration in Africa*, Fifth Session of the Committee on Trade, Regional Cooperation and Integration, E/ECA/CRTCI/5/5, ECA: Addis Ababa.

ECE (2001) *ECE Strategy for a Sustainable Quality of Life in Human Settlements in the 21st Century*, ECE/HBP/120, New York and Geneva: UN.

—— (2004) *Symposium on Social Housing. Summary Report*. Online: www.unece.org/hlm/prgm/hmm/social%20housing/UNECE_Report_FIN.pdf (accessed October 2008).

—— (2005) *UNECE Strategy for Education for Sustainable Development*, UN Economic and Social Council, CEP/AC.13/2005/3/Rev. 1, New York and Geneva: UN.

—— (2006) *Guidelines on Social Housing. Principles and Examples*, ECE/HBP/137, New York and Geneva: UN.

ECLAC (2002) *Statistical Yearbook – Economic Commission for Latin America and the Caribbean*, Santiago: ECLAC.

—— (2006a) *Shaping the Future of Social Protection: Access, Finance, and Solidarity*, Montevideo: Uruguay. Online. Available HTTP www.sedi.oas.org/ddse/puente_caribe/documents/ECLAC_Social%20Protection%202006.pdf (accessed October 2008).

—— (2006b) *Report of the High-Level Ministerial Dialogue on Social Security and Sus-*

tainable Social Development in the Caribbean, LC/CAR/L.92. Online: www.cepal.org/publicaciones/PortOfSpain/2/LCCARL92/L.92.pdf (accessed October 2008).
—— (2007) *Employment and Labor Insertion Policies to Overcome Poverty*, Conceptual Note, Washington, 13 and 14 September 2007.
Economist, The (2002) 'Brazil's Presidential Election: The Meaning of Lula for Latin American Democracy. How Good for Brazil', 5 October.
Elman, R.A. (1996) *Sexual Politics and the European Union: The New Feminist Challenge*, Oxford: Berghahn Books.
ESCAP (2001) *Working towards Social Integration in the ESCAP Region*, Social Policy Paper No. 3, New York: UN.
—— (2007a) *Committee on Emerging Social Issues*, E/ESCAP/CESI(4)/L.2. Online: www.unescap.org/ESID/Committee2007/English/CESI4_L2E.pdf (accessed October 2008).
—— (2007b) *Ten as One: Challenges and Opportunities for ASEAN Integration*, ESCAP Series on Inclusive Sustainable Development No. 1, Bangkok: ESCAP.
ESCWA (2005) *Towards Integrated Social Policies in Arab Countries. Framework and Comparative Analysis*, E/ESCWA/SDD/2005/4, New York: UN.
—— (2007) *Operationalizing Social Policy in the ESCWA Region, Peer-review Meeting.* Online: www.escwa.un.org/information/meetings/editor/Download.asp?table_name=eventDetails&field_name=id&FileID=73 (accessed November 2008).
—— (2008a) 'The Social Policy Report II: From Concept to Practice', *Aide Mémoire for the Expert Group Meeting*, Amman.
—— (2008b) *Integrated Social Policy Report II: From Concept to Practice* (accessed online November 2009).
Estevadeordal, A., Frantz, B. and Nguyen, T.R. (eds) (2004) *Regional Public Goods, from Theory to Practice*, New York: IDB and ADB.
European Commission (2000) *The European Community's Development Policy*, COM(2000) 212 final, 26.4.2000, Brussels.
—— (2001) *Promoting Core Labour Standards and Improving Social Governance in the Context of Globalisation*, COM(2001)416, 18.4.2001, Brussels.
—— (2003) *Communication from the Commission to the Council and to the European Parliament. The European Union and the United Nations: The Choice of Multilateralism*, COM 526 final:5, Brussels.
—— (2004a) *Joint Report on Social Inclusion.* DG Employment and Social Affairs. Luxembourg: Office for Official Publications of the European Communities; Online: http://ec.europa.eu/employment_social/spsi/docs/social_inclusion/final_joint_inclusion_report_2003_en.pdf (accessed May 2007).
—— (2004b) 'The Cohesion Fund: A Boost for European Solidarity', *Inforegio Panorama*, No. 14, September, Brussels: European Communities Publications Office.
—— (2004c) *The Social Dimension of Globalization: The EU's Policy Contribution on Extending the Benefits to All*, COM(2004)383, 18.5.2004, Brussels.
—— (2004d) *Developing Countries, International Trade and Sustainable Development: The Function of the Community's Generalised system of Preferences (GSP) for the Ten-year Period from 2006 to 2015*, COM(2004) 461 final.
—— (2005) *Europa: Your Europe: Enforcing Your Rights and European General Guides.* Online: http://ec.europa.eu/youreurope/nav/en/citizens/services/eu-guide/enforcing-rights/enforcing-rights_en.pdf (accessed July 2005).
—— (2006) *Regional Policy Inforegio.* Online: http://ec.europa.eu/regional_policy/objective1/results_en.htm (accessed March 2008), http://ec.europa.eu/regional_policy/

objective1/cofund_en.htm (accessed 6 June 2006), http://ec.europa.eu/regional_policy/funds/procf/cf_en.htm (accessed 9 August 2006).

—— (2007a) *Competition Policy*. Online: http://europa.eu/pol/comp/overview_en.htm (accessed December 2007).

—— (2007b) *Latin America. Regional Programming Strategy 2007–2013*, 12.07.2007 (E/2007/1417). Online: http://ec.europa.eu/external_relations/la/rsp/07_13_en.pdf (accessed May 2008).

European Communities (2000) 'Charter of Fundamental Rights of the European Union', *Official Journal C 364/1*. Online: http://eur-lex.europa.eu/LexUriServ/LexUriServ.do?uri=OJ:C:2000:364:0001:0022:EN:PDF (accessed 18 December 2000).

European Court of Human Rights (2004, 2005) *Subject Matter of Judgments before the Court*. Online: www.echr.coe.int/ECHR/EN/Header/Case-Law/Case-law+information/Subject+matter+of+judgments/ (accessed December 2007).

—— (2008) *Convention for the Protection of Human Rights and Fundamental Freedoms as Amended by Protocol No. 11*. Online: www.echr.coe.int/nr/rdonlyres/d5cc24a7-dc13–4318-b457–5c9014916d7a/0/englishanglais.pdf (accessed March 2008).

European Court of Justice (2007) *Table alphabétique des matières 1985–2001*, pp. 182–740. Online: http://curia.europa.eu/fr/content/outils/tm.pdf (accessed March 2008).

European Economic and Social Committee (EESC) (2003) *European Social Dialogue and Civil Dialogue: Differences and Complementarities*, citing a speech by Daniela Obradovic, Brussels: EESC Pamphlet.

—— (2006) *Opinion of the European Economic and Social Committee on the Representativeness of European Civil Society Organizations in Civil Dialogue*, SC/023-CESE 240/2006, Brussels. Online: http://eesc.europa.eu/sco/registrations/documents/avis/ces240–2006_ac_en.pdf (accessed November 2007).

—— (2006) *Group III Various Interests*. Online: www.eesc.europa.eu/groups/3/ (accessed November 2007).

European Union (2008) 'Economic Partnership Agreement between the CARIFORUM States, of the One Part, and the European Community and its Member States, of the Other Part', L. 289/1/3, *Official Journal*. Online: http://trade.ec.europa.eu/doclib/docs/2008/february/tradoc_137971.pdf (accessed January 2009).

Eurostat (2008a) *Table: Social Benefits (Other than Social Transfers in Kind) Paid by Government (ESA95 Code D.62)*, Public Finance Data Navigation Tree. Online: http://epp.eurostat.ec.europa.eu/portal/page?_pageid=1996,45323734&_dad=portal&_schema=PORTAL&screen=welcomeref&close=/B/B1/B12&language=en&product=Yearlies_new_economy&root=Yearlies_new_economy&scrollto=133 (accessed March 2008).

—— (2008b) *Table: Total Expenditure on Social Protection per Head of Population in PPS*. Online: http://epp.eurostat.ec.europa.eu/tgm/table.do?tab=table&language=en&pcode=dae11024&tableSelection=1&footnotes=yes&labeling=labels&plugin=0 (accessed March 2008).

Evans, P. (2005) 'Counter-hegemonic Globalization: Transnational Social Movements in the Contemporary Global Political Economy', in T. Janoski, A. Hicks and M. Schwartz (eds) *Handbook of Political Sociology*, New York: Cambridge University Press, pp. 655–70.

Falkner, G. (1998) *EU Social Policy in the 1990s: Towards a Corporatist Policy Community*. London and New York: Routledge.

—— (2003) 'The EU's Social Dimension', in M. Cini (ed.) *European Union Politics*, Oxford: OUP, pp. 264–77.

FAO (2008) *Asia Pacific Food Situation Update*, Bangkok: FAO Regional Office for Asia and the Pacific.

Farrell, M. (2004) *The EU and Inter-Regional Cooperation: In Search of Global Presence*, UNU-CRIS Working Paper 2004/9, Bruges: United Nations University Comparative Regional Integration Studies.

—— (2005) 'The Global Politics of Regionalism: An Introduction', in M. Farrell, B. Hettne and L. Van Langenhove (eds) *Global Politics of Regionalism. Theory and Practice*, London: Pluto Press.

Farrell, M., Hettne, B. and Van Langnehove, L. (2005) (eds) *Global Politics of Regionalism. Theory and Practice*, London: Pluto Press.

FEALAC (2002) 'Economy and Society', Co-Chairs' Statement, Working Group Meeting, 7–8 March, Tokyo.

—— (2003) 'Final Report', Economy and Society Working Group, August.

—— (2006) 'IV Economy and Society Working Group Meeting', 7–8 June, Tokyo.

—— (2008) 'Final Report', Sixth Meeting of the Economy and Society Working Group, 25–26 November, Quito, Ecuador.

Feffer, J. (2007) 'Another World', *World Beat*, 2(19). Online: www.fpif.org/fpifzines/wb/4203 (accessed 30 June 2008).

Financial Times (2007) *European Immigration.* Online: http://www.ft.com (accessed 20 August 2007).

French-Davis, R. and Devlin, R. (1998) *Towards an Evaluation of Regional Integration in Latin America in the 1990s*, Working Paper, Instituto para la integración de Al y el Caribe (INTAL) Banco Interamericano de Desarrollo (BID).

Friedan, B. (1963; 2nd edn 1982) *The Feminine Mystique*, London: Gollancz/Harmondsworth: Penguin.

Gamble, A.M. and Payne, A.J. (eds) (1996) *Regionalism and World Order*, London: Macmillan.

GCIM (2005) *Migration in an Interconnected World: New Directions for Action*, Switzerland: The Global Commission on International Migration.

Geyer, R.R. (2000) *Exploring European Social Policy*, Cambridge: Polity Press.

Giam, G. (2006) 'Haze Problem: Bilateral Pressure on Indonesia Works Best', Singapore Andle. Online: www.singaporeangle.com/2006/10/haze-problem-bilateral-pressure-on.html (accessed 13 October 2006).

Gibb, R. (2007) 'Regional Integration in Post-apartheid Southern Africa', *Tijdschrift voor Economische en Sociale Geografie*, 98(4): 421–35.

Giddens, A., Diamond, P. and Liddle, R. (eds) (2006) *Global Europe, Social Europe*, Cambridge: Polity.

Gilson, J. (2005) 'New Interregionalism? The EU and East Asia', *Journal of European Integration*, 27(3): 307–26.

Goetschy, J. (2002) 'The European Employment Strategy, Multi-level Governance and Policy Coordination: Past, Present and Future', in J. Zeitlin and D. Trubeck (eds) *Governing Work and Welfare*, Oxford: OUP.

—— (2006) 'Taking Stock of Social Europe: Is There Such a Thing as a Community Social Model?', in M. Jepsen and A. Serrano Pascual (eds) *Unwrapping the European Social Model*, Bristol: Policy Press, pp. 47–92.

Gonzales, J. (2007) *An Evaluation of the Impact Assessment Studies of the EPAs on the Caribbean and Sub-Saharan Africa. What Scope for the ILO?*, ILO Discussion Paper.

Graham, K. and Felício, T. (2006) *Regional Security and Global Governance*, Brussels: VUB Press.

Granger, C. and Siroën, J.-M. (2006) 'Core Labour Standards in Trade Agreements: From Multilateralism to Bilateralism', *Journal of World Trade*, 40(5): 813–36.

Greven, T. (2005) *Social Standards in Bilateral and Regional Trade and Investment Agreements: Instruments, Enforcement, and Policy Options for Trade Unions*, Occasional Paper 16, Dialogue on Globalization, Geneva: Friederich Ebert Stiftung.

Grugel, J. (2005) 'Citizenship and Governance in Mercosur: Arguments for a Social Agenda', *Third World Quarterly*, 26(7): 1061–76.

—— (2006) 'Regionalist Governance and Transnational Collective Action in Latin America', *Economy and Society*, 35(2): 209–31.

Gudynas, E. (2005) '"Open Regionalism" or Alternative Regional Integration?', Americas Program, Silver City, NM: International Relations Center. Online: http://americas.irc-online.org/am/2904 (accessed 27 April 2008).

Hagemann-White, C. (2006) *Combating Violence against Women: Stocktaking Study on the Measures and Actions taken in Council of Europe Member-States*, Strasbourg: Council of Europe.

Hantrais, L. (1995; 2nd edn 2000) *Social Policy in the European Union*, Basingstoke: Macmillan.

Hasan, A. (2001) *Role of Human Capital in Economic Development: Some Myths and Realities*, LDC Series No. 6. ESCAP Publication (ST/ESCAP/2174), pp. 3–14.

Hänggi, H. (2000) 'Interregionalism: Empirical and Theoretical Perspectives', Paper for Dollars, Democracy and Trade Workshop, Los Angeles, 18 May.

Hawthorne, S. (2007) *Unbundling Water from Land.* Online: www.bilaterals.org/article.php3?id_article=6921 (accessed 17 September 2008).

Held, D. (2004) *Global Covenant: The Social Democratic Alternative to the Washington Consensus*, Cambridge: Polity.

Hettne, B. (1999) 'The New Regionalism: A Prologue', in B. Hettne, A. Inotain and O. Sunkel (eds) *Globalism and the New Regionalism*, London: Macmillan.

—— (2003) *Regionalism, Interregionalism and World Order: The European Challenge to Pax Americana*, American University Council on Comparative Studies Working Paper Series No. 3. Online: www.american.edu/academic.depts/ccs/working_paperhettne.pdf (accessed 17 March 2003).

—— (2006) 'Beyond the "New" Regionalism', in A. Payne (ed.) *Key Debates in New Political Economy*, Oxon: Routledge, pp. 128–60.

Hooghe, L. and Marks, G. (2001) *Multi-level Governance and European Integration*, Lanham: Rowman and Littlefield.

Houte, W. (1996) 'Globalization, Regionalization and Regionalism: A Survey of Contemporary Literature', *Acta Politica*, XXXI: 164–81.

HSA (2006) 'Cochabamba Manifesto', Declaration presented to the Presidents during the South American Community of Nations Summit in Cochabamba, Bolivia, 13 December. Online: www.commonfrontiers.ca/Bolivia/documents/final_declaration_Dec13_06.html (accessed 27 March 2008).

—— (2006a) 'Conclusiones de la Sesión Temática Agricultura, Tierra y Territorio', Social Summit for the Integration of the Peoples, Cochabamba, Bolivia, 6–9 December. Online: www.movimientos.org/noalca/integracionpueblos/show_text.php3?key=8806 (accessed 27 March 2008).

—— (2006b) 'Conclusiones y Propuestas de la Sesión Temática del Agua', Social Summit for the Integration of the Peoples, Cochabamba, Bolivia, 6–9 December. Online: www.movimientos.org/noalca/integracionpueblos/show_text.php3?key=8755 (accessed 27 March 2008).

—— (2006c) 'Conclusiones sobre Derechos Sociales', Social Summit for the Integration of the Peoples, Cochabamba, Bolivia, 6–9 December. Online: www.movimientos.org/noalca/integracionpueblos/show_text.php3?key=8769 (accessed 27 March 2008).

—— (2006d) 'Conclusiones de la Mesa Temática de Energía', Social Summit for the Integration of the Peoples, Cochabamba, Bolivia, 6–9 December. Online: www.movimientos.org/noalca/integracionpueblos/show_text.php3?key=8726 (accessed 27 March 2008).

—— (2006e) 'Conclusiones: Financiamento para los Derechos y la Integración de los Pueblos', Social Summit for the Integration of the Peoples, Cochabamba, Bolivia, 6–9 December. Online: www.movimientos.org/noalca/integracionpueblos/show_text.php3?key=8771 (accessed 27 March 2008).

—— (2006g) 'Conclusiones: Propuestas de la Mesa de Migraciones y Ciudadanía', Social Summit for the Integration of the Peoples, Cochabamba, Bolivia, 6–9 December. Online: www.movimientos.org/noalca/integracionpueblos/show_text.php3?key=8725 (accessed 27 March 2008).

—— (2006i) 'Final Declaration', Fifth Hemispheric Meeting of Struggle Against Free Trade Agreements and for the Integration of the People, La Havana, Cuba, 15 April. Online: www.movimientos.org/noalca/vencuentro/show_text.php3?key=6991 (accessed 27 March 2008).

—— (2006j) 'Civil Society Organizations on the Road to the Construction of the South American Community Of Nations', Call from Civil Society to South American Presidents presented to the Ministers and Vice-ministers of the SACN in Santiago, Chile, 22–23 November. Online: www.art-us.org/node/191 (accessed 27 March 2008).

—— (2007) 'Declaracion de Montevideo', Final Declaration, Southern Peoples Summit 'Todos los Pueblos, toda la Esperanza', Montevideo, Uruguay, 17 December. Online: www.rbrasil.org.br/content,0,0,2257,0,0.html (accessed 27 March 2008).

—— (2007a) 'Manifiesto de Santiago', Final Declaration, Summit for Friendship and Integration of the Iberoamerican Peoples, Santiago, Chile, 9 November. Online: www.cumbredelospueblos2007.cl/node/96 (accessed 27 March 2008).

—— (2008) 'Declaración Seminario UNASUR: Intereses en Disputa', Rio de Janeiro, Brazil, 13 March. Online: www.asc-hsa.org/node/298 (accessed 27 March 2008).

Huber, D. (1999) *A Decade which Made History. The Council of Europe 1989–1999*, Strasbourg: Council of Europe Publishing.

ICFTU (2008) *Trade Unions and Bilaterals: Do's and Don'ts – a Trade Union Guide*, Brussels.

Ichiyo, M. (2002) 'Neo-Liberal Globalization and People's Alliance', Speech at People's Plan 21 General Assembly, Rajabhat Institute, Bangkok, 22–23 June Online: www.jca.apc.org/ppsg/en/Documents/muto200206.html (accessed 1 September 2008).

IDB (2004a) *Single Based Social Security for* MERCOSUR, ATN:OC-9258-RG. Online: www.iadb.org/int/redes/rpg/index.aspx?mid=50&cid=180&scid=191 (accessed September 2008).

—— (2004b) *Common Population Census in CARICOM – ATN/OC-10157-RG*. Online: www.iadb.org/int/redes/rpg/index.aspx?mid=50&scid=200&cid=180 (accessed September 2008).

—— (2006) 'Effective Policies to Meet the MDGs Agenda in the Caribbean', *Minutes*. Online: http://www.iadb.org.NEWS/detail.cfm?artid=2858&language=En&id=2858&CFID=323783&CFTOKEN=65636281 (accessed September 2008).

—— (2007) 'Employment and Labor Insertion Policies to Overcome Poverty', Conceptual note, Washington, DC, 13–14 September. Online: http://www.iadb.org.NEWS/

detail.cfm?artid=2858&language=En&id=2858&CFID=323783&CFTOKEN=65636281 (accessed September 2008).

Iglesias, E. (2000) 'Twelve Lessons from Five Decades of Regional Integration in Latin America and the Caribbean', Presentation to the Conference Celebrating the 35th Anniversary of the Institute for the Integration of Latin America and the Caribbean (INTAL), Buenos Aires, November. Online: www.iadb.org/INT/Trade/1_english/2_WhatWeDo/Documents/c_OtherPubs/Speeches/e_talk%20points%20intal%2035%20years%20Eng.pdf (accessed 15 June 2008).

Illanes, M.A. and Riesco, M. (2007) 'Developmental Welfare State and Social Change in Chile', in M. Riesco (ed.) *Latin America, A New Developmental Welfare State Model in the Making?*, London: Palgrave-Macmillan, pp. 378–424.

ILO (2007) *Labour and Social Trends in ASEAN 2007: Integration, Challenges and Opportunities*, Bangkok: ILO Regional Office for Asia and the Pacific.

—— (2008) *Social Dimension of Economic Partnership Agreements between European Union and African Countries*, ILO Bureau for Workers' Activities.

Inayat, M. (2007) 'The South Asian Association for Regional Cooperation', in Bailes, A.J.K., Gooneratne, J., Inayat, M., Khan, J.A. and Singh, S. (eds) *Regionalism in South Asian Diplomacy*, SIPRI Policy Paper No. 15, Stockholm: SIPRI.

INFOSAN (2006) *IFOSAN Information Note No. 4/2006 (14 August 2006) – Controlling Avian Influenza*. Online: www.cphln.ca/CPHLN/src/documents/EN_Note_4_2006_AvianInfluenza.pdf (accessed 7 October 2008).

INTAL (2008) *Intrumentos Básicos de Integración, Cronología*. Online: www.iadb.org/intal/cronologia.asp?idioma=esp&cid=237&aid=1311 (accessed 26 March 2008).

IOM (2008) *Migration in Southeast Asia*. Online: www.iom-seasia.org/ (accessed August 2008).

ISACPA (2004) *An Engagement with Hope: SAARC Development Goals (SDGs) 2005–*2010. Online: www.saarc-sec.org/data/pubs/rpp. 2005/pdfs/Tables/Table-2.26.pdf.

—— (2006) *Vision 1440 H-A: A Vision for Human Dignity – Summary*, May. Online. _and_Targets.doc (accessed October 2008).

IsDB (2008) *The 33rd Annual Report 1428H 2007–2008*. Online: www.isdb.org/irj/portal/anonymous?NavigationTarget=navurl://0b4fc07088549fb613bee94900acd775 (accessed October 2008).

Isella, C. and Tejada Gómez, A. (1996) *Canción con Todos*, performed by César Isella, Mercedes Sosa, Aute, León Gieco, Piero and others, Quito, June. Online: www.youtube.com/watch?v=gjNdfopY00k.

Jeffery, C. (2002) 'Social and Regional Interests: ESC and Committee of the Regions', in J. Peterson and M. Shackleton (eds) *The Institutions of the European Union*, Oxford: OUP, pp. 326–46.

Jepsen, M. and Serrano Pascual, A. (eds) (2006) *Unwrapping the European Social Model*, Bristol: Policy Press.

Jocelyn-Holt, A. (1999) *La Independencia de Chile*, Santiago: Planeta.

Kanyenze, G., Kondo, T. and Martens, J. (2006) *The Search for Sustainable Development in Southern Africa*, Harare: ANSA Secretariat.

Keck, M.E. and Sikkink, K. (1999) 'Transnational Advocacy Networks in International and Regional Politics', *International Social Science Journal*, 51(159): 89–101.

Keet, D. (2007a) *Economic Partnership Agreements: Responses to the EU Offensive against ACP Developmental Regions*, The Hague: TransNational Institute.

—— (2007b) 'Alternative Regional Strategies in Africa', *Global Social Policy*, 7(3): 262–5.

Keet, D. and Bello, W. (2004) *Linking Alternative Regionalisms for Equitable and Sustainable Development*, Amsterdam: Transnational Institute.

Kohler, G. and Keane, J. (2006) *Social Policy in South Asia: Towards Universal Coverage and Transformation for Achieving the Millennium Development Goals.* Online: http://www.unicef.org/rosa/Social_Policy_Workshop_Report.pdf (accessed November 2008).

Kwon, H.J. (2005) 'An Overview of the Study: The Developmental Welfare State and Policy Reforms in East Asia', in Kwon, H.-J. (ed.) *Transforming the Developmental Welfare State in East Asia*, London: Palgrave-Macmillan, pp. 1–23.

Leibfried, S. and Pierson, P. (eds) (1995) *European Social Policy: Between Fragmentation and Integration*, Washington, DC: Brookings Institution.

Lipschutz, A. (1955) 'El Problema Racial en la Conquista de América y el Mestizaje', in J. Cademártori (1972) *La Economía Chilena*, Santiago: Cormorán.

Lisbon Council (2008) *European Social Model.* Online: www.lisboncouncil.net/index.php?option=com_content&task=view&id=8&Itemid=57 (accessed 23 June 2008).

Lisbon Treaty (2007) 'Treaty of Lisbon Amending the Treaty on European Union and the Treaty Establishing the European Community', signed at Lisbon, 13 December. *Official Journal 2007/C 306/01.* Online: http://eur-lex.europa.eu/JOHtml.do?uri=OJ:C:2007:306:SOM:EN:HTML (accessed 17 December 2007).

Lovecy, J. (2002) 'Gender Mainstreaming and the Framing of Women's Rights in Europe: The Contribution of the Council of Europe', *Feminist Legal Studies*, 10(3–4): 271–83.

MacMahon, R. (2008) *The Rise in Bilateral Free Trade Agreements*, Council on Foreign Relations. Online: www.cfr.org.publication/10890 (accessed 16 September 2008).

Macmullen, A. (2004) 'Intergovernmental Functionalism? The Council of Europe in European Integration', *Journal of European Integration*, 26(4): 405–29.

Mansfield, E.D. and Milner, H.V. (1999) 'The New Wave of Regionalism', *International Organization*, 53: 589–627.

Marshall, K. and Butzbach, O. (eds) (2003) *New Social Policy Agendas for Europe and Asia: Challenges, Experience, and Lessons*, Washington, DC: World Bank.

Martin, M. *et al.* (2008) *TIMSS 2007 International Science Report: Findings from IEA's Trends in International Mathematics and Science Study at the Fourth and Eighth Grades.* Chestnut Hill, Mass.: TIMSS & PIRLS International Study Center, Boston College. Online: http://timss.bc.edu/TIMSS2007/sciencereport.html (accessed 8 October 2008).

Mattli, W. (1999) *The Logic of European Integration: Europe and Beyond*, Cambridge: Cambridge University Press.

Maydell, V.B., Borchardt, K. and Henke, K.D. (2006) *Enabling Social Europe*, Berlin and Heidelberg: Springer.

Mello, F. (2006) 'Introducción ¿Por qué Integración Regional?', in *Integración en América Latina: apuntes para debatir la Integración de los Pueblos*, Sao Paulo: Alianza Social Continental (ASC), Campaña Brasileña contra el ALCA/OMC and Red Brasileña por la Integración de los Pueblos (REBRIP), pp. 7–12. Online: www.rebrip.org.br/projetos/clientes/noar/noar/UserFiles/20/File/Publica%E7%F5es%20REBRIP/cartilhaintegracaoespanholtexto.pdf (accessed 13 July 2008).

Moravcsik, A. (2005) 'The European Constitutional Compromise and the Neofunctionalist Legacy', *Journal of European Public Policy*, 12(2): 349–86.

Mullis, I.V.S., Martin, M.O., Kennedy, A.M. and Foy, P. (2007) *PIRLS 2006 International Report: IEA's Progress in International Reading Literacy Study in Primary School in 40 Countries*, Chestnut Hill, MA: TIMSS & PIRLS International Study Center, Boston College. Online: http://pirls.bc.edu/pirls2006/intl_rpt.html (accessed 08 October 2008).

—— (2008) *TIMSS 2007 International Mathematics Report: Findings from IEA's Trends in International Mathematics and Science Study at the Fourth and Eighth Grades*, Chestnut Hill, MA: TIMSS & PIRLS International Study Center, Boston College. Online: http://timss.bc.edu/TIMSS2007/mathreport.html (accessed 8 October 2008).

Musgrave, R.A. and Musgrave, P.B. (2003) 'Prologue', in I. Kaul *et al.*, *Providing Global Public Goods: Managing Globalization*, New York and Oxford: Oxford University Press.

Narine, S. (2002) *Explaining ASEAN: Regionalism in Southeast Asia*, Boulder, Colo: Lynne Rienner Publishers.

Nesadurai, H. (2003) 'Attempting Developmental Regionalism through AFTA: The Domestic Sources of Regional Governance', *Third World Quarterly*, 24(2): 235–53.

Nuera, A.C. (2007) 'Engaging the Drafting of the ASEAN Charter', in A.C. Nuera and E.R. Rillorta (eds) *Understanding the ASEAN: Building the ASEAN People's Capacity to Engage a Truly People-centered ASEAN*, Philippines: South East Asian Committee for Advocacy (SEACA).

Ocampo, J.A. (2006) *Regional Financial Co-operation*, Baltimore, Md.: Brookings Institution Press.

Ocampo, J.A. and Martin, J. (2003) *Globalization and Development: A Latin American and Caribbean Perspective*, Santiago, Chile: ECLAC.

ODI (2009) *A Development Charter for the G-20*, London: ODI.

ODI/ECDPM (2008) *The New EPAs: Comparative Analysis of their Content and the Challenges for 2008. Final Report*, March 2008. Online: http://www.ecdpm.org (accessed May 2008).

Olivet, C. (2005) 'Unravelling Interregionalism Theory: A Critical Analysis of the New Interregional Relations between Latin America and East Asia', Paper presented at the Sixth Conference of REDEALAP, Buenos Aires, December.

Orbie, J. and Tortell, L. (2008) *The European Union and the Social Dimension of Globalization, How the EU Influences the World*, London and New York: Routledge.

ORIT (2005) 'Labour Platform for the Americas'. Online: www.cioslorit.net/arquivo_up/laboursPlata.pdf (accessed 25 June 2008).

Ortiz, I. (2007) *Social Policy*, New York: UNDESA.

—— (ed.) (2001) *Social Protection in Asia and the Pacific*, Asian Development Bank. Online: www.adb.org/Documents/Books/Social Protection/prelims.pdf (accessed November 2008).

Page, S. (2000) *Regionalism among Developing Countries*, Basingstoke: Macmillan-ODI.

PAHO/WHO and CARICOM (2006) *Report of the Caribbean Commission on Health and Development*. Online: www.who.int/macrohealth/action/PAHO_Report.pdf (accessed September 2008).

Pinheiro Guimarães, S. (2007) *El mundo multipolar y la integración sudamericana*, Santiago: CENDA. Online: www.cendachile.cl/pinheiro_integracion (accessed 14 March 2008).

Platform of European Social NGOs (2006) *Social Platform Annual Report 2006*. Online: http://cms.horus.be/files/99907/MediaArchive/Annual%20reports/Final%20AR%20 2006-En.pdf (accessed November 2007).

Podesta, B., Gomez Galán, M., Jacome, F. and Grandi, J. (2000) *Ciudadanía y mundialización. La sociedad civil ante la integración regional*, Madrid: CIDEAL, CEFIR and INVESP.

Richards, D.G. (1997) 'Dependent Development and Regional Integration', *Latin American Perspectives*, 24(6): 133–55.

Richards, G. and Kirkpatrick, C. (1999) 'Reorienting Interregional Co-operation in the Global Political Economy: Europe's East Asian Policy', *Journal of Common Market Studies*, 37(4): 683–710.

Rieger, E. and Leibfried, S. (2003) *Limits to Globalization*, Cambridge: Polity.

Riesco, M. (2007) *Latin America, a New Developmental Welfare State Model in the Making?*, London: Palgrave Macmillan/UNRISD.

Rillorta, E.R. (2007) 'Civil Society Engagements with the ASEAN', in A.C. Nuera and E.R. Rillorta (eds) *Understanding the ASEAN: Building the ASEANP People's Capacity to Engage a Truly People-centered ASEAN*, Philippines: South East Asian Committee for Advocacy (SEACA).

Room, G. (1993) *Anti-poverty Action Research in Europe*, Bristol: SAUS Publications.

Rüland, J. (2002) *The European Union as an Inter- and Transregional Actor: Lessons for Global Governance from Europe's Relations with Asia*, National Europe Centre Paper no. 13, Australian National University.

SAARC Charter (1985) Online: www.saarc-sec.org/data/CharterDay2006/nepfm.htm.

SAARC Secretariat (2002a) *Convention on Regional Arrangements for the Promotion of Child Welfare in South Asia*, Kathmandu: SAARC Secretariat.

—— (2002b) *Convention on Preventing and Combating Trafficking in Women and Children for Prostitution*, Kathmandu: SAARC Secretariat.

—— (2004a) *Social Charter of the South Asian Association for Regional Cooperation*, Kathmandu: SAARC Secretariat.

—— (2004b) *SAARC – A Profile*, Kathmandu: SAARC Secretariat.

SADC (2006) *Media Release: The African Development Bank Grants to SADC UA20.000.000.* Online: www.sadc.int/archives/read/news/784 (accessed October 2008).

Saguier, M.I. (2007) 'The Hemispheric Social Alliance and the Free Trade Area of the Americas Process: The Challenges and Opportunities of Transnational Coalitions against Neo-liberalism', *Globalizations*, 4(2): 251–65.

Sakellaropoulos, T. and Bergman, J. (eds) (2004) *Connecting Welfare Diversity within the European Social Model*, Antwerp and Oxford: Intersentia.

Sané, P. (2006) in Social Aspects of Regional Integration: IFSP High-Level Symposium, Montevideo, 21–24 February 2006. Online: http://portal.unesco.org/shs/en/files/9229/11401047741montevideo.sumposium.pdf/montevideo_symposium.pdf (accessed 8 April 2009).

SAPA Working Group on ASEAN (2006a) *Submission on the Economic Pillar*, Submissions to the Eminent Persons Group on the ASEAN Charter, Singapore, 28 June. Online: www.asiasapa.org/pdf/docs/SAPA_submission_ASEAN_Charter_econ.pdf (accessed 9 March 2008).

—— (2006b) *Submission on the Socio-Cultural Pillar and Institutional Mechanism*, Submissions to the Eminent Persons Group on the ASEAN Charter, Quezon City, Philippines, 10 November. Online: www.focusweb.org/philippines/component/option,com_docman/task,doc_download/gid,4/Itemid,49/ (accessed 9 March 2008).

—— (2007) *Analysis of the ASEAN Charter.* Online: www.asiasapa.org/pdf/docs/ASEAN_Charter-SAPA_Analysis.pdf (accessed 9 March 2008).

—— (2008) *Background.* Online: www.asiasapa.org/ (accessed 10 March 2008).

SAPSN (2000) 'Making Southern African Development Cooperation and Integration a People-Centered and People-Driven Regional Challenge to Globalisation', Declaration to the Governmental Summit of the Southern African Development Community (SADC), Windhoek, Namibia, 1–7 August. Online: http://sapsn.wordpress.com/2000/08/10/declarationwindhoek/ (accessed 20 March 2008).

—— (2006) 'Reclaiming SADC for People's Solidarity and Development Cooperation', declaration from People's Summit Parallel to the Intergovernmental and Heads of State SADC Summit, Maseru, Lesotho, 14–18 August. Online: http://sapsn.wordpress.com/2006/08/20/declarationmaseru/ (accessed 20 March 2008).

—— (2007) 'Reclaiming SADC for People's Solidarity and Development Cooperation: Let the People Speak', Declaration from People's Summit Parallel to the Intergovernmental and Heads of State SADC Summit, Lusaka, Zambia, August. Online: http://sapsn.wordpress.com/2007/08/18/declarationlusaka/ (accessed 20 March 2008).

Schoeman, M. (2002) 'From SADCC TO SADC and Beyond: The Politics of Economic Integration', Paper presented at International XIII Congress of the International Economic History Association, Buenos Aires, July. Online: http://eh.net/XIIICongress/Papers/Schoeman.pdf (accessed 25 June 2008).

Scholte, J.A. (2004) 'Civil Society and Democratically Accountable Global Governance', *Government and Opposition*, 39(2): 211–33.

—— (2005) 'The Sources of Neoliberal Globalization', Overarching Concerns Programme, United Nations Research Institute for Social Development (UNRISD) Paper No. 8. Online: www.unrisd.org/ (accessed 25 June 2008).

SELA (2008) *Social Dimension of Integration: Guidelines for an Action Plan in the Areas of Health, Education, Housing, and Employment*, UNU-CRIS Working Papers (W-2008/4). Online: www.cris.unu.edu/fileadmin/workingpapers/W-2008–4.pdf (accessed 10 January 2009).

Sen, A.K. (1999) *Beyond the Crisis: Development Strategies in Asia*, Singapore: Institute of Southeast Asian Studies.

Seoane, J., Taddei, E. and Algranati, C. (2005) 'The New Configurations of Popular Movements in Latin America', in A. Boron and G. Lechini (eds) *Politics and Social Movements in an Hegemonic World: Lessons from Africa, Asia and Latin America*, Buenos Aires: CLACSO, Consejo Latinoamericano de Ciencias Sociales. Online: http://bibliotecavirtual.clacso.org.ar/ar/libros/sursur/politics/Algranati.rtf (accessed 19 March 2008).

Serbin, A. (1997) 'Globalización y Sociedad Civil en los Procesos de Integración', *Nueva Sociedad*, 147: 44–55.

—— (2004) 'Entre la Globalofobia y el Globalitarismo: Sociedad Civil, Movimientos Sociales y Globalización en América Latina y el Caribe', in J.M. Gómez (ed.) *América Latina y el (des)orden global neoliberal*, Buenos Aires: CLACSO.

Sinclair, S. and Traynor, K. (2004) 'Divide and Conquer: The FTAA, U.S. Trade Strategy and Public Services in the Americas'. Online: www.bilaterals.org/article.php3?id_article=1211 (accessed 17 September 2008).

Söderbaum, F. (2004) 'Modes of Regional Governance in Africa: Neoliberalism, Sovereignty Boosting, and Shadow Networks', *Global Governance*, 10: 419–36.

—— (2007) 'Regionalisation and Civil Society: The Case of Southern Africa', *New Political Economy*, 12(3): 319–37.

Söderbaum, F. and Taylor, I. (2008) *Afro-regions – The Dynamics of Cross-border Microregionalism in Africa*, Stockholm: Nordiska Afrikainstitutet, Elanders Sverige AB.

Söderbaum, F. and Van Langenhove, L. (2005) 'Introduction: The EU as a Global Actor and the Role of Interregionalism', *Journal of European Integration*, 27(3): 249–62.

Solidum, E. (2003) *The Politics of ASEAN: An Introduction to Southeast Asian Regionalism*, Singapore: Eastern Universities Press.

Spooner, D. (2004) 'Trade Unions and NGOs: The Need for Cooperation', *Development in Practice*, 14(1): 19–33.

Springer, B. (1994) *The European Union and its Citizens: The Social Agenda*, Westport, Conn.: Greenwood Press.

Suleiman, E. (2004) *The Dismantling of Democratic States*, Princeton, NJ: Princeton University Press.

Tarrow, S. (2001) 'Transnational Politics: Contention and Institutions in International Politics', *Annual Review of Political Science*, 4: 1–20.

Tavares, R. (2006) 'Understanding Regional Peace and Security: A Framework for Analysis', Gothenburg University, unpublished Ph.D. dissertation.

Taylor, V. (2003) 'Civil Society of the Southern Africa Development Community', ICSW Brief Paper. Online: http://www.icsw.org (accessed 9 April 2009).

Telò, M. (2005) *Europe: A Civilian Power? European Union, Global Governance, World Order*, Houndmills: Palgrave Macmillan.

Tercera, La (2009) 'Columna de Juan Emilio Cheyre', January: 2.

Thakur, R. and Van Langenhove, L. (2006) 'Enhancing Global Governance through Regional Integration', *Global Governance*, 12(3): 233–40.

—— (2008) 'Enhancing Global Governance through Regional Integration', in A. Cooper, C.W. Hughes and P. De Lombaerde (eds) *Regionalization and Global Governance. The Taming of Globalisation?*, London and New York: Routledge.

Therborn, G. (1995) *European Modernity and Beyond – The Trajectory of European Societies, 1945–2000*, London: Sage.

Threlfall, M. (2002) 'The European Union's Social Policy: From Labour to Welfare and Constitutionalised Rights?', in R. Sykes, C. Bochel and N. Ellison (eds) *Social Policy Review 14*, Bristol: Policy Press, pp. 171–94.

—— (2003) 'European Social Integration: Harmonization, Convergence, and Single Social Areas', *Journal of European Social Policy*, 13(2): 121–39.

—— (2007) 'The Social Dimension of the European Union: Innovative Methods for Advancing Integration', *Global Social Policy*, 7(3): 271–93.

UN (2004) *A More Secure World: Our Shared Responsibility*, report of the High-Level Panel on Threats, Challenges and Change, A/59/565. Online: http://daccessdds.un.org/doc/UNDOC/GEN/N05/270/78/PDF/NO527078.pdf?OpenElement (accessed 10 December 2008).

—— (2006a) *Report of the Secretary-General: A Regional–Global Security Partnership: Challenges and Opportunities*, document S/2006/590, New York: UN.

—— (2006b) *Delivering as One: Report of the Secretary-General's High Level Panel*, New York: UN.

UNAIDS (2007) *Asia: AIDS Epidemic Update: Regional Summary*, Geneva: UNAIDS and WHO.

—— (2008) *Report on the Global AIDS Epidemic*, Geneva: UNAIDS.

UNCTAD (2007) *Trade and Development Report 2007: Regional Cooperation for Development*, Geneva: UNCTAD.

UNDESA (2003) *Monterey Consensus on Financing for Development*, DPI/2329-October 2003-20M, New York: UN Department of Public Information. Online: http://www.un.org/esa/sustdev/documents/Monterrey_Consensus.htm.

—— (2005) *Report on the World Social Situation: The Inequality Predicament*, New York: UN Division for Social Policy and Development.

—— (2007) 'Technical Cooperation. An African Social Policy to Manage Globalization', *DESA News*, 11(1). Online: www.un.org/esa/desa/desaNews/v11n01/techcoop.html (accessed September 2008).

—— (2008) *UN Youth Flash* 5(3). Online: www.un.org/esa/socdev/unyin/documents/flashv5no3.pdf (accessed September 2008).

UNDP (1994) *Human Development Report. New Dimensions of Human Security*. Online: http://hdr.undp.org/en/reports/global/hdr1994/chapters/ (accessed March 2009).

—— (2002a) *Human Development Report*, New York and Oxford: Oxford University Press. Online: http://hdr.undp.org/en/media/HDR_2002_EN_Complete.pdf (accessed March 2009).

—— (2002b) *Social Protection in an Insecure Area: A South–South Exchange on Alternative Social Policies. Responses to Globalization. Final Report.* Inter-Regional Workshop, Santiago, Chile, 14–17 May. Santiago: UNDP. Online: http://videos.cep.cl/sw2002/Informe_Final/SW2002_Final_Report.html (accessed 17 November 2004).

—— (2007) *2007 Consolidated Work Plan, Regional Centres in Bangkok and Colombo.* Online: http://regionalcentrebangkok.undp.or.th/documents/about/Workplan_Asia-Pacific_Regional_Centres-2007.pdf (accessed September 2008).

—— (2007) *Human Development Report 2007/2008: Fighting Climate Change – Human Solidarity in a Divided World*, New York: UNDP.

UNDP/UNU-CRIS (2009) *Delivering Human Security through Multi-level Governance.* Online: www.cris.unu.edu/fileadmin/user_upload/HSPaper.pdf (accessed April 2009).

UNESCO (2006) Buenos Aires Declaration calling for a New Approach to the Social Science Policy Nexus. Online: http://portal.unesco.org/shs/en/ev.php-URL_ID=9004&URL_DO=DO_TOPIC&URL_SECTION=201.html (accessed March 2008).

UNICEF (2008) 'Regional Policy Makers' Symposium on Social Protection in South Asia. Synthesis Report', Dhaka, Draft.

UNICEF ROSA (2006) *State of the SAARC Child 2005.* Online: http://www.unicef.org/rosa/Final_The_State_of_SAARC_Child_2005-Feb-27-06.pdf (accessed November 2008).

UNRISD (2003) *Late Industrializers and the Development of the Welfare State*, Geneva: UNRISD.

UNSG (2005) *In Larger Freedom. Towards Security, Development and Human Rights for All*, Report of the Secretary-General of the United Nations for Decision by Heads of State and Government in September 2005, A/59/2005. Online: http://daccessdds.un.org/doc/UNDOC/GEN/N05/270/78/PDF/NO527078.pdf?OpenElement (accessed 10 December 2008).

—— (2006) *Report of the Secretary General on the Themes of the 2006 ECOSOC Coordination Segment*, New York: UN.

UNU-CRIS (2008) *Deepening the Social Dimension of Regional Integration: An Overview of Recent Trends and Future Challenges in the Light of the World Commission on the Social Dimension of Globalization*, ILLS Discussion Paper No. 188, Geneva: ILO. Online: www.ilo.org/public/english/bureau/inst/download/dp18808.pdf (accessed 28 August 2008).

Van Langenhove, L. (2009) 'The UN Security Council and Regional Organisations: A Difficult Partnership', in J. Wouters, E. Drieskens and S. Biscop (eds) *Belgium in the UN Security Council: Reflections on the 2007–2008 Membership*, Mortsel: Intersentia.

Van Langenhove, L. and Costea, A.C. (2007) 'The EU as a Global Actor and the Emergence of "Third-Generation" Regionalism', in P. Foradori, P. Rosa and R. Scartezzini (eds) *Managing a Multilevel Foreign Policy*, Lanham, Md: Lexington Books.

Van Langenhove, L. and Marchesi, D. (2008) 'The Lisbon Treaty and the Emergence of Third Regional Integration', *European Journal of Law Reform*, X(4): 477–96.

Väyrynen, R. (2003) 'Regionalism: Old and New', *International Studies Review*, 5(1): 25–51.

Veltmeyer, H. (2004) *Civil Society and Social Movements: The Dynamics of Intersectoral Alliances and Urban–Rural Linkages in Latin America*, UNRISD Programme Papers on Civil Society and Social Movements, 10. Geneva: UN Research Institute for Social Development. Online: www.unrisd.org/ (accessed 25 June 2008).

Waddington, C. (2003) 'International Migration Policies in Asia', Paper presented at the Regional Conference on Migration, Development and Pro-Poor Policy Choices in Asia organized by RMMRU, Bangladesh and DFID, Dhaka, Bangladesh, 22–24 June.

Wallace, H. (2005) 'An Institutional Anatomy and Five Policy Modes', in W. Wallace, H. Wallace and M. Pollack (eds) *Policy-making in the European Union*, 5th edn, Oxford: OUP, pp. 49–90.

Warleigh-Lack, A. (2008) 'Studying Regionalization Comparatively: A Conceptual Framework', in A.F. Cooper, C.W. Hughes and P. De Lombaerde (eds) *Regionalisation and Global Governance. The Taming of Globalization?*, London and New York: Routledge.

WCSDG (2004) *A Fair Globalization: Creating Opportunities for All*, Geneva: International Labour Office – World Commission on the Social Dimension of Globalisation.

WHO (2003) *Investing in Health of the Poor: Regional Strategy for Sustainable Health Development and Poverty Reduction.* Online: http://www.who.int/macrohealth.documents/en/strategypaperpaper_final_july28.pdf (accessed November 2008).

—— (2008) *Cumulative Number of Confirmed Human Cases of Avian Influenza Reported to WHO*, A/(H5N1), 10 September. Online: www.who.int/csr/disease/avian_influenza/country/cases_table_2008_09_10/en/index.html (accessed 7 October 2008).

Wikström, K. (2008) 'Abortion Rights: Still a Fight in Europe', *International Viewpoint. Online Magazine* IV404, September. Online: www.internationalviewpoint.org/spip.php?article1523 (accessed December 2008).

Wilfred, J.E. (1998) 'The New Regionalism', *The Economic Journal*, 108(449): 1149–61.

Williamson, J. (2002) *Did the Washington Consensus Fail?*, Washington, DC: Institute for International Economics. Outline of remarks at the Center for Strategic and International Studies. Online: www.iie.com/publications/papers/williamson1102.htm (accessed 06 November 2002).

Wilson, D. and Purushothaman, R. (2003) *Dreaming with BRICs. The Path to 2050*, Global Economics Paper No. 99. Economic Research from the GS Financial Workbench, Goldman Sachs Group.

Wiman, R., Voipio, T. and Ylönen, M. (2007) *Comprehensive Social Policies for Development in a Globalising World*, Helsinki: Ministry for Foreign Affairs in Cooperation with the Ministry of Social Affairs and Health and STAKES, the National Research and Development Centre for Welfare and Health.

World Bank (2002) *World Development Indicators Database*, Washington, DC: World Bank. Online: www.worldbank.org (accessed April 2004).

—— (2004) *Urban Population in World Bank Regions by City Size*, Washington, DC: World Bank. Online: www.worldbank.org/urban/env/population-regions.htm (accessed 28 July 2006).

—— (2006) *Global Economic Prospects 2006: Economic Implications of Remittances and Migration*, Washington, DC: World Bank.

Yeates, N. (2001) *Globalisation and Social Policy*. London: Sage.

—— (2005) *Globalisation and Social Policy in a Development Context: Regional*

Responses, Social Policy and Development Programme Paper No. 18, Geneva: United Nations Research Institute for Social Development.

—— (2007) 'World-regionalism and Social Policy: The Asia–Europe Meeting (ASEM) Process', *Cosmopolis*, 2007/1.

—— (ed.) (2008) *Understanding Global Social Policy*, Bristol: Policy Press.

Yeates, N. and Deacon, B. (2006) *Globalism, Regionalism and Social Policy: Framing the Debate*, UNU-CRIS Occasional Papers (O-2006/6). Online: www.cris.unu.edu/fileadmin/workingpapers/20060418154630.O-2006–6.pdf (accessed 20 September 2008).

Zeitlin, P., Pochet, P. and Magnusson, L. (2005) *The Open Method of Coordination in Action: The European Employment and Social Inclusion Strategies*, Bern, Berlin, Brussels, Frankfurt, New York, Oxford and Vienna: P.I.E.–Peter Lang.

Interviews

Rajeev Kher, Junior Secretary for South Asia, Indian Ministry of Commerce, New Delhi, 21 February 2008.

Rajeev Kumar, Director, SAARC and SAFTA, Indian Ministry of Commerce, New Delhi, 21 February 2008.

Vinay Mohan Kwatra, Economic and Finance Division, SAARC Secretariat, Kathmandu, 26 February 2008.

Hassan Shifau, Social Affairs, SAARC Secretariat, Kathmandu, 26 February 2008.

Rishi Ram Ghimire, Poverty Eradication and Information Unit, SAARC Secretariat, Kathmandu: 27 February 2008.

Index